ECONOMIC TRENDS
IN THE SOVIET UNION

EDITED BY

ABRAM BERGSON AND SIMON KUZNETS

HARVARD UNIVERSITY PRESS
Cambridge, Massachusetts
1963

© Copyright, 1963, by the President and Fellows of Harvard College

Distributed in Great Britain by Oxford University Press, London

Library of Congress Catalog Card Number 63–9548

Printed in the United States of America

PREFACE

The present volume represents the result of a cooperative inquiry into Soviet economic growth undertaken at a conference sponsored by and supported by a grant from the Committee on Economic Growth of the Social Science Research Council. The conference was held at Princeton, New Jersey, on May 6–8, 1961. In a sense the volume is a sequel to one on *Soviet Economic Growth: Conditions and Perspectives* (Evanston, 1953), which was edited by one of the undersigned and set forth the proceedings of a conference held at Arden House, Harriman, New York on May 23–25, 1952.

The focus of the more recent meeting, however, was somewhat different from that of the earlier one, and there is a corresponding difference between the resulting publications. When Soviet growth was considered at the earlier conference, a main concern was to examine past trends, but throughout an attempt was made also to gauge future prospects. For the more recent conference, the different contributors were again asked to examine past trends. But it was felt that rather than attempt to appraise future prospects they might usefully extend their inquiries in another way — by undertaking comparisons with the experience of other countries. The contributors were asked to make comparisons, where feasible, with the experience of the United States in particular, although that of other countries might also be considered. The papers submitted to the conference were prepared in this light, and the present volume is oriented accordingly.

Since the death of Stalin (March 5, 1953), there has been a marked change in the policy of the Soviet government on the publication of statistical information. The government often has continued, as it did before, to suppress economic data, but lately it has been releasing a sharply increasing volume of such information. In publishing economic data, it has also sought sometimes to observe higher reporting standards than it did previously, although in the crucial sphere of agriculture old deficiencies seem only to have been supplanted by new ones, while standards elsewhere surely still leave much to be desired. Partly because of these gains in respect of quantity and quality of statistical data available, Western scholars have been able to complete in the years since the Arden House meeting a number of fruitful studies on the Soviet economy. In considering again the theme that had been explored earlier, the participants at the Princeton conference could take account of this new work.

In examining past trends, contributors to the Arden House volume focused especially on the period beginning with 1928, the year when the First Five Year Plan was initiated. This has also been done here, but the earlier inquiries necessarily had to stop with the late forties or first years in the fifties while here it has been possible to consider more recent years as well. The period of the five year plans in the USSR has been notably turbulent. For this reason, the feasibility of considering a longer period has been a very real advantage for purposes of gauging trends.

But, by the same token, it is regrettable that in extending the interval considered contributors to the present volume often could not reach beyond 1958 or 1959, these being the terminal dates for underlying serial data used. Moreover, this limitation is the more significant since, as it has turned out, trends established in the fifties prior to 1958 and 1959 frequently have not persisted since with their earlier force. In any event, in appraising the import of the facts set forth in this volume the reader should consider that while the latest years have yet to be systematically studied, economic growth in Soviet Russia clearly has slowed down. Thus from Soviet *official* data we may compute these rates of growth:

	Average annual increase (percent)		
	1950–58	1958–61	1950–61
Agricultural production	5.8	1.9	4.8
Industrial production	12.1	10.1	11.5
National income	10.9	7.6	10.0

Western scholars have many reasons to think that rates such as these, derived from official statistics, are often significantly inflated, but undoubtedly there has been a retardation such as is shown.

The economic growth of Soviet Russia has long been a subject of almost universal interest. Some may feel that the interest has often been excessive, so far as it has betrayed a willingness to appraise the novel social system of that country primarily by reference to material and with little regard to political and social aspects. But the growth of the Soviet economy is still a momentous theme, meriting scholarly inquiry. Surveying afresh as they do different facets, the essays gathered together in this volume should contribute to further understanding of this topic.

In addition to authors of papers published herewith, a number of scholars participated in the conference — some as appointed discussants and other less formally. However, all contributed not only to the conference itself but to the present volume, for in revising their papers for publication the authors have taken into account comments that were made on them. It is therefore a pleasure to acknowledge the debt thus incurred to Joseph Berliner, James Blackman, Herbert Block, Morris Bornstein, Evsey Domar, Alexander Eckstein, Alexander Erlich, Walter Galenson, Alexander Gerschenkron, Raymond Goldsmith, David Granick, Rush Greenslade, Chauncey Harris, Leon Herman, Hans Heymann, Jr., Donald Hodgman, Oleg Hoeffding, Holland Hunter, Joseph Kershaw, Herbert Levine, Nancy Nimitz, Lloyd Reynolds, Harry Schwartz, Jaroslav Vanek, Lazar Volin, Murray Weizman, and Peter Wiles.

As was indicated, the conference was sponsored by and supported by a grant from the Committee on Economic Growth of the Social Science Research Council. The conference also benefited much from the opportunity provided by the Woodrow Wilson School of Princeton University to use its facilities. The papers on national income, capital stock, and consumption standards were initially prepared as research memoranda for The RAND Corporation, and are now published with the kind permission of that organization. Grateful acknowledgement is also due to the National Bureau of Economic Research for permission to use unpublished materials. Last but by no means least, the volume has benefited throughout from the thorough editing given it by Mrs. Lillian Weksler.

Abram Bergson
Simon Kuznets

Cambridge, Massachusetts
July 1962

CONTRIBUTORS TO THIS VOLUME

Abram Bergson — Professor of Economics and Member, Executive Committee of Russian Research Center, Harvard University; Consultant, The RAND Corporation

Janet G. Chapman — Consultant, The RAND Corporation

Warren W. Eason — Assistant Professor of Economics, Princeton University

Franklyn D. Holzman — Professor of Economics, Tufts University; Associate, Russian Research Center, Harvard University

D. Gale Johnson — Professor of Economics and Dean, Division of the Social Sciences, University of Chicago

Norman M. Kaplan — Economist, The RAND Corporation; Professor of Economics, University of Rochester

Simon Kuznets — Professor of Economics, Harvard University; Chairman, Committee on Economic Growth, Social Science Research Council

Raymond P. Powell — Associate Professor of Economics, Yale University

CONTENTS

TABLES

ECONOMIC TRENDS
IN THE SOVIET UNION

I

NATIONAL INCOME

Abram Bergson*

1. Introduction

Soviet national income is a theme that might be elaborated upon in different ways, but for present purposes it will be appropriate to focus on two related topics: (i) the rate of growth of total output, and (ii) the rate of growth of factor productivity. Also, in considering the latter I refer especially, at least for major inputs, to an aspect that lately has been receiving increasing attention: the productivity of different factors taken together. I try to explore these matters in a comparative way. Thus, in examining Soviet trends I also compare them with corresponding trends in the United States.

In considering developments in the USSR, we are interested primarily in the period of the five-year plans. In 1928, when this period begins, the

* This chapter was originally prepared as a report for The RAND Corporation; however, any views expressed in it are those of the author and should not be interpreted as reflecting the views of The RAND Corporation or the official opinion or policy of any of its sponsors.

The study was aided by access to the facilities of the Russian Research Center of Harvard University.

USSR was producing a total output on the order of $170 per capita, in terms of 1929 dollar prices. In the United States we had surpassed this level in the first decade after the Civil War. Considering circumstances such as these, it sometimes is suggested that in contrasting Soviet growth under the five-year plans with that in the United States, we should focus on an early period for the latter. Such a comparison should be of interest, but no more so than one in which reference is to a recent period for the USA as well as for the USSR. In any event, a comparative study of Soviet and American growth can be undertaken from different standpoints. To contrast the Soviet performance with that of the United States in both early and recent years is in order where the concern is mainly to gain insight into the Soviet growth process and perhaps ultimately into the weighty but elusive question of the comparative "economic efficiency" of competing social systems. In this essay, therefore, I endeavor to make both comparisons.

I have only recently completed a substantial study on Soviet national income.[1] In addition to compiling measures of income, I try on this basis to gauge comparative growth in the USSR and the USA. While I can add little to what has been said before, a brief review will make this a more rounded survey.

Although calculations of output per unit of inputs are by now familiar for the United States, in attempting to compile such data for the USSR and to compare their trends with those in the United States, I tread on relatively new ground. But when one considers the difficulties involved it is easy to feel that novelty may be about all that can be claimed for this effort. Perhaps most importantly, in calculating general factor productivity, one ordinarily aggregates inputs by using as weights "market-determined" factor income shares. Unfortunately, the Soviet price system fails to provide us with meaningful data of this sort. By experimenting with alternative sets of "synthetic" factor income shares, however, we may be able to limit the range of speculation on this important theme.

The data should be viewed in the light of diverse outstanding circumstances, particularly the fact that by the outset of the period considered the USSR generally had done little more than recover economically from the losses suffered during the World War, Revolution, and Civil War,[2] and that the interval then saw in its early years not only the first important applications of still novel techniques of central planning but also an extraordinary reorganization of agriculture with attendant extraordinary losses of capital and skill. Moreover, at a later point it witnessed

---

[1] Abram Bergson, *The Real National Income of Soviet Russia Since 1928* (Cambridge, Mass., 1961); hereafter cited as *Real SNIP*.

[2] *Ibid.*, pp. 6ff.

still more cataclysmic events under the impact of a great war fought furiously over the territory of the USSR itself. Pertinent events in the periods considered for the USA do not need mention here.

2. Growth of Soviet National Income

For purposes of appraising trends in Soviet national income, reference is made to Tables I.1 and I.2. Essentially, I rely here on *Real SNIP*, but the computations made previously for 1928–1955 have been extrapolated to 1958. Also, in *Real SNIP* attention is focused on *gross* national product. It is now possible to compile corresponding data on *net* national product, and the latter may be of greater interest here than the former.

In *Real SNIP* gross national product is computed in terms of prevailing ruble prices, but a partial revaluation is made to exclude sales taxes and include subsidies; in other words, after revaluation, output is in effect in terms of ruble factor cost. National income data are supposed to provide a partial basis for the appraisal of one or another or both of two abstract ultimates: production potential and welfare. The revaluation in terms of ruble factor cost while adjusting for outstanding distortions in ruble prices is supposed to make the national income data more indicative of production potential. Possibly, there is also a gain for appraisal of welfare, but in this case welfare must be viewed from the standpoint not of consumers' utilities, but of planners' preferences. The cited figures on the Soviet net national product correspond to those compiled previously on the Soviet gross national product in terms of ruble factor cost.

In *Real SNIP* two main series were derived in terms of the latter standard. In both cases, 1937 is taken as a base but the two series differ regarding the "index number formula" applied. One series is of the conventional sort: output in all years is computed in terms of values prevailing in the base year. The other is somewhat novel: obtained as a composite, it is intended to approximate serial data where in the comparison of each given year with the base year, output is computed in terms of given-year values. According to familiar theoretic reasoning, a given change in production potential may mean different things regarding production capacity depending on the "commodity structure." Thus, with a given change in production potential a country may experience a relatively large change in capacity to produce commodity mixes that are predominantly industrial and a relatively small change in capacity to produce commodity mixes that are predominantly agricultural. Both series should provide observations on the change over a period of years in capacity to produce the commodity mix prevailing in the base year. But, while at best neither calculation is very reliable in this regard, the one in terms of a given-year factor cost

Table I.1

USSR and USA: National Product, Factor Inputs, and Factor Productivity, Selected Years

USSR[a] (1937 = 100)

Item	Nature of measurement	1928	1937	1940	1950	1958
Net national product	In 1937 ruble factor cost	67.1	100.0	110.3	132.7	225.5
	As composite, 1937 base	38.1	100.0	110.3	129.9	221.0
Employment	Number of workers adjusted for non-farm hours	72.5	100.0	111.8	120.4	132.5
Reproducible fixed capital	In 1937 rubles	41.0	100.0	126.4	133.2	311.4
	As composite, 1937 base	36.1	100.0	126.4	124.0	282.7
Farm land	Acres	83.5	100.0	101.1	98.3	131.4
Livestock herds	In 1937 rubles	147.3	100.0	117.5	108.0	139.4
Selected inputs	With 1937 weights[b]	69.7	100.0	113.7	120.4	165.1
		71.9		111.9	119.1	147.4
		70.3		113.2	119.5	163.5
Net national product per worker, adjusted for nonfarm hours	With output in 1937 ruble factor cost	92.6	100.0	98.7	110.2	170.2
	With output as composite, 1937 base	52.6	100.0	98.7	107.9	166.8
Net national product per unit of reproducible fixed capital	With output in 1937 ruble factor cost and capital in 1937 rubles	163.7	100.0	87.3	99.6	72.4
	With output and capital as composite, 1937 base	105.5	100.0	87.3	104.8	78.2
Net national product per unit of selected inputs	With output in 1937 ruble factor cost and inputs using 1937 weights[b]	96.3	100.0	97.0	110.2	136.6
		93.3		98.6	111.4	153.0
		95.4		97.4	111.0	137.9
	With output as composite 1937 base and inputs using 1937 weights[b]	54.7	100.0	97.0	107.9	133.9
		53.0		98.6	109.1	149.9
		54.2		97.4	108.7	135.2

USA[c] (1929 = 100)

Item	Nature of measurement	1869/78	1899/1908	1929	1948	1954	1957
Net national product	In 1929 dollars	11.3	43.0	100.0	—	—	—
	In 1954 dollars	—	—	100.0	162.5	—	225.3
Employment	Number of workers adjusted for nonfarm hours	32.5	74.2	100.0	108.5	120.3	125.8
Reproducible fixed capital	In 1929 dollars	9.8	43.9	100.0	—	—	—
	In 1947/49 dollars	—	—	100.0	105.8	131.0	146.7
Farm land	Acres	39.2	80.4	100.0	99.0	96.6	91.0
Livestock herds	In 1929 dollars	53.8	101.5	100.0	—	—	—
	In 1947/49 dollars	—	—	100.0	97.1	105.8	104.3
Selected inputs	With 1929 weights	28.2	68.4	100.0	107.7	—	129.1
	With 1954 weights	—	—	100.0	107.4	121.4	128.0
Net national product per worker adjusted for nonfarm hours	With output in 1929 dollars	34.8	58.0	100.0	—	—	—
	With output in 1954 dollars	—	—	100.0	150.0	—	179.1
Net national product per unit of reproducible fixed capital	With output and capital in 1929 dollars	115.3	97.9	100.0	—	—	—
	With output in 1954 dollars and capital in 1947/49 dollars	—	—	100.0	—	—	—
Net national product per unit of selected inputs	With output in 1929 dollars and inputs using 1929 weights	40.1	62.9	100.0	153.6	—	153.6
	With output in 1954 dollars and inputs using 1954 weights	—	—	100.0	151.3	—	176.0

[a] Data for 1940–58 adjusted for territorial changes.

[b] Alternative figures correspond to different weights used in aggregating inputs, as given on p. 19. Thus, for the top figures, weights A were used; for the middle figures, weights B; and for the bottom figures, weights C.

[c] The entries for decade intervals are computed from annual averages for the decade.

Notes: The dash (—) indicates that data are not available.

Here and for later tables, where sources and methods are not given, see appendix.

Table I.2
USSR and USA: National Product, Factor Inputs, and Productivity, Average Annual Rate of Growth for Selected Periods (percent)

Item	Nature of measurement	USSR 1928–58	1928–58 effective years	1928–40	1940–50	1950–58
Net national product	In 1937 ruble factor cost	4.1	4.8	4.2	1.9	6.8
	As composite, 1937 base	6.0	7.0	9.3	1.7	6.8
Employment	Number of workers adjusted for non-farm hours	2.0	2.3	3.7	0.7	1.2
Reproducible fixed capital	In 1937 rubles	7.0	8.1	9.8	0.5	11.2
	As composite, 1937 base	7.1	8.2	11.0	−0.2	10.9
Farm land	Acres	1.5	1.8	1.6	−1.3	3.7
Livestock herds	In 1937 rubles	−0.2	−0.2	−1.9	−0.8	3.2
Selected inputs	With 1937 weights[a]	2.9 / 2.4 / 2.9	3.4 / 2.8 / 3.3	4.2 / 3.8 / 4.1	0.6 / 0.6 / 0.5	4.0 / 2.7 / 4.0
Net national product per worker adjusted for nonfarm hours	With output in 1937 ruble factor cost	2.1	2.4	0.5	1.1	5.6
	With output as composite, 1937 base	3.9	4.5	5.4	0.9	5.6
Net national product per unit of reproducible fixed capital	With output in 1937 ruble factor cost and capital in 1937 rubles	−2.7	−3.1	−5.1	1.3	−3.9
	With output and capital as composite, 1937 base	−1.0	−1.1	−1.6	1.9	−3.6
Net national product per unit of selected inputs	With output in 1937 ruble factor cost and inputs using 1937 weights[a]	1.2 / 1.7 / 1.2	1.4 / 1.9 / 1.4	0.1 / 0.5 / 0.2	1.3 / 1.2 / 1.3	2.7 / 4.0 / 2.8
	With output as composite, 1937 base and inputs using 1937 weights[a]	3.0 / 3.5 / 3.1	3.5 / 4.1 / 3.6	4.9 / 5.3 / 5.0	1.1 / 1.0 / 1.1	2.7 / 4.1 / 2.8

USA[b]

Item	Nature of measurement	1869/78–1899/1908	1899/1908–1929	1929–57	1929–48	1948–57
Net national product	In 1929 dollars	4.6	3.4	—	—	—
	In 1954 dollars	—	—	2.9	2.6	3.7
Employment	Number of workers adjusted for non-farm hours	2.8	1.2	0.8	0.4	1.7
Reproducible fixed capital	In 1929 dollars	5.1	3.3	—	—	—
	In 1947/49 dollars	—	—	1.4	0.3	3.7
Farm land	Acres	2.4	0.9	-0.3	-0.1	-0.9
Livestock herds	In 1929 dollars	2.1	0.1	—	—	—
	In 1947/49 dollars	—	—	0.2	-0.2	0.8
Selected inputs	With 1929 weights	3.0	1.5	0.9	0.4	2.0
	With 1954 weights	—	—	0.9	0.4	2.0
Net national product per worker adjusted for nonfarm hours	With output in 1929 dollars	1.7	2.2	2.1	2.2	—
	With output in 1954 dollars	—	—	—	—	2.0
Net national product per unit of reproducible fixed capital	With output and capital in 1929 dollars	-0.5	0.1	—	—	—
	With output in 1954 dollars and capital in 1947/49 dollars	—	—	—	—	—
Net national product per unit of selected inputs	With output in 1929 dollars and inputs using 1929 weights	1.5	1.8	1.5	2.3	...
	With output in 1954 dollars and inputs using 1954 weights	—	—	2.0	2.2	1.7

[a] Alternative figures correspond to different weights used in aggregating inputs, as given on p. 19. Thus for the top figures, weights A were used; for the middle figures, weights B; and for the bottom figures, weights C.

[b] Where the terminal date is a decade, the rate of growth is based on an annual average centered at the middle of the decade.

Note: The dash (—) indicates that data are not available; the symbol . . . that they are negligible.

may well be more so than the one in terms of base-year ruble factor cost. Both series on gross national product have been used here to derive two corresponding series on net national product.[3]

To repeat, the revaluation of national income in terms of ruble factor cost is only partial. Moreover, as a valuation standard, ruble factor cost itself leaves something to be desired. Then too, despite a substantial effort the calculations necessarily are inexact. While the resultant errors are not likely to cumulate in any serious way, the deficiencies in valuation procedures, particularly in early years, probably give rise to something of an upward bias. The bias is only compounded (although probably to a less extent than might be supposed) by the omission from national income of home processing, an activity that dwindles in relative importance as industrialization proceeds.[4]

[3] To one familiar with the theory of national income computation, the case for given-year (as distinct from base-year) weights for purposes of compiling measures pertinent to production potential probably is readily perceived, but to my knowledge this matter was first elaborated by Dr. Richard Moorsteen in a talk which he gave at The RAND Corporation in the summer of 1958. Dr. Moorsteen has since discussed this question in "On Measuring Production Potential and Relative Efficiency," *Quarterly Journal of Economics,* August 1961. With special reference to Soviet circumstances, I discuss it in *Real SNIP,* chap. 3. I have also benefited from discussion with Dr. Moorsteen on the related question referred to below concerning the index number formula to be employed in the aggregation of inputs.

[4] For the series in terms of 1937 ruble factor cost, one possible source of upward bias is eliminated. Thus, of two compilations made previously in terms of 1937 ruble factor cost use is made of that involving extension of the revaluation within retail sales. While it was felt that this extension yielded rates that were nearer the mark, in *Real SNIP* it was convenient to focus on the series involving the more restricted revaluation. The former series yields a slightly slower rate of growth than the latter for 1928–37: gross national product grows 0.7 of a percentage point less rapidly than with the less extended revaluation. For 1937–48 and 1937–54, the two series do not differ consequentially.

On the other hand, ruble factor cost still includes somewhat arbitrary profit charges, and omits any systematic allowance for rent and interest. Deduction of the former and inclusion of illustrative charges for the latter reduce the average annual rate of growth of gross national product 0.4 of a percentage point for 1928–37. The rate also shows a slight reduction during 1937–50 and 1950–55. For effective years during 1928–55 the rate of growth falls 0.3 of a percentage point.

Where the purpose is to appraise production potential, agricultural labor services are valued ideally at the same rate as industrial labor services requiring similar skill and entailing similar "disutility." Since in 1937 collective farmers earned about 1,600 rubles per man-year, while industrial wage earners on the average earned some 2,800 rubles per year, this condition appears unlikely to have been fulfilled in the USSR, but no effort was made in *Real SNIP* to adjust for this aspect. From a recomputation made to allow for agricultural rent, we may judge that especially in the early years, revaluation of agricultural labor services would also reduce somewhat the rate of growth.

Although *Real SNIP* might be read somewhat differently, I believe that for purposes of appraising production potential, all money income differentials between the farm and industry for labor of similar skill and disutility tend to be distorting. This is so even where the differentials equalize differences in living costs due to locational and institutional factors, for with such a differential relative prices fail to conform (as is ideally desired) to rates of transformation.

The inclusion in the net national product of a significant variety of, but by no means

According to a recent computation by Dr. Morris Bornstein, which for 1950–55 is in close accord with *Real SNIP*, the Soviet gross national product grows at a somewhat higher rate during 1955–58 than during 1950–55. According to a tentative computation in *Real SNIP*, the rate of growth during 1955–58 is about the same as during 1950–55. Neither calculation, however, allows for the probably significant upward bias in Soviet official data on agricultural output for recent years. Here in extending the *Real SNIP* series for 1928–55 to 1958, I therefore assume that during 1955–58 output grows somewhat less rapidly than during 1950–55. The two series compiled in *Real SNIP* show the same growth in national income during 1950–55 and probably little error is entailed in the assumption that this is also true for 1955–58.[5]

From the *Real SNIP* figures on gross, I derive corresponding figures on net national product by means of estimates of depreciation charges taken from or calculated on the basis of data compiled in a forthcoming inquiry by Dr. Richard Moorsteen and Professor Raymond Powell into the capital stock of the USSR. The charges rest on Soviet asset longevity figures which curiously turn out to be similar to those employed by Professor Kuznets in comparable computations for the United States. While the Moorsteen-Powell data on depreciation are in terms of prevailing ruble prices, I believe they may be used with a minimum of error to adjust the *Real SNIP* output data in terms of ruble factor cost.[6]

---

all, home processing at factor cost would reduce the rate of growth of output in 1937 ruble factor cost during 1928–37 some 0.3 of a percentage point. The relative decline in home processing presumably occurred primarily in these early years.

[5] On the data considered in the extrapolation, see *Real SNIP,* chap. 15; and M. Bornstein, "A Comparison of Soviet and United States National Product," in Joint Economic Committee, 86th Congress of the United States, 1st Session, *Comparisons of the United States and Soviet Economies* (Washington, 1959), part II.

[6] In *Real SNIP* all outlays classified in Soviet statistics as "capital repairs" (as distinct from "current repairs") are viewed as "final" product and included in gross national product. Here, before deducting depreciation, I omit from gross national product one-half of such outlays on capital repairs. The measures obtained are, I believe, more nearly comparable than they would otherwise be with the Commerce Department data for the USA after which the *Real SNIP* computations are patterned and which I use in comparing the growth of national income in the USSR and in the USA. While the share of capital repairs deducted is arbitrary, an alternative adjustment would have hardly any effect on measures that are of interest here.

In their study of capital stock, Moorsteen and Powell compile data on the volume of outlays on capital repairs in terms of 1937 ruble prices. With the aid of deflators for fixed capital investment implied in *Real SNIP,* I have derived corresponding figures in terms of the prices of other years that are needed for adjustment of the *Real SNIP* data on gross national product in terms of given-year values. As with depreciation, the fact that the data are in terms of prevailing ruble prices poses no problems.

To return to depreciation, from the Moorsteen-Powell computations alternative series on depreciation are or may be compiled. I use here a series representing depreciation on basic assets excluding capital repairs. Since some capital repairs are still treated here as a final product, some allowance should properly be made for their depreciation, but it did not seem advisable to use a second Moorsteen-Powell series where depreciation is

Under the five-year plans, Soviet national income has grown at a rapid tempo, although hardly one such as might be suggested by familiar Soviet official claims. Thus, during the entire period 1928–58, the Soviet net national product, in terms of 1937 ruble factor cost, is found to grow at an average rate of 4.1 percent annually. On the basis of the alternative computation obtained as a composite, the corresponding figure is 6.0 percent. These rates of growth and others, where in order, have been adjusted somewhat roughly for the changes in Soviet boundaries that occurred in the period studied, chiefly in 1939 and 1940.[7] The figures just given, however, are averages where all years in the period including the four war years are counted. For present purposes, probably of more interest are the rates of growth obtained on the assumption that the entire increase in output is attributable to the 26 peacetime years: 4.8 and 7.0 percent, respectively. Actually, the Russians did not regain their prewar level of production until 1948. The expansion of output to this level and beyond, it is true, was facilitated by reparations and by the availability for a time of partially damaged plants which could be renovated and restored to full use with limited investments. Nevertheless, the alternative

---

computed in a manner conforming to Soviet accounting theory which yields total charges twice those given by the series I employ. Essentially, for the second series, depreciation is charged both on basic investments and on capital repairs. Moreover, in the case of capital repairs the charge is related not to actual outlays on capital repairs but to outlays called for by Soviet accounting norms. Since outlays in accord with such norms are presupposed by the Soviet asset longevity figures, theoretically, there is something to be said for this approach, but I hesitate to rely on the Soviet norms. In any event, under this approach the depreciation charges would tend to be less comparable than those actually relied upon with the depreciation data for the USA, and this is of concern here. Of course, if the alternative were employed, we would still have to exclude from the Soviet gross national product one-half of the total capital repairs, but this would occasion no difficulty.

The elements of the calculation of the net national product described here are shown in the appendix.

Reference here and elsewhere to unpublished calculations of Moorsteen and Powell is with the kind permission of the authors and The RAND Corporation.

[7] As in *Real SNIP*, chap. 13, I assume that the territories incorporated in the USSR in 1939 and later add, in each year, 10 percent to the total output produced within the pre-1939 boundaries. For the various factor inputs in the USSR, referred to later in this chapter, I assume that the relation of new territories to those within the pre-1939 boundaries is the same as that for total output. By implication, therefore, the territorial acquisitions do not affect the relation of output to the different inputs. For reproducible fixed capital, this adjustment simply reverses the one made in compiling the unadjusted series from which I start. Or rather, this is so for 1940, but there is no basis to proceed differently here for 1950–55. For inputs other than fixed capital (employment, farm land, and livestock herds), the stated assumption is rather arbitrary, but the resultant errors in my calculations cannot be consequential. See *Real SNIP*, chap. 13; Abram Bergson and Hans Heymann, Jr., *Soviet National Income and Product, 1940–48* (New York, 1953), p. 233; and TSU, *Narodnoe khoziaistvo SSSR v 1958 godu* (Moscow, 1959), pp. 386–387, 445–446 (hereafter cited as *Narodnoe khoziaistvo 1958*).

rates of growth must still be considered a conservative representation of the elusive aspect in question: what Soviet growth might have been if there had been no war. Following Professor Gregory Grossman, I will refer to measures which impute to nonwar years Soviet growth for periods spanning the war as rates of growth for "effective years."

While growth is generally swift, it fluctuates in different intervals. The tempo also depends on the formula. Thus, during 1928–40, with valuation at 1937 ruble factor cost, output grows 4.2 percent annually. With valuation at ruble factor cost of the given year, the corresponding figure is more than twice as great: 9.2 percent. As already explained, particularly for the early years, my calculations are inexact and probably subject to an upward bias, but output clearly grew rapidly. For 1940–50, an interval spanning the war, the rate of growth sharply declined according to either formula, although much more so where valuation is at ruble factor cost of the given year. During 1950–58 the tempo is again relatively high: 6.8 percent annually, according to either measure. By implication, the rate of growth during this interval exceeds that during 1928–40 where valuation is at 1937 ruble factor cost. Where valuation is at ruble factor cost of the given year, it equals or falls short of the corresponding tempo for 1928–40. Thus, to the interesting question whether growth is tending to accelerate, proceed without change, or slow down, the answer awkwardly depends on the formula.

Although the two formulas often diverge (to repeat) the one in which valuation is at ruble factor cost of the given year may be more indicative of changes in capacity to produce the base-year mix than that where valuation is at ruble factor cost of 1937. By implication, in this sense, growth during 1928–58 may have been more rapid than the more conventional computation suggests. Also, growth in the same sense probably is not accelerating as the more conventional computation suggests. Rather, the tempo may not be changing; or alternatively, it may actually be slowing down.

Obviously, the data on the Soviet net national product in terms of alternative index number formulas bear on the familiar question of the effect, where use is made of the same formula, of a change in base year on index numbers of physical volume. Since I have discussed this matter in detail in chapter 12 of *Real SNIP*, it may suffice to say here that so far as a shift from a very "early" to a "late" base year reduces the increase in "real" national income my calculations conform to expectations as formulated in Professor Alexander Gerschenkron's well-known hypothesis. Moreover, the high degree of relativity of the measures to the base year that is observed in early years seems understandable in view of the violent structural changes occurring under the early Soviet five-year plans.

3. Growth of National Income: USSR Versus USA

For the national income of the United States, one necessarily turns to the computations of Professor Simon Kuznets and the U.S. Department of Commerce. Accordingly, for comparison with the Soviet data, in Tables I.1 and I.2, I present corresponding figures for the United States compiled from these computations. For years before 1929, I use Professor Kuznets' calculations of the U.S. net national product in terms of 1929 dollar prices. Since the calculations for the USSR were patterned after those of the U.S. Department of Commerce, net national product has essentially the same meaning here as in the Commerce Department calculations. As is well known, Professor Kuznets conceives of the net national product somewhat differently from the Commerce Department, but his data are used only for selected years and for these years the comparisons, I believe, are not consequentially affected by this feature. While Professor Kuznets' calculations generally are in terms of 1929 dollar prices, because of the nature of the computation they may sometimes significantly reflect dollar prices of the given year. For reasons which will become evident, this is not undesirable for my purposes. But as Professor Kuznets makes clear, his computations are often crude in any event. Although here too the errors are difficult to quantify, in early years, particularly, there may be some tendency toward an upward bias.[8]

[8] I refer in this chapter to data compiled in Simon Kuznets' *Capital in the American Economy: Its Formation and Financing* (Princeton, 1961), and use his variant III, the one statistically most comparable with the Commerce Department calculations.

On the nature and import of the difference in scope between Kuznets' and the Commerce Department's concept of net national product, see Simon Kuznets, "Long-Term Changes in National Income of the United States of America since 1870," in Simon Kuznets, ed., *Income and Wealth of the United States* (Cambridge, England, 1952), pp. 29ff. On reasons for thinking that Professor Kuznets' computations may materially reflect given-year prices, see *Real SNIP,* chaps. 7 and 14. As was explained, particularly in early years my real national income data may be subject to something of an upward bias for various reasons, among them the undervaluation of farm labor services and omission of home processing. Although Professor Kuznets is not explicit on the matter, his measures of real national income must also reflect an undervaluation of farm labor services, especially in early years. As Professor Kuznets makes clear, his measures are affected by the omission of home processing.

Professor Kuznets also considers as sources of bias the "increase in the extent of hauling, distribution, and other services" and "higher costs in cities." For present purposes, where the concern is with production potential, I doubt that such activities are properly viewed in this way, although the trends in question must be related to the undervaluation of farm labor services, and no doubt there is much to be said for Professor Kuznets' approach if the concern is with welfare. Moreover, as Professor Kuznets acknowledges, the adjustment he suggests for the bias in question, together with that caused by the omission of home processing, entailing an increase in household consumption in 1869/78 of 50 percent, represents "a rather generous allowance" (see Kuznets, "Long-Term Changes," p. 60). Nevertheless, if we adjust consumption for 1869/78 in this way and increase consumption for 1899/1908 correspondingly by, say, 25 percent, the annual rate of growth of net national product over the interval falls only 0.5 of a percentage point.   •

For years since 1929, I use national income data published by the Department of Commerce. In their latest revision these data are in terms of 1954 dollar prices. Unfortunately, the Commerce Department publishes figures in constant prices only on gross national product, but corresponding data on net national product can be derived. Although hardly devoid of error, the Commerce Department calculations must be statistically among the most reliable available on national income, and their quality should not be unduly impaired by the adjustment for depreciation, which is based chiefly on Kuznets' data in terms of replacement cost.[9]

In order to gauge comparative trends in output, either series for the USSR may be used, and for the USA, only one series is at hand for any given interval, but conceivably additional measures for either country might be derived. In fact, as will appear, something is known about further alternatives in any event. Which sorts of data should be compared in the two countries? Although the pertinent methodological issue is rarely explored, I think there will be no dissent if I observe certain principles set forth in chapter 14 of *Real SNIP*. Essentially, comparisons may be useful where the measures for each country are (as here) in local prices. Preferably, the same index number formula should be applied in the two countries, although the effect of a change in formula is also of interest. If possible, the data for each country should also be in terms of prices that are more or less contemporaneous with the period in question. Furthermore, the base years for the two countries might well be similarly located in the respective intervals in question, although one also wishes to know the effect on the results of a shift in the base year.

Given these principles, my findings are much the same as those reached previously. The data permit us to compare the Soviet performance under the five-year plans with that of the United States in both recent and early times. For the USA, attention may be usefully directed to two intervals in particular, 1929–57 and 1869/78–1899/1908. Let us compare first the Soviet performance with that of the United States in the recent period. The net national product of the USSR grows during 1928–58 at an average

---

In Table I.1, I incorporate in the index for 1869/78 an allowance for a 5 percent under-coverage which Professor Kuznets indicates is probable. This is quite apart from the omission of home processing.

[9] The figures on gross national product since 1929 in dollar prices of 1954 are from U.S. Department of Commerce, *U.S. Income and Output*, Washington, 1958, pp. 118–119. In the same prices, depreciation is estimated to be $22.6 billions in 1929, $34.4 billions in 1954, and $48.4 billions in 1957.

For depreciation in 1929 and 1948 I use the Kuznets estimates of depreciation on nonwar goods, excluding depletion. From depreciation in terms of current replacement cost, corresponding figures in terms of 1954 replacement cost are obtained by use of the inflators for private investment in fixed capital implied in the Commerce Department national income calculations in terms of 1954 prices. Kuznets' estimates of depreciation are available only up to 1955, but once the corresponding figure in 1954 dollars is obtained, it can be extrapolated to 1957 with a minimum of error.

annual rate of 4.1 percent where output is valued at 1937 ruble factor cost and of 6.0 percent where output is valued at ruble factor cost of the given year. The corresponding figures for effective years are 4.8 and 7.0 percent. In contrast, the net national product of the USA, valued at 1954 prices, grows during 1929–57 at an average annual rate of but 2.9 percent. For comparison with the Soviet series in 1937 ruble factor cost, according to the guiding methodological principles, one might wish to consider data for the USA in terms of prices of, say, the late thirties. Similarly, for comparison with the Soviet series in ruble factor cost of the given year, it would be preferable to use USA data compiled according to a corresponding formula. Judging from information compiled previously, each of these recomputations would raise the rate of growth of the U.S. output only a fraction of a percentage point.[10] The conclusion must be that Soviet output tends systematically to grow more rapidly than ours. The Russians outpace us where measures for both countries are in appropriate base-year values, and they do so the more where measures are in appropriate given-year values.

For the USSR, the allowance made for the war necessarily is arbitrary. Besides, the period also witnessed in its early years the first efforts at central planning and the collectivization drive with its resultant losses and dislocations. Under the circumstances, therefore, it may be of interest to compare the performance of the two countries, where for the USSR reference is to recent postwar years, say, 1950–58: here the Soviet margin over us is marked no matter which measure is considered. For the USA, too, the period considered was surely complex, but curiously, if for this country, reference is made instead to, say, the years 1948–57, the comparison is not markedly affected.

Turning now to the comparison of the Soviet performance under the five-year plans with that of the United States during 1869/78–1899/1908, the pertinent Soviet measures are as before, but for the USA, output grows at an average annual rate of 4.6 percent. For the USA, output is calculated in terms of 1929 dollars, but depending on the measures for the USSR, reference should properly be made either to data in terms of dollar prices of, say, the late 1880's or to data in terms of dollar prices of the given year. Regrettably, from such additional information as could be found, the effect of each of these two further recomputations is conjectural. But where reference for both countries is to measures in appropriate base-year values, probably neither country markedly outpaces the other. Where reference for both countries is to measures in appropriate given-year values the outcome is especially speculative, although one wonders whether the USA tempo could match that of the USSR. Thus the shift in base year for the United States even over a long interval to a relatively

[10] *Real SNIP*, chap. 14, pp. 265ff.

early date might not have as large an impact on real national income as that observed for the USSR when the base year is shifted from 1937 to 1928. Nevertheless, the facts on this important matter are still unsettled, for the effect of a shift in base year on U.S. national income measures still has to be systematically investigated.

In view of the terminal dates selected, and, in the early intervals, of the use of decade averages as the terminal figures, the growth rates calculated for the United States probably reflect (as one would wish here) secular trends rather than the fluctuations due to business cycles.

To attempt to translate relative trends in national income into relative trends in production potential is only to compound uncertainties, but I think the presumption must be, nevertheless, that since 1928, and especially in recent years, the Russians have expanded capacity to produce their commodity mixes of the late thirties more rapidly than we have to produce our commodity mixes of that time. Comparison of the growth of Soviet capacity since 1928 regarding Soviet commodity mixes of the late thirties with the growth of our capacity in the latter decades of the last century regarding our mixes of, say, the late 1880's might possibly show that the Russians match or surpass us in this respect, too, although this is conjectural.

Although neither the Commerce Department nor Kuznets refers explicitly to the matter, the data from both presumably are pertinent to both production potential and welfare. The corresponding figures for the USSR bear primarily on the former, and for this reason, the comparisons are best considered as relating to this aspect.

To repeat, the same change in a country's production potential may mean different changes in its capacity to produce different commodity mixes. With the same change in its capacity to produce different mixes, there may be different changes in its production potential. Granting that each country increased its production capacity in the manner described, must we not consider still that production potential may have varied incommensurately? Indeed, in view of the Russians' notable concentration on industry at the expense of agriculture and services, is this not likely to have been so? Thus, could not the Russians have outpaced us regarding output but not regarding production potential, and simply because the gains realized in the latter respect in both countries permitted larger increases in the production of the Soviet mixes than in that of ours?

These familiar questions are properly the subject of a separate inquiry, but it may not be amiss to summarize a tentative standpoint taken on them in chapter 14 of *Real SNIP*. Most likely both countries have in fact experienced disproportionate changes in capacity to produce different mixes. Actually, in the case of the USSR, changes of this kind are already implied in the alternative series on output that have been considered.

Nevertheless, the disproportions are probably not as favorable to the Russians as has been supposed. At least this seems so where the Soviet performance since 1928 is compared with that of the United States in a contemporary period. On the other hand, if the comparison is between the Soviet performance since 1928 and that of the United States in the latter decades of the last century, the Russians may be at an advantage.

4. TRENDS IN SOVIET FACTOR PRODUCTIVITY

The results of the attempt to relate trends in output to trends in major inputs taken together for the USSR are shown in Tables I.1 and I.2. In compiling these measures, I consider the two series on net national product, but in each case compare output with an aggregate of the following inputs:

Employment. A calculation made previously for 1928–55 has been here extended to 1958. Essentially, employment is the sum of: (i) average employment during the year in nonfarm, civilian occupations as determined chiefly from Dr. Warren Eason's computations; (ii) agricultural employment in terms of "full-time" equivalents as estimated for 1928 from a Soviet official calculation and for 1937 and later years from data compiled by Miss Nancy Nimitz; (iii) the penal labor force, which was negligible in 1928, and is assumed to total 3.5 millions in 1940 and 1950, and 2 millions in 1958; and (iv) the armed forces as determined from diverse information, including data released by Khrushchev in his speech before the Supreme Soviet on January 14, 1960. It is difficult to appraise the possible errors that result. The data on agricultural employment almost inevitably are rather crude. The figures on penal labor are also quite arbitrary, but at least in respect to trends for the entire period 1928–58 an error at this point could hardly be consequential. While the precise form of measurement varies somewhat among sectors, employment is more or less in terms of man-years. In the tables the figures cited also allow in the case of civilian, nonfarm workers for changes in hours, as indicated by trends in industry alone. Information at hand on trends in the agricultural work day under the five-year plans is conflicting: possibly there was no change to speak of; possibly as a result of collectivization, hours declined.[11]

[11] For the underlying data on employment in man-years for 1928–55, before adjustment for changes in nonfarm hours and in boundaries, see *Real SNIP*, appendix K. For 1958, employment in these terms is 93.6 million, constituted as follows: civilian, nonfarm, 50.1 million; farm, 37.9; military, 3.6; and penal, 2.0.

On civilian, nonfarm and farm employment, I consider particularly data in *Narodnoe khoziaistvo 1958*, pp. 655–659; and in TSU, *Sel'skoe khoziaistvo SSSR* (Moscow, 1960), p. 450. On the armed forces, see *Pravda*, January 15, 1960. Perhaps wrongly, no allowance is made for a further decline in penal labor below the assumed 1955 level. The employment equivalent of changes in nonfarm hours for 1928–55 is determined from data in *Real SNIP*, appendix H. For 1958, normal working hours are taken to be 113 percent of those prevailing in 1937 (see *Narodnoe khoziaistvo 1958*, p. 665).

In this initial inquiry, it seemed best not to attempt to adjust employment for changes in occupational or skill structure. Although measures of factor productivity with this adjustment are useful in that they tend to reflect forces other than changes in the quality of the labor force, the adjustment is not easily made. In any event, the measures of factor productivity are still of interest if (as is so without the adjustment) they reflect qualitative changes in labor.[12]

Reproducible fixed capital. I rely here on the computations by Moorsteen and Powell. "Reproducible fixed capital" is understood to include producers' durables and buildings and structures of all kinds. Moorsteen and Powell measure the fixed capital stock both gross and net of depreciation. The latter aspect is more appropriate here, although interestingly the two series move closely together and for practical purposes the choice between them is of little import. The data are also compiled in terms of ruble prices of different years. For the moment, attention is directed to those valued at 1937 ruble prices but later I shall refer to an alternative composite, 1937 base series similar to the one compiled for national income. The composite, 1937 base series is derived from the Moorsteen-Powell computations in terms of the prices of different years.

The volume of net fixed capital assets at any date is the sum of the stock of fixed capital, net of depreciation and on hand on January 1, 1928, and the total net investment in fixed capital from that time to the date in question. Because of limitations on Soviet data underlying the net stock of fixed capital on hand on January 1, 1928, this item may possibly be overstated as much as 30 percent. As the share of the initial stock in the total on hand at any date dwindles in the course of time, the rate of growth necessarily is affected, particularly in early years.[13]

Gross fixed capital investment in the period since January 1, 1928, is determined, also probably with an appreciable margin of error, from a computation much the same as that made in *Real SNIP*: for producers' durables, outlays in current prices, computed from Soviet data, are deflated by price indexes compiled by Moorsteen; for construction, outlays in constant prices are assumed to vary with the physical volume of material

[12] Among the qualitative changes in question, under conditions of industrialization by far the most outstanding are those associated with the shift in relative numbers of workers on the farm and in industry. Nevertheless, logically before any adjustment is made for qualitative changes in labor one needs to consider whether, because of the possible undervaluation of farm labor services, national income may not be distorted to begin with. Once one has allowed for this latter aspect, the adjustment for qualitative changes in labor is correspondingly less than that generally assumed to be appropriate. See also fn. 4 on the possible effect on Soviet national income of an allowance for the undervaluation of farm labor services.

[13] For intervals considered in the tables the rates of growth of the fixed capital stock in 1937 prices based on a January 1, 1928, stock reduced 30 percent are as follows: 1928–58, 8.3 percent; 1928–58 (effective years), 9.6 percent; 1928–40, 12.6 percent; 1940–50, 0.9 percent; and 1950–58, 11.5 percent.

inputs into construction, computed by Powell. Depreciation is deducted on a basis already indicated. As a result of the war, the Russians are supposed to have lost one-third of the fixed capital on hand at the time of the German attack. While this is a rather arbitrary figure, under alternative assumptions that the losses totaled 15 percent and 50 percent of the prewar stock, the assets on hand on January 1, 1950, vary only 8 percent from the amount calculated initially.[14]

This is not the place to discuss the thorny question of the theoretic basis for the measurement of "real" capital stock, but it should be observed that in 1937 Soviet fixed capital goods were subject, to only an inconsequential degree, directly or indirectly, to the famous "turnover tax" and as a result of a price reform of the previous year subsidies were no longer the major feature that they had been in this area. By implication, capital goods prices in 1937 probably conform more or less to the ruble factor cost standard in terms of which national income has been valued. Broadly speaking, capital goods prices also tend to conform to ruble factor cost in years for which such prices enter into my composite, 1937 base series.

The data on Soviet fixed capital evidently represent *capacity*. While a computation of factor productivity on this basis is of interest, one might also wish to consider data representing employment, but such information is not available. However, because of the increase in shift work, employment probably has increased more rapidly than capacity.

Farm land. Here we use the total sown area given by Soviet official statistics. Although on the eve of the five-year plans vast areas of the USSR were still uncultivated, in terms of climate or soil or both much of this land was either inferior or entirely unsuitable for agriculture. By the same token, the expansion of the sown area since 1928 undoubtedly has been associated with a significant decline in quality. While this has been true of the whole period, it must have been especially so in the years since 1954 as the sown area has sharply increased under Khrushchev's New Lands Program.[15]

No account could be taken of this qualitative deterioration. While in

---

[14] As already explained, fixed capital stock excludes capital repairs and is net of depreciation. Since I have classified as "final" product one-half of expenditures on capital repairs, it might have been preferable to use a series in which capital repairs to this extent are included along with basic assets in the stock of fixed capital, but after an allowance for depreciation. For present purposes, however, I believe the series actually used is more appropriate than either of two others that Moorsteen and Powell compile. In both cases, all outlays on capital repairs are included, but in one the charge for depreciation is doubled while in the other it is increased 50 percent. On the rationale of the former calculation, see fn. 6; the latter is simply an arbitrary variant of this.

By appropriate averaging, Moorsteen-Powell data for January 1 have been centered on July 1.

[15] *Narodnoe khoziaistvo 1958*, pp. 386–387.

neglecting qualitative changes I am only continuing a procedure adopted in the case of employment, unhappily in the case of farm land there hardly is any basis such as there was before to desire such changes to be reflected in the measures of factor productivity rather than in those of factor inputs.

Livestock herds. Herd numbers for different sorts of livestock (cows, other cattle, hogs, sheep and goats, and horses) given by Soviet official data, are aggregated in terms of the average ruble prices realized on the farm in 1937. Estimates of the latter were compiled for *Real SNIP* by Dr. George Karcz. No account is taken of changes in animal weights or productivity. These usually declined markedly in the thirties, but by the end of the period studied were probably as high as or higher than they had been on the eve of the five-year plans.[16]

So much for inputs that are aggregated. In summing them, as already explained, I use as weights three sets of "synthetic" factor income shares (Table I.3).

Table I.3
USSR: Weights Used in Aggregating Factor Inputs

Item	Weights A		Weights B		Weights C	
	Billion rubles	Percent	Billion rubles	Percent	Billion rubles	Percent
Employment	179.9	70.4	179.9	80.5	179.9	67.5
Reproducible fixed capital	46.2	18.1	18.5	8.3	46.2	17.3
Farm land	22.4	8.8	22.4	10.0	33.6	12.6
Livestock herds	7.0	2.7	2.8	1.3	7.0	2.6
All	255.5	100.0	223.6	100.0	266.7	100.0

All three tabulations are highly arbitrary. Moreover because of the nature of their derivation the income shares indicated are somewhat different even in principle from "market-determined" shares usually employed in calculations of this sort. There is a corresponding change in the concept of factor productivity, although one hardly entailing any loss of interest. Essentially, the usual "market-determined" factor income shares are supposed to correspond ideally to relative marginal productivities of different factors. For the "synthetic" factor income shares considered, the desideratum perhaps is best thought of as being instead that the shares correspond ideally to relative marginal productivities not

[16] For the underlying herd figures, see *ibid.*, pp. 445–446. On livestock prices in 1937, see *Real SNIP,* appendix G

necessarily as they actually are but as they would be if one abstracts from any special efficiencies or inefficiencies of the social system considered. In this way, the latter tend to be reflected not in the measures of total inputs but in the measures of factor productivity.

As to the derivation, I assign to employment in all three cases a measure of importance corresponding to the total wages and other labor income earned in the USSR in 1937 (in the case of farm households some of the earnings might be more properly classified as agricultural rent). For reproducible fixed capital, for weights A and C, I allow for a net return of 20.0 percent annually on the stock on hand on July 1, 1937. For weights B, the rate of return is reduced to 8.0 percent. In the USA, in 1929, private capital (excluding agricultural land) generally earned an average net return of 6.89 percent. But because of the relatively limited capital stock in the USSR in 1937, even with an assumed rate of 20.0 percent, the total income accruing to reproducible fixed capital amounts to but 25.7 percent of all Soviet labor income in the same year. This is no more than the corresponding relation that prevailed in the United States in 1929, 26.0 percent. As we go back to relatively early dates in U.S. history, however, there is hardly any evidence of any sharp increase in the net return to capital above the 1929 level. Although this might mean different things, it is possibly wrong to suppose (as one is tempted to do) that the relative shortage of capital in the USSR calls for the imputation of a notably high return to it.

For farm land, in the case of weights A and B, the assumed weight means that agricultural rent equals 40.0 percent of Soviet farm labor income in 1937. For weights C, agricultural rent is 60.0 percent of the latter. The former relation is about the same as that for the USA in 1929. Compared with farm labor income, however, agricultural rent in the USA tends to be greater in earlier than in recent years. For livestock herds, I allow in all cases the same net return as for reproducible fixed capital.[17]

---

[17] The total wage and other labor income earned in the USSR in 1937 is the sum of "total net income, currently earned," exclusive of "imputed rent," of all Soviet households in 1937 and Soviet employers' contributions to social insurance, as given in Abram Bergson, Hans Heymann, Jr., and Oleg Hoeffding, *Soviet National Income and Product, 1928–48: Revised Data,* The RAND Corporation Research Memorandum, RM-2544, March 1, 1960. According to the Moorsteen-Powell calculations, the Soviet stock of reproducible fixed capital net of depreciation on July 1, 1937, totaled 231.1 billion rubles in 1937 prices. The weights assigned reproducible fixed capital are calculated from this magnitude and the assumed rate of return. The weight assigned farm land is calculated from the assumed relation to farm labor income and the magnitude of the latter given in Bergson, Heymann, and Hoeffding; 56.0 billion rubles.

On the relative earnings of different factor inputs in the USA in 1929 and on pertinent trends in earnings over time, see pp. 30–33.

The comparative relations between the stock of reproducible fixed capital and labor income for the two countries may have an interest of their own. So, too, may the farm land-man ratios that may be derived from the data on factor inputs:

While the factor income shares used as weights in aggregating inputs are "synthetic," they refer to circumstances prevailing in the USSR in 1937. By the same token, all three input series might be viewed as being in terms of base-year weights. Where output is measured in terms of values of the given year, it might be more appropriate to aggregate inputs in terms of given-year weights, although the case for doing so perhaps is not as strong as would be supposed.[18]

According to a computation based on such given-year weights, however, the over-all trends of output per unit of inputs would not be changed consequentially although the tempo of increase for early years might be somewhat reduced and that for later years somewhat increased. In this computation, weights A for inputs are imputed to the given year in each comparison with 1937. Evidently, this recalculation illustrates the effect of the use of given-year weights for inputs on the assumption that relative factor prices vary inversely with relative inputs.[19]

	Reproducible fixed capital ÷ *labor income, all sectors, local prices*	*Acres of farm land per "man-year" employed*
USSR, 1937	1.28	8.9
USA, 1929	3.77	47.5

[18] In general, in calculating factor productivity should we employ the same index number formula in aggregating inputs as is used in measuring total output? If only for reasons of convenience, one is inclined to do so. As mentioned above, there may also be a theoretic case for this procedure, but it will depend on the degree to which the marginal rate of substitution between inputs tends not to depend consequentially on the prevailing output mix. Also, I assume that if between any two years the concern is in the case of output to obtain observations on the change in capacity to produce the output mix of the base year, the concern in the case of inputs is to obtain observations on the "equivalent variation" in the input mix of the base year. Alternatively, if in the case of output one desires observations on the change in capacity to produce the output mix of the given year, supposedly in the case of inputs the aim is to obtain observations on the "equivalent variation" in the input mix of the given year.

[19] The results of the recomputation of the average annual rate of growth of net national product per unit of inputs follow, together with the figures obtained originally by use of weights A for the base year. In both calculations, output is the composite, 1937 base series: With inputs with weights A imputed to 1937, for 1928–58, 3.0 percent; 1928–58 (effective years), 3.5 percent; 1928–40, 4.9 percent; 1940–50, 1.1 percent; and 1950–58, 2.7 percent. With inputs with weights A imputed to given year, for 1928–58, 3.1 percent; 1928–58 (effective years), 3.6 percent; 1928–40, 4.0 percent; 1940–50, 1.2 percent; and 1950–58, 4.0 percent.

In the recomputations, in addition to imputing weights A to the given year, the composite, 1937 base series for fixed capital is used instead of that in terms of 1937 prices. Because construction is represented by material inputs, however, the Moorsteen-Powell data on fixed capital in terms of the prices of different years probably fail to reflect fully the effect of a shift in base year. By the same token, the impact of the change from 1937 to given-year prices must also be dampened.

In the calculations employing base-year weights, I aggregate inputs arithmetically in terms of these weights. According to familiar theoretic reasoning, inputs might preferably be aggregated geometrically. The following alternative series illustrate the effect of such a recomputation on the average annual rate of growth of net national product at 1937 ruble factor cost per unit of inputs aggregated according to weights A: With inputs

In calculating output per unit of inputs, I consider four factor inputs, of which three (labor, reproducible fixed capital, and farm land) are of a major sort, but those considered are still not exhaustive of factor inputs in the USSR. More to the point, the distinction between items to be treated as factor inputs and items to be treated as sources of change in factor productivity is necessarily somewhat conventional, but one might wish to include in aggregate factor inputs at least one other: inventories. Nevertheless, when this inquiry was being organized it was felt that the inclusion of inventories could not materially affect the results, and this is indeed the case if we may rely on new estimates of Soviet inventories which Professor Powell made available to me recently. Thus, if inventories are included with factor inputs, output per unit of inputs grows, at an annual rate from 0.1 to 0.3 percent lower than the tempos previously computed.[20]

Among the items reckoned here in total factor inputs is farm land. In some inquiries into factor productivity, an attempt is made to treat as inputs all natural resources, including not only farm land, but also extractive wealth and urban land. Although here, as for farm land, changes in quality pose an awkward problem to say the least, extension of the inputs aggregated in this way might be to the good. This has not been possible here and consequently extractive wealth and urban land must be viewed as sources of change in factor productivity, but I think this represents no serious loss.

To come finally to the results: where output is valued at 1937 ruble factor cost, during 1928–58 net national product per unit of inputs grows at an average annual rate of 1.2 to 1.7 percent. With output valued at ruble factor cost of the given year, net national product per unit of inputs grows at an average annual rate of 3.0 to 3.5 percent. For "effective years" during 1928–58, the corresponding figures are 1.4 to 1.9 and 3.5 to 4.1 percent, respectively. Although these computations leave much to be

---

aggregated arithmetically, for 1928–58, 1.2 percent; 1928–58 (effective years), 1.4 percent; 1928–40, 0.1 percent; 1940–50, 1.3 percent; and 1950–58, 2.7 percent. With inputs aggregated geometrically, for 1928–58, 1.3 percent; 1928–58 (effective years), 1.5 percent; 1928–40, negligible; 1940–50, 1.3 percent; and 1950–58, 3.5 percent. Use of the geometric aggregation reduces the rate of growth of output per unit of inputs in early years and increases it in recent years, but the effect throughout is limited.

The nature of the aggregation is related to the effect on a shift from base-year to given-year weights. Thus, where given-year weights are taken to be the same as base-year weights a shift to the former affects the results where aggregation is arithmetic but not where aggregation is geometric. Hence, with the geometric aggregation, the same input series might equally well be compared with either of the two output series. By the same token, the effect of geometric aggregation of inputs is not additive to that due to the use of given-year weights.

[20] To measure the effect of the inclusion of inventories, I use the calculation based on weights A, and the variant of this calculation obtained when inventories are included with a weight corresponding to a 20 percent return on the assets on hand in 1937. The inventory data were compiled by Professor Powell as part of the inquiry in collaboration with Dr. Moorsteen into the Soviet capital stock.

desired, I conclude that under the five-year plans output has tended systematically to grow more rapidly than the inputs. This is true for either measure of output, but the margin between output and inputs is larger when output is in terms of ruble factor cost of the given year.[21]

As for national income, so for factor productivity, the tempo varies in different intervals. For 1928–40, net national product, at 1937 ruble factor cost, per unit of inputs grows at an average annual rate of 0.1 to 0.5 percent. With the alternative valuation of output, the corresponding figures are far greater, 4.9 to 5.3 percent. When we consider the crudity of my calculations for these early years, we must conclude that with the former sort of measure net national product per unit of inputs grew little if at all, and may even have decreased. For output valued at given-year ruble factor cost, however, a markedly rapid rate was achieved.

During 1940–50, either measure of net national product per unit of inputs grows 1.0 or somewhat more than 1.0 percent annually. This suggests that despite the war, output grew somewhat more rapidly than inputs. For 1950–58 the two measures are again in essential accord: with output valued at 1937 ruble factor cost, net national product per unit of inputs grows 2.7 to 4.0 percent annually; with output valued at given-year ruble factor cost, the corresponding figures are 2.7 to 4.1 percent. Thus, in either case, growth was relatively rapid, but as for national income, the answer to the interesting question of whether compared with prewar years there is acceleration or retardation depends on the computation. With output at 1937 ruble factor cost, the tempo accelerates. With output at given-year factor cost, the tempo is either broadly the same as in prewar years or declines somewhat.

In measuring output per unit of inputs, we also provide a basis to appraise the part of the increase in output "accounted for" by the increase in productivity as distinct from the part "due to" the increase in the volume of inputs employed.[22] Thus, for the period as a whole perhaps as much as three-tenths or even two-fifths of the over-all growth of output valued at 1937 ruble factor cost is explicable in terms of the increase in productivity. For output in terms of given-year ruble factor cost, the share of over-all growth due to the change in productivity appears to be appreciably greater. During 1928–40, the increase in productivity contributes in the former case little or nothing to the growth of output and in

---

[21] For national income per unit of inputs, it is difficult to judge the allowance for the effects of the war reflected in the average rate of growth for effective years during 1928–58. In 1950, output per unit of inputs was still but 11.2 to 13.6 percent above 1940 (with inputs aggregated according to weights A) and this increase was probably realized during the reconstruction period. By implication, output per unit of inputs hardly increased during the war, and may very well have declined. By the same token, the allowance made for the war is not apt to err markedly if at all on the generous side.

[22] See fn. 35, below.

the latter about as much as during the entire period 1928–58. For both calculations, the increase in productivity accounts for about one-half or more of the increase in output during 1940–50, and something more or less than this share during 1950–58.

The role of different factors in the growth of aggregate inputs is difficult to gauge because of the need here to employ rather arbitrary weights. But it is nevertheless of interest that for 1928–58 as a whole aggregate inputs by any computation grow more rapidly than labor, the input with the predominant weight. This is due solely to the notable expansion of re-producible fixed capital, which grows more than three times as rapidly as employment. Of the two remaining inputs considered, farm land tends to grow somewhat more slowly than employment, while livestock herds actually decline. By implication, the growth of reproducible fixed capital more than offsets these two lagging inputs, so far as aggregate inputs are concerned.

During 1928–40 and again during 1950–58, the pattern of structural change is broadly similar to that for 1928–58, but the divergence between reproducible fixed capital and employment is in the first interval smaller and in the second much greater than during the entire period 1928–58. Also land and livestock herds lag even more behind employment during 1928–40 than they do during 1928–58, while after 1950 they both finally outpace the latter. During 1940–50, all inputs either increase little or decline, but employment very likely increases as much as if not more than the others.

In calculating output per unit of inputs, we seek ultimately to appraise the sources of growth of production potential. As was explained, where we are concerned with production potential, the measure with valuation in terms of given-year ruble factor cost may be more indicative of changes in capacity to produce the base-year mix than that with valuation in terms of 1937 ruble factor cost. With 1937 the base year, the implication is that per unit of inputs capacity to produce the mix of that year over the period 1928–58 may have grown at a higher tempo than the computation with output valued at 1937 ruble factor cost might indicate. Similarly, a rela-tively high rate may also have been realized during 1928–40, although the latter computation suggests the contrary. Then, too, if productivity is conceived in this way it is seen that during 1950–58 the tempo is rapid and may approach that which prevailed during 1928–40, but, the 1937 ruble factor cost computation to the contrary notwithstanding, there may have been no acceleration compared with the earlier period. Possibly there was some retardation. During 1940–50, capacity to produce the base-year mix grows at a limited rate according to either computation.

Factor productivity is the result of complex forces and for this reason the plausibility of measures of this feature is not easy to appraise. But if capacity to produce the 1937 mix grew more rapidly than inputs over the period studied this surely is understandable. The five-year plans, it is true, saw many developments that were adverse to productivity, most notably the disorganization and loss of skills under wholesale collectivization and the dislocation of war. As factor productivity is computed here, one must also reckon as an adverse factor the decline in average quality of land, and no doubt this was reinforced by diminishing returns to other natural resources, particularly in extractive industries. But the period also witnessed an unprecedented transformation in technology and a marked increase in labor skill, and these developments alone very likely more than offset the adverse factors.

The technological transformation rested to a great extent on borrowing from abroad, but if due account is taken of this fact the progress achieved in productivity despite resource limitations serves as an indicator of the "economic efficiency" of the Soviet social system. Nevertheless, one wonders also at the role in the rising factor productivity of such efficiency in the familiar and more restricted sense of effectiveness of "resource allocation," where labor skill is given. This is difficult to gauge, but at the outset of the period studied the Russians were taking their first steps in comprehensive, central planning, and it is likely that as they gained experience in this complex work they were able to allocate resources with greater effectiveness. Hence, this too may have been a factor in the rising productivity. Of course, whether the concern is with economic efficiency in this restricted or in some more general sense, calculations of the sort made here can be illuminating only with regard to trends over time as distinct from absolute levels realized at any one time. In any complete account, of course, the latter must also be considered.

Collectivization and the attendant disorganization and loss of skills occurred during 1928–40. Moreover, although not important for the entire period 1928–58, the wholesale purges of the late thirties must also have been adverse to productivity in the prewar interval. Then, too, the late thirties witnessed a rapid expansion in defense, and in various ways this also may have worked in the same direction. But granting all this, if per unit of inputs capacity to produce the 1937 mix grew at a relatively rapid tempo during 1928–40, this is not surprising when we consider that technological progress must have been especially marked at this time.

While the war brought great dislocation, in the munitions sector it also brought further technological progress, and in many sectors technological progress must also have been rapid during reconstruction. But all things considered, there seems little basis to question that for the decade 1940–50 productivity grew at only a modest rate. For 1950–58, per unit of inputs capacity to produce the 1937 mix is found to grow again at a rapid rate, possibly comparable to that prevailing before the war. In trying to appraise this result, we must remember that in the fifties the technological transformation continued apace, although probably not as swiftly as during prewar years; the Russians experienced no such adversities as hampered progress in earlier years; the government no doubt was able to eliminate many inefficiencies that had developed in the years of war and reconstruction; and the many economic reforms introduced by Stalin's successors, despite their adverse aspects, probably have on balance had a positive effect on productivity.

The findings regarding factor productivity should also be viewed in the perspective of the comparative trends observed in different inputs. Most importantly, since the introduction of new technology often depends on initiation of new capital investments, the rapid expansion of the capital stock is in itself something of a testimonial to the pace of the technological transformation that occurred.[23]

From the data compiled, one may compute not only output per unit of inputs generally but also output per unit of one or another input. Of the different calculations of the latter sort, however, only two are of particular interest: in one case output is related to employment, in the other to reproducible fixed capital. Trends under the five-year plans regarding output per unit of employment have been discussed in *Real SNIP,* and those regarding output in relation to fixed capital are being considered by Moorsteen and Powell. Furthermore, what could be said in either regard is more or less implied in our discussion of trends in output per unit of inputs generally and in the structure of inputs. Accordingly, the data on output per worker and on output per unit of reproducible fixed capital (Tables I.1 and I.2), are presented only for reference purposes. Interesting as these topics are, I do not attempt to explore them here.[24]

[23] See fn. 35, below.

[24] The data, however, may help us to understand an outstanding feature: the sharp decline under the five-year plans in output per unit of reproducible fixed capital. In theoretic discussions of economic growth it sometimes is assumed that the capital coefficient, that is, the volume of reproducible fixed capital per unit of output, is fairly stable as growth proceeds. While reference usually is to reproducible capital, the implication is that this might also be true of reproducible fixed capital. To my knowledge, the validity of this supposition is still to be investigated in any systematic way empirically, but if the sharp increase in the capital coefficient observed for the USSR under the five-year plans turns out to be unique, it is not difficult to understand why. In the course of economic development, the capital stock ordinarily grows more rapidly than the labor force. By the same token, there must also be a tendency toward diminishing returns to capital. But ordinarily, also, technological progress may offset this aspect largely if not entirely. For the USSR, however, since the capital stock increases radically in relation to the labor force, the tendency towards diminishing returns is correspondingly accentuated, and technological progress although probably marked is only a partial offset.

While I suspect the foregoing is the crux of the matter, no doubt other factors, too, are present, and among other things one inevitably wonders whether there may not be some evidence here of inefficiency in Soviet planning.

Data set forth below on output per unit of reproducible fixed capital in the USA fail to show any precise constancy, but the variation over long periods is relatively limited, at

5. Trends in Factor Productivity: USSR Versus USA

Although output per unit of inputs has been computed previously for the United States, for comparison with the data for the USSR it seemed best to make a fresh calculation. The results appear in Tables I.1 and I.2. In calculating output per unit of inputs, the two series on the net national product of the USA, one for 1929 and earlier years in terms of 1929 dollars and the other for 1929 and later years in terms of 1954 dollars, are related to two series of inputs. Both sets of inputs are aggregates corresponding to those used for the USSR, and they differ chiefly in the weights employed, although some of the series for the individual inputs also differ somewhat. The following input series were used:

Employment. In both input measures, I rely mainly on a compilation made in *Real SNIP*. Essentially, for years up to 1929, employment is the sum of: (i) the labor force in nonagricultural branches after allowance for unemployment; and (ii) the number of farmers, together with the number of agricultural employees in terms of their assumed full-time equivalent. Under both headings, I use Professor Jacob Schmookler's adaptation of the basic Fabricant data. For 1929 and later years, calculations by Kuznets and the Commerce Department yield employment in all sectors in terms of its full-time equivalent. Obviously, at least for early years, the figures leave something to be desired. To allow for changes in the hours of nonfarm workers, I rely on data compiled by Dewhurst and his associates.[25] In accord with the procedure followed for the USSR, no allowance is made for changes in the farm working day, but the latter has tended to decline systematically during periods considered here. As for the USSR, no allowance is made for qualitative changes in employment.

Reproducible fixed capital. Two related but distinct series are used, one where total inputs are compared with output in 1929 dollars and the other where total inputs are compared with output in 1954 dollars. For the former, I rely chiefly on Professor Raymond Goldsmith's perpetual inventory data in terms of 1929 dollars. By summing Goldsmith's "structures" and "producers' durables," net of depreciation, I believe I obtain figures comparable in scope with those for Soviet reproducible fixed capital.

least in comparison with the Soviet experience. Interestingly, however, the capital stock also grows in relation to the labor force much less in the United States than in the USSR. By implication, for the USA diminishing returns to capital should have been less pronounced and hence more easily offset by technological progress than has been so for the USSR.

[25] The data on employment, before adjustment for nonfarm hours, are: for 1869–78, 12.4 million; 1899–1908, 29.1 million; 1929, 44.9 million; 1948, 54.0 million; 1954, 61.6 million; and 1957, 64.5 million. After adjustment for nonfarm hours, they are: for 1869–78, 14.6 million; 1899–1908, 33.3 million; 1929, 44.9 million; 1948, 48.7 million; 1954, 54.0 million; and 1957, 56.5 million. All figures are either taken from, or derived by use of, sources and methods described in *Real SNIP,* chap. 14. Data for 1954 are needed because this is a weight year in the aggregation of inputs.

Because of limitations in the underlying data and calculations, Goldsmith feels that his estimate of reproducible wealth for any particular date may err by as much as 10 to 20 percent or even more, but the margin of error is probably smaller in comparisons made over long intervals. Goldsmith's data are available only for years since 1896. To obtain a corresponding estimate for 1869/78, I follow him in linking his measures with similar data of a census type compiled by Kuznets. The Kuznets data differ somewhat in scope from Goldsmith's, and also are more crude than his.[26]

For the compilation of total inputs for comparison with output in 1954 dollars, I again rely on data on reproducible fixed capital compiled by Goldsmith by his perpetual inventory method. These are the results of a forthcoming computation that is for the most part in terms of 1947/49 dollars, although for 1929–45 the figures are obtained through a partial recomputation of data in 1929 dollars. As before, I use the sum of Goldsmith's structures and producers' durables, net of depreciation.[27] The data on fixed capital for the USA, like those for the USSR, refer to stocks rather than employment.

Farm land. For both total input measures, I use "farm cropland" as given in the U.S. census returns. For terminal dates not coinciding with or near a census date, the figures are obtained by extrapolation or interpolation. Because the census returns on farm cropland begin only with 1879, the estimate for 1869/78 is especially crude. As with the data for the USSR, those for the USA are in physical units and do not allow for changes in quality. For the USA, quality may have deteriorated materially in early years when the acreage was expanding rapidly. Since 1929, however,

[26] The absolute figures on reproducible fixed capital in terms of 1929 dollars are (in billions): for 1869/78, 22.4; for 1899/1908, 100.6; and for 1929, 228.9. In Raymond W. Goldsmith, *A Study of Saving in the United States* (Princeton, 1956), III, 20, end-of-the-year data are given for the U.S. stock of structures and producers' durables in 1929 dollars. The 1929 figure used here is the total of the assets in these two categories, recentered on July 1. For 1899/1908, the figure is the average of the end-of-the-year totals of assets in the two categories. The figure for 1869/78 actually pertains to the mid-point of this interval (that is, end of 1873), and is extrapolated from an estimate of 30.5 billions in 1929 prices for reproducible fixed capital for 1880. The latter figure is obtained by linking to Goldsmith's calculations corresponding data he has compiled for earlier years from calculations by Kuznets. For the latter, see Raymond W. Goldsmith, "The Growth of Reproducible Wealth of the United States of America from 1805 to 1950," in Kuznets (ed.), *Income and Wealth in the United States,* pp. 306–307. To obtain totals comparable with those for later years, I sum the following Goldsmith-Kuznets asset categories: nonfarm residences, agricultural structures and equipment, nonagricultural business structures and equipment, and government structures and equipment.

[27] The absolute figures on reproducible fixed capital in 1947/49 dollars are (in billions): for 1929, 474.3; for 1948, 501.8; for 1954, 621.5; and for 1957, 695.7. With Professor Goldsmith's kind permission, I refer to a mimeographed appendix, issued in July 1960, to his forthcoming *National Wealth of the United States in the Postwar Period.* The figures given in this source pertain to the end of the year and have been recentered here on July 1. Also, the figure for 1929 is adjusted to allow for the break in Goldsmith's series in 1945.

farm cropland has tended to contract somewhat, and quality should have improved.[28]

Livestock herds. For the most part, the data are those compiled by Goldsmith. As for reproducible fixed capital, for comparison with output in 1929 dollars, Goldsmith's data in 1929 dollars are used. For comparison with the output in 1954 dollars, his figures in 1947/49 dollars are used. The underlying calculations take into account changes in numbers of different herds but not in quality. While this was also so for the data for the USSR, no doubt livestock quality has tended to improve more in the USA than in the USSR.[29]

As was explained, two sets of weights are used to aggregate inputs. The set based on 1929 factor incomes is used for the purpose of deriving a series on total inputs to be related to net national product in 1929 dollars and the set based on 1954 factor incomes is used for the purpose of deriving a corresponding series to be related to net national product in 1954 dollars. The weights are given in Table I.4. The figures represent the

Table I.4
USA: Weights Used in Aggregating Factor Inputs

Item	Calculated factor incomes, 1929		Calculated factor incomes, 1954	
	Billions of dollars	Percent	Billions of dollars	Percent
Employment	60.69	77.0	234.2	84.8
Reproducible fixed capital	15.77	20.0	38.1	13.8
Farm land	1.89	2.4	3.2	1.2
Livestock herds	0.45	0.6	0.6	0.2
All	78.80	100.0	276.1	100.0

[28] Farm cropland for the end of 1873 (the mid-point of 1869/78) is taken as 14 to 15 percent below that for 1879 as given in U.S. Department of Commerce, *Historical Statistics of the United States, 1789–1945* (Washington, 1949), p. 121. This is in view of the indicated change in farm land as a whole from 1869 to 1879. Farm cropland for the end of 1903 (the mid-point of 1899/1908) and for 1929–54 is either taken or interpolated from data given in *ibid.*, p. 121; in U.S. Department of Commerce, *Statistical Abstract of the United States, 1958* (Washington, 1958), p. 612; and in the *Statistical Abstract of the United States, 1959* (Washington, 1959), p. 614. The corresponding figure for 1957 is based on the change from 1954 to 1957 in "harvested crops — acreage used for specified purposes," given in *ibid.*, p. 653.

[29] The average annual value of livestock herds in 1929 prices for 1899/1908 and a corresponding figure for July 1, 1929, are computed from end of the year figures in Goldsmith, *A Study of Saving*, III, 21. The value of livestock herds for the end of 1873 (mid-point of the interval 1869/78) is extrapolated roughly from a Goldsmith-Kuznets figure for 1880 in Goldsmith, "The Growth of Reproducible Wealth," p. 307. For data in 1947/49 dollars for July 1, 1929, 1948, 1954, and 1957, I recentered end-of-the-year figures in Goldsmith's forthcoming *National Wealth in the Postwar Period.*

results of an attempt to determine from U.S. Department of Commerce tabulations of national income the earnings imputable to the factors in question. Thus, for employment, the figures are intended to include in addition to actual compensation of employees the returns of entrepreneurs imputable to their labor services. The latter are determined in the light of calculations by Professor D. Gale Johnson. For each year reproducible fixed capital is credited essentially with the average return earned in that year on capital generally, exclusive of various items, among them agricultural land. For data on the capital stock, I refer again to Goldsmith. On agricultural rent, we have computations by Johnson. Livestock herds are arbitrarily credited with the same rate of return as reproducible fixed capital.[30]

The year 1954 saw a recession in the USA, but interestingly the growth of total inputs during 1929–57 is hardly affected if instead of 1954, 1929 is used as the weight year (compare Tables I.1 and I.2).[31]

[30] For 1929, the weight for employment is the sum of: (i) compensation of nonfarm employees, from data in *U.S. Income and Output*, pp. 126–127 and 200, and U.S. Department of Commerce, *National Income, 1954 Edition*, p. 178, calculated at $49.79 billions; (ii) agricultural labor income, including imputed labor income of farm entrepreneurs, which according to D. Gale Johnson "Allocation of Agricultural Income," *Journal of Farm Economics*, November 1948, p. 728, amounted to $5.19 billions; (iii) imputed labor income of nonfarm entrepreneurs, $5.71 billions—following D. Gale Johnson, "Functional Distribution of Income in the United States," *Review of Economics and Statistics*, May 1954, p. 177, I impute to labor services 65 percent of the earnings of nonfarm entrepreneurs, which according to *U.S. Income and Output*, pp. 126–127, amounted to $8.79 billions.

From Goldsmith's data, the total stock of reproducible fixed capital in the United States on July 1, 1929, may be calculated at $228.9 billions at current prices. The figure for the income of this factor, therefore, implies an average return of 6.89 percent. The rate of return is calculated by relating these two aspects: (i) All property income earned, excluding agricultural rent, estimated to be $23.53 billions on this basis: national income amounted to $87.81 billions (see *U.S. Income and Output*, pp. 126–127), or to $86.11 billions, after the adjustment of depreciation to a replacement cost basis; from this I deduct labor income as calculated above, $60.69 billions, and agricultural rent, $1.89 billions (see immediately below). (ii) The total "national wealth," excluding consumers' durables, monetary gold and silver, and agricultural and public land on July 1, 1929, which from Goldsmith's data totaled $341.5 billions in current values.

Agricultural rent, including earnings of farm structures, in 1929 is given in Johnson, *Journal of Farm Economics*, November 1948, p. 728. Considering the comparative shares of land and structures in total farm real estate values before the war, I take agricultural rent, exclusive of earnings of farm structures, to be $1.89 billions. According to Goldsmith's data, U.S. livestock herds were worth $6.5 billions at current prices in 1929 and I allow here the rate of return imputed to reproducible fixed capital.

The weights for 1954 are derived by essentially the same methods and sources. However, the average rate of return on "national wealth," excluding consumers' durables, monetary gold and silver, and agricultural and public land, is 4.99 percent.

[31] Data on total inputs cited in the tables are obtained by arithmetic aggregation, but geometric aggregation has even less effect on output per unit of inputs in the USA than in the USSR. Thus, for 1929–57 the rate of growth of output per unit of inputs (based on 1954 weights) remains unchanged at 2.0 percent a year. There is no perceptible change either for 1929–48 or 1948–57. For 1869/78–1899/1908, the rate of growth declines 0.1 percent (based on 1929 weights).

For the USA as for the USSR, the factor inputs considered are not all-inclusive. But for the period 1929–57, relatively reliable data on inventories are available for the USA. Interestingly, inclusion of this input has no perceptible effect on the growth of output per unit of inputs.[32]

In contrasting trends in output per unit of inputs in the USSR and USA, we face again the question as to the sorts of data that can be appropriately compared. On output I try to observe the guiding principles outlined above. On inputs we might wish to consider data in terms of the base year and formula employed for output, but this would only compound the difficulties in the way of proceeding in a methodologically impeccable manner. As for total output, we compare the Soviet performance under the five-year plans with that of the United States during each of two intervals, 1929–57 and 1869/78–1899/1908.

We consider first the comparison with the U.S. performance during 1929–57. In the USSR with output valued at 1937 ruble factor cost, the net national product per unit of inputs grows during 1928–58 at an average annual rate of 1.2 to 1.7 and for effective years at an average rate of 1.4 to 1.9 percent. With output valued at ruble factor cost of the given year, the corresponding figures are 3.0 to 3.5 and 3.5 to 4.1 percent. In the former case, inputs are aggregated as is appropriate in terms of weights pertaining to 1937. In the latter, use is made again of these weights, but if (as is desired) weights pertaining to the given year were substituted, it seems doubtful that the results would be seriously affected. In the USA, the net national product per unit of inputs grows during 1929–57 at an average annual rate of 2.0 percent. Here output is valued at dollar prices of 1954 and inputs are aggregated in terms of 1954 weights, but as we have already seen, revaluations of output appropriate for comparison with the two Soviet measures would have little effect, and I believe this is also true of the corresponding revaluations of inputs that are called for.[33]

I hope I am not being insensitive to the limitation of the data if I conclude that where measures are in appropriate base-year values neither country much outpaces the other, although the USA may have some margin of superiority. Where the measures are in appropriate given-year values, however, output per unit of inputs may well be growing more rapidly in the USSR than in the USA.

[32] In 1929–57, inventories (derived from Goldsmith's data) grow more rapidly than all other inputs considered (with 1929 as 100, the former stand at 188 and the latter at 128 in 1957), but at the prevailing return on capital (see fn. 30), their weight is limited: 1.7 percent of the total for all inputs, including inventories.

[33] On this aspect, I refer to the comparative results obtained in aggregating U.S. inputs in terms of 1929 and 1954 weights (Tables I.1 and I.2). Regrettably, for fixed capital in both computations we have to use data in terms of 1947–49 prices. At least for the years in question, however, I doubt that measures of the U.S. stock of fixed capital could be materially affected by index number relativity. For this reason, the two input series would be little changed if for fixed capital we had used data in 1929 prices and in 1954 prices.

For 1950–58 the USSR appears to outpace the USA no matter what measure is considered. This is so whether reference is made for the USA to the entire period 1929–57 or to the interval 1948–57.

I turn to the comparison with the U.S. performance during 1869/78–1899/1908. For the USA, net national product per unit of inputs increases at an average annual rate of 1.5 percent. Here output is valued at dollar prices of 1929 and inputs are aggregated in terms of 1929 weights. I have already commented on the possible effect on the rate of growth of the net national product of changes in base year and formula. As to the effect of corresponding changes for inputs, a further computation may be illuminating. If inputs are reaggregated with weights pertaining to *circa* the end of the 1880's (as anyone acquainted with the pertinent data will be aware, they are very crude), net national product per unit of inputs grows annually during 1869/78–1899/1908 0.1 of a percentage point less than was computed initially.[34]

In sum, the comparative trends in this case are uncertain indeed. Nevertheless, where measures are in appropriate base-year values, the presumption is that neither country outpaces the other very decidedly. Where measures are in appropriate given-year values, there may well be a margin in favor of the Russians, although this is speculative.

In appraising comparative trends in factor productivity, we arrive at a basis for gauging the comparative contributions to the growth of output

[34] The weights, intended to represent factor shares in terms of 1890 prices and quantities of 1884–93 or end of 1888 are: employment, $7.24 billion (75.2 percent); reproducible fixed capital, $1.69 billion (17.6 percent); farm land, $0.52 billion (5.4 percent); livestock, $0.17 billion (1.8 percent); all, $9.62 billion (100.0 percent).

Regarding the underlying calculations: chiefly on the basis of Kuznets' data, I take national income during 1884–93 to be $10.50 billion in 1890 prices; in the light of computations in Johnson, *Review of Economics and Statistics,* May 1954, pp. 178–179, I take all labor service income to be 69.0 percent of national income; considering the findings in Kuznets, "Long-Term Changes," p. 86, I take reproducible fixed capital to earn 6.89 percent, the same as in 1929; from the Goldsmith-Kuznets computations I take the stock of reproducible fixed capital toward the end of 1888 to be $24.5 billions in 1890 prices; in view of data in Kuznets, "Long-Term Changes," p. 89, I take all agricultural income to be 16.5 percent of the national income during 1884–93; considering calculations in Johnson, *Journal of Farm Economics,* November 1948, p. 728, I take agricultural rent to be 30.0 percent of total agricultural income; and I impute to livestock herds, which are indicated by Goldsmith-Kuznets calculations to have been worth in 1890 about $2.6 billions in current prices, an average return of 6.89 percent.

Reaggregation of inputs in terms of the foregoing weights required data on inputs for the base data. As determined by use of the sources and methods employed in deriving U.S. inputs for other years, the figures are (percent of 1929): employment, adjusted for nonfarm hours, 1884–93, 53.5; reproducible fixed capital, end of 1888, in 1929 dollars, 24.3; farm land, end of 1888, acres, 59.3; livestock herds, end of 1888, in 1929 dollars, 93.8.

If, for reaggregation, data on reproducible fixed capital and livestock herds, in terms of prices of *circa* 1890, could have been used, the calculated rate of increase in output per unit of inputs would probably have been further reduced. The magnitude of the reduction is conjectural, although the Moorsteen-Powell measures of Soviet fixed capital in terms of alternative prices (as embodied in the two series considered here) may shed some light in this regard.

that are made by productivity. Thus, where measures are in base-year values, output was found to have grown more rapidly in the USSR during 1928–58 than in the USA during 1929–57. This Soviet margin of superiority is due entirely to the more rapid increase in inputs. In fact, this increase in inputs may have offset the lag of the USSR behind the USA in output per unit of inputs. Where measures are in given-year values, the Russians excel us even more regarding total output, but while the more rapid increase in inputs in the USSR is still a major factor, the Russians may also have benefited from a more rapid increase in factor productivity. If with either measure the Russians in recent postwar years markedly outpace us regarding output, the relatively rapid increase in their inputs is a partial explanation but a higher tempo of factor productivity is probably also a factor.

Where the USSR during 1928–58 is compared with the USA during 1869/78–1899/1908 and measures are in base-year values, neither country much surpasses the other regarding output. At the same time inputs appear to grow at about the same rate in the two countries. By the same token, the contribution of factor productivity to the increase in output may have been broadly similar too. If measures are in given-year values, the Russians may have matched or surpassed us regarding the tempo of growth of total output, but the pace of increase of inputs is again much the same in the two countries. Accordingly, the relative tempos regarding output were determined by the relative tempos regarding factor productivity.

From the data compiled, we may also contrast trends in input structures in the two countries. Thus, although the USSR during 1928–58 experiences a more rapid increase in inputs generally than the USA during 1929–57, the relative tempos for different inputs vary markedly. For livestock herds, the USSR experiences a decline and the USA an increase; while for land, the situation is the reverse. Considering effective years, employment in the USSR increases three times as fast as in the USA; for reproducible fixed capital, the Soviet tempo is more than five times ours. If we consider for the USSR the years 1950–58, and for the USA the years 1948–57, the rate of increase in total inputs in the former still materially exceeds that in the latter, but this is despite the fact that the Soviet tempo for employment is about the same as or less than that in the USA. The Russians, however, surpass us regarding all other inputs, and in the case of reproducible fixed capital their tempo is still nearly three times that of the USA even though for the latter the expansion is far more rapid than during 1929–57.

If reference for the USSR is to 1928–58 and for the USA to 1869/78–1899/1908, total inputs in the two countries probably increase at about the same rate. Moreover, the tempos are also not very disparate for employment and farm land, but for livestock herds the USSR lags behind the USA while for reproducible fixed capital the Soviet tempo is markedly above that in the USA, although in the USA the rate of expansion is high and has not since been equaled by us during any lengthy interval.

Appraisal of comparative trends in production potential per unit of inputs is even more hazardous than that in total production potential, but while both measures of output are pertinent to production potential, those calculated with given-year values may be more indicative of changes in capacity to produce the base-year commodity mix. By implication, in respect of the rate of increase in capacity to produce a base-year commodity mix per unit of inputs, the USSR during 1928–58 may have matched or surpassed the USA during 1929–57, although according to computations with output in terms of base-year prices, the former seemingly matches or falls short of the latter. Whichever measure is considered, in very recent years, the USSR appears to outpace the USA in capacity to produce a base-year commodity mix per unit of inputs. If reference is to the USSR during 1928–58 and to the USA during 1869/78–1899/1908, the comparison again seems more favorable to the USSR than it did previously, although it still is conjectural whether that country enjoys any superiority to speak of.

Finally, we must remember that the base-year commodity mixes in the two countries are different. As explained previously, one wonders whether the Russians could have derived any decided advantage from this fact where the comparison is with the USA during 1929–57, but very possibly they are favored where the comparison is with the USA during 1869/78–1899/1908.

What follows regarding comparative "economic efficiency"? If my imperfect data are to cast light on this matter, due regard must be given to still other complexities: (i) As computed, factor productivity in the USSR is adversely affected by a decline in the average quality of land. Possibly this was also a feature in the USA during 1869/78–1899/1908, when our acreage increased rapidly, but not during 1929–57, when our acreage declined. (ii) For both countries, factor productivity is also adversely affected by limitations in extractable natural resources and urban land. I suspect that neither country enjoys any marked advantage in this respect, although the USSR benefits somewhat where the comparison is with the USA during 1929–57. (iii) In transforming its production methods under the five-year plans, the USSR has been able to borrow technology from abroad on an extraordinary scale. Although in early stages the USA also obtained technology from abroad, the borrowing hardly could have been comparable to that of the USSR under the five-year plans. The Russians are favored still more when the comparison is with the USA during 1929–57. (iv) Technological progress has also been greatly facilitated in the USSR by the government's ability, owing to its authoritarian control over investment, to establish and maintain a notably rapid rate of growth of reproducible fixed capital.[35]

The foregoing aspects must be considered where the concern is with "economic efficiency" generally. If economic efficiency is understood in the restricted sense concerning the effectiveness of "resource allocation," we must also bear in mind that differences in performance regarding factor productivity may in some degree reflect differences in improvement in the quality of the labor force. Finally, in whichever sense economic efficiency is construed, my data necessarily bear on progress realized over time rather than on the absolute level achieved at any one time.

It may be hoped that further inquiry will facilitate our appraisal of these complexities. Meantime, I think I may safely conclude that there is little evidence that Soviet socialism is nearly as efficient as its proponents hold. This system no doubt has been underrated, however, by many Western critics.

For the USA as for the USSR, I have compiled data not only on output per unit of inputs but on output per worker and per unit of reproducible fixed capital (Tables I.1 and I.2). As before, this is done only for reference purposes, and no attempt is made to explore these matters.[36]

[35] In recent writings on economic growth, the assumption has often been made that the pace of technological progress is independent of that of the growth of capital stock. While one can imagine theoretic circumstances where this would be so, the contrary situation where the two are significantly interrelated is surely more realistic. Moreover, if such an interrelation does exist, it should be particularly important in the case of the USSR under the five-year plans, where, because of the vast possibilities of borrowing from abroad, the technological horizon from the beginning has been notably wide.

I alluded earlier to the problem of the theoretic basis for the measurement of the real capital stock. When technological progress is related to the growth of the capital stock generally, almost inevitably it is "nonneutral" as between different capital goods. Granted that technological progress depends on the increase in the capital stock, it is my impression that we shall rarely if ever be able to measure the latter exclusive of technological progress. In any case, I doubt that this desideratum has been achieved in either the Soviet or the American capital stock data employed here. By implication, in trying to grasp the impact of my calculations regarding economic efficiency, we face still another complexity and one difficult to gauge: to some extent technological progress is apt to be reflected not in output per unit of inputs but in inputs.

In this chapter, output per unit of inputs has been taken to demonstrate the relative shares of the increase in output that are "due" on the one hand to the increase in factor productivity and on the other to the increase in factor inputs. This is in accord with a customary and I believe defensible usage. But in view of the foregoing, the disaggregation of the increase in output that is accomplished must have a rather conventional character. It provides a point of departure but is hardly a final basis for appraisal of causality in any deep sense.

[36] See fn. 24.

APPENDIX

Derivation of Net National Product

In this appendix we show the derivation of the data on net national product of the USSR used in this chapter. Net national product at 1937 ruble factor cost is obtained by deducting from gross national product in 1937 ruble factor cost, mainly from *Real SNIP,* one-half the capital repairs included in the latter and also an allowance for depreciation. In *Real SNIP* a composite, 1937 base series on gross national product is compiled from data in terms of 1937, 1950, and 1928 ruble factor cost. In order to obtain a corresponding series on net national product it was necessary to adjust additionally in the manner described pertinent figures on gross national product in 1950 and 1928 ruble factor cost.

For each base year, the elements in the computations described are shown in Table I.5.

Table I.5
USSR: Calculation of Net National Product
(billions of rubles)

Year	Gross national product	Adjustment for capital repairs	Depreciation	Net national product
In ruble factor cost (or ruble prices) of 1937				
1928	141.1	0.6	3.3	137.2
1937	215.6	2.0	9.1	204.5
1940	261.9	2.0	11.9	248.0
1950	322.4	5.7	18.1	298.6
1955	464.7	9.7	29.0	426.0
1958	562.3	12.4	42.7	507.2
In ruble factor cost (or ruble prices) of 1950				
1937	478.4	4.9	24.4	449.1
1950	694.1	13.1	39.4	641.6
1955	1000.3	22.2	62.6	915.5
1958	1210.4	27.9	90.6	1091.9
In ruble factor cost (or ruble prices) of 1928				
1928	29.56	0.30	2.00	27.26
1937	81.30	1.69	7.97	71.64

Before their use in the derivation of the index numbers in Table I.1, the foregoing data on the national product were adjusted for territorial changes, as already described. In the case of gross national product in 1937 ruble factor cost, the estimate for 1928 is that in which the revaluation at ruble factor cost is extended within retail sales. See p. 8, fn. 4.

II

LABOR FORCE

WARREN W. EASON

The material presented in this chapter is confined to those aspects of labor utilization under industrialization that are essentially economic and susceptible to measurement. The relevance of a number of institutional questions will be indicated at several points, but there will be no opportunity to examine these questions at length within the limits of the chapter.[1]

The chapter is organized under three broad headings: the quantitative dimensions of over-all labor supply, including the total number of persons who work or who are considered available for work, by age and sex, with reference to given periods of time; the "qualitative" dimensions of over-all labor supply, including the skills and general competence derived from formal education and training as well as from experience on the job;[2] and the allocation of labor in accordance with the demand for labor, by area,

[1] The institutional questions together with those of an economic nature will be considered in my *Labor Problems in the Industrialization of the USSR* (forthcoming).
[2] Other qualitative aspects, including health and general physical condition, and effort and efficiency applied to the job, will not be discussed.

industry, and occupation. Some specific comparisons are made with developments in the United States.

One purpose, underlying all others, is to present summary statistics on the Soviet labor force. In this respect, we are in a much more fortunate position than we were, for example, at the Arden House conference on Soviet economic growth, held (at Harriman, New York) in the spring of 1952. At that time, the Soviet government had released no figure on the total labor force since the late 1920's; there was an almost complete lack of official statistics on the total postwar population, its structure by age and sex, and the pattern of birth and death rates and postwar employment figures were available for only one sector of the labor force (wage and salary workers) for only a few years.[3]

Although serious shortcomings still remain, the picture is much improved. For example, we now have: (i) employment figures for major economic sectors covering most postwar years, appearing in the statistical handbooks published since 1956 [4] and culminating in the recent release of comprehensive data on employment in agriculture;[5] (ii) aggregate demographic data including total population as well as the number by age and sex, from the census of 1959,[6] and related series on births and deaths, age, specific mortality rates, etc.;[7] (iii) also from the 1959 census, data on the population according to economic activity, including total labor force and its distribution by major economic categories;[8] and (iv) related data on education and training and on the skill of various groups in the labor force. The available data for the prewar period, these postwar figures, and selected comparable figures for 1939 and 1940 that have appeared in recent publications make it possible to approach the question of the labor force in Soviet industrialization with a firmer statistical foundation than was available ever before.[9] Perhaps it will be well to summarize the principal findings before getting into the body of the paper.

[3] Warren W. Eason, "Population and Labor Force," in Abram Bergson, ed., *Soviet Economic Growth: Conditions and Perspectives* (Evanston, 1953), pp. 101–122 and appendixes A and C.

[4] From TSU, *Narodnoe khoziaistvo SSSR: statisticheskii sbornik* (Moscow, 1956), to TSU, *Narodnoe khoziaistvo SSSR v 1959 godu: statisticheskii ezhegodnik* (Moscow, 1960).

[5] TSU, *Sel'skoe khoziastvo SSSR: statisticheskii sbornik* (Moscow, 1960).

[6] TSU, *Uroven' obrazovaniia, natsional'nyi sostav, vozrastnaia struktura, i razmeshchenie naseleniia SSSR po respublikam, kraiam i oblastiam* (Moscow, 1960).

[7] TSU, *Zdravookhranenie v SSSR: statisticheskii sbornik* (Moscow, 1960), pp. 36–46.

[8] TSU, "O raspredelenii naseleniia SSSR po obshchestvennym gruppam, otrasliam narodnogo khoziaistva i zaniatiiam i ob urovne obrazovaniia rabotnikov fizicheskogo i umstvennogo truda," *Vestnik statistiki*, 1960, no. 12, pp. 3–21.

[9] In many respects the recent information simply confirms estimates (and some guesses) made on the basis of partial information previously available. In other respects, important revisions have been indicated, for example, in the estimates of war losses, particularly with respect to males. Nor are the recent figures unaffected by the usual kind of Soviet obscurantism. But on balance the stock of official statistics on population and labor force has improved markedly.

With respect to the quantitative dimensions of over-all labor supply:
The average rate of population (and labor force) growth since 1928 has
been much lower than that projected on the basis of preplan birth and
death rates. Primarily because of World War II and the difficulties of
the early 1930's, but also because of a relatively greater secular decline
in fertility rates than mortality rates, the average rate of population increase on comparable territory since 1928 has been about 0.8 percent per
year, compared with 2 percent or more in the late 1920's. If projected rates
had prevailed, the population would now be more than 300 million instead of 215 million.

Rural or agricultural "overpopulation" was potentially a serious problem in 1928 — although the Soviet Union as a whole is not densely popu-
lated — because arable land is a relatively small fraction of the total land
area, and because there was already a surplus agricultural population of 10
to 20 percent.[10] The decline in the rate of population growth after 1928
tended to reduce this surplus, or at least to prevent it from becoming
more serious, and thereby tended to remove a major obstacle to raising
over-all labor productivity.

Trends in age distribution associated with the reduced rate of population growth, that is, toward a higher proportion of the population in the
working ages and a lower proportion of children and young people, also
enhanced the attainment of per capita economic goals. The relative decline
of the nonproductive elements in the population reduced the pressure
of consumption on production and permitted a higher rate of investment
(nonconsumption) than otherwise would have been the case. Under a
normal projection based on the pattern of births and deaths at the beginning of the plans, the proportion of children and young people in the
population would have remained relatively high. The Russians have thus
been spared some of the possible effects of a "population explosion." [11]

The growing deficit of males in the population — a result of World War
I and the Civil War, the period of the early 1930's, and especially World
War II — in and of itself has kept the ratio of the females to the total
labor force larger than it otherwise would have been, and it may also have
helped to sustain the relatively large proportion of the female population
that was in the labor force.

In general, the percentage of the population in the labor force has remained relatively high. The proportion age 10 to 15 declined sharply and

[10] Nancy Baster, *Agricultural Overpopulation in the USSR* (unpublished essay written
for the Certificate of the Russian Institute, Columbia University). According to Soviet
sources cited by Mrs. Baster, there was a surplus in agriculture with respect to production
at the then existing levels of technology, assuming some full-time equivalent labor force
as the number necessary for production.

[11] See United Nations, *The Determinants and Consequences of Population Trends*
(New York, 1953), chaps. 12 and 15.

the proportion age 60 and over moderately, but the proportion of working ages has not changed much. As a result, when taken together with the indicated changes in the age distribution of the population, the percentage of the total population in the labor force has declined only moderately, from 57 percent in 1926 to 53 percent in 1939, and 52 percent in 1959.

The average number of persons actually working during the year, expressed as a percentage of the labor force, has increased since 1928, largely because females in the labor force have actually worked a greater share of the time that they have available. All the measures of labor supply indicate an increase since 1928, but the rate varies with the measure used. The choice of measure depends upon the analytical problem at hand.

Until recently, man power resources have been abundant, compared with capital and arable land. The recruitment and allocation of labor for industry, therefore, has not been a serious drain on the agricultural labor force, and Soviet manpower policies, by the standards of the more industrialized countries, have appeared to be wasteful of labor. But the rate of growth of over-all labor supply has now declined and if the pace of industrialization is to continue, this decline must be offset by more effective utilization of labor. Demographic forces growing out of World War II have compelled the USSR to face relatively suddenly the problem of increasing scarcity of human resources that would have come about more gradually as part of the industrialization process itself.

With respect to the qualitative dimensions of over-all labor supply: One outstanding fact is that at the beginning of the period of rapid industrialization steps had already been taken to raise skill and competence. In 1928 the nucleus of an industrial labor force already existed; and significantly, in view of the full range of educational requirements of an expanding economy, the early elementary grades already encompassed relatively high proportions of the relevant age groups.

From this starting point, the Russians moved in several well-defined directions to develop a labor force with the skills and experience required. In terms of numbers affected, the primary method was through experience on the job, including on-the-job training. This method was widely used to develop lower and intermediate skills, but it accounts even today for the background of the majority in white collar occupations.

At the same time, the educational system has expanded, with particular attention to the demands of the national economy for trained personnel. The rate of growth of institutions of higher learning and of schools for specialized secondary education, their curricula, and the size of the student body, all reflect this economic orientation. Although the majority of the labor force still comprises persons *without* such training, the number of formally trained persons entering the labor force has been rising. The educational reform of 1958 may be seen as an attempt to adjust the rate at which the educational system is turning out individuals with different levels of formal education to the demands of the economy for labor in terms of quality.

With respect to the recruitment and allocation of labor in accordance with the demand: Compared with other industrializing countries, the urban population and the nonagricultural labor force have increased relatively rapidly since 1928. However, the urban population still comprises less than half of the total population, and the nonagricultural labor force came only recently to include as much as half of the total civilian labor force.

The rural population and the agricultural labor force, on the other hand, have declined relatively little in absolute terms during most peacetime years since 1928. The increase in the urban population has been more or less equivalent to the natural increase of the total population, and the increase in the nonagricultural labor force has been of the same order of magnitude as the natural increase in the population of working ages.

It seems, therefore, that, up to this point, the Russians have had no difficulty in supplying the demands of industry for labor. Further evidence appears in the relatively large amount of labor still used in collective and state farm agriculture, and in the millions of persons still occupied on the "fringe" of the labor force, that is, on a partial, intermittent, and part-time basis in subsidiary or other private economic activity (particularly agricultural).

However, with the greatly reduced age-cohorts (born during the war) now entering the working ages, the over-all problem of labor recruitment and allocation enters a new phase. If the continuing demands of industry are to be met, more labor will have to be supplied by means of an absolute reduction in the agricultural labor force, and we can also expect increased effort to draw the fringe labor force as well as those outside the labor force into full participation. In general, under these changing conditions of labor scarcity, one can expect greater refinements in policies affecting the recruitment, allocation, and utilization of labor.

1. The Quantitative Dimensions of Over-all Labor Supply

Definition and Measurement

Labor supply in quantitative terms reflects the size and rate of growth of population, the proportion of population by age and sex in the labor force, the average number of persons actually working as a percent of the labor force, and the number of hours worked. Labor supply may therefore be defined and measured in many different ways. We begin with some clarifying remarks, because the observations and conclusions about trends in supply depend in part on the measure employed.

In the broadest sense, we may equate "labor supply" with the *labor force,* the latter defined to include persons "having an occupation," that is, persons who work for pay or profit plus persons who contribute without pay to the principal productive effort of the head of the household. The measure includes all persons who are "usually" so occupied, and therefore refers to no particular period of time. The total number of persons having an occupation thus includes those who work part-time, intermittently, or seasonally, as well as those who work full-time.

This broad and loosely constructed measure of the labor force is typically utilized with respect to relatively underdeveloped countries — where agricultural activity is dominant; where a major portion of economic activity is performed by individuals or households; where much of what is produced does not enter a market or state distribution network; and where, therefore, no sharp distinction is made between household and other activity. An example of this definition in practice is the gainful worker concept used in U.S. censuses through 1930.

At the other extreme, the labor force may be defined to include individuals only when they are actually working — using a workday as the basic unit. The measure is then one of the number of persons working on a given day, or the corresponding average full-time equivalent number of persons working (man-days of work) over a given period of time. In the latter case, part-time, intermittent, or seasonal work is an appropriate fraction of a full-time person.

Between these two extremes a number of variations in terms of the time dimension are possible, including, for example, the method followed by the United States in the decennial censuses beginning with 1940, as well as in the monthly survey of the labor force, based on an individual's status during a given "census week." [12]

The broader definition was embodied in pre-Soviet and early Soviet census methods and applied to an economy where the overwhelming majority of the labor force were members of individual peasant households working in agriculture and handicrafts, and more than half of the total labor force consisted of helping family members. Aggregate measures according to the narrower definition have more recently come to the fore, reflecting in part the major share in economic activity of State and co-operative enterprises, which keep current records on employment. The report on the labor force from the 1959 Soviet census includes data on both the number having an occupation and the annual average level of employment for wage and salary workers and collective farmers.[13]

In this study, three measures of labor supply will be used: the *total*

[12] See A. J. Jaffe and C. D. Stewart, *Manpower Resources and Utilization: Principles of Working Force Analysis* (New York, 1951), chap. 2.
[13] "O raspredelenii naseleniia," pp. 3–21.

labor force, meaning the number in the broader sense above, the *labor force of working ages* (16 to 59), and the *average annual number of persons actually working,* meaning the number in the narrower sense above.

Trends in the Total Labor Supply

√ *The total labor force.* The total labor force increases only 0.5 percent per year between 1926 and 1939, and 0.3 percent per year between 1940 and 1959 (on comparable territory), but is expected to increase 1.4 percent per year between 1959 and 1975 (Table II.1).

√*The labor force of working ages* (*16 to 59*). For 1926–39 and 1940–59, the rate of increase of the labor force of working age is higher than that for the total labor force; for the projection to 1975, it is lower; and for shorter time periods during 1950–60, the two are about equal. The average rate of increase of the labor force of working ages — ranging from 1.3 percent during 1926–39 to 0.6 percent during 1940–59, and 1.1 percent during 1959–75 — thus varies less than that for the total labor force. The relatively greater variation in the latter reflects the changes in the labor force outside the working ages. An important factor here is the sharp decline in the 1930's in the proportion of population age 10 to 15 in the labor force, and the absolute decline in the number of such persons by 1959.

√ *The average number of persons actually working.* In the process of industrialization, the average number of persons actually working typically increases as a percentage of the total labor force, through the movement of labor from agriculture to industry, and through the reduction of seasonal variation and part-time work in agriculture (by mechanization and improved organization). In the course of this development in the Soviet Union, much of the labor force has been socialized — as seen in the increase in the number of wage and salary workers (of State enterprises), the collectivization of agriculture, and the widening of the producer cooperative network — while the number of persons occupied solely in private economic activity has declined. The homestead garden plot of collective farmers has always been officially considered subordinate to the work of the collective farm, although it still attracts a large proportion of the work time of the collective farmer and his family.

The measure we seek is the average annual number of man-days actually worked in all branches of the economy, divided by some conventional figure for the possible number of man-days of work in a full-time man-year, by branches. Although such estimates for all branches of the economy are very likely drawn up by the Central Statistical Administration of the USSR, no aggregate measure has ever been published. Data for certain branches have been made available for certain years —

Table II.1
USSR, 1926–1975 and USA, 1860–1975: Annual Rates of Increase
of the Labor Force, Total and Working Ages
(percent)

Period	Total labor force	Labor force of working ages[a]
USSR		
1926–39	0.5	1.3
1940–50	−0.6	−0.2
1950–55	2.3	2.4
1955–60	1.3	1.3
1960–65	0.9	0.3
1965–70	1.6	1.3
1970–75	1.8	1.6
1926–39	0.5	1.3
1940–59	0.3	0.6
1959–75	1.4	1.1
USA		
1860–70	2.1	—
1870–80	3.1	3.0
1880–90	2.9	—
1890–1900	2.2	2.2
1900–10	2.3	2.5
1910–20	1.4	1.4
1920–30	1.6	1.5
1930–40	0.6	0.9
1940–50	1.3	1.2
1950–60	1.3	1.3
1960–65	1.4	1.4
1965–70	1.6	1.6
1970–75	1.4	1.4

[a] USSR group is 16 to 59; USA age group is 14 to 64, except for 1870–80, when it is 16 to 59.
Notes: USSR: calculated from Table II.3 and Warren W. Eason, *Soviet Manpower*, appendix Table R1, adjusted (preliminary) for recent data from the 1959 Soviet census. In this and in all other tables in this chapter, territory for 1939 and earlier years is that before the annexations of late 1939; all other dates refer to present territory. USA: calculated from Clarence D. Long, *The Labor Force Under Changing Income and Employment* (Princeton, 1958), pp. 285–287, 317, and from U.S. Bureau of the Census, "Projections of the Labor Force in the United States, 1955 to 1975," *Current Population Reports*, series P-50, no. 69, October 1956, p. 13.
The dash (—) indicates that data are not available.

either as reported by all establishments, in the case of wage and salary workers and cooperative handicraftsmen, or as estimated from sample budget surveys (including the data from the surveys themselves) in the case of collective farmers.

The principal difficulty is that the data for private and collective farming for different dates (1926, 1939, and 1959) are not entirely comparable.
Those for 1926 and 1939 are based on the average annual number of
persons working each *workday*. Such averages are available separately for
males, for females, and for both sexes. Those for 1939 and 1959 are based
on the average annual number of persons working at least one day (on
the collective farm) each month, but only for both sexes. In other words,
the 1926 and 1959 data are not comparable. Furthermore, the absence of
data by sex for 1959 prevents any comparison of the prewar and postwar
periods by sex. Finally, the data for 1959 do not permit the distinction
required in the case of persons who work on the collective farm (in a
given month) and *also* on their homestead garden plot.

Despite these shortcomings of the data, the general trend seems clear.
The annual average number of persons actually working increased absolutely and as a percentage of the labor force after 1926 (Table II.2). Between 1926 and 1939 the number working each work-day increased from
59.7 to 69.7 percent of the total labor force. The average annual number
including collective farmers who worked at least one day per month comprised 77.9 percent of the labor force in 1939 and 85.7 percent in 1959.

The percentages rose for several reasons. First, the proportion of the
labor force of nonworking ages in the total declined; and this group tends
to work a smaller percentage of a full-time year than the labor force of
working ages. Second, the proportion of wage and salary workers rose
from 11.4 percent of the total labor force in 1926 to 38.9 percent in 1939,
and 55.5 percent in 1959 (Table II.14 on p. 84). Most of this increase
took place in nonagricultural occupations. Third, the average annual
number of persons actually working in agriculture as a percentage of the
total labor force in agriculture has increased considerably since 1926
because the *combination* of collective farm plus homestead farm work has
demanded a larger share of the collective farmer's available time than
private farming did (in 1926) of the private farmer. This is especially true
for females. The relative amount of time spent on the collective farm
proper in 1939 was not high, since many farmers preferred to work on
their own homestead plot, but the contribution to collective farm work
has apparently increased since then due to the requirement that each able-
bodied collective farm member work a specified number of labor days.
Seasonal variation in collective farm work has also declined.[14]

For the most part the increase in the average annual number of persons
actually working as a percentage of the total labor force consists of an increase in female labor. Between 1926 and 1939, the average number of

[14] Warren W. Eason, *Soviet Manpower* (an unpublished PhD thesis on deposit with the
Columbia University Library, 1959), appendix Table Q3, and TSU, *Sel'skoe khoziaistvo
SSSR*, pp. 460–461.

Table II.2
USSR: Labor Force and Average Annual Number of Persons Actually Working, by Sex, 1926–59
(in thousands unless otherwise indicated)

Both sexes and Males

Item	Persons 1926	Persons 1939	Persons 1959	Change per year (%) 1926–39	Change per year (%) 1939–59	Persons 1926	Persons 1939	Persons 1959	Change per year (%) 1926–39	Change per year (%) 1939–59
	Both sexes					Males				
Labor force										
Total	84,500	90,000	109,000	0.5	0.3	45,300	49,700	55,200	0.8	−0.2
Working ages	67,000	78,600	98,800	1.3	0.6	35,700	43,700	50,200	1.7	0.1
Average annual number of persons working each workday	50,400	62,800	—	1.3	—	32,800	37,600	—	1.2	—
Percent of total labor force	59.7	69.7	—			72.4	75.7	—		
Average annual number of persons working each workday, except collective farmers working at least one day per month	—	70,200	93,400	—	0.7	—	40,100	—	—	—
Percent of total labor force	—	77.9	85.7			—	80.4	—		

Females and Females (as % of both sexes)

Item	Persons 1926	Persons 1939	Persons 1959	Change per year (%) 1926–39	Change per year (%) 1939–59	1926	1939	1959
	Females					Females (as % of both sexes)		
Labor force								
Total	39,200	40,300	53,800	0.2	0.9	46.4	44.8	49.4
Working ages	31,300	34,900	48,600	0.9	1.1	46.7	44.4	49.2
Average annual number of persons working each workday	17,600	25,200	—	3.0	—	34.9	40.1	—
Percent of total labor force	45.0	62.5	—			—	—	—
Average annual number of persons working each workday, except collective farmers working at least one day per month	—	30,100	—	—	—	—	42.9	—
Percent of total labor force	—	74.9	—			—	—	—

Notes: Data derived from Table II.3; Eason, *Soviet Manpower*, Table 22 and appendix Tables Q2 and Q3; and the 1959 census. The dash (—) indicates that data are not available.

males working each workday increased 1.2 percent per year, and the average number of females 3.0 percent per year. In the process, the average number of working females increased from 45.0 to 62.5 percent of the female labor force. For males, the corresponding increase was from 72.4 to 75.7 percent. Furthermore, much of the latter gain should be attributed to the relative decrease in the labor force of nonworking ages, not to a higher proportion of available time worked by males of working ages.

This pattern of growth may have continued in the postwar period, but there is little reason to think so. It is true that the total number of females in the labor force increased from 44.8 percent of both sexes in 1939 to 49.4 percent in 1959 (Table II.2); the average annual number of female wage and salary workers increased from 38 percent of both sexes in 1939 to 47 percent in 1959; and the number of females in the collective farm labor force increased from 54.3 percent of both sexes in 1939 to 60 percent in 1959 (Table II.14 on p. 84). However, none of these developments is necessarily associated with a tendency of females to work an increased proportion of available time (as they did between 1926 and 1939). Most importantly, the increased proportion of females in the total labor force is specifically related to the increased male deficit in the population. The greater burden on women to provide the family livelihood, however, may also have enhanced their motivation to work a higher proportion of available time.

Conclusions regarding the labor supply. Changes in the quantitative dimensions of the Soviet labor supply depend to a considerable degree on the measure employed. The choice varies with the problem at hand. For example, for questions related to *productivity,* actual labor inputs are required, and the average annual number of persons actually working — or the number of man-hours — seems appropriate. The noteworthy feature of this measure for the Soviet Union is the sharp increase in the proportion actually worked of the total available labor time of the female labor force, resulting in a relatively rapid rate of increase compared with the total labor force. On the other hand, for questions concerned with a surplus or underemployed element in the labor force, both the total labor force and the number actually working must be considered. The narrowing of the difference between the two measures since 1926, together with the lowered rate of population growth and changes in age structure, comprise much of the evidence on the reduction or elimination of a labor surplus. Finally, the long-run pattern of growth of Soviet labor supply is perhaps best reflected in the rate of growth of the labor force of working ages, in recognition of the close relationship between long-run labor supply and population growth.

In describing trends in the labor supply, we referred to relationships between population growth and labor supply and to variations in the proportion of the population in the labor force. We should consider each of these factors to understand better the forces at work in the Soviet Union.

Labor Supply and the Pattern of Population Growth

The Soviet Union entered the period of rapid industrialization and the five-year plans (1928) with a peacetime tradition of high birth and death rates and relatively high rate of population growth, possibly more than 2 percent per year.[15] The population was "young" in age distribution, and in terms of specific age groups and the sex ratio bore the effects of World War I and the Civil War, when mortality rates were high and birth rates low. Long-run projections made at the time, however, indicated continued rapid growth, a gradual aging of the population, and the elimination of the demographic deficits of the early Soviet period.[16] Future labor supply was therefore projected on the basis of a continued rapid rate of increase of the population of working ages.

The actual pattern of population growth after 1928 was different from that projected. In most peacetime years, and especially in the last decade, the USSR has experienced a decline in fertility and mortality rates, common to industrializing countries, although compressed in time. For the longer run, these are the more important developments. At the moment, however, the Soviet Union is still living in the demographic shadow of World War II, when mortality rates were high and fertility rates low.

The implication of these developments for labor supply is that there are considerably fewer people of working ages than there would have been if the original projections of 1928–30 had materialized; and that the pattern of recent years is dominated by substantial irregularities in the distribution of the population by age and sex, and by marked changes in the rate of growth of the population of the working and reproductive ages, resulting directly and indirectly from World War II.

The rate of population growth.[17] For the period as a whole — roughly from the 1926 census to the 1959 census, but excluding the estimated population of the territories annexed in 1940 and 1945 — the average rate of population increase is approximately 0.8 percent per year. This is lower than the long-run average which includes the Imperial Russian period: from 1850 to the present, on Soviet territory, the population increased

---

[15] The annual rate of increase during the late 1920's derived from reported crude birth and death rates is about 2.4 percent. However, as indicated in Eason, *Soviet Manpower*, chap. II and appendix M, corrections for relatively greater underreporting of deaths than births could reduce the rate to 2 percent or less.

[16] See Frank Lorimer, *The Population of the Soviet Union: History and Prospects* (Geneva, 1946).

[17] Portions of this summary are from Warren W. Eason, "The Soviet Population Today: An Analysis of the First Results of the 1959 Census," *Foreign Affairs*, July 1959.

slightly more than 1.0 percent per year, and in the fifty-year period before 1850, on Imperial Russian territory, slightly less than 1.0 percent per year.

One reason for the lower rate of increase over the past three decades, of course, is the demographic effects of World War II, referred to above: between the 1939 and 1959 censuses the average rate of population increase on comparable territory was only 0.5 percent per year. But the *peacetime* rate of population increase since the start of the industrialization drive has also been less than for earlier years. In 1931–34, the rate of population growth must have declined to near zero or even less, due to higher death rates and lower birth rates resulting from collectivization and the food shortages. Although population growth recovered by the later 1930's, the impact of these few early years was severe enough to reduce the average rate of population increase for 1926–39 to 1.23 percent per year, or only a little more than one-half of the rate that Soviet planners had anticipated. Nevertheless, this rate was higher than that of many other countries in these years.

The rate of population growth since 1950 has been about 1.6 percent per year — slightly less than before the start of the industrialization drive.

The moderate decline in the rate of population growth under peacetime conditions conceals a relatively sharp decline in both birth and death rates since the late 1920's. The evidence indicates a crude birth rate of about 25 per thousand now, compared with more than 40 on the eve of the industrialization drive; a death rate of 7.2 compared with 18; and average life expectancy of 67 years compared with 44 years. Standardization for changes in age structure compared with the 1920's would lower the present birth rate and raise the death rate somewhat, and one can say that for comparable age distributions the rates are about one-half those of 35 years ago.[18]

The future rate of growth of the Soviet population depends primarily on expected trends in fertility. The low death rate precludes a further significant decline, judging by the experience of other countries; in fact, as the Soviet population ages, the crude death rate may rise to some extent. Future trends in the birth rate, on the other hand, are obscure. From a long-run point of view, for reasons given in the source cited in fn. 18, the prediction of a continued decline in fertility rates is about as reasonable as the prediction of a return to higher rates.

In the short run, however, trends in the crude birth rate will reflect the relatively small number of persons born during World War II and now passing through the child-bearing ages. Even if fertility rates remain constant, the relative decline in the number of women of child-bearing ages

[18] Some of the reasons for the trends in births and deaths are examined in Eason, *Soviet Manpower,* chap. II.

which has already begun will reduce the crude birth rate by as much as 5 per thousand. With time this effect will become less important, and long-run fertility trends will again have a dominant effect on the crude birth rate after 1975 or 1980.

The distribution by ages. The pattern of change in the distribution of population by age is related to the pattern of change in birth and death rates, and in particular to the incidence of the national crises beginning with World War I. Declining birth rates tend to reduce the percentage of the population in the younger age groups. Declining infant mortality tends to operate in the other direction. General improvements in conditions affecting mortality other than infant mortality tend to have a relatively minor influence on the age distribution of the population.

Between the censuses of 1897 and 1939, changes in the distribution of the population by broad age groups were gradual and in the following directions: a declining proportion age 0 to 15, from 40.6 to 37.7 percent of the total; a rising proportion age 16 to 59 (the working ages), from 52.5 to 55.5 percent; and essentially a constant proportion age 60 and over, from 6.8 to 6.9 percent. These changes seem to be dominated by the abnormal years of the period, including World War I, the Civil War, and the early 1930's. Except for these years, relatively high birth rates and gradually declining infant mortality tended to raise the proportion of young people in the population.

If we compare 1939 with 1959, we find that World War II sharply reduced the proportion age 0 to 15 from 37.7 to 30.4 percent; increased the proportion age 16 to 59 from 55.5 to 60.2 percent; and also increased the proportion age 60 and over from 6.9 to 9.4 percent. Thus, despite war losses approaching 25 million adults, the proportions of adults age 16 to 59 and 60 and over were a good deal higher in 1959 than 1939. The lower birth rates and higher infant mortality rates of the war outweighed the high military losses and excess civilian deaths.

The effect of military and other losses on labor supply was to a degree recouped immediately after the war by the entry into the working ages of cohorts born in the late 1920's. In the latter period, with few exceptions, the birth rate was high; and persons born then were young enough during the war to escape many of its hazards. In other words, although total labor supply right after the war was smaller than it would have been in the absence of war, the rate of increase of the population of working ages from 1946 to 1958 was probably greater than at any time in the past.[19]

In more recent years the growth of the population of working ages, as already noted, has been dominated by the entry of age groups born during

[19] The rate of increase was high partly because relatively large numbers were entering the working ages, but also because the numbers leaving the working ages, reflecting losses during the war, were by the late 1940's relatively small.

the war. The situation starting in 1950 may be summarized as follows: between 1950 and 1955, the increase in the number of persons of both sexes age 16 to 59 was 12.3 million and between 1955 and 1960, 8 million; between 1960 and 1965, the increase will be an estimated 1 million; after 1965 this downward trend will be reversed, with projected increases of almost 8 million between 1965 and 1970 and more than 10 million between 1970 and 1975.

The implications for the *proportion* of the total population in the working ages depend on fertility rates after 1960. The proportion age 16 to 59 will decline after 1960 in any event, thereby reversing trends since 1897, although the decline will be greater if rising fertility rates are assumed. The proportion age 60 and over will increase so that by 1975 it will be roughly equal to that in the United States at the present time.

The sex ratio. It is statistically correct and undoubtedly valid to say that the burden of the Soviet revolution and the building of an industrialized socialist state (if we include its defense) fell much more heavily on males than females. In 1897 there were approximately the same number of males as females and the sex ratio was 99 males per 100 females. By 1926, reflecting World War I and the Civil War, there were 5 million fewer males than females, and the sex ratio was 94. By 1939, due to the conditions of the early 1930's, there were 7 million fewer males than females and the sex ratio had declined to 92, although under normal conditions it would have increased.

The effect of World War II on the sex ratio in the Soviet Union staggers the imagination. The 1959 census reports 114.8 million females and 94 million males, an absolute deficit of 20.8 million males. By calculating backward, using published birth rates and certain assumptions with respect to the distribution of mortality by sex, we estimate that in 1950 there were about 25 million fewer males than females in the adult population, and the sex ratio for the total population was about 80 males per 100 females.

Thus it may be inferred that population war losses — civilian and military — were borne to a large degree by males.[20] An estimated 45 million total war losses comprises 25 million persons who were alive in 1940 and who would not have died if there had not been a war, and 20 million persons who would have been born and survived. Of the 25 million excess deaths other than among infants, no more than 10 million can be accounted for as males in military service, leaving 15 million excess civilian deaths, of which 11 million were males and 4 million females. The reasons for three times as many male deaths as female outside the military service during and after the war, over and above the number who would have

---

[20] The derivation of the estimates of war losses is given in Eason, "The Soviet Population Today."

died under normal conditions, are discussed in "The Soviet Population Today."

According to the 1959 census, the male deficit is now confined to the population age 32 and over. Barring war or other turmoil, the male deficit as a major social and economic problem should lessen. But in all probability it will not be entirely eliminated, because in the Soviet Union as in other countries, even under peacetime conditions, life expectancy for females (67 years in 1954–55) exceeds that for males (61 years).[21]

The Proportion of the Population in the Labor Force

The broad relationship between the population and the labor force in the Soviet Union seems fairly clear. Compared with many other countries, a large percentage of the population has always been engaged in economic activity. In the Imperial Russian and early Soviet periods, characterized, as we have said, by a predominantly agricultural and household economy, virtually all able-bodied persons of both sexes participated in primary economic activity at least part of the year — and were counted as having an occupation or in the labor force.

The reports from the census of 1959 give us the proportion of the population in the labor force for 1959 and, less precisely, 1939 — the first from census sources since 1926 and the first from any source since the official estimates of 1931.[22] The relationship between total labor force and population by age and sex for the census dates is given in Table II.3. All the data for 1926, the population data by age and sex for 1939 and 1959, and the total labor force of both sexes for 1959 are from the censuses. The number of males and females in the labor force in 1959, and the number of males, females, and both sexes in the labor force in 1939 are estimated with a reasonably small margin of error. The distribution of the labor force in 1939 and 1959 by age groups is estimated from the corresponding population in the labor force by age and sex. These assumptions reflect the general trends after 1926 inferred from fragmentary noncensus data and certain relationships in the 1926 data and yield the census totals for the labor force, males and females, for 1939 and 1959.

The share of the labor force in the population declined from 57.5 percent in 1926 to 52.2 percent in 1959. This decline, in the face of an increasing proportion of the working age population (16 to 59) in the total, reflects a decline in the proportion of the labor force in specific age and sex groups.

---

[21] The low male deficit in 1897 is consistent with available data on life expectancy — 33 years for females and 31 years for males — a smaller difference than at present (see TSU, *Narodnoe khoziaistvo SSSR v 1956 godu* [Moscow, 1957], p. 270).

[22] The 1931 data, calculated for the control figures of 1932, appear in A. Ia. Pleshchitser, *Sotsial'nye sdvigi v dinamike naseleniia SSSR* (Kazan', 1932), p. 9, and are reproduced in Eason, *Soviet Manpower*, appendix L.

Table II.3
USSR: Population and Labor Force, by Age and Sex, 1926, 1939, and 1959
(In thousands unless otherwise indicated)

Age groups	1926			1939			1959		
	Population	Labor force	Percent	Population	Labor force	Percent	Population	Labor force	Percent
Both sexes									
10 to 15	20,800	12,200	58.7	25,600	6,000	23.4	17,200	2,000	11.6
16 to 59	78,800	67,000	85.0	94,000	78,600	83.6	125,700	98,800	78.6
60 and over	9,800	5,300	54.1	11,200	5,400	49.1	19,700	8,200	43.2
10 and over	109,400	84,500	77.2	130,800	90,100	68.9	162,600	109,000	67.0
Total	147,000	84,500	57.5	170,600	90,100	52.8	208,800	109,000	52.2
Males									
10 to 15	10,500	6,400	61.0	12,800	3,100	24.2	8,600	1,000	12.1
16 to 59	37,300	35,700	95.7	44,700	43,700	97.8	55,300	50,200	90.8
60 and over	4,300	3,200	74.4	4,300	3,100	72.1	6,600	4,000	60.6
10 and over	52,100	45,300	86.9	61,800	49,900	80.7	70,500	55,200	78.3
Total	71,000	45,300	63.8	81,700	49,600	61.1	94,000	55,200	58.7
Females									
10 to 15	10,300	5,800	56.3	12,800	2,900	22.7	8,600	1,000	11.4
16 to 59	41,500	31,300	75.4	49,400	34,900	70.6	70,400	48,600	69.0
60 and over	5,500	2,100	38.2	6,900	2,400	34.8	13,100	4,200	32.0
10 and over	57,300	39,200	68.7	69,100	40,200	58.2	92,100	53,800	58.4
Totals	76,000	39,200	51.3	88,900	40,200	45.3	114,800	53,800	46.9

Note: Sources and methods are given in the appendix.

Most important statistically is the decline in the percentage of the population age 10 to 15 in the labor force, from an estimated 58.7 percent in 1926 to 23.4 percent in 1939, and 11.6 percent in 1959. This decline largely reflects increased attendance at school. Universal education for grades 1 to 4 (roughly ages 8 to 11) was achieved by the mid-1930's, and the number in grades 5 to 7 (roughly ages 12 to 14) increased 9 million between 1926 and 1939. If we assume that school attendance effectively eliminates the labor force contribution of such individuals, it explains the decline in the proportion of the population age 10 to 15 in the labor force from 1926 to 1939. The 23.4 percent figure for 1939 is sufficient to encompass a relatively high proportion of persons age 12 to 15 in *rural* areas still in the labor force. By 1959 the 11.6 percent of the population age 10 to 15 in the labor force is consistent with the fact that attendance in grades 5 to 7 was almost universal, and that attendance in grades 8 to 10 (roughly ages 14 to 16 in the postwar period) had increased three times compared with 1939, even in rural areas.

On the other hand, the figures may overstate the true decline in the proportion of the population age 10 to 15 in the labor force, since the censuses exclude from the labor force all persons attending school who are not *at the same time* working for pay. Individuals who work a few summer months in private agriculture would have been counted (by the censuses, taken in the winter months) in a category tantamount to having an occupation (helping family member) if they were *not* attending school at the time of the census, but they would have been counted as not having an occupation if they were attending school. Increased school attendance therefore is a major factor in the decline in the proportion of the population age 10 to 15 in the labor force; but the number of persons actually working a few months in the summer (while attending school) did not decline proportionately. In short, it is likely that more young people age 10 to 15 work on the private garden plots of collective farmers and wage and salary workers than is indicated by the numbers in the labor force for 1939 and 1959 in Table II.1.

The proportion of the population age 60 and over in the labor force also shows a drop. The decline to 1939 reflects rural-urban migration, since the proportions of the rural and urban populations age 60 and over in the labor force are held constant. By comparison with many other countries, particularly with respect to females, these percentages are high.[23] The slight decline to 32 percent by 1959 for females age 60 and over is not

[23] See United Nations, *Demographic Yearbook, 1948* (New York, 1949), p. 232. Differences in concepts make for difficulties in international comparisons of the number in the labor force; see United Nations, *Application of International Standards to Census Data on the Economically Active Population,* Population Studies no. 9 (New York, 1951).

necessarily significant, in view of possible error in the estimating procedure used.

The percentage of females age 16 to 59 in the labor force has remained relatively high. The decline from 75 percent in 1926 to 69 percent in 1959 is the net result of rural-urban migration (from rural areas where in 1926 the corresponding proportion was 85 percent, to urban areas with 40 percent) and the assumption (based on inferences from employment data by sex) that the percentage for urban areas increased after 1926. For 1939, the figure of 97.8 percent of males age 16 to 59 in the labor force excludes only those who are physically or mentally unable to work. The decline to 90.8 percent in 1959 reflects the increase in the number of persons on pensions.[24]

In summary, except for the lowered proportion for young people age 10 to 15, and the somewhat lowered proportion for males ages 16 to 59 and 60 and over, the proportion of the Soviet population in the labor force remains relatively high. The percentages are compared with data for the United States in Table II.4. There is an over-all stability in the United States proportions, with a declining proportion of the older males in the labor force more or less balanced by a rising proportion of females.[25] According to Long (pp. 20–26), this over-all stability is also present in other countries. However, neither the United States (as a whole) nor any other country examined by Long began with as high a proportion of the population other than males of working ages in the labor force as the Soviet Union. A decline in the Soviet percentage was therefore almost certainly to be expected. Perhaps the relevant comparison is with the nonwhite groups in the United States. Long writes: "The stability for the United States has been due to the behavior of the native white population. Both colored and foreign-born have reduced their participation by impressive amounts." (p. 21).

Will the proportions in the labor force of females age 16 and over, and of males age 60 and over, decline in the future in the Soviet Union? This is likely in the long run, especially with rising living standards and the easing of the housing crisis. In the short run, however, the pressure appears to be increasing to draw housewives and others into the labor

[24] No official source can be cited for the relationship between the lowered percentage in the labor force and the (reported) higher number of pensioners, the latter including more than 12 million persons "with their primary source of income from pensions" out of a total of 20 million pensioners, according to the 1959 census. But examination of alternative assumptions to explain the sharp drop in the reported male labor force (all ages) compared with the male population age 16 to 59 suggests this explanation. Considering the war losses in both military and civilian life (21 million killed) among males, the possibility that some 4 million males age 16 to 59 are now on pensions and unable to work does not seem unreasonable.

[25] Long, chap. 13. These changes are not apparent in the age groups shown in Table II. 4, which were selected for comparability with the Russian.

Table II.4

USA, 1870–1950 and USSR, 1926–1959: Labor Force as Percent of Population, by Age and Sex

Age groups	USA									USSR		
	1870	1880	1890	1900	1910	1920	1930	1945	1960	1926	1939	1959
Both sexes												
10 to 15	—	—	—	—	—	—	—	—	—	58.7	23.4	11.6
16 to 59	—	—	—	—	—	—	—	—	—	85.0	83.6	78.6
60 and over	—	—	—	—	—	—	—	—	—	54.1	49.1	43.2
10 and over	44.4	47.3	49.0	49.9	50.7	50.4	49.5	47.8	49.4	77.2	68.9	67.0
Total	32.5	34.7	37.0	38.1	39.4	39.4	39.8	40.1	39.7	57.5	52.8	52.2
Males												
10 to 15	19.3	24.4	—	—	—	—	—	—	—	61.0	24.2	12.1
16 to 59	91.0	93.4	—	—	—	—	—	—	—	95.7	97.8	90.8
60 and over	64.2	64.3	—	—	—	—	—	—	—	74.4	72.1	60.6
10 and over	74.9	78.7	79.2	79.5	78.6	78.3	76.2	72.2	72.9	86.9	80.7	78.3
Total	—	—	60.0	60.9	61.5	61.4	61.3	60.5	58.2	63.8	61.1	58.7
Females												
10 to 15	7.0	9.0	—	—	—	—	—	—	—	56.3	22.7	11.4
16 to 59	15.7	17.1	—	—	—	—	—	—	—	75.4	70.6	69.0
60 and over	5.4	5.2	—	—	—	—	—	—	—	38.2	34.8	32.0
10 and over	13.3	14.7	17.0	18.8	20.8	21.2	22.0	23.3	26.5	68.7	58.2	58.4
Total	—	12.8	12.8	14.3	16.1	16.5	17.7	19.6	21.5	51.3	45.2	46.9

Notes: USA data from Long, *The Labor Force*, pp. 285–288; USSR data from Table II.3.
The dash (—) indicates that data are not available.

force, in large measure to compensate for the decline in the rate of growth of the population of working ages. For the next decade, therefore, the percentage of females in the labor force will probably not decrease, and the percentage of males will probably increase due to the aging of the population.

2. The Qualitative Dimensions of Over-all Labor Supply

In many respects the Soviet Union began rapid industrialization with the same dearth of skills and experience as other underdeveloped countries. On the eve of the First Five-Year Plan, approximately 80 percent of the population was dependent on agricultural or other rural sources of income, and agricultural production methods were small-scale and simple, involving some 25 million independent peasant households.

In some respects, the quality of the labor supply was worse than in other countries, as a result of unique conditions: after 1917 many of the most experienced and qualified people were eliminated from positions of responsibility for essentially political reasons.

In other respects, however, the country was less underdeveloped than frequently imagined, at least in terms of the skill, education, and experience requirements of an urban and industrial labor force. The rural population was still below that of India and similar countries, where almost 90 percent live in rural areas. Industrialization, urbanization, and capital formation had already been in process for almost 50 years, creating a sizable nucleus of an industrial labor force. And the educational system was already fairly well established by the standards of underdeveloped countries, although far short of that required by a fully industrialized society.

But in relation to the ambitious goals of the five-year plans, vast and far-reaching changes in the qualifications of the labor force and population were in order. As a result, beginning in 1928 — through the expansion of the educational system, the large-scale movement of the population to urban areas and to nonagricultural employment, the mechanization of some farm work, and incessant indoctrination through the press and radio — the population was rapidly industrialized. In addition, the advance of personnel in terms of skills and experience led to the formation of cadres of professional, technical, and managerial manpower which now encompass some 15 percent of the total labor force.

A comprehensive list of the qualitative dimensions of over-all labor supply would include: (i) health and general physical condition; (ii) skills and general competence derived from formal education and training; (iii) skills and general competence derived from experience on the job; and (iv) effort and efficiency applied to the job. Because of limitations of space, the first and fourth aspects will not be discussed, although their importance in any complete analysis of labor supply must be recognized.

The problem of improving skills and general competence through some combination of formal education and experience on the job raises a number of questions of which the following will be considered as particularly germane here: (i) the distribution of skills — low-level, intermediate, and high-level — required by the industrialized work process; (ii) the establishment of a broad, minimum amount of education, acclimatization, and general commitment to work in the industrialized setting, on the part of the broad mass of the labor force. Particular attention will be paid to the relative importance in the Soviet Union of formal education and training versus the acquisition of experience on the job.

The Development of Skills and Specialized Experience

In the development of the skills and specialized experience required by labor under industrialization — running from high-level administrators, managerial and technical personnel, to the relatively unskilled production-line personnel — the USSR has moved in two directions: it has placed *primary* emphasis on the acquisition of skills and competence on the job and it has developed the system of specialized education slowly but deliberately, tailoring curriculum and programming to the needs of the economy, ordering the number of graduates so as to increase gradually the share of specialized personnel in the total.

The relative importance of on-the-job training and experience is seen in the data from the censuses of 1939 and 1959 (Table II.5). In 1939, 87.7 percent of the total labor force, 50.2 percent of white collar workers, and 95.7 percent of blue collar workers (including farmers) had completed no more than an elementary school education. By 1959 the number in this category still included more than half of the total labor force (57.7 percent) and 68.4 percent of blue collar workers, but only 11.6 percent of white collar workers. However, even in 1959, less than half of white collar workers (47.6 percent) and only 1.4 percent of blue collar workers had received either higher education or specialized secondary education, that is, had received formal specialized education off the job for their skill or profession.[26]

The formal education achieved varies by occupation (Table II.6). Unfortunately, the categories of formal education beyond elementary school

[26] It is difficult to tell whether training in Labor Reserve Schools or in factory apprentice programs is counted as specialized secondary education, although according to the usual method of reporting it would not be. Factory training programs, of course, constitute formalized on-the-job training, and the Labor Reserve System, instituted in 1940, is an attempt to supply equivalent training in lower level vocational skills outside the factory (see Nicholas DeWitt, *Education and Professional Employment in the USSR* [Washington, 1961], chap. III). It should also be noted that the census of January 15, 1959, was taken before the reorganization of the educational system, promulgated in 1958, had been put into effect.

Table II.5

USSR: General and Specialized Education Among the Major Categories of the Labor Force, Censuses of 1939 and 1959
(percent)

Category	Total	Not completing lower or upper secondary education, higher education, or specialized secondary education	Completing lower or upper secondary education, higher education, or specialized secondary education		
			Total	Completing lower or upper secondary education	Completing higher education or specialized secondary education
1939					
Blue collar workers	100.0	95.7	4.3	—	—
Wage earners	100.0	91.8	8.2	—	—
Collective farmers[a]	100.0	98.5	1.5	—	—
White collar workers	100.0	50.2	49.8	—	—
Total labor force[b]	100.0	87.7	12.3	—	—
1959					
Blue collar workers	100.0	68.4	31.6	30.2	1.4
Wage earners	100.0	61.4	—	—	—
Collective farmers[a]	100.0	78.8	—	—	—
White collar workers	100.0	11.6	88.4	40.8	47.6
Total labor force[b]	100.0	57.7	43.3	32.4	10.9

[a] Excludes supervisory personnel and specialists.

[b] Excludes persons working exclusively in private, subsidiary agriculture.

Notes: From "O raspredelenii naseleniia," p. 16.

The dash (—) indicates that data are not available.

Table II.6
USSR: White Collar Workers, by Selected Occupations, Completing Seven or
More Years of Education, Censuses of 1939 and 1959
(percent of total in occupation)

Occupation	1939	1959
Teachers and scientific workers	89.2	99.1
Legal personnel	68.4	98.7
Economists, planners, and statisticians	78.0	97.9
Medical workers	67.4	96.9
Workers in cultural and related activities	59.4	95.8
Clerical personnel	62.4	94.3
Agronomists, veterinarians, et cetera	62.2	93.6
Accountants, bookkeepers	53.5	92.7
Engineering-technical personnel	63.0	91.0
Leading personnel in state administration	35.9	90.8
Artists, et cetera	64.4	89.4
Management of enterprises and collective farms	28.5	85.3
Communications workers	36.8	79.2
Trade, supply, food services, et cetera	18.2	73.7
Workers of communal enterprises	19.7	56.1
All white collar workers	49.8	88.4

Note: From "O raspredelenii naseleniia," pp. 20–21.

are not listed separately by occupation, and we cannot distinguish, for example, between those who received formal training as engineers and those who completed either lower or upper secondary school and then went on to qualify as engineers on the job. The latter procedure was undoubtedly significant in most if not all of the occupations listed; we can calculate from Table II.5 that 46.2 percent of *total* white collar workers whose education went beyond elementary school completed lower or upper secondary education but were trained specifically for their occupations on the job.

The percentage of white collar workers by occupation completing more than elementary school education varies considerably — ranging in 1939 from 89.2 percent of teachers and scientific workers to 18.2 percent of workers in trade, supply, and food services, compared with an average of 49.8 percent for all white collar workers. The average is higher in 1959, and the spread between the highest percentage (99.1) and the lowest (56.1) is narrower than in 1939.

The reliance of the Russians on on-the-job training should not be surprising. A similar pattern has existed in the United States and elsewhere. Concerning the engineering profession in the United States, for example, Blank and Stigler state, ". . . this profession is only a little over half way through the long transition from training through experience to training through formal education." [27] Such emphasis in the earlier stages of economic development "is not a peculiarly Russian phenomenon; it was and remains a characteristic of American industrial training as well." [28]

↲ The experience of the Soviet Union lends support to the view that major strides in raising the quality of labor can be made without elaborate and extensive educational facilities. Working on the job is not *ipso facto* "training," although it is so up to a point. Some organization and supervision as well as instructional skill may also be required. The advantage of on-the-job training in the early stages of industrialization is that it conserves scarce resources, that is, the special facilities which would otherwise be required for teaching the workers, and teaching the teachers. If the quality of the results is not high, it is at least wasteful of the most plentiful resource (labor). In the early 1930's, on-the-job training by rough-and-ready methods was combined with the hiring of workers (by enterprises) in numbers that would have been called excessive under any other conditions. But the resulting training of masses of new workers constituted perhaps the most important output of industrial enterprises.

If the emphasis on on-the-job training in the early stages of development is not unusual by comparison with other countries, its variability among occupations is significant, as is the increasing importance of formal education in all occupations.

The incidence of formal education beyond elementary school is highest in occupations requiring technical or specialized knowledge (for example, teachers and scientific workers), and it is lowest in those which are of low priority in the national economy (as in trade and communal services) or which involve the more generalized abilities of supervision and control (as in enterprise management). The latter may reflect the greater importance of political reliability than of specialized knowledge or managerial know-how (through education) during many of these years.

↲ In other words, the Soviet Union has tended to emphasize formal education in those occupations which stand most to benefit from formal methods of instruction on a full-time basis, and which are specialties deemed relatively important for the national economy. As a result, formal education has been limited to a relatively small fraction of occupations.

However, formal education has been increasing in importance. But it is much less important than frequently imagined — or, to be more exact, is more selective than, for example, in the United States. In the case of higher education, it is selective in terms of the proportion of the relevant age groups admitted, the priority assigned to particular occupational

[27] David M. Blank and George J. Stigler, *The Demand and Supply of Scientific Personnel* (New York, 1957), p. 8.

[28] Walter Galenson, "Industrial Training in the Soviet Union," *Industrial and Labor Relations Review*, July 1956, p. 562.

groups, and the incidence of higher education within broad occupational groups.

The outstanding example of selectivity is the case of engineers and certain other specialists. According to Table II.7, the number of persons graduating from higher educational institutions — as engineers, medical doctors, and agricultural specialists — since the late 1920's, is approximately double that of the United States. But in all other specialties combined, the number in the Soviet Union is less than half that of the United States. Present trends in enrollment probably will tend to increase this disparity.[29]

Table II.7
USSR, 1928–59 and USA, 1926–58: Number of Graduates
of Higher Institutions, by Selected Fields

Field	USSR	USA	USSR as percent of USA
Engineers	1,117,800	620,300	180.0
Medical doctors	420,000	181,700	231.2
Agricultural specialists	389,000	166,400	233.9
Science majors	430,000	704,400	61.0
Sum of above	2,357,000	1,672,800	140.9
Humanities, social sciences, etc.	1,772,300	5,198,600	34.1
Totals	4,129,300	6,871,400	60.1

Note: From DeWitt, p. 453. Higher educational institutions for the USSR include universities and institutes, and for the USA, colleges and universities.

In respect to higher education, therefore, the Soviet Union has concentrated its efforts on relatively technical fields which can be expected to have the most direct effect on economic development. This carefully focused use of higher education, even after 30 years of economic development, shows little sign of changing. The fact that the entering class in higher education in 1959 comprised about 12 percent of the population age 18, compared with 32 percent for colleges and universities in the United States, will tend to perpetuate the over-all relationship shown in Table II.7, in which the total number of graduates of higher educational institutions in the Soviet Union since 1928 has equaled only 60 percent of those in the United States.

A final indication of the relatively narrow and specialized use of higher education — together with an indication of the wider use of specialized secondary education — is given in Table II.8. Among the "intelligentsia," the number with higher education comprised 8.6 percent in 1926, 7.8

[29] DeWitt, *Education and Professional Employment in the USSR,* pp. 452ff.

Table II.8

USSR: Educational Background of the "Intelligentsia" and "Leading Personnel," Selected Years, 1926–58

Formal specialized education completed	"Intelligentsia" [a]						"Leading personnel" [b]	
	1926		1937		1956		1958	
	(thousands)	(percent)	(thousands)	(percent)	(thousands)	(percent)	(thousands)	(percent)
Higher education (professional)	233	8.6	749	7.8	2,633	17.0	2,510	26.7
Specialized secondary education (semiprofessional)	288	10.6	1,440	15.0	3,624	23.4	3,196	34.0
No formal specialized education completed ("praktikal")	2,204	80.8	7,402	77.2	9,203	59.6	3,694	39.3
Totals	2,725	100.0	9,591	100.0	15,460	100.0	9,400	100.0

[a] Includes administrators, managers and supervisors, government bureaucrats and party functionaries, academicians and scientists, professionals and technicians, teachers and medical doctors, some white collar employees, military officers, and university students.
[b] Includes leading administrative, managerial, and specialized personnel.
Note: Data derived from DeWitt, pp. 482, 487.

percent in 1937, and 17.0 percent in 1956. DeWitt includes in this category "administrators, managers and supervisors, government bureaucrats and party functionaries, academicians and scientists, professionals and technicians, teachers and medical doctors, some white-collar employees, military officers, and even university students." Thus, in this group of high-level personnel, the proportion with higher education was relatively low in 1926 and has only doubled in 30 years. The proportion of intelligentsia with secondary specialized education, however, is somewhat higher even in 1926, and has increased at a more rapid rate. This suggests that even for the broad group of upper echelon personnel, semiprofessional training has been and continues to be — in terms of numbers affected — the relatively more important basis for technical competence.

These observations hold even if we concentrate on the "leading administrative, managerial, and specialized personnel" alone. In 1959, only 26.7 percent had completed higher education but 34.0 percent had completed specialized secondary education, while 39.3 percent had completed no specialized training (although some may have completed part of such courses of study).[30]

The Problem of General Educational Minimums

Underlying the problem of developing specific skills is the problem of raising the general educational level, through formal schooling. The development of a program with this aim has received high priority in the Soviet Union, partly as an end in itself — witness the publicity given the sharp rise in the literacy rate by 1939 — and partly to increase the effectiveness of the media of mass communications, in addition to providing the basis for raising the quality of the labor force.

With the beginning of industrialization the USSR moved swiftly to implement a program of basic general education, and by the middle 1930's primary education through grade 4 was essentially universal for persons passing through the relevant age groups. It may well be that this would have been done in any event, that is, the sizable amount of resources required would have been assigned in accord with the highest priority attached to the goals. As a matter of fact, the major share of the resources required had already been committed in 1928, and even as early as 1914.

[30] The relative emphasis on higher and specialized secondary education may have contributed to a rather curious relationship in Table II.6. With the increase in formal education between 1939 and 1959, the majority of occupations listed retained their relative position on the scale. Engineering-technical personnel, however, hold a lower relative position in 1959 than 1939, and this may be due to the composite categorization (in Table II.6) of all those completing more than elementary school. Compared with other occupations, the relative influence of those with specialized secondary school training among engineers in 1939 may have been greater than those with higher education *as engineers* in 1959. Only adequate data by categories of higher education would clarify this point.

This is evident from the statistics. A total of approximately 10 million persons was enrolled in grades 1 to 4 in 1928, including more than half, and possibly as high as 80 percent, of the population in the formally corresponding age groups (8 to 11).[31] These relationships reflect to a certain degree the expansion of the network of primary grades during the 1920's: from 6.6 million pupils in 1922–23 to 10.3 million in 1928, according to *Kul'turnoe stroitel'stvo.* On the other hand, part of this expansion during the 1920's constituted a reconstruction of the network, which had been destroyed during World War I, the Revolution, and the Civil War. Perhaps the most significant fact, therefore, is that in 1914–15 there were 7.4 million pupils (on territory comparable to the Soviet Union in 1939) in grades 1 to 4, or only 3 million less than in 1928 (*ibid.*). (The total population, on comparable territory, was only slightly greater in 1928.)

This high proportion of the corresponding population in grades 1 to 4 in 1928, moreover, was not confined to urban areas. Allowing for the shortcomings of the data, it seems reasonable to conclude that more than half of the *rural* population age 8 to 11 was enrolled in grades 1 to 4.

The achievement of universal elementary education (grades 1 to 4) by the middle or later 1930's, although significant in several respects, nevertheless must be interpreted as something less than a total effort from an economic resources point of view, in the light of the educational network already existing on the eve of the plans.

A second respect in which the Soviet educational effort beyond that required by the demand for a skilled labor force appears relatively modest is the rate of expansion of the secondary school network. Despite the long-run goal of universal education through secondary school, and the avowed aim of the early 1930's to reach this goal with all possible speed, enrollment increased much more slowly in secondary schools than in primary schools.

During the 1920's, the vast majority of pupils completing the elementary grades did not continue in school, and in all probability entered the labor force (around age 12). During the 1930's, the proportion enrolled in grades

---

[31] This statement must be approximate for several reasons. According to TSU, *Kul'turnoe stroitel'stvo SSSR: statisticheskii sbornik* (Moscow, 1956), p. 122, there were 10.3 million pupils in grades 1 to 4 in 1928 and 9.5 million at the beginning of the school year during which the 1926 census was taken. A total of 9.5 million equals 85 percent of the population age 8 to 11 (the formally relevant ages), and we can presume approximately the same percentage for 1928. However, the number of pupils enrolled in grades 1 to 4 undoubtedly includes children younger than 8 and older than 11. This follows from our general knowledge and also from the fact that in periods when attendance was obligatory or otherwise approached universal levels, the total number of pupils in grades 1 to 4 was actually 10 or 20 percent *greater* than the population age 8 to 11 (for 1959, age 7 to 10). This result is obtained for the *urban* population in 1926 and for the total population in 1939 and 1959.

5 to 7 rose steadily, although even by the eve of World War II their number accounted for little more than half of those completing grades 1 to 4. DeWitt (pp. 142–143) indicates that education through the lower secondary levels (pre-reform, grades 5 to 7; post-reform, grades 5 to 8) is still not universal in the rural areas, although this goal should be reached soon.

In sharp contrast to the increases in enrollment in grades 1 to 4 — and to a lesser degree in grades 5 to 7 — during the 1930's, the expansion in enrollment in upper secondary education (grades 8 to 10) was very modest, paralleling closely that of enrollment in higher and specialized secondary education. Between 1948 and 1958, however, the number of persons enrolled, successively, in grades 5 to 7 and 8 to 10 increased markedly. But this increase must be due in part to the release of facilities and teachers, as children born during the war passed through the elementary grades.

Thus between 1948 and 1952, the number enrolled in grades 5 to 7 increased 8 million or about 50 percent; and between 1948 and 1956, the number enrolled in grades 8 to 10 increased 4 million, or five times. Over the same years, however, total enrollment in all elementary and secondary grades, as well as the number of schools, remained essentially constant, while the number of teachers increased about 20 percent.[32] Largely as a result of underlying demographic movements, the USSR in these years was able to raise significantly the average grade at which pupils left elementary and secondary school, at the cost of only a modest increase in the total resources going to elementary and secondary education.

By the same token, however, the USSR also increased sharply the number of individuals with the educational requirements — and the motivation — for continuing their formal education. This developed into a problem of some proportions, aggravated by the changes in the rate of growth of the labor force of working ages caused by the entry of the age-cohorts born during the war. The solution was the educational reform of 1958, which brought the rate at which advanced schools turn out people of given ages more into line with the rate at which these people are being supplied (demographically speaking) to the national economy.

The Educational Reform of 1958

The essence of the reform of the educational system launched in 1958 is to replace seven-year schools by eight-year schools, and to make eight-year education obligatory for all; and to replace ten-year schools by eleven-year schools. Although eight years of education are now obligatory, the number who may avail themselves of the 9th, 10th, and 11th years on a full-time basis is strictly limited and depends on merit. Further-

[32] *Kul'turnoe stroitel'stvo*, pp. 80–81 and 122–123.

more, priority for entrance into higher training (universities and institutes) is now to be given to those who not only have completed eleven years but who also have had production line experience. Thus, many who complete eleven years without interruption will be forced to go to work before continuing their education full-time; and those who go to work after eight years will have to achieve the 9th to 11th years while they work. Widened facilities for such part-time education are being developed, particularly within factories.

The rationale of the reform is essentially one of bringing the supply of formally educated labor into line with the demand, subject to the conditions of limiting formal education to those in occupations requiring highly technical or specialized knowledge and which are also specialties deemed important for the national economy, and of relying wherever possible on secondary specialized education — which can be entered from the 8th grade — rather than on higher education.

The problem the reform was designed to solve may be given some perspective with reference to the United States. We are experiencing at the present time the situation where "managers, administrators, scientists, engineers, and skilled technicians [are increasing] as a percentage of total employment, while the proportion of manual workers and other less skilled employees [diminishes]." [33] This has a number of implications for our economy — more narrowly, in terms of recruiting and training higher level manpower; more broadly, in terms of the impact of the changing structure of the labor force in an upward direction on such things as the nature and vitality of the labor movement and the conduct of labor relations.

In its present stage, Soviet economic development is considerably below that of the United States in terms of demand for high-level man power, even allowing for the Soviet administrative (ministerial) superstructure.[34] Furthermore, as a general rule, Soviet enterprises are operating at considerably lower levels of technology and organization than U.S. plants. Present and prospective plans for modernization will modify but not eliminate the differential. Emphasis in production, moreover, is on a limited diversity of product, on the mass production of a relatively narrow selection of commodities.

The implication of these considerations for the demand for man power, in terms of broad levels of skill and experience, is that the Soviet economy is still based on the broad mass of manual and semiskilled labor — on the proletariat, in a basic sense of the word. Consistent with this condition are the attempts of Soviet authorities to keep the administrative and

[33] Samuel E. Hill and Frederick Harbison, *Manpower and Innovation in American Industry* (Princeton, 1959), p. 3.

[34] David Granick, "Soviet-American Management Comparisons," in Joint Economic Committee, 86th Congress of the United States, 1st Session, *Comparisons of the United States and Soviet Economies* (Washington, 1959), part I, p. 146.

technical superstructure of production enterprises within relatively narrow limits. It remains to be seen whether the introduction of higher levels of technology and organization in the future will mean a shift away from demands for the mass of labor to a rapidly widening demand for persons with higher skills, as is now taking place in the United States. It is in these terms — of the distribution of the labor force by broad skill categories, taking into account developments in the rate of growth of the labor force — that the primary reason given for the recent broad-scale reorganization of the whole educational system finds its principal defense.

The reorganization has two major aspects. First, if trends to 1958 had continued, in a relatively few years universal secondary education would have been established; but under the reorganization, the vast majority of students are prevented from attending school full-time beyond the 8th grade. Second, preference in entrance to many branches of advanced training is now given to persons with at least two years of production line experience, providing they have also completed their secondary education.

The reorganization, thus, will direct a greater share of the training effort into preparation for the more ordinary production line jobs — a greater share, that is, than if the reorganization had not taken place. Since these jobs require only a limited amount of formal education, a substantial fraction of the population of school age will be channeled into the ordinary work force. These individuals will be able to complete their secondary education on the job and to compete for entry at a later date into the higher educational institutions. At *best* the reorganization postpones or lengthens the period of time required for persons now coming of age to acquire advanced training. At *worst* (from the standpoint of the personal ambitions of the school-age persons involved) a higher proportion will never obtain advanced training.

The program will thus increase the average age of the students receiving advanced training in universities and institutes. It will attract initially the older people who have been on the production line a number of years and who until now have not been able to compete academically with those coming directly from secondary schools. It will delay the entrance into higher education of many individuals now in secondary schools.

By drawing people immediately from the relatively large "middle group" in the labor force (born from about 1925 to 1940), the new program will tend to redress any imbalance in the proportion of trained and untrained people which occurred when this group passed through the ages heretofore devoted to advanced training. It will tend to maintain a balance — in terms of formal skills and administrative competence and age structure — between the "middle group" and the relatively small "junior group" (born after 1940).

The aims of the reorganization are couched in ideological terms — to bring the young people "closer to the facts of economic life." This should be viewed not so much as a return to the old faith, or as a renewal of the proletarian spirit for its own sake — although this is also involved — but as a reaction to the demands of economic efficiency and the effective use of man power resources at present levels of technology and organization.

There was a relative shortage of skilled and higher level man power in the 1930's, and the expanding educational work operated to fill the need. But the expansion seems to have overextended itself. What seems to have been developing in the Soviet Union up to the reorganization, in fact, is a relative shortage of individuals trained or otherwise available for manual and semiskilled labor, and also a declining respect for ordinary work on the part of persons completing secondary training and looking forward to further education. If the prereorganization trends had continued, if universal education through the equivalent of our high school had been attained, and if a greater number had gone on to advanced training, who would have manned the assembly lines, at least on the scale that the present levels of technique and economic organization imply? This question probably would have arisen to some degree in any event. But the evident note of urgency and the fairly drastic nature of the reorganization almost certainly reflect the impact of the present substantial decline in the number of persons entering the work ages, due to the lowered birth rate in World War II.

Formalized education and the accompanying aspirations to something better than the position of a worker in industry developed gradually in other industrialized countries; and the man-power base of the economy in the United States was broadened in part by mass immigration. The spread of something approaching universal secondary education in the United States, perhaps not by chance, coincides with the widening demand for persons with more than rudimentary skills. The educational system of the Soviet Union, on the other hand, has grown more rapidly than others. Perhaps it has succeeded too well in accomplishing its purpose, especially in the light of the recent changes in the rate of growth of the labor force. The reorganization of the system serves to bring it into line with the "realities of economic life" — to paraphrase the language of the reorganization itself — at the present stage of economic development.

3. THE ALLOCATION OF LABOR

The impact of industrialization on labor is nowhere more apparent than in the reallocation and redistribution of labor by area, industry, and occupation. Indexes reflecting some of these changes will be discussed in this section. Where feasible, some indication will be given of differences in the rate and direction of change in labor allocation and distribution between the Soviet Union and other countries in the course of industrialization.

The Distribution of the Population by Urban and Rural Areas

The expansion of industry and trade in Imperial Russia and the Soviet Union, as in other countries, has gone hand in hand with the growth of urbanized areas. Between 1850 and 1860, the urban population (on Soviet territory) doubled absolutely, and increased from 5.5 to 11.3 percent of the total (Table II.9). Between 1860 and 1914, a period in which the rate of industrialization, in terms of output, was relatively high, the urban population increased to almost 3 times its 1860 level. However, the demand for industrial and other nonagricultural labor was not enough, given the rate of growth of the population, to alter significantly the proportion of the population in urban areas, which remained near 12 percent of the total through the last quarter of the 19th century, increasing to 14.6 percent by the beginning of World War I. The war itself caused an increase of 5 million persons in the urban population, from 14.6 to 18.2 percent of the total.

This trend was sharply reversed during the Revolution, Civil War, and the early period of the New Economic Policy. Even in terms of Table II.9, which is not based on a uniform definition of an urban area for Imperial Russia and the Soviet Union, urban population declines from 25.6 million in 1918 to 21.4 million in 1923, or from 18.2 to 16.1 percent of the total.[35] In terms of a consistent definition of an urban area, as much as one-third or more of the urban population left the urban areas by the early 1920's, reflecting the large-scale remigration of population to rural areas as well as population emigration.[36] During economic recovery under the NEP, the trends were once again reversed, and the urban population increased both absolutely and relatively.

By 1928, therefore, 18.4 percent of the population was urban. This actually represents about the same proportion *consistently defined* as prevailed in Imperial Russia during the last quarter of the 19th century. The net result of the succession of sharply contrasting periods over the 70 years since the beginning of industrialization on Soviet territory is a practically unchanged degree of urbanization of the population.

From a qualitative point of view, however, the population was undoubt-

[35] Urban area for the pre-Soviet years in Table II.9 includes only those places officially designated as cities or possessing municipal self-government. The data for the Soviet years also include localities which are predominantly nonagricultural, by occupations. The minimum population for this purpose ranges from 500 to 2,000, depending on the types of occupation. Thus, the proportion for 1897 comparable with 1926 might be near 20 percent, or even higher, rather than the indicated 12.4 percent. Trends during the Imperial Russian years are probably not affected by this problem. For further discussion, see Eason, *Soviet Manpower*, pp. 82–89.

[36] E. Z. Volkov, *Dinamika naseleniia SSSR za vosem'desiat let* (Moscow, 1930), p. 201.

Table II.9

Imperial Russia and USSR, 1850–1960 and USA, 1820–1960: Total, Urban, and Rural Population

Year[a]	Imperial Russia and USSR Population (in thousands)			Percent		USA Population (in thousands)			Percent	
	Total	Urban	Rural	Urban	Rural	Total	Urban	Rural	Urban	Rural
1820	—	—	—	—	—	9,638	693	8,945	7.2	92.8
1830	—	—	—	—	—	12,866	1,127	11,739	8.8	91.2
1840	—	—	—	—	—	17,069	1,845	15,244	10.8	89.2
1850	57,076	3,118	53,958	5.5	94.5	23,192	3,544	19,648	15.3	84.7
1860	61,720	6,993	54,727	11.3	88.7	31,443	6,217	25,226	19.8	80.2
1870	65,208	8,040	57,168	12.3	87.7	38,558	9,902	28,656	25.7	74.3
1880	78,592	10,159	68,433	12.9	87.1	50,156	14,130	36,026	28.2	71.8
1890	92,822	11,816	81,006	12.7	87.3	62,948	22,106	40,841	35.1	64.9
1897	103,906	12,870	91,036	12.4	87.6	—	—	—	—	—
1900	109,593	14,058	95,535	12.8	87.2	75,995	30,160	45,835	39.7	60.3
1910	130,354	18,586	111,768	14.3	85.7	91,972	41,999	49,973	45.7	54.3
1914	139,912	20,445	119,467	14.6	85.4	—	—	—	—	—
1918	140,903	25,643	115,261	18.2	81.8	—	—	—	—	—
1920	137,093	22,867	114,226	16.7	83.3	105,711	54,158	51,553	51.2	48.8
1923	133,467	21,435	112,032	16.1	83.9	—	—	—	—	—
1926	147,028	26,314	120,714	17.9	82.1	—	—	—	—	—
1928	149,900	27,600	122,300	18.4	81.6	—	—	—	—	—
1929	153,100	29,200	123,900	19.1	80.9	—	—	—	—	—
1930	155,600	30,900	124,700	19.9	80.1	122,775	68,955	58,820	56.2	43.8
1931	158,100	32,000	126,100	20.2	79.8	—	—	—	—	—
1932	160,700	36,300	124,400	22.6	77.4	—	—	—	—	—
1933	160,600	39,700	120,900	24.7	75.3	—	—	—	—	—
1934	160,600	41,000	119,500	25.6	74.4	—	—	—	—	—
1935	160,500	—	—	—	—	—	—	—	—	—

Year										
1936	162,200	47,000	115,200	29.0	71.0	—	—	—	—	—
1937	164,100	—	—	—	—	—	—	—	—	—
1938	167,300	—	—	—	—	—	—	—	—	—
1939	170,557	56,125	114,432	32.9	67.1	—	—	—	—	—
1940	196,300	62,000	134,300	31.6	68.4	131,669	74,424	57,246	56.5	43.5
1941	198,700	62,800	135,900	31.6	68.4	150,697	88,927	61,770	59.0	41.0
1950	178,700	68,700	110,000	38.4	61.6	150,697	97,468	54,230	64.0	36.0
1951	181,800	72,100	109,700	39.7	60.3	—	—	—	—	—
1952	184,900	75,500	109,400	40.8	59.2	—	—	—	—	—
1953	188,100	78,900	109,200	41.9	58.1	—	—	—	—	—
1954	191,100	82,300	108,800	43.1	56.9	—	—	—	—	—
1955	194,500	85,700	108,800	44.1	55.9	—	—	—	—	—
1956	197,900	89,100	108,800	45.0	55.0	—	—	—	—	—
1957	201,400	92,600	108,800	46.0	54.0	—	—	—	—	—
1958	205,000	96,200	108,800	46.9	53.1	—	—	—	—	—
1959	208,700	99,900	108,800	47.9	52.1	—	—	—	—	—
1959	208,827	99,978	108,849	47.9	52.1	—	—	—	—	—
1960	212,300	103,700	108,600	48.8	51.2	179,323	125,268	54,055	69.9	30.1

a For USSR, January 1, except that reference is to census dates for 1897, 1923, 1926, 1939, and 1959. The census for 1923 included only urban areas.

Notes: Sources and methods are given in the appendix.

The dash (—) indicates that data are not available.

edly more urbanized. Through migration and remigration, after 1914 a larger proportion of the population had been exposed to urban life than is reflected in the statistics, and a growing proportion of the urban population had become acclimated to an urban way of life.

With the beginning of the five-year plans, urbanization was greatly accelerated. By 1939, the urban population had more than doubled and the rural population had declined, with the result that the urban population increased from 18.4 to 32.9 percent of the total. The annexation of territory in 1940 reduced this percentage only slightly.

Although the average rate of increase after 1928 was substantial, the pattern of increase in the first years was very irregular, as may be seen from the following data:[37] Net rural-urban migration (in thousands) in 1929 was 1,392; in 1930, 2,633; in 1931, 4,100; in 1932, 2,719; in 1933, 772; in 1934, 2,452; and in 1935, 2,527. The increase in urban population in 1929 was 1,700; in 1930, 1,100; in 1931, 4,300; in 1932, 3,400; in 1933, 1,300; in 1934, 3,000; and in 1935, 3,000. Except for 1930, the increase in the total urban population each year is somewhat greater than net rural-urban migration, as one would expect when the natural increase of the urban population is taken into account. The greatest increases took place in 1931 and 1932, reflecting the flight from the countryside following the mass collectivization of agriculture.

Considering the 12-year intercensal period as a whole (1926–39), the urban population increased 29.8 million, 23 million by net migration to areas which by 1939 had been classified urban, and the remainder by natural population increase. Net migration, in turn, is the sum of 18.5 million migrants (net) to areas which were urban at the beginning of the period (according to the lists of the 1926 census) and 4.5 million migrants whose status was changed from rural to urban by the time of the 1939 census. The total population of these areas of changed status was 5.8 million.

Between 1940 and 1960, the urban population on comparable territory increased from 62 to 104 million, or from 32 to 49 percent of the total. A further absolute decline in the rural population is implied by these figures, from 134 million in 1940 to 109 million in 1960.

The sources of increase in the urban population in recent years appear to be similar to those for 1926–39. Of the 17 million increase in urban population from 1950 to 1955, more than 9 million were migrants from rural areas.[38] Thus, more than 53 percent of the increase is due to migra-

---

[37] The increase in urban population is calculated from Table II.9, including a two-year average for 1934 and 1935. Net rural-urban migration is from TSUNKHU, *Sotsialisti-cheskoe stroitel'stvo SSSR, 1936* (Moscow, 1936), p. 545.

[38] *Pravda*, February 3, 1955.

tion, compared with 63 percent between 1926 and 1939.[39] If the fraction of the increase due to the reclassification of areas from rural to urban was the same as in the intercensal period, or about 20 percent,[40] these data imply a somewhat higher rate of natural increase of the urban population from 1950 to 1955 than in the intercensal period. This is not necessarily inconsistent with lower crude birth rates for the total population in recent years, because the fall in the birth rate during 1931–34 was probably more than proportionately an urban phenomenon.

The increase of the urban population from 1955 to 1960 is somewhat greater (18 million) than in the preceding five years, but interpretation of this difference must await further information about the reclassification of areas for the purposes of the 1959 census.

With almost one-half of the population now living in urban areas, the Soviet Union is among the more urbanized countries of the world, although its urban population proportion is well below that of the following countries:[41] for Argentina, it is 61 percent of the total population; for Denmark, 61 percent; for West Germany, 60 percent; for the United Kingdom, 80 percent; for Australia, 69 percent; and for New Zealand, 61 percent.

The Soviet Union now has the same percentage of its population in urban areas as the United States had about 1910. The Soviet Union began the five-year plans with about the same percentage of its population in urban areas as the United States in 1860 — or earlier, since the Soviet definition would count as urban some areas which were counted as rural in the United States. However, Soviet urbanization during the 1930's was more rapid than in the United States after 1860: the urban population of the USSR doubled in about the first ten years of industrialization and only in the first twenty years in the United States. Also, the percentage of the population in urban areas doubled in less than twenty years in the Soviet Union, but in almost forty years in the United States.

The comparison seems to reflect both a more rapid rate of migration of the population from rural to urban areas in the Soviet Union, and the fact that attrition in World War II fell more heavily on former rural residents in the predominantly "peasant" army. Urbanization proceeded less rapidly in the United States despite the fact that during the 19th century, a relatively large proportion of a sizable immigrant population settled in urban areas, tending thereby to increase the urban population more rapidly than otherwise would have been the case.

[39] From the data above: migration of 18.5 million as a percentage of the total increase in urban population of 29.8 million.

[40] From the data above: 5.8 million as a percentage of 29.8 million.

[41] *Demographic Yearbook, 1948*, pp. 214–219.

Allocation by Industry

The distribution of the labor force by agricultural and nonagricultural ✓ *occupations.* Closely related to the distribution of the population by rural and urban areas, but a better index of the change in labor allocation, is the distribution of the labor force by agricultural and nonagricultural occupations. From the absolute data in Table II.10, and the percentage rates of increase in Table II.11, several observations may be made about the pattern of growth and redistribution of the labor force between these two major sectors of economic activity under Soviet conditions.

The over-all rate of increase of the nonagricultural labor force since 1928 appears relatively high, but it shows wide variation among the various subperiods. The rate of increase of 8.7 percent per year between 1928 and 1939 is greater than for any ten-year period in the United States since 1820. On the other hand, the rate of 3.0 percent per year between 1950 and 1959 is less than in the United States for any decade before about 1910. The increase of only 0.5 percent per year between 1940 and 1950, of course, reflects the war.

The percentage distribution of the labor force between agricultural and ✓ nonagricultural occupations has also changed more rapidly than in other countries. Restricting the comparison to countries where the preindustrialization data indicate a proportion of the population in agricultural occupations of 70 percent or more (in 1928 in the Soviet Union it was 82 percent), using ten-year intervals, and beginning with the earliest data available for the other countries, the proportion of the labor force in agricultural occupations declined to below 50 percent in the course of three decades in the Soviet Union, but took four decades for Sweden, five for the United States, six for Japan, and ten for France.[42]

Despite the rapid rates of change away from agriculture in over-all terms, only during 1930–33, 1936–37, and 1940–50, was there an absolute decline in the agricultural labor force. The first of these periods is associated with the collectivization drive, food shortages, and population losses, and may also reflect the increase in the number of children attending primary school. The decline between 1936 and 1937 appears in the collective farm labor force and is largely unexplained, except perhaps by the political events of the time. The decline between 1940 and 1950 is related to the war, and if annual data were available the decline might be restricted to a shorter time period.

In the other years, that is, for 1925–29, 1934–36, 1937–39, and 1950–59, the absolute change in the agricultural labor force was negligible. This trend during normal years raises some questions as to the forces at work

[42] Simon Kuznets, "Quantitative Aspects of the Economic Growth of Nations: II. Industrial Distribution of National Product and Labor Force," *Economic Development and Cultural Change,* Supplement to volume V, no. 4, July 1957, pp. 82ff.

Table II.10

USSR, 1925–1959 and USA, 1820–1960: Agricultural and Nonagricultural Labor Force

Year	USSR[a] Labor force (in thousands) Total	Nonagric.	Agric.	USSR[a] Percent Nonagric.	Agric.	USA Labor force (in thousands) Total	Nonagric.	Agric.	USA Percent Nonagric.	Agric.
1820	—	—	—	—	—	2,881	812	2,069	28.2	71.8
1830	—	—	—	—	—	3,932	1,159	2,773	29.5	70.5
1840	—	—	—	—	—	5,420	1,700	3,720	31.4	68.6
1850	—	—	—	—	—	7,697	2,795	4,902	36.3	63.7
1860	—	—	—	—	—	10,533	4,325	6,208	41.1	58.9
1870	—	—	—	—	—	12,925	6,075	6,850	47.0	53.0
1880	—	—	—	—	—	17,392	8,807	8,585	50.6	49.4
1890	—	—	—	—	—	23,318	13,380	9,938	57.4	42.6
1900	—	—	—	—	—	29,073	18,161	10,912	62.5	37.5
1910	—	—	—	—	—	37,371	25,779	11,592	69.0	31.0
1920	—	—	—	—	—	42,434	30,985	11,449	73.0	27.0
1925	81,200	11,800	69,400	14.5	85.5	—	—	—	—	—
1926	82,300	13,500	68,800	16.4	83.6	—	—	—	—	—
1926	84,500	12,800	71,700	15.1	84.9	—	—	—	—	—
1927	84,200	14,500	69,700	17.2	82.8	—	—	—	—	—
1928	86,100	15,500	70,600	18.0	82.0	—	—	—	—	—
1929	87,400	16,400	71,000	18.8	81.2	—	—	—	—	—
1930	89,500	18,100	71,400	20.2	79.8	48,830	38,358	10,472	78.6	21.4
1931	88,000	21,400	66,600	24.3	75.7	—	—	—	—	—
1932	88,600	24,100	64,500	27.2	72.8	—	—	—	—	—
1933	88,800	26,000	62,800	29.3	70.7	—	—	—	—	—
1934	89,100	25,900	63,200	29.1	70.9	—	—	—	—	—
1935	89,300	27,100	62,200	30.3	69.7	—	—	—	—	—
1936	90,900	28,600	62,300	31.5	68.5	—	—	—	—	—
1937	89,600	32,600	57,000	36.4	63.6	—	—	—	—	—
1938	89,700	34,700	55,000	38.7	61.3	—	—	—	—	—
1939	89,800	34,800	55,000	38.8	61.2	—	—	—	—	—
1940	100,800	40,800	60,000	40.5	59.5	52,148	42,986	9,162	82.4	17.6
1950	(97,000)	(43,000)	(54,000)	44.3	55.7	58,600	50,500	8,100	86.2	13.8
1959	109,000	56,200	52,800	51.6	48.4	—	—	—	—	—
1960	—	—	—	—	—	71,000	66,000	5,000	92.9	7.1

[a] For USSR, July 1, except for census years, when reference is to census dates.

Notes: USSR, 1939 and 1959 are from Table II.14 on p. 84; other years are from Eason, *Soviet Manpower*, appendix Tables K1 and K2, with "discrepancies in derivation" distributed between agricultural and nonagricultural categories in proportion to that implied for 1938 by the 1939 census data. USA data are from U.S. Department of Commerce, *Historical Statistics of the United States, 1789–1945* (Washington, 1949), p. 63; and *Statistical Abstract of the United States, 1960* (Washington, 1960), p. 91.

The dash (—) indicates that data are not available.

Table II.11
USSR, 1926–1959 and USA, 1820–1960: Annual Rates
of Increase of the Nonagricultural Labor Force

Period	Percent
USSR	
1926–39	8.7
1940–50	0.5
1950–59	3.0
1926–34	9.2
1934–39	7.7
USA	
1820–30	3.6
1830–40	3.9
1840–50	5.1
1850–60	4.4
1860–70	3.4
1870–80	3.8
1880–90	4.3
1890–1900	3.1
1900–10	3.6
1910–20	1.9
1920–30	2.2
1930–40	1.2
1940–50	1.2
1950–60	1.9

Note: Derived from Table II.10.

under Soviet conditions in the fulfillment of demands for nonagricultural labor out of agricultural labor reserves. Even allowing for an increase in cropped plowland of about 20 percent between 1928 and 1937 and 30 percent (on comparable territory) between 1940 and 1959,[43] the fact that the increase in the nonagricultural labor force for most years since 1928 could be provided essentially out of the net increase in the total labor force does not present the image of an economy sorely pressed to find man power resources for redistribution in the direction of nonagricultural employment. And even after 30 years, including wartime population losses, 48 percent of the total labor force (and 53 percent of the civilian labor force) remains in agricultural employment.

Considering these facts, a conclusion that "for all practical purposes, there are no more great reserves of labor in agriculture to be tapped," [44]

[43] TSU, *Posevnye ploshchadi SSSR* (Moscow, 1957), I, 6–7; TSU, *Sel'skoe khoziaistvo SSSR*, p. 29.
[44] Leon Herman, "The Labor Force: Who Does What," *Saturday Review*, January 21, 1961, p. 35.

does not seem justified. The Russians are still far from the goal of indus-trialization: to reduce the proportion of the labor force in agricultural occupations to a fraction of the total. This process has already been essen-tially completed in the United States where the agricultural man power now accounts for only 7.1 percent of the total.

It is therefore difficult to infer from Soviet trends since 1938 the future pattern of change under normal conditions. In an earlier discussion, Kershaw assumed an absolute decline in the agricultural labor force in order to supply industry with labor and to achieve the projected agricul-tural production goals of 1970.[45] But if the pattern and rate of economic growth in the Soviet Union now require that the agricultural labor force be decreased absolutely, with half of the total labor force still in agricul-tural occupations, why was this not required in the past? It may be relevant to point out that, although the underlying conditions are some-what different, the agricultural labor force did not decline absolutely in the United States until after 1920, when it comprised about 25 percent of the total, and the decline has been substantial only in the last decade or so. Interestingly, in terms of the proportion of the labor force in agriculture, the Soviet Union is only now where the United States was in the first decade of its industrialization drive.[46]

In these respects, therefore, the Soviet Union is at an early stage of industrialization.[47] There is still a sizeable pool of man power on the farms, and if conditions were normal, it should not be difficult to reassign it to industry on an economically rational basis and with no drastic or sudden institutional changes.

In two respects, however, conditions are not normal. First, currently the rate of growth of the total labor force is declining — a temporary phenomenon, but one which has put a special strain on the allocative mechanism. From a longer run point of view, improvements in production methods and farm management are a necessary prerequisite for the release of man power to industry. Soviet planners and administrators have found it difficult to make these improvements in the past 30 years, and labor continues to be wasted on the farms. It is no wonder, therefore, that the Soviet government expresses continuing concern over the ways and means by which productivity can be increased in agriculture and labor duly re-leased for nonagricultural work. Their concern is not so much with the underlying relationships between labor supply and demand that require

[45] Joseph A. Kershaw, "Agricultural Output and Employment," in Bergson, ed., *Soviet Economic Growth*, p. 308.

[46] The relevant comparison would be with the civilian labor force in the Soviet Union, according to which about 53 percent are in agricultural occupations, or the same as in the United States in 1870.

[47] There is no real contradiction between this observation and the one above to the effect that the country has become relatively urbanized. The difference is in the rural nonfarm population, which is relatively small in the Soviet Union.

these changes, but with the institutional prerequisites to economic changes that have proved so intransigent in the Soviet Union. The statistics may continue to show a rate of redistribution of the labor force between agricultural and nonagricultural occupations which is not too different from that in other developing countries, but the solution of the institutional problems required to do this will probably entail extraordinary efforts on the part of the Soviet administrators.

The distribution of the civilian nonagricultural labor force among major branches of industry. The distribution of the civilian nonagricultural labor force among major branches of industry in the Soviet Union resembles in many ways that of other industrializing countries, but there are also significant differences. We compare the Soviet Union in 1928 and 1959 with the United States in 1870, 1910, and 1959 (Table II.12). These dates for the Soviet Union are the only ones for which internally consistent and otherwise comparable data are available. It is recognized that 1928 is a preplan year and that no data for the 1930's are included in the comparison, but several problems of comparability that are posed can more easily be dealt with after having made the comparison in terms of 1928 and 1959.

Table II.12
USSR, 1928–1959 and USA, 1870, 1910, and 1959:
Civilian Nonagricultural Employment by Sector
(percent)

Sector	USSR		USA		
	1928	1959	1870	1910	1959
Industry	45	40	40	33	33
Construction	8	11	12	6	7
Transportation and communications	12	13	10	12	8
Commerce	9	8	12	19	22
Government and other services	26	28	26	31	29
Totals	100	100	100	100	100

Note: Derived from Table II.13 on p. 82, except for USSR, 1928, which is derived by distributing the nonwage and salary category for 1928 in Table II.13 (28.3 percent) in proportion to the respective number employed according to the 1926 census.

It is not surprising, first, that the proportion of the labor force in commerce is (and has been) larger in the United States than in the Soviet Union, and that the proportion in transportation and communications is about the same at comparable stages of development.[48] Perhaps less

[48] According to the 1897 census, about 10 percent of the nonagricultural labor force of Imperial Russia was in commerce.

expected is the fact that government and other services combined absorb about the same proportion of the nonagricultural labor force in the two countries, although government alone would be higher for the Soviet Union and services for the United States.

Probably the most interesting aspect is that in the early stages of industrialization the proportion of the labor force in industry and construction is almost identical in the two countries — 53 percent in the Soviet Union in 1928 and 52 percent in the United States in 1870.[49] This proportion was essentially unchanged in the Soviet Union in 1959, although the industrial component had declined and construction increased, but the proportion for the United States had declined to 39 percent in 1910 and 40 percent in 1959, a change complemented by the higher proportion in commerce. These changes reflect basic differences in the pattern of growth in the two countries, once the Soviet rapid industrialization drive got under way.

Comparable data for the 1930's probably would reveal still higher proportions of the labor force in the USSR in industry and construction, at the expense of government and other services. Of *wage and salary employment* only, the proportion in industry increased somewhat by the end of the 1930's, but returned to the original order of magnitude after that (Table II.13). The proportion in construction more than doubled by 1932 and has remained relatively high since, except during 1937–40.

Comparison in these terms ignores the substantial and varying nonwage and salary group in the nonagricultural labor force — comprising 28.3 percent of the total in 1928, 14.5 percent in 1932, 22.0 percent in 1940, and 3.1 percent in 1959. In Table II.12, the percentage for 1928 is distributed in proportion to the appropriate data from the 1926 census, and the percentage for 1959, since it is small, is distributed in proportion to wage and salary employment alone. There is no adequate basis for such a calculation for the other years considered in Table II.13.[50]

Allocation by Occupation

The distribution of the labor force by major occupational groups. The major occupational groups for which more or less consistent data are

[49] Although 1928 is a preplan year and not representative of the industrialization drive, it can be expected to embody the results of industrialization over the preceding 70 years at a slower pace.

[50] Readily available data after the 1926 census are in the form of establishment statistics, covering wage and salary workers and one or two other categories, but exclude forced labor and certain other groups. Data for the United States in these tables include self-employed persons as well as wage and salary workers. The recently released data from the USSR 1939 and 1959 censuses give some basis for *total* nonagricultural employment and therefore total nonwage and salary worker employment — as in Table II.13 — but none for the distribution of the latter by industrial categories.

Table II.13

USSR, 1928–1959 and USA, 1870–1959: Civilian Nonagricultural Employment by Sector, Selected Years
(percent)

Item	1928	1929	1930	1931	1932	1933	1934	1935	1936	1937	1940	1945	1950	1959
USSR														
Civilian nonwage and salary	28.3	27.6	22.1	16.0	14.5	23.3	17.7	16.7	15.6	21.0	22.0	—	5.8	3.1
Wage and salary														
Industry	28.3	28.3	31.1	33.5	34.0	31.1	32.9	34.9	35.9	33.5	29.6	—	37.1	38.4
Construction	5.1	6.2	9.6	12.5	13.2	9.4	10.4	8.9	7.8	6.5	6.7	—	10.8	10.6
Transportation and communications	10.1	9.7	10.2	10.5	10.2	10.2	11.6	11.2	11.1	10.3	10.5	—	12.1	12.7
Commerce	4.3	4.8	6.0	7.0	8.1	7.5	8.1	8.1	8.1	7.7	8.9	—	8.9	8.4
Government and other services	23.9	23.4	21.0	20.5	20.0	18.5	19.3	20.2	21.5	21.0	22.3	—	25.3	26.8
Total nonagricultural	100.0	100.0	100.0	100.0	100.0	100.0	100.0	100.0	100.0	100.0	100.0	—	100.0	100.0
Wage and salary														
Industry	39.4	38.7	40.0	39.9	39.8	40.5	40.0	41.9	42.5	42.4	37.9	38.3	39.4	39.6
Construction	7.1	8.5	12.3	14.9	15.4	12.3	12.7	10.7	9.2	8.2	8.6	10.1	11.5	11.0
Transportation and communications	14.1	13.2	13.1	12.5	11.9	13.3	14.1	13.5	13.2	13.1	13.4	14.1	12.8	13.1
Commerce	6.1	6.6	7.7	8.3	9.5	9.8	9.8	9.8	9.6	9.8	11.4	10.1	9.5	8.6
Government and other services	33.3	32.0	26.9	24.4	23.4	24.1	23.4	24.1	25.4	26.5	28.7	27.4	26.8	27.7
Total wage and salary	100.0	100.0	100.0	100.0	100.0	100.0	100.0	100.0	100.0	100.0	100.0	100.0	100.0	100.0

Item	1870	1880	1890	1900	1910	1920	1930	1940	1950	1959
USA										
Industry	39.6	41.9	40.0	41.0	32.7	34.3	38.2	31.6	31.6	33.2
Construction	11.9	9.7	10.6	9.2	5.8	5.7	3.6	6.3	4.9	7.1
Transportation and communications	10.0	9.7	10.9	11.3	11.7	12.4	13.2	10.4	7.6	8.1
Commerce	12.4	13.4	13.4	13.7	19.0	18.5	17.2	21.4	21.8	22.3
Government and other services	26.1	25.3	25.0	24.8	30.8	29.1	27.8	30.3	34.1	29.3
Total nonagricultural	100.0	100.0	100.0	100.0	100.0	100.0	100.0	100.0	100.0	100.0

Notes: Except for 1959, USSR wage and salary employment data and all USA data are derived from David Redding, *Nonagricultural Employment in the USSR, 1928–55* (unpublished PhD dissertation on deposit with Columbia University library, 1958), pp. 59, 75. USSR nonwage and salary data are derived from Table II.10 and data for 1959 are calculated from *Narodnoe khoziaistvo 1959*, pp. 558–589.

The dash (—) indicates that data are not available.

available for the USSR are really socioeconomic groups based on the type of income received, including wage and salary workers, cooperative handicraftsmen, noncooperative handicraftsmen, collective farmers, private farmers, "bourgeoisie" (those who hire others to produce a marketable product), unemployed, and the military. Data from the censuses of 1926, 1939, and 1959, for these groups are reproduced in Table II.14. Because of the nature of the grouping, comparisons are difficult to make with other countries (except perhaps in the Communist bloc), but we can relate the parts of the labor force to the whole.

Heretofore, the total labor force estimated from establishment and other sector statistics has been considerably less than the total labor force estimated from the population and hypothetical percentages of the population (by age and sex) in the labor force. It now turns out that both of these estimates differ from the census results.

Estimates for the date of the 1959 census, but based on the official Soviet estimate of 200 million total population as of April 1956, compared with the census results are (in millions):[51] The total labor force, as of the census date, that was estimated from population is 117.3 million. That estimated from establishment and other sector statistics is 107.0. The difference, thus, is 10.3. The total labor force from the census is 109.0. The excess of the estimate from the population over the census figure was 8.3.

There are three reasons for the difference of 8.3 million between the labor force estimated from the population and that reported by the census. First, the estimate was based on population projections which comprised more persons of working ages and less age 60 and over than are reported in the census. Second, a higher proportion of the population age 10 to 15 was assumed to be in the labor force than is implied by the census results. On the other hand, the estimating procedure tries to account for youths age 10 to 15 who actually worked for a month or two in the summer although attending school full-time in the winter months. On this basis, therefore, the census total may *understate* the "true" total labor force. Third, no allowance was made in the estimates for males age 16 to 59 and 60 and over who receive pensions and are totally disabled.

The labor force estimated for the census date from establishment and other sector statistics (107 million) is 2 million less than the labor force from the census, resulting in a 10.3 million residual compared with labor force estimated from population. The 2 million may be accounted for in part by statistical discrepancies in procedure, but an additional factor may be the inclusion of some categories not covered in the establishment statistics, such as forced labor, in the major occupational groups of the census. The latter possibility is illustrated by the comparison of the num-

---

[51] The precensus estimates are from Eason, *Soviet Manpower*, p. 456.

Table II.14
USSR: Total Labor Force by Major Occupational Groups, by Sex, Censuses of 1926, 1939, and 1959

Occupation	1926 Both sexes	1926 Males	1926 Females	1926 Percent females	1939 Both sexes	1939 Males	1939 Females	1939 Percent females	1959 Both sexes	1959 Males	1959 Females	1959 Percent females
In thousands												
Wage and salary workers	9,600	6,600	3,000	31.3	34,900	23,000	11,900	34.1	60,500	33,100	27,400	45.3
Nonagricultural	(8,400)	(5,800)	(2,600)	31.0	(28,800)	(18,600)	(10,200)	35.4	(51,000)	(27,100)	(23,900)	46.9
Agricultural	(1,200)	(800)	(400)	33.3	(6,100)	(4,400)	(1,700)	27.9	(9,500)	(6,000)	(3,500)	36.8
Coop. handicraftsmen	1,500	1,100	400	26.7	2,200	1,700	500	22.7	1,400	1,300	100	71.4
Noncoop. handicraftsmen					400	200	200	50.0	200	100	100	50.0
Collective farmers					36,300	16,600	19,700	54.3	33,300	13,500	19,800	59.5
Private farmers[a]	70,500	35,300	35,200	49.9	12,600	4,400	8,200	65.1	10,000	3,500	6,500	65.0
"Bourgeoisie"	1,300	1,100	200	15.4	—	—	—	—	—	—	—	—
Employed labor force	82,900	44,100	38,800	46.8	86,400	45,900	40,500	46.9	105,400	51,600	53,800	51.0
Unemployed	1,000	600	400	40.0	—	—	—	—	—	—	—	—
Civilian labor force	83,900	44,700	39,200	46.7	86,400	45,900	40,500	46.9	105,400	51,600	53,800	51.0
Military	600	600	0	0	3,400	3,400	0	0	3,600	3,600	0	0
Total labor force	84,500	45,300	39,200	46.4	89,800	49,300	40,500	45.1	109,000	55,200	53,800	49.4
Nonagric. labor force	12,800	9,200	3,600	28.1	34,800	23,900	10,900	31.3	56,200	32,200	24,000	42.7
Agric. labor force	71,700	36,100	35,600	49.7	55,000	25,400	29,600	53.8	52,800	23,000	29,800	56.4
Percent												
Wage and salary workers	11.4	14.6	7.6		38.9	46.6	29.4		55.5	60.0	50.9	
Nonagricultural	(10.0)	(12.8)	(6.6)		(32.1)	(37.3)	(25.2)		(46.8)	(49.1)	(44.4)	
Agricultural	(1.4)	(1.8)	(1.0)		(6.8)	(8.9)	(4.2)		(8.7)	(10.9)	(6.5)	
Coop. handicraftsmen	1.8	2.4	1.0		2.5	3.5	1.3		1.2	2.4	0.2	
Noncoop. handicraftsmen					0.4	0.4	0.5		0.2	0.2	0.2	
Collective farmers					40.4	33.7	48.6		30.6	24.6	36.7	
Private farmers[a]	83.4	77.9	89.8		14.0	8.9	20.2		9.2	6.3	12.0	
"Bourgeoisie"	1.5	2.5	0.6		—	—	—		—	—	—	
Employed labor force[e]	98.1	97.4	99.0		96.2	93.1	100.0		96.7	93.5	100.0	
Unemployed	1.2	1.3	1.0		—	—	—		—	—	—	
Civilian labor force	99.3	98.7	100.0		96.2	93.0	100.0		96.7	93.5	100.0	
Military	0.7	0.3	0		3.8	6.9	0		3.3	6.5	0	
Total labor force	100.0	100.0	100.0		100.0	100.0	100.0		100.0	100.0	100.0	
Nonagric. labor force	15.1	20.3	9.2		38.8	48.5	26.9		51.6	57.3	44.7	
Agric. labor force	84.9	79.7	90.8		61.2	51.5	73.1		48.4	42.7	55.3	

a Includes individual farmers and persons occupied solely in subsidiary agricultural activity.

Notes: Sources and methods are given in the appendix.
The dash (—) indicates that data are not available.

ber of wage and salary workers in industry, construction, and transportation and communications, according to the censuses of 1939 and 1959, with the number reported by establishments for corresponding dates (in millions) : For 1939, the census figure was 23.7 million and for 1959, 36.6. The noncensus figure for 1939 was 17.4 and for 1959, 32.5. The difference between these figures for each year suggests more than poor statistics or *de facto* unemployment; it suggests forced labor or others not reported in establishment statistics, a possibility reinforced by the smaller difference in 1959 than 1939, in line with knowledge of the trends in forced labor. Another aspect to be considered in this connection is the total of 3.4 million for the military on the date of the census, January 17, 1939, a number not supported by several fairly clear references in major sources of the time. The true figure in January was probably not more than 2 million, although 3.4 million is not out of the question for the end of 1939.

Trends in the number of wage and salary workers in nonagricultural occupations, and the distribution by sex. The expansion of nonagricultural employment for most years has appeared as an increase in the number of wage and salary workers (state enterprises). The number of wage and salary workers has thus increased more rapidly than total nonagricultural employment and now comprises almost all nonagricultural employment. Data on the number of wage and salary workers in nonagricultural occupations by sex are given in Table II.15.

The demand for wage and salary workers was satisfied during the 1930's partly by the supply of man power already in the urban areas, consisting of unemployed persons and those in other categories of the urban labor force, partly by the migration of labor from rural to urban areas, and partly by drawing persons into the labor force.

The demand for industrial and other nonagricultural labor is and will continue to be reflected in the increase in the number of wage and salary workers. We gain some appreciation of what this means in terms of allocative pressures if we compare the increase in the number of wage and salary workers with the increase in the labor force of working ages (Table II.16).

The rate of increase in the number of wage and salary workers has declined from one broad period to another. Between 1926 and 1939 the average increase was 10.7 percent per year, and between 1939 and 1959, 2.9 percent per year. But even if we eliminate the effects of the war and the early 1930's, and consider only normal years of regular and continuous increase, the average rate of increase declined from 5.6 percent per year between 1934 and 1939 to 4.3 percent per year between 1950 and 1960.

The increase in the number of wage and salary workers has exceeded that of the labor force of working ages by less and less. The excess was 75 percent in 1926–39, and 10 percent in 1939–59, 31 percent in 1934–39 and 11 percent in 1950–60. In other words to a declining degree the num-

Table II.15
USSR: Wage and Salary Workers in Nonagricultural Occupations, by Sex, 1922/23–1960
(in thousands unless otherwise indicated)

Year[a]		Both sexes	Males	Females	Percent female
1922/23		5,629	4,196	1,433	25.5
1923/24		6,032	4,500	1,532	25.4
1924/25		6,951	5,226	1,725	24.8
1925/26		8,407	6,276	2,132	25.4
1926	Census	8,484	5,890	2,594	30.6
1926/27		9,115	6,712	2,403	26.4
1928		9,923	7,270	2,653	27.0
1929	Jan. 1	10,724	—	—	—
1929		10,592	7,729	2,863	27.0
1930	Jan. 1	12,979	9,527	3,452	26.6
1931	Jan. 1	14,645	10,669	3,976	27.1
1931	July 1	13,909	9,889	4,020	28.9
1932	Jan. 1	16,930	12,148	4,782	28.2
1932	July 1	20,073	14,460	5,613	28.0
1933	Jan. 1	18,495	12,799	5,696	30.8
1933	July 1	20,052	13,996	6,056	30.2
1934	Jan. 1	20,550	14,150	6,400	31.1
1934	July 1	19,892	13,367	6,525	32.8
1935	Jan. 1	19,506	13,206	6,300	32.3
1935	July 1	20,344	13,745	6,599	32.4
1936	Jan. 1	22,062	14,539	7,523	34.1
1936	July 1	20,587	13,649	6,938	33.7
1937	Jan. 1	21,355	14,062	7,292	34.1
1937	July 1	23,060	14,928	8,078	35.0
1938	Jan. 1	21,803	14,237	7,566	34.7
1938	July 1	22,597	14,733	7,864	34.8
1939	Jan. 1	23,803	15,210	8,593	36.1
1939	July 1	23,054	14,801	8,253	35.8
1937	Jan. 1	24,311	15,499	8,812	36.2
1937	July 1	26,011	16,309	9,702	37.3
1938	Jan. 1	24,507	15,439	9,068	37.0
1938	July 1	25,440	15,951	9,489	37.3
1939	Jan. 1	25,157	16,113	10,044	38.4
1939	Census	25,495	15,781	9,714	38.1
1940		26,640	16,437	10,200	38.3
1941		28,800	18,600	10,200	35.4
1945		29,000	17,500	11,500	38.4
1946		30,200	—	—	—
1947		24,800	11,200	13,600	54.8
1948		28,900	—	—	—
1949		30,000	—	—	—
1950		31,900	—	—	—
1951		33,600	—	—	—
1952		35,800	19,600	16,200	45.3
1953		37,300	—	—	—
1954		38,900	—	—	—
1955		39,000	—	—	—
1956		41,800	—	—	—
1957		42,300	23,200	19,100	45.2
1958		44,700	24,500	20,200	45.2
1959	Jan. 1	46,400	24,900	21,500	46.3
1959	July 1	48,600	25,900	22,700	46.7
1960		51,000	27,100	23,900	46.9
		50,800	—	—	—
		(54,800)	—	—	—

[a] Dates are averages for the year, except as indicated.

Notes: Sources and methods are given in Eason, *Soviet Manpower*, appendix E, adjusted for postwar noncensus data according to information in *Narodnoe khoziaistvo 1956*, pp. 204–206; *Narodnoe khoziaistvo 1958*, pp. 658–659, 644; *Narodnoe khoziaistvo 1959*, pp. 588, 594; and TSU, *Sel'skoe khoziaistvo SSSR*, pp. 451, 458.

The dash (—) indicates that data are not available.

Table II.16

USSR: Increases in the Labor Force of Working Ages and in the Number of Wage and Salary Workers in Nonagricultural Occupations, by Sex, Censuses of 1926, 1939, and 1959; Estimates of 1934–39 and 1950–60; and Projections for 1960–65

Period and category		Increase in the labor force of working ages, 16 to 59 (thousands) (1)	Increase in the number of wage and salary workers in nonagricultural occupations (thousands) (2)	Average annual change (percent) (3)	Column 2 minus column 1 (thousands) (4)	Column 2 as percent of column 1 (5)
Changes during intercensal periods[a]						
1926–39	Both sexes	11,600	20,300	10.7	+8,700	175
	Males	8,000	12,700		+4,700	159
	Females	3,600	7,600		+4,000	121
1939–59	Both sexes	20,200	22,200	2.9	+2,000	110
	Males	6,500	8,500		+2,000	130
	Females	13,700	13,700		0	100
1926–59	Both sexes	31,800	42,500	5.8	+10,700	134
	Males	14,500	21,200		+6,700	151
	Females	17,300	21,300		+4,000	123
Estimated changes during normal periods[b]						
1934–39	Both sexes	4,800	6,300	5.6	+1,500	131
	Males	3,300	2,700		−600	81
	Females	1,500	3,600		+2,100	240
1950–60	Both sexes	17,300	19,200	4.3	+1,900	111
	Males	10,800	9,500		−1,300	88
	Females	6,500	9,700		+3,200	149
Projected changes (both sexes)[c]						
1960–65		1,600	8,000	2.9	+6,400	500

[a] Census data calculated from Tables II.2 and II.3.
[b] Labor force of working ages calculated from the same source as in Table II.3; wage and salary workers calculated from data in Table II.15.
[c] Labor force of working ages calculated from same source as in Table II.3; wage and salary workers from Seven-Year Plan (1959–1965).

ber of wage and salary workers has increased at the expense of other sectors of the labor force.

The number of female wage and salary workers (in nonagricultural occupations) has increased more rapidly than the number of males, and females now comprise about 50 percent of the total number of wage and salary workers, compared with 27 percent at the beginning of the plans (see Table II.15). The absolute increase in the number of male wage and salary workers was greater than that in the number of females from 1926 to 1939 and less from 1939 to 1959; but the relative increase in the number of females was greater through the end of the war. Since the war, the sex ratio among wage and salary workers in nonagricultural occupations has remained essentially unchanged.

The planned goal for 1965 for wage and salary workers involves a much lower rate of increase (2.9 percent per year) than the actual rates in the past. In this particular five-year period the over-all picture in labor supply is tight. If the goal is to be reached, this will be partly through the increase of the population of working ages and of the population age 60 and over.[52] The rather substantial remainder, however, must come from the family members of rural and urban workers, now in intermittent, partial, and part-time private economic activity, and by a net reduction in other sectors such as collective farming and possibly the military, and conceivably by a further reduction in forced labor.

After 1965, the growth of the population of working ages will recover to somewhat below earlier normal rates, and will support the major share of continued growth in the number of wage and salary workers at past rates, placing relatively modest demands on other branches of the labor force.

The distribution of wage and salary workers by occupational categories. The question of quality in labor was discussed in section 2 from the standpoint of supply. In the present section we look at quality in terms of the structure of employment. The five categories used by the USSR for this purpose — wage earners, apprentices, engineering-technical personnel (including management), salaried employees (principally office help), and service personnel (such as janitors) — are roughly correlated with quality in terms of skill and administrative responsibility. The percentage distribution of wage and salary workers in industry by these categories for 1928–59 is given in Table II.17, together with administrative and management personnel as a percentage of total wage and salary workers in all branches for 1952–59.

Wage earners comprise the same percentage of the total now — 82 percent — as in 1928. Immediately after 1930, however, wage earners had declined to 75 percent of the total. Two percentage points of this decline can be explained by the relative increase in "apprentices," resulting from the influx of unskilled labor from the farms during 1931. The subsequent decline in the percentage of apprentices can be explained by the increased reliance on schools for training, both separate from and attached to factories.

The remainder of the decline appears as an increase of engineering-technical-salaried employees from 9 percent in 1928 to 14 percent in 1932. Although it is difficult to tell from the available data, which are not appropriately subdivided before 1932, this was probably predominantly a

---

[52] In recent years there has been a proportionate increase in the number of wage and salary workers in agricultural occupations, that is, the number employed by state farms and agricultural units attached to enterprises. The effect of a continuation of these trends on the demand and supply conditions with respect to nonagricultural wage and salary workers is not clear. Partly this will be a matter of changing the structure of agricultural organization and, in effect, substituting state farm production (and wage and salary employment) for collective farm production (and membership in what is technically a producer cooperative).

Table II.17

USSR: Percentage Distribution of Wage and Salary Workers in Industry, by Occupational Categories, 1928–59

Occupation	1928	1930	1931	1932	1937	1940	1950	1955	1956	1957	1958	1959
Wage earners	82	83	78	75	78	75	80	82	82	82	83	83
Apprentices	5	4	7	7	3	3	2	2	2	2	2	2
Engineering-technical personnel[a] } Salaried employees	9	9	11	14	14	15	14	13	13	13	13	13
Service personnel	4	4	4	4	5	7	4	3	3	3	2	2
Total	100	100	100	100	100	100	100	100	100	100	100	100

	1952	1954	1955	1958	1959
Administrative and management personnel as percent of wage and salary workers, all branches	14.6	14.0	12.4	10.2	9.7

a Includes management personnel.

Note: All except administrative and management personnel, 1928–31, derived from TSUNKHU, *Narodnoe khoziaistvo SSSR: statisticheskii spravochnik, 1932* (Moscow-Leningrad, 1932), p. 429; 1932–55, from TSU, *Promyshlennost' SSSR: statisticheskii sbornik* (Moscow, 1957), p. 23; 1956–59, from *Narodnoe khoziaistvo 1959*, p. 138.

Administrative and management personnel from *Narodnoe khoziaistvo 1959*, p. 595.

relative increase in the proportion of salaried employees rather than engineering-technical and managerial personnel. In other words, an exceptionally large proportion of the increases in the work force of enterprises
during the critical year of 1931 comprised office workers — related undoubtedly to the exceptionally large increase in the number of female
employees during 1931–32.

The trends in Table II.17 must be seen in the light of the broad changes
in the demand for personnel, by the categories listed, in the course of
industrialization. General reference to this point has already been made in
the discussion about the educational reform. Hill and Harbison (pp.
16–56) have reported a proportion of production workers in 1947 in a
sample of 50 industrial enterprises in the United States which is (as an
order of magnitude) not unlike that reported for all industry in the USSR
in the 1950's. Most important, however, they report a significant decline in
the proportion in the last decade or so, which they relate to fundamental
changes in industrial organization at a later stage of economic development. The other side of the coin is a relative increase in managerial and
technical personnel.

From this point of view, we may conjecture that in the USSR the
demand for industrial man power may shift toward managerial and higher
level technical personnel. For the present, however, the data are consistent
with the view that the demand for personnel in these categories is that of
an economy at a lower level of development than the United States. Interestingly, administrative and management personnel as a percentage of the
total number of wage and salary workers in all branches, declines from
about 14 percent in 1954 to 10 percent in 1958 and 1959. However, these
data probably reflect the reduction in personnel in the government superstructure, particularly in connection with the reorganization of the administrative framework instituted in 1957, and not in the enterprises themselves. Until we can isolate this effect, these data cannot be used as a basis
for conclusions about the internal structure of the labor force in industrial
enterprises.

The constant proportion of engineering-technical-managerial-salaried
personnel in the total (14 percent in 1932 and 13 percent in 1955) conceals a *rising* proportion of those in the engineering-technical-managerial
category proper (from 5 percent in 1932 to 9 percent in 1955). A corresponding trend has been shown for the United States by Hill and Harbison.
On the other hand, without adequate data for 1928–32 it is difficult to
interpret the trend after 1932. The figure of 5 percent for managerial-
engineering-technical personnel in 1932 may be exceptionally low for the
given level of technology and industrial organization (if so, it is probably
lower than in 1928), in which case the higher figures of 7 percent in 1937
and 9 percent in 1940 might represent something more normal. The fact

that the proportion has remained unchanged between 1940 and 1955 tends to support this view.

The decline in the proportion of salaried employees and the rise in the proportion of production workers, on the other hand, could be explained in terms of the stated policy — beginning in the 1930's, but re-emphasized in the 1950's — to reduce office staffs and to put these people to work in "production."

With the reform of the educational system, stressing the provision of an adequate supply of production workers, one can foresee the proportions of Table II.17 remaining more or less constant for the next decade (or two), as they have in the past decade. Sooner or later, however, with higher levels of industrial technology and increasing complexity of economic organization, the proportion of production workers may be expected to decline and that of managerial-technical personnel to rise, raising questions affecting allocation as well as the qualitative dimensions of labor supply.

Summary and Conclusions

In surveying trends in the allocation of labor by area, industry, and occupation, we distinguished between those of a longer-run variety and those which reflect the particular circumstances of relatively short periods of time.

From a longer-run point of view we observed that the redistribution of labor into categories associated with industrialization and growth — that is, from rural to urban areas and from agricultural to nonagricultural occupations — has proceeded at a relatively rapid rate, but that with half of the labor force still in agricultural occupations (and half of the population in rural areas) the process of redistribution still has a long way to go.

Because the industrialization drive began with more than 80 percent of the labor force in agricultural occupations, the requirements of industry and other nonagricultural sectors for man power in most of the interim years have been met without a net drain on the agricultural sector that might have necessitated drastic reorganization of agricultural production methods to release labor and maintain production. And because more than half of the civilian labor force is still in agriculture, the process under normal conditions might be expected to continue—with gradually increasing pressures for structural and institutional changes in agriculture to provide man power for industry. Three considerations, however, are intensifying the problem: the first is the temporary decline in the rate of growth of over-all labor supply; the second is the substantial reduction in the possible shift of labor from other nonagricultural activities (including forced labor) into wage and salary employment; and the third is the fact that the Soviet Union has experienced special difficulties of an institutional nature in raising agricultural labor productivity.

Also from a longer-run point of view, the redistribution of labor within the nonagricultural sector, by industry and occupation, is broadly similar to that in the United States since 1860 — reflecting the universal attributes of the industrialization process — but there are also a number of important differences. The similarities are most evident in the occupational distribution — by categories of wage earner, engineering-technical personnel, et cetera — suggesting a similar structure of management and distribution of skills at the same stage of development. The differences are more apparent in the higher proportion in industry and construction in the Soviet Union after 1928 and the lower proportion in commerce.

It was shown to be equally important, in understanding the pattern of redistribution of labor in the early stages of Soviet industrialization, to examine the changes which reflect the particular circumstances of relatively short periods of time.

The first of these is 1928–30, a period of gradual adaptation to the forces embodied in the First Five-Year Plan. Any trends apparent in this initial period are of a longer-run sort. With 1931, however, came the upheaval related to collectivization. Most trends were greatly accelerated: the rate of increase of the urban population and nonagricultural labor force, the relative shift of the nonagricultural labor force to wage and salary employment, the increase in employment in construction (and possibly also industry), and the relative increase in the number employed in all industry as engineering-technical personnel and salaried employees. The proportion employed in industry as wage earners, however, declined, and the proportion employed as apprentices increased, an indication of large numbers of individuals entering industry with no experience. For several years after 1931, short-run developments in some cases paralleled long-run trends; in others a temporary plateau was reached; and in still others, the movement was irregular and even erratic.

These were times of great change and turmoil, clearly reflected in labor redistribution. In certain respects the redistribution required by industrialization was greatly hastened by the events of one or two years. Although some of the developments tended to be averaged out in the long run, the whole process of change, particularly from a social point of view, was speeded up. Perhaps from a political point of view, in terms of establishing itself clearly in the driver's seat of planned economic development, it was even necessary for the Soviet government to take strong steps quickly. But from an economic point of view, erratic changes and abrupt reversals are not the most efficient way to adapt resources to changing requirements. It is therefore likely that purely allocative needs in the short run were not well served by the changes observed.

It is difficult to draw conclusions about the postwar period, because most of the indexes relating to the allocation of labor begin with 1950 or later, and because the indicated changes are relatively modest. The very persistence of change, however, suggests that trends during this period — as well as the other normal period before the war — may reveal the underlying structural and economic forces influencing labor allocation and redistribution at this particular stage of development. The data also suggest that one major phase in labor allocation may be drawing to a close. The new phase — reflecting short- and long-run shifts in labor supply and demand — is characterized by greater attention to new and improved methods of allocating and redistributing labor.

APPENDIX

Notes to Table II.3

The data for 1926 are from the census.

The labor force data for 1939 were derived by adjusting the estimates in Eason, *Soviet Manpower*, p. 449, to conform to the recently published results of the 1939 census. Only a relatively minor adjustment was needed, and it was confined to the estimate of the rural population age 12 to 15 in the labor force.

Given the proportions of the population in the labor force by age and sex for 1939, the labor force by age and sex for 1959 is estimated from the reported number of males and females of all ages in the labor force and the number of males and females by age and sex in the population as follows: (i) The proportion of males and females age 10 to 15 in the labor force is assumed to be one-half the corresponding proportion for 1939. (ii) The proportion of females age 16 to 59 in the labor force is assumed to be the same in 1959 as 1939, to the nearest 100,000 in the labor force. This makes it possible to derive the number of females age 60 and over in the labor force. (iii) Given the total number of males in the labor force (from the census) and the number age 10 to 15, it is evident that the proportion of the population age 16 and over in the labor force is significantly below that of 1939, due presumably to the total disability incurred by war. The difference compared with 1939 is distributed in proportion to the population in the respective age groups, 16 to 59 and 60 and over.

Notes to Table II.9

USSR

Total Population

1860–1941: see Eason, *Soviet Manpower*, appendix N.

1950–59: calculated from 1959 census total population by means of published annual birth and death rates.

1959 census and 1960: *Narodnoe khoziaistvo 1959*, p. 10.

Urban Population

1860–1941: see Eason, *Soviet Manpower*, appendix N.

1950–55: derived from the urban population for 1956 by applying the average increase of 3.4 million per year, from the statement by Khrushchev in *Pravda*, February 3, 1955, that "for the last five years the urban population has increased by approximately 17 million persons."

1956–58: derived from urban population in 1959 by interpolating between average growth of 3.4 million for 1950–55 and 3.8 million reported during 1960.

1959–60: *Narodnoe khoziaistvo 1959*, p. 10.

USA

1820–1940: *Historical Statistics,* p. 5.

1950: U.S. Census of Population: 1950, vol. II, *Characteristics of the Population:* part I, United States Summary (Washington, 1953), pp. 1–5.

1960: *Statistical Abstract of the United States, 1962* (Washington, 1962), p. 19.

Notes to Table II.14

The estimating procedure for 1939 and 1959 is fairly complex and will be summarized very briefly.

Although the data on the labor force from the censuses of 1939 and 1959 constitute a significant improvement in terms of coverage and detail over earlier data, they are not in most instances in a form required by the categories of Table II.14. The total labor force of both sexes for 1959 comes close to that form, except that collective farm tractor drivers are listed as wage and salary workers instead of collective farmers. But the number of males and females in the labor force for 1959 are available only for the labor force net of persons working in subsidiary private agriculture, and only for "productive" and "nonproductive" branches of the economy. The labor force of both sexes for 1939 is distributed only by productive and nonproductive branches, and the number of males and females are reported only for labor force net of persons working in subsidiary private agriculture.

The estimating procedure, therefore, involves setting up relationships among the reported distributions of the census data, and between census and non-census data (establishment statistics).

In the final estimates, persons hired by collective farms are counted as wage and salary workers; cooperative handicraftsmen are listed separately, although the census groups them with wage and salary workers; and collective farm tractor drivers are listed under collective farmers.

III

CAPITAL STOCK

Norman M. Kaplan*

In the last four months of 1959, the Russians undertook a detailed inventory and revaluation of capital, that is, of buildings, structures, producers' durables, and other fixed assets in place. The purposes of this chapter are to describe the revaluation procedures; to present and comment on the primary results, the 1960 capital values; and to draw some implications from the results — primarily, some intertemporal and international comparisons of the distribution of capital.

The capital revaluation has yielded not only January 1, 1960, capital values but also capital indexes for the 1928–60 period. Although the latter are of considerable interest in themselves and are useful in apprais-

* This chapter was originally prepared as a report for The RAND Corporation; however, any views expressed in it are those of the author and should not be interpreted as reflecting the views of The RAND Corporation or the official opinion or policy of any of its sponsors.

This chapter is part of a forthcoming monograph on Soviet capital formation, hereafter cited as *Kaplan*.

I make use of an unpublished monograph by Professor Raymond Goldsmith, and I am very grateful to him for permission to use the results. Finally, I am indebted to Mr. Abram Bergson and Mr. Oleg Hoeffding for helpful comments.

ing the reliability of the capital values, limitations of space force me to omit examination of the indexes from this material.

1. THE 1959 CAPITAL REVALUATION

The objectives of the capital inventory and revaluation[1] are stated as follows: to measure more accurately the amount and structure of capital; to provide a more accurate basis for determining depreciation allowances (which before the revaluation were determined from decreed percentages applied to capital at original cost) and, thereby, for determining costs and prices; to determine the real wear-and-tear of capital, so as to improve the planning of replacements and spare parts; to provide a uniform valuation of capital among enterprises, so as to improve various aspects of financial planning; and to verify the presence of assets in enterprises, independently of entries for them on the books of the enterprises.

To these ends, capital as of January 1, 1960,[2] is inventoried and valued at its replacement cost in terms of July 1, 1955, prices and the unified cost estimates introduced in 1956. This valuation scheme reflects the most recent general price change in the USSR and the costs used for investment planning since 1956. Later price changes appear to be scattered and small: some have occurred for railroad rolling stock, ships, agricultural machinery, and some construction materials;[3] some wage rates and other producers' durables prices may also have changed. Thus, a valuation scheme

---

[1] There is a substantial Soviet literature on the capital revaluation, but I have neither examined it in detail nor attempted a systematic survey of it. My account is based primarily on P. Bunich, *Pereotsenka osnovnykh fondov* (Moscow, 1959). Additional information comes from: TSU, *Narodnoe khoziaistvo SSSR v 1959 godu* (Moscow, 1960), hereafter cited as *Narodnoe khoziaistvo 1959*; K. Vinogradov, "Obraztsovo provesti perepis' zhilishchnogo fonda na 1 ianvaria 1960 g.," *Vestnik statistiki,* 1959, no. 7, pp. 22–28; F. Pankratov, "Ob inventarizatsii fondov v sviazi s ikh pereotsenkoi," *Vestnik statistiki,* 1959, no. 6, pp. 49–58; Anon., "Pereotsenka osnovnykh fondov nachalas'," *Vestnik statistiki,* 1959, no. 9, pp. 3–5; V. Petropavlovskii, "Prakticheskoe primenenie sbornika ukrupnennykh pokazatelei stoimosti zhilykh i kommunal'nykh zdanii," *Vestnik statistiki,* 1959, no. 9, pp. 50–53; V. Gorelik and A. Monastyrskii, "O sostavlenii otchetov po pereotsenke i opredeleniiu iznos osnovnykh fondov," *Vestnik statistiki,* 1959, no. 12, pp. 49–62; N. Monakhov, "Kak pol'zovatsia sbornikami ukrupnennykh pokazatelei stoimosti zdanii i sooruzhenii dlia pereotsenki osnovnykh fondov," *Vestnik statistiki,* 1959, no. 7, pp. 54–65; A Beliakov, "Nekotorye itogi pereotsenki osnovnykh fondov SSSR," *Vestnik statistiki,* 1960, no. 10, pp. 3–11; E. Ivanov and V. Iubovskii, Book reviews, *Finansy SSSR,* 1959, no. 10, pp. 89–92; F. Pankratov, "Uspeshno provesti pereotsenku osnovnykh fondov kolkhozov," *Vestnik statistiki,* 1960, no. 11, pp. 18–23. Where possible and unambiguous, subsequent citations are to author only.

Probably the most serious deficiency in this account is the failure to study the 138 price and cost handbooks prepared for the revaluation. To do so, and especially to compare the data with previously available data, would be a major undertaking; hence my reliance on secondary Russian sources for a description of methods.

[2] Organizations are instructed to include assets to be delivered or completed between the date of the inventory and January 1, 1960.

[3] For 1959 price changes in specific construction materials, see S. Stoliarov, *O tsenakh i tsenoobrazovanii v SSSR* (Moscow, 1960), pp. 67–68.

close to present prices has been used but with no attempt to take post-1956 changes into account.

The capital revaluation does not extend to all organizations or to all kinds of assets. Subject to the revaluation are state and cooperative organizations, enterprises, and institutions required to set aside allowances for depreciation. Except for those types of assets not subject to revaluation regardless of ownership, all capital of such organizations is to be revalued whether related to the primary or secondary activity of the organization. Thus, an industrial enterprise is required to inventory and revalue not only its industrial capital but also its housing and other nonproductive capital. The organizations and sectors excluded entirely from the revaluation are: collective farms; private capital, whether agricultural, housing, or other; administrative institutions (such as ministries and departments); schools and higher educational institutions; hospitals and clinics; central scientific and technical libraries; and unspecified others.

Two groups of assets are excluded from revaluation even when found in organizations subject to the revaluation: One consists of assets with relatively short service lives and, hence, whose original and replacement costs are not very different: essentially, tools and implements *("instrument; proizvodstvennyi, khoziaistvennyi, kontorskii inventar'; proizvodstvennye prinadlezhnosti")*. These assets are to be included in the January 1, 1960, capital values at original cost. A second group consists of relatively unimportant assets whose revaluation is difficult. Most important among those mentioned specifically are: perennial plantings; land improvement and irrigation structures and related assets; and productive and draft livestock. No mention is made of the values at which such assets are included when they belong to organizations subject to the revaluation. Nevertheless, it seems clear that these are also included at original cost at least in the organizations' reports. The reports which organizations subject to the revaluation are required to submit include both groups of assets as "assets not subject to revaluation" and have columns only for original cost and postrevaluation replacement cost.

To enable organizations to revalue their machinery, equipment, and rolling stock, 102 price handbooks have been prepared which list all types of producers' durables — including machinery no longer produced by domestic industry and imported machinery — and their replacement values. The replacement value is the July 1, 1955, wholesale price *(optovaia tsena)* plus: packaging and tare charges when these are not included in the wholesale price; warehousing expenses; installation, lining, enameling, and facing expenses; average transportation expenses when wholesale prices are f.o.b. manufacturer; expenditures on the equipment foundation; design and miscellaneous other charges; and zonal price differentials. Since the inventory lists producers' durables by model number and type, the appropriate replacement value is found by determining the wholesale price from the relevant handbook and making whatever additions are necessary.[4]

To enable organizations to revalue their buildings and structures, 36 handbooks provide the necessary valuations. The valuations provided are consolidated values, for example, values per cubic meter of a building or per linear meter of a pipeline. The buildings are classified by type — such as a metallurgical factory building, railroad station, apartment building, or hospital. Each type is further classified into major components — such as basic building, basement, or fencing; by number of stories; and by the material from which the walls are constructed. Within each type of building, there is an average value per cubic meter (or other physical unit) for each relevant subgroup, differentiated by 10 regions.

Each type of building is also described in terms of the technical characteristics most frequently encountered. Adjustment coefficients are provided for the differences in technical characteristics between the typical building and that being evaluated. For example, if the typical building has brick walls which account for 30 percent of total value and which are 2.5 bricks thick, and the building being evaluated has walls only 2 bricks thick, the value per cubic meter of the typical building is to be reduced 6 percent, that is, $0.30 - (0.30 \times 0.8)$. However, if the building being evaluated is obsolete in some technical respect, the revaluation is made to accord with the consolidated values for an analogous building with contemporary standards.

Where the basic building has ancillary structures or installations, or lacks some facilities normally included, these are valued separately and added or subtracted.[5] Where the building is unique and cannot be related to any type described in the handbooks, price indexes are to be used to translate original into replacement cost.[6]

Structures other than buildings are evaluated in essentially the same way as buildings, that is, primarily by means of consolidated values per

---

[4] The components of complex equipment are valued separately and added. For example, a drilling rig is valued by aggregating the values of such equipment as the hoist, the rotor, or the crown block.

In those cases where machinery that is no longer produced by domestic industry and imported machinery are not specifically listed in the price handbooks, their valuations are obtained from the prices of analogous contemporary machinery and adjustment coefficients which express the differences in the performance of the machinery.

[5] For detailed examples of such additions and subtractions, see Monakhov, pp. 59–65; and Petropavlovskii, pp. 50–53.

[6] Bunich, p. 56, gives an example of such a calculation in which the indexes are 2 with $1940 = 1$ and 1.5 with $1945 = 1$. It is interesting to observe that Raymond P. Powell's price indexes for construction inputs are 1.99 with $1940 = 1.00$ and 1.36 with $1945 = 1.00$ (see *A Materials-Input Index of Soviet Construction, Revised and Extended,* The RAND Corporation, Research Memorandum RM-2454, September 28, 1959, p. 85).

unit of volume, area, or length. Such values are also provided in the handbooks by types of structures, classified into major components, by design differences, and by materials used.

One distinction between the revaluation of structures and producers' durables seems significant. The revaluation of producers' durables, apart from imported machinery and machinery no longer produced, is straightforward. The proliferation of price handbooks is due primarily to the variety of durables involved; the handbooks represent a collation of prices at which transfers have occurred. Given the full listing of durables by type and model number, few problems of valuation arise. Indeed, there is little discussion in the literature on the revaluation of machinery.

On the other hand, the instructions and examples with respect to the valuation of structures are voluminous, involved, and detailed. The values in the handbooks are for typical structures, with many correction factors to take account of departures from typicality. Moreover, the handbook values are not a collation of available costs: (i) the level of aggregation is higher than that used in previous derivations of cost estimates which are in terms of intermediate outputs — cubic meters of concrete foundation, square meters of wood flooring, cubic meters of brick wall, et cetera; (ii) at least in some cases, replacement value apparently means not the cost of replacing the old structure exactly but that of replacing it by a similar structure with current specifications. Thus, the handbooks appear to provide a new compilation of price information: essentially, average prices plus the numerous correction factors necessary to apply such average prices to the specific valuation problem, given the extreme heterogeneity of structures. I do not mean to suggest that something is wrong with these procedures. My only point is that the price information is new and its relationship to the previously available price data, unclear.

In addition to revaluing inventoried capital, the Russians have undertaken to measure real wear-and-tear or depreciation (*iznos*). Three kinds of depreciation are distinguished: the physical wear-and-tear resulting from the use of the asset; the depreciation due to productivity increases in the production of the asset; and the obsolescence of old assets due to the appearance of new assets with greater productivity in use. The last two are said to be reflected in the constant-price replacement values — obsolescence, via the valuation of assets no longer produced. Only physical wear-and-tear is measured separately from the basic valuations.

The diverse methods employed in measuring physical wear-and-tear can be classified broadly into two groups. One general method determines the technical conditions of the asset by direct examination or from data in the technical descriptions; and voluminous materials provide criteria for measurement.[7] A second general method compares elapsed service life or

[7] For example, for a foundation that can be examined directly, the criteria for good

past output with the norms for service life or output; and again volum- inous materials state the relevant norms. Whichever general method is employed, the result is a measure of wear-and-tear for each asset inven- toried, and in many cases separate measures for major components of the asset.

From an organizational point of view, the capital revaluation was a major undertaking. Under the over-all supervision of the Central Statis- tical Administration, the highest levels of the administrative hierarchy participated in the preparation of handbooks, instructions, reporting forms: the State Planning Commission, the State Committee on Con- struction Affairs, the Ministry of Finance, as well as the various ministries, republican councils of ministers, sovnarkhozy, and scientific and project- making institutes.

The time-table of the undertaking was somewhat as follows:

(i) Since 1939, there have been repeated statements of the urgency of a general inventory and revaluation of capital. Before 1958, however, there were only: inventories and revaluations for particular sectors or areas, such as the postliberation inventories in areas occupied during the war; and experimental inventories, such as the 1952 flour mill inventory, for methodological purposes associated with the 1959 inventory.[8]

(ii) The first steps in the 1959 inventory and revaluation occurred in the second half of 1958 and the first half of 1959. In this period, the organizations, enterprises, and institutions prepared the original itemiza- tion of assets and the technical data on each. These steps were checked, regularized, and corrected by the statistical and financial organizations. In May and June of 1959, there were nationwide instructional conferences on the inventory and revaluation. Commissions were created in each sov- narkhoz, ministry, and department, and in each enterprise and organiza- tion to conduct the final inventory and revaluation.[9]

(iii) From September through December 1959, the inventory, revalua- tion, and measurement of wear-and-tear were completed by the organiza- tions, enterprises, and institutions. In January 1960, the results were reported to the Central Statistical Administration.

(iv) From February through May 1960, the Central Statistical Admin- istration collated the reports and prepared the over-all results which were

condition with a 0- to 10-percent reduction of value for wear-and-tear are no distortion, a true bond, a rubble slab and span of good quality, no declination in the base, and a dry cellar. Where the foundation is inaccessible to direct examination, there must be a base without declinations or cracks, a wall bond without distortions, and no sagging. Similar lists are given for 11- to 20-percent, 21- to 30-percent, et cetera, reductions of value.

[8] For a brief account of the pre-1959 inventories, see *Kaplan,* Table C-6, note 5.

[9] In *Vestnik statistiki,* 1959, no. 9, pp. 4–5, there are complaints that in some ministries and sovnarkhozy these initial steps were inadequately attended to. There are also ad- monitions to work harder on the inventory and revaluation.

examined and approved by the highest economic organizations — ministries, sovnarkhozy, et cetera — before release. Thus, little time elapsed between receipt of the reports by the Central Statistical Administration and release of the aggregate results in *Narodnoe khoziaistvo 1959*, published on August 20, 1960.[10] Although such speed may be explained by the use of machine tabulation,[11] it is also possible that the published results are preliminary and that amendments, corrections, and further details may be forthcoming.

At about the time of the general capital inventory and revaluation, a separate housing census was taken under the supervision of the Central Statistical Administration.[12] To provide information on housing utilization, organizations responsible for socialized housing in urban and rural areas were required to report their housing stocks on January 1, 1960, and various technical and utilization data about their housing; no separate inventory, however, was required because it was already part of the general capital inventory.

The housing census also covered private housing which was omitted from the general capital inventory and required a separate inventory. Between January 2 and January 12, 1960, all owners of private housing except collective farm members and private farmers were required to report their square meters of housing and various technical and utilization characteristics of that housing. The separate housing census thus fills one of the gaps in the general capital inventory — the stock of private housing other than that of collective farm members and private peasants.

According to *Vestnik statistiki*, 1960, no. 11, pp. 18–23, preparations are now under way for a revaluation of collective farm capital under the supervision of the Central Statistical Administration. The initial inventory was scheduled for completion on December 1, 1960. Instructions and price handbooks were to be published in the spring of 1961. In August–November 1961, the final inventory, revaluation, and measurement of wear-and-tear were to be completed by collective farms. The Central Statistical Administration was then to collate the results and determine the January 1, 1962, capital values. However, no results have been published as yet.

Two aspects of the collective farm capital revaluation are of special interest here. First, the replacement costs are those used in the general 1959 capital revaluation, that is, July 1, 1955, wholesale prices for producers' durables and the consolidated values, at July 1, 1955, prices and

---

[10] The manuscript of *Narodnoe khoziaistvo 1959* was received by type-setters on May 14, 1960 (*ibid.*, p. 896). The tables on capital values may have been filled in some time later. To my knowledge, the first appearance of a ruble figure resulting from the revaluation was in *Pravda*, July 16, 1960 — a figure of "more than 2,400 billion rubles" for state and cooperative capital.

[11] Gorelik and Monastyrskii, p. 51.

[12] Vinogradov, pp. 22–28.

1956 cost estimates, for structures. The existing handbooks were to be abridged to eliminate assets not used in collective farms and extended to cover structures from local building materials. The same replacement costs are said to be used in order to permit a comparative analysis of collective farm and state farm capital efficiency. This implies that the prices paid by collective farms differ at a given time from the wholesale prices of state farm purchases. Second, livestock is to be excluded from the 1961 revaluation since all livestock had been revalued on January 1, 1959, at procurement (*"zakupochnye"*) prices. Thus another gap in the 1959 capital inventory and revaluation can be filled by data available to the Central Statistical Administration.

2. THE PRIMARY RESULTS OF THE 1959 REVALUATION

The primary published results of the 1959 revaluation are: January 1, 1960, capital values gross of wear-and-tear by segments of the economy; January 1, 1960, capital values gross of wear-and-tear by types of assets; the relationships between January 1, 1960, capital values at replacement and at original cost; and wear-and-tear as percentages of January 1, 1960, capital values. The results are presented in Tables III.1, III.2, and III.3, and require the following comments:

(i) The sector classifications in Table III.1 are the generally familiar ones, but a few details should be added.[13] Construction includes both contract and force-account construction and project-making organizations. Agriculture includes forestry. Housing includes structures the floor space of which is wholly or predominantly used for residence purposes — hotels and hostels as well as permanent dwellings. Municipal services include sewage organizations, bath houses, laundries, barbershops, and similar enterprises; and urban roads and other municipal improvements. Banks, insurance organizations, state administration, party, trade union, and other social organizations are included in "public health, et cetera." (Hereafter, "public health, education, science, art, and others" will be referred to elliptically as "public health.") Finally, the classification is *not* an establishment classification: the assets of an industrial enterprise are classified by activities — its primary assets in industry, its subsidiary agricultural assets in agriculture, its workers' supply section in trade, its creche in education, its apartment building in housing, et cetera.

(ii) The capital values by branches of industry in Table III.1 are the product of the percentage distribution and the industry total given in *Narodnoe khoziaistvo 1959,* pp. 67 and 68. The propriety of the calculation is indicated by: the reference to the percentage distribution as origi-

---

[13] For the meaning of the sector classifications see Norman M. Kaplan, "Capital Formation and Allocation," in Abram Bergson, ed. *Soviet Economic Growth* (Evanston, 1953), p. 50. Additional remarks here are from Bunich, pp. 50–53.

Table III.1

USSR: January 1, 1960, Capital Values at July 1, 1955, Replacement Costs by Segment of the Economy (billions of rubles)

Sector	Capital value	Branch of industry	Capital value
Productive capital, including livestock	1,739.3	Electric power production	95.2
Industry	800.1	Fuels	136.0
Construction	54.4	Coal	70.4
Agriculture	419.2	Petroleum extraction	37.6
Transportation	367.5	Petroleum refining	15.2
Communications	19.9	Gas	5.6
Procurement	20.9	Other (residual)	7.2
Material-technical supply and sales	11.5	Chemicals	39.2
Trade and public feeding	41.6	Building materials	42.4
Other sectors of material production	4.2	Cement	8.0
Nonproductive capital	1,225.4	Glass, china, and pottery	4.8
Housing	941.5	Ferrous metallurgy	76.8
Municipal services	59.7	Nonferrous metallurgy	33.6
Public health, education, science, art, and others	224.2	Machine-building and metalworking	162.4
Total capital, including livestock	2,964.7	Timber, woodworking, and paper	47.2
Excluding private capital	2,438	Light industry	36.0
In organizations subject to revaluation	2,001.1	Textiles	25.6
		Apparel	4.0
		Leather, fur, boots and shoes	4.8
		Other (residual)	1.6
		Food industry	72.8
		Fish	20.8
		Meat	6.4
		Milk and butter	6.4
		Flour and groats	7.2
		Other (residual)	3.2
		Other branches	53.6
		Total industry	800.1

Note: Data from *Narodnoe khoziaistvo 1959*, pp. 65, 67, 68; and Beliakov, p. 4.

Table III.2
USSR: January 1, 1960, Capital Values at July 1, 1955,
Replacement Costs by Type of Assets
(billions of rubles)

Item	All capital	Industrial capital
Total capital, including livestock	2,964.7	800.1
Buildings and structures	2,185.4	490.6
Total capital in organizations subject to revaluation	2,001.1	788.9
Buildings	896.6	217.1
Transmission facilities; structures other than buildings	538.2	265.6
Power equipment	83.5	65.0
Operating equipment	259.9	190.7
Measurement and control devices and laboratory equipment	13.5	6.0
Transportation equipment	151.4	31.9
Tools	1.7	1.0
Implements	17.4	5.8
Other capital	38.9	5.8

Note: Data from *Narodnoe khoziaistvo 1959*, p. 69.

nating from the data of the revaluation; the discussions of the results of the revaluation which refer to both the sector and branch of industry distributions; and the nature of the divergences between the previously published 1958 and 1960 distributions.[14]

In one respect, the branch of industry classification is an establishment classification: the industrial capital of an establishment which produces more than one product is placed in the branch to which its major output belongs.[15] The materials underlying the capital revaluation provide little additional information on the scope of the industrial branches. In the absence of contrary indications, the industrial classifications in Table III.1 are taken to be essentially the same as those described elsewhere.[16]

[14] On these points, respectively, see *Narodnoe khoziaistvo 1959*, p. 68; Beliakov, pp. 4–5; and *Kaplan*, Table E-1, note 3.

There is some question as to the relevant industry total: all industrial capital is 800.1 billion rubles and that in organizations subject to revaluation is 788.9 billion rubles (Table III.2). I have used the former figure; if the latter is correct, each industry value in Table III.1 should be reduced 1.4 percent.

[15] Bunich, p. 53.

[16] See *Kaplan*, chap. 4. The scope of the classification is derived from earlier information on distributions of industrial capital at original cost and from an assumed stability in nomenclature. The main points are as follows:

(i) Electric power production includes transmission lines and substations.

(ii) Fuels include the extraction of peat and other minor fuels, the coke industry, and the output of other coal, petroleum, and shale products.

(iii) Chemicals, building materials, and ferrous and nonferrous metallurgy include the mining of the relevant ores and raw materials.

(iv) Machine-building and metalworking include: (a) machine-building proper; (b)

Table III.3

USSR: The Effect of Revaluation on Capital at Original Cost and the Ratio of Wear-and-Tear to Capital at Replacement Cost, January 1, 1960

(percent)

Sector	Ratio of revalued capital to capital at original cost	Ratio of wear-and-tear to capital at replacement cost
Total capital[a]	112.4	25
Productive capital	106.3	26
Industry	98.0	25
Construction	89.0	27
Agriculture (state)	107.4	26
Transportation	132.9	29
Communications	124.3	30
Procurement	115.1	26
Material-technical supply and sales	109.4	25
Trade and public feeding	108.2	26
Other sectors	137.0	27
Nonproductive capital	129.3	22
Housing	132.7	23
Municipal services	119.5	24
Public health, education, science, art, and other	116.0	21

Type of assets	Ratio of revalued capital to capital at original cost		Ratio of wear-and-tear to capital at replacement cost
	All capital	Industrial capital	
Total capital[a]	112.4	98.0	25
Buildings	121.6	98.7	22
Transmission facilities; structures other than buildings	126.8	106.2	26
Power equipment	91.5	90.3	29
Operating equipment	89.7	90.3	30
Measurement and control devices and laboratory equipment	88.9	90.7	25
Transportation equipment	92.0	97.4	31

[a] In organizations subject to revaluation.

Note: Data from *Narodnoe khoziaistvo 1959*, pp. 72–75.

(iii) The asset classifications in Table III.2 require the following general remarks.[17] Buildings include housing as well as nonresidence buildings. Structures other than buildings refer to engineered objects not connected with physical transformations of commodities, such as mine shafts, oil wells, roads, dams, bridges, and pipe lines. Transmission facilities (*"peredatochnye ustroistva"*) are those used for the conversion, conveyance, and transmission of energy. These three categories constitute the stock of construction.

Power equipment is that used for the production of thermal and electrical energy and for their conversion to mechanical energy, for example, generators, transformers, and steam turbines. Operating equipment is that requiring power and used for mechanical, heating, and chemical operations on materials. Measurement and control devices and laboratory equipment and transportation equipment are more or less self-explanatory, although each includes a variety of items. Tools and implements are a miscellany of small-valued and/or short-lived items such as benches, store counters, safety devices, vats, containers, office equipment, fire-fighting equipment, and libraries. Other capital, by elimination of identified categories, consists primarily of livestock but also of long-lived plantings and land improvement items.

The last three categories in Table III.2 — tools, implements, and other capital — represent assets which are reported at original cost. Indeed, the assets reported at original cost are said to be about 3 percent of the capital of organizations subject to the revaluation[18] and these three categories account for 2.9 percent of the total.

(iv) The classification by type of asset in Table III.3 is the same as that in Table III.2 but excludes tools, implements, and other capital. From

---

repair plants such as locomotive repair plants, ship repair yards, and industrial equipment and motor vehicle repair plants; (c) the production of metal wares and consumers' durables; and (d) the production of structural steel members and welding work. Though not mentioned specifically, the production of military equipment is believed to be included also.

(v) Timber and woodworking include the felling, hauling, and floating of timber as well as sawmills, the plywood industry, prefabricated houses and structural parts, furniture, and matches.

(vi) The food industry includes beverages, tobacco, and fishing as well as food processing proper.

(vii) In addition to an unspecified component, "other branches" (in Table III.1) include: (a) the rubber and asbestos industry, 0.4 percent of total capital at original cost on January 1, 1956; (b) printing and publishing, also 0.4 percent on January 1, 1956; (c) the abrasive and graphite industry, 0.1 percent of January 1, 1960, industrial capital at July 1, 1955, prices; and (d) a miscellany of identified branches such as musical instruments and parts, school supplies, toys and games, and scientific equipment. For further details see *Kaplan,* Table E-1, note 2; and Bunich, pp. 52–53.

[17] The classifications are discussed in Bunich, pp. 37–46.

[18] L. Volodarskii, "Pereotsenka osnovnykh fondov narodnogo khoziaistva SSSR," *Planovoe khoziaistvo,* 1960, no. 10, p. 7.

Tables III.2 and III.3, the original-cost capital values can be computed for each category of assets. The total of these values and the capital values in Table III.2 for tools, implements, and other capital yields an original cost capital value (1,780.5 billion rubles) that is consistent with the 2,001.1 figure in Table III.2 and the ratio of revalued capital to capital at original cost (1.124) in Table III.3. Hence the relevant total in the distribution by type of assets (Table III.3) is all capital of organizations subject to the revaluation; and tools, implements, and other capital are not shown because they are included at original cost.

The sectors listed in Table III.3 are the same as those in Table III.1, except that agriculture refers to state organizations only. Since the ratios for total capital in both parts of Table III.3 are the same, the total in the sector distribution also refers to all capital of organizations subject to the revaluation. However, whether the sector data in Table III.3 refer to distributions of that total is problematic because of the absence of precise sector capital values of that scope. Calculations with respect to the ratios of revalued to original-cost capital lead me to believe that the productive sectors do refer to capital of organizations subject to the revaluation; but the nonproductive sectors are more inclusive.[19] The point

[19] The calculations are analogous to those for the distributions by type of assets. Given the component ratios in Table III.3, the capital values in Tables III.1 and III.2, and certain estimates (pp. 110–112), one can compare the implied and the stated ratios (or capital values). The calculations and argument are as follows:

(i) For productive capital, I substitute the industry figure in Table III.2 for that in Table III.1 and, using the other, nonagricultural sector data from Table III.1, observe an implied ratio of revalued to original-cost capital of 1.065. Since the agricultural ratio is 1.074, something else is excluded with a ratio less than 1.063, the ratio for all productive capital. Suppose tools, implements, and other capital — with a ratio of 1.000 — are included in the total for productive capital but not in the sectors. The 1.063 ratio for all productive capital and the indicated capital values and ratios for nonagricultural productive capital imply a capital value of 100 billion rubles for state agriculture excluding livestock and agricultural tools and implements. This is consistent with the 419 figure for all agriculture, the estimates of about 220 billion rubles for collective farm capital and 40 to 60 billion rubles for private agricultural capital (p. 111–112), and the assumption that a large part of tools, implements, and other capital belongs in state agriculture. Hence, the productive sectors refer to the capital of organizations subject to the revaluation and account for 1,470 billion rubles thereof.

(ii) If nonproductive capital refers to the capital of organizations subject to the revaluation, the housing component is about 450 to 475 billion rubles (p. 111). The ratios for all nonproductive capital and its components, and the capital values for municipal services in Table III.1 and for housing just indicated, imply that of 224 billion rubles in public health, 59 to 62 billion rubles belong to organizations subject to the revaluation. Although this seems large (p. 111), it is certainly not impossible.

(iii) The trouble is that 1,470 billion rubles of productive capital with a ratio of 1.063 and 569 or 597 billion rubles of nonproductive capital with a ratio of 1.293 are inconsistent with total capital of 2,001 billion rubles in organizations subject to the revaluation (Table III.2) and a 1.124 ratio for that total. That is, the 1,470 figure and the ratios for total, productive, and nonproductive capital imply 645 billion rubles for nonproductive capital. (To yield 1.293 for nonproductive capital, that 645 billion rubles must include about 510 billion rubles for housing, which is inconsistent with other information on the

is not trivial for it implies that the Central Statistical Administration has revalued at least part of the nonproductive capital that has not been revalued by organizations subject to the general inventory and revaluation (pp. 113 and 115).

Because the wear-and-tear ratios by sectors in Table III.3 do not yield sharply divergent results with alternative sector weights, it is difficult to distinguish alternative hypotheses. Nevertheless, I conclude that the sector classification of wear-and-tear ratios refers to the capital of organizations subject to the revaluation for two reasons: the numerical results are consistent with this hypothesis[20] and the wear-and-tear estimates are the product of data developed in the course of the inventory for which no readily available substitutes appear to exist. The implications of this conclusion are that the sector classifications *differ* with respect to the two sets of ratios in Table III.3 and that some of the capital in public health in Table III.1 belongs to organizations subject to the revaluation.

(v) The ratios of capital at replacement cost to capital at original cost by types of assets in Table III.3 conceal considerable variation within categories. Thus, it is stated that assets with replacement cost greater than original cost show an excess of 466.8 billion rubles and those with

---

distribution of buildings in organizations subject to the revaluation.) Or, alternatively, the 569 and 597 billion ruble figures for nonproductive capital and the ratios for total productive and nonproductive capital imply, respectively, 1,295 and 1,360 billion rubles for productive capital.

(iv) These calculations can be made to yield internally consistent ruble values and ratios if we assume that within nonindustrial and nonagricultural productive capital, there are substantial amounts — at least 100 billion rubles — of capital in sectors with relatively large ratios that belong to organizations *not* subject to the revaluation. But this seems to me impossible since, if construction is excluded because of its ratio, the relevant sectors contain only 465 billion rubles of capital (Table III.1) and none seems a likely repository for relatively large amounts of capital belonging to organizations *not* subject to the revaluation.

(v) From the foregoing calculations, I conclude that nonproductive capital and its components do not refer to the capital of organizations subject to the revaluation. Furthermore, if the capital values for components of nonproductive capital in Table III.1 are used in conjunction with the corresponding ratios in Table III.3, a ratio of 1.286 is obtained for all nonproductive capital — as against 1.293 in Table III.3. Since the two ratios are so close, I conclude that the nonproductive sectors include more than the capital of organizations subject to the revaluation. They are not all inclusive, however: the capital values for housing and municipal services in Table III.1 and the ratios for all nonproductive capital and its components in Table III.3 imply a figure of 168 billion rubles for public health, and the total is 224 billion rubles.

[20] That is, $(1,470 \times 0.26) + (530 \times 0.22) = 500$, where: 1,470 and 530 are estimates of the productive and nonproductive capital, respectively, of organizations subject to the revaluation (fn. 19); and 0.26 and 0.22 are the corresponding wear-and-tear ratios from Table III.3. The 500 billion rubles are 25 percent of total capital subject to the revaluation and correspond to other ruble figures stated for January 1, 1960, wear-and-tear (Table III.1 and p. 110.) Moreover, transfer of about 25 billion rubles from productive capital to nonproductive capital leaves the result unchanged.

On the other hand, the use of the productive and nonproductive capital values in Table III.1 as weights yields 720 billion rubles, or 24 percent of total capital.

original cost greater than replacement cost an excess of 246.4 billion rubles.[21] The difference between these two figures — 220.4 billion rubles — is the same as the excess of replacement cost over original cost for all assets, either as stated in the source of the two figures or as calculated from Tables III.2 and III.3. Yet the same calculation for the categories of assets in Tables III.2 and III.3 yields an excess of replacement over original cost of only 273 billion rubles for buildings and structures and an excess of original over replacement cost of only 53 billion rubles for producers' durables.

Nevertheless, the ratios of capital at replacement cost to capital at original cost tend to exceed unity for buildings and structures and to be less than unity for producers' durables. The same tendency appears in the sector ratios in Table III.3 where the ratio for nonproductive capital — all, or virtually all, buildings and structures — appreciably exceeds that for productive capital. This, of course, is a consequence of differences in price movements, either diminished or heightened by differences in average age. The differences in price changes are cited as explanations by Soviet sources.[22]

The ratios of wear-and-tear to capital value also differ appreciably between structures and producers' durables. And again, the classification in Table III.3 conceals to some extent the variation in the ratios — reportedly from 18 to more than 32 percent for less aggregative segments of the economy.[23] Finally, the amount of wear-and-tear at replacement values placed on the books of organizations as of January 1, 1960, is stated to be 502 billion rubles, about twice that then on the books at original cost, and the difference is explained as a consequence of price level changes.[24]

(vi) From the relationships among the data in Tables III.1 and III.2, several aspects of the capital values can be clarified.

The difference between total socialized capital and total capital in organizations subject to the revaluation (Table III.1) is 437 billion rubles, which represents collective farm capital and the capital of budget organizations.[25] In the sector distribution, the 437 billion rubles appear essentially in agriculture and public health.[26]

[21] Volodarskii, p. 7.

[22] Beliakov, p. 6, and Volodarskii, p. 9.

[23] Beliakov, p. 8, and Volodarskii, p. 11.

[24] Beliakov, p. 8.

[25] Budget organizations are those whose expenditures are entirely financed from the state budget and whose revenues are budget revenues. The difference is described in this way in Beliakov, p. 4 and the description is supported by the account of the revaluation in Bunich, pp. 32–33.

[26] Small amounts appear elsewhere, for example, 11.2 billion rubles in industry representing subsidiary enterprises of budget organizations. Not all capital in public health is included in the 437 billion rubles; for example, a creche or a stadium operated by an industrial enterprise is placed in public health. From calculations described below, however,

The difference between total capital including livestock and total capital excluding private capital is 527 billion rubles. This amount represents primarily private housing and private livestock.[27]

Total capital excluding that in organizations subject to the revaluation is 964 billion rubles (Table III.1). Of this amount, somewhat over 750 billion rubles represent buildings and structures (Table III.2).[28] Thus, in the sum of private capital, collective farm capital, and the capital of budget organizations, about 200 billion rubles represent assets other than buildings and structures — primarily, livestock and collective farm producers' durables.

It is stated that of the total value of buildings in organizations subject to the revaluation, "more than" 50 percent is accounted for by housing, about 40 percent by productive buildings (except trade buildings), and about 10 percent by nonproductive buildings (including trade buildings); and that about three-fourths of the capital in trade is buildings.[29] Since three-fourths of trade plus all of municipal services equal about 10 percent of all buildings in organizations subject to the revaluation, only a small amount of buildings in organizations subject to the revaluation fall in public health. That amount is the sum of durables and structures other than buildings in municipal services, and capital belonging to budget organizations in municipal services (if any). The total amount of capital in organizations subject to the revaluation that falls in public health is equal to the sum indicated immediately above plus the value of durables and structures other than buildings that fall in public health and belong to organizations subject to the revaluation. Since municipal services as a whole account for only 60 billion rubles and since durables in public health cannot be very large, the amount of capital in question cannot reasonably exceed 40 to 50 billion rubles, and I would guess it to be about 25 billion rubles.

Finally, the indicated distribution of buildings implies that of the total value of buildings in organizations subject to the revaluation, about 450 to 475 billion rubles represent housing and about 330 to 360 billion rubles, productive buildings, excluding those in trade.

The foregoing calculations make other estimates possible. Collective farm capital is at least 213 billion rubles: that is, 437 billion rubles for capital in collective farms and budget organizations, minus 224 billion

---

it appears that the overwhelming portion of such capital belongs to budget organizations. On these points, see Bunich, pp. 32–33, 50, and p. 52, fn. 1; Tables III.1 and III.2.

[27] Beliakov, p. 4.

[28] That is, $2,185.4 - 896.6 - 538.2 = 750.6$. The "somewhat over" does not refer to the 0.6 but rather to the inclusion of transmission facilities in the second item and their exclusion from the first. The value of transmission facilities is believed to be relatively small.

[29] Beliakov, pp. 5 and 7.

rubles in public health, plus the small amount of capital in public health that belongs to organizations subject to the revaluation (say, 25 billion rubles), minus 11 billion rubles of capital in industry that belong to budget organizations. Private housing is about 470 to 490 billion rubles: that is, 942 billion rubles for all housing minus 450 to 475 billion rubles for housing belonging to organizations subject to the revaluation (socialized housing).[30] Private capital other than housing — livestock and other items — is 40 to 60 billion rubles: or, 527 billion rubles of private capital minus 470 to 490 billion rubles of private housing. The distribution of collective farm assets is somewhat as follows: 55 billion rubles of buildings and structures and 170 billion rubles of other assets; or 75 billion rubles of buildings and structures and 150 billion rubles of other assets.[31]

(vii) Rough as they are, the previous calculations appear to be internally consistent and illuminate an important methodological question underlying the capital values in Table III.1. Consider capital other than that belonging to organizations subject to the revaluation. Is such capital included at original cost, at July 1, 1955, replacement cost, or at some other valuation? Of the capital belonging to organizations subject to the revaluation, some components are reported by those organizations at original cost. Though the Central Statistical Administration itself might have revalued such components — particularly, livestock — there is no evidence that it has done so. Any errors here, however, are trivial because a portion thereof — short-lived tools and implements, at least — are at valuations which are virtually identical with July 1, 1955, replacement costs.

The important components of present concern are private capital, collective farm capital, and the capital of budget organizations. Individually and in the aggregate they are significant shares of total capital. How are they valued?

It should be observed first that the housing and livestock censuses provide a measure of physical capital in these sectors, and capital data at original cost are available for other components. Thus, the Central Statistical Administration could have obtained the relevant capital values at

---

[30] The housing of local soviets is subject to the revaluation, according to Bunich, p. 32.

[31] As indicated above, total capital excluding that in organizations subject to the revaluation is 964 billion rubles, of which buildings and structures account for more than 750 billion rubles. Take buildings and structures to be 755 billion rubles and other assets 210. Subtracting private capital other than housing from the 210 billion rubles, I obtain 150 to 170 billion rubles for collective farm assets other than buildings and structures. From the 755 billion rubles, I subtract: (i) private housing, 470 to 490 billion rubles; (ii) buildings and structures in industry that belong to organizations *not* subject to the revaluation, about 10 billion rubles (Table III.2); and (iii) buildings and structures in such areas as public health, that belong to organizations *not* subject to the revaluation, about 200 billion rubles (Table III.1 and p. 111). The result is 55 to 75 billion rubbles for collective farm buildings and structures.

July 1, 1955, prices — in part by direct valuations of physical units, in part by means of price indexes. Is there any evidence that this has been done?

First, consider private housing. The value of the January 1, 1960, stock of private housing is about the same as that of socialized housing — 470 to 490 billion rubles out of 942 billion rubles for all housing. In terms of floor space, the January 1, 1959, stocks of housing are (in millions of square meters) : socialized, 524; private urban, 257; and private rural, 430.[32] In terms of floor space, the stock of private housing is about a third greater than that of socialized housing. The value per unit of floor space in private housing is, therefore, 75 to 80 percent of the value per unit in socialized housing. The *direction* of this inequality is consistent with the hypothesis that July 1, 1955, costs are used throughout. At a specified set of replacement costs, the value per unit of floor space should be less in private than in socialized housing because of differences in construction materials used, in quality of construction, and in amenities provided. I am unprepared to say, however, that the *magnitude* of the inequality is precisely that implied by qualitative differences and comparable valuations — that 0.8 square meter of socialized housing is equivalent to 1 square meter of private housing. It is possible that the qualitative differences are, on the average, much larger, and either the valuations for private housing reflect purchases of building materials at retail prices or the valuations measure the cost of replacing existent private housing by improved rather than identical housing.[33]

In any event, private housing is not included in Table III.1 at *original* cost. According to *Narodnoe khoziaistvo 1958* (p. 641), a substantial portion of total private urban housing must be prewar housing: in 1940, floor space in private urban housing was 60 percent, and in 1926, 45 percent, of that on January 1, 1959. The corresponding percentages for private rural housing are even greater. Given the large increases in construction prices between the prewar years and 1959, the inclusion of private housing at original cost would yield a much smaller capital value, relative to that for socialized housing, than Table III.1 and the associated data indicate.

What about collective farm capital? As indicated above, the collective farm component of total capital is somewhat more than 213 billion rubles. There are several indications that this is not an original cost capital figure. According to *Narodnoe khoziaistvo 1959* (p. 423), collective farm in-

---

[32] See TSU, *Narodnoe khoziaistvo SSSR v 1958 godu* (Moscow, 1959), p. 641 (hereafter cited as *Narodnoe khoziaistvo 1958*); and S. Strumilin, "Chto takoe kommunizm," *Oktiabr'*, 1960, no. 3, p. 141.

[33] Although there are indications that the latter principle of valuation is followed, the example provided in the case of structures suggests a much more limited application (see Bunich, p. 55).

divisible funds are 185.7 billion rubles on January 1, 1960, and 167.6 billion rubles on January 1, 1959. These data, however, reflect the revaluation of livestock in terms of the new 1958 procurement prices which were much higher than pre-1958 prices: January 1, 1959, indivisible funds before the revaluation of livestock — that is, with pre-1958 livestock increments at pre-1958 valuations — are only 123.6 billion rubles. The differences between indivisible funds and productive capital are insufficient to bring the January 1, 1960, total at original cost to anything like 213 billion rubles.[34]

According to *Narodnoe khoziaistvo 1958* (p. 368), productive capital in all socialized agriculture at original cost is 149.5 billion rubles on January 1, 1954, 223.8 on January 1, 1957, and 248.9 on January 1, 1958. If these data are extrapolated to January 1, 1960, on the basis of either the average annual 1954–58 rate of increase or the 1957–58 rate of increase, the result is 310 to 320 billion rubles. On January 1, 1960, state agriculture accounts for 100 to 150 billion rubles at July 1, 1955, prices with a 7 percent differential between replacement and original cost; hence, 7 to 10 billion rubles must be added to reflect the revaluation of state agricultural capital.[35] The result, 315 to 330 billion rubles, is considerably short of total agricultural capital in Table III.1 minus private capital other than housing, that is, 419 billion rubles minus 40 to 60 billion rubles.

[34] The differences are: indivisible funds exceed capital because they include bank accounts earmarked for investment purposes; indivisible funds include nonproductive as well as productive capital; and physical assets financed from bank loans apparently enter indivisible funds only when or to the extent that, such loans are repaid. Bank funds apparently varied from 6 to 10 percent of total indivisible funds in the 1951–57 period (see P. Pavlov, *Snashivanie i amortizatsiia osnovnykh fondov* [Moscow, 1957], p. 43, and V. Chuvikov, "Kolkhoznyi stroi-velichaishee zavoevanie Oktiabria," *Ekonomika sel'skogo khoziaistva,* 1957, no. 7, p. 33). Nonproductive capital at original cost increased from 2.4 billion rubles on January 1, 1951, to 3.7 billion rubles on January 1, 1955, 4.6 billion rubles on January 1, 1958, and 5.7 billion rubles on January 1, 1959 (see Pavlov, p. 43, and A. Rumiantseva, *Obshchestvennye fondy kolkhozov* [Moscow, 1960], p. 24). The January 1, 1960, balance of unpaid long-term bank loans to collective farms was 23.6 billion rubles, a small part of which represents loans for purposes other than investment, that is, the purchase of mineral fertilizers (see the statistical supplement to *Vestnik statistiki,* 1960, no. 2, pp. 90–91).

To obtain a January 1, 1960, productive capital figure at original cost, I make the following adjustments to the January 1, 1959, figure of 123.6 billion rubles: I subtract 6 percent, or 7 billion rubles to exclude bank funds; I subtract 6 billion rubles to exclude nonproductive capital; I add 18 billion rubles to reflect the 1959 increment to capital on the assumption that the increment is approximately equal to the increment in indivisible funds; and I add 23 billion rubles of outstanding bank loans. The result is about 150 billion rubles.

[35] See Table III.3, and fn. 19. Also, some amount should probably be subtracted to reflect nonagricultural capital in subsidiary enterprises which appear elsewhere in the sector distribution. Nonagricultural capital accounts for from 7 to 9 percent of the total productive capital in the 1951–59 period (TSU, *Sel'skoe khoziaistvo SSSR* [Moscow, 1960], p. 386). However, the amount of such capital that appears elsewhere is unknown and, accordingly, I make no adjustment for nonagricultural capital.

Collective farm capital in 1960 is stated to exceed 180 billion rubles, of which buildings and structures represent one-third, livestock 30 percent, and machinery another 30 percent.[36] The implied magnitude for livestock indicates that the livestock revaluation is reflected in the data.[37] Thus, even with the livestock revaluation, collective farm capital is considerably below 213 billion rubles.

From all this I conclude that collective farm capital is *not* valued at original cost. Presumably, the Central Statistical Administration has valued the livestock component directly and has used price indexes to revalue the other components from original cost data. Again I am unable to comment on the accuracy of the valuations for want of detailed price information and capital values. The direction of the revaluation, however, appears to be correct: the emphasis of the Soviet discussion is to suggest that the original cost valuations are too low.[38] In any event, more accurate collective farm capital values and an estimate of the error involved in the collective farm component of total capital in Table III.1 must await the results of the detailed inventory and revaluation now under way.

No recent original cost capital values for budget organizations have been published. Hence, one cannot compare capital values. Original cost values do exist for budget organizations and, at least for those components which also appear in other state organizations, the price handbooks provide the relevant valuations. By using such valuations and price indexes, the Central Statistical Administration could obtain replacement cost capital values. The calculations in connection with Table III.2 suggest that it has done so (see fn. 19).

[36] See N. Nikitin, "O pereotsenke osnovnykh fondov kolkhozov," *Uchet i finansy v kolkhozakh i sovkhozakh,* 1960, no. 11, p. 24. The date of the capital figure is given only as "now," but the article was published in late 1960.

[37] At original cost, collective farm livestock was about 20 billion rubles in the 1952–55 period (Pavlov, p. 43). On January 1, 1958, livestock in all socialized agriculture was 36 billion rubles according to the original cost capital data, and the share of livestock in total productive capital at original cost declined slightly between January 1, 1958, and January 1, 1959 (see *Narodnoe khoziaistvo 1958,* p. 368; and TSU, *Sel'skoe khoziaistvo SSSR,* p. 386). Given the extrapolation of original cost capital to January 1, 1960 (p. 114) and the January 1, 1959, share of livestock in the total, the livestock figure on January 1, 1960, for all socialized agriculture appears to be about 45 billion rubles. Thus, the implied collective farm livestock figure of 55 to 60 billion rubles indicates that the effects of the January 1, 1959, revaluation of collective farm livestock are incorporated in the data.

[38] See Nikitin, pp. 24–25. The explanations advanced are: that original cost values for buildings and structures generally omit the value of labor participation in kind and of the use of internal transportation facilities; and that machinery and equipment are purchased by collective farms from the machine tractor stations in 1958 and 1959 at prices which reflect not replacement cost but depreciated values determined by regional commissions fixing those prices.

However, at least one offset occurs: the purchases by collective farms of building materials at retail prices and of machinery at wholesale prices plus a special markup.

The capital value including collective farm capital and the capital of budget organizations is described in *Narodnoe khoziaistvo 1959* (p. 65) in essentially the same way as the capital of organizations subject to the revaluation: the 2,438 figure in Table III.1 is stated to be at "present prices" and the 2,001.1 figure at "present (replacement) values." Finally, when the January 1, 1960, capital values are considered along with the capital indexes, the results suggest at least roughly consistent price levels for the various components of January 1, 1960, capital.[39]

For the foregoing reasons, I take all the components of the January 1, 1960, capital values in Table III.1 to be, at least roughly, at July 1, 1955, prices. The important reservations are with respect to the accuracy of the calculations of private capital, collective farm capital, and the capital of budget organizations.

3. Some Implications

The availability of Russian capital data and the recent appearance of several monographs on American capital formation make possible various intertemporal and international comparisons which have been missing in discussions of Russian economic development. Here, I attempt four comparisons: of Russian investment and capital; of Russian and American distributions of capital by segment of the economy; of Russian and American distributions of capital by type of assets; and of Russian and American ratios of capital to gross national product.

Each of these is tentative and for much the same reasons. Although as yet I have found no emetic ingredients, the Russian capital values are still in an ingestive stage. I am not as fluent with American data as I should be; others who are more fluent will, I hope, correct any errors or omissions. Various adjustments are necessary to achieve comparability of the basic measures, but the data required for such adjustments tend to be absent or inadequate. Finally, I am unprepared to comment on some elementary aspects of the comparisons: (i) in the absence of a comparative study of ruble prices and the dollar prices in terms of which the U.S. data are compiled, it is impossible to know to what extent the capital distributions reflect significant differences between ruble and dollar price relatives; (ii) in the absence of the necessary data, it is impossible either to add capital consumption to available American net capital values or to subtract all wear-and-tear from available Russian gross capital values and, thereby, to know to what extent the comparisons are vitiated by the admixture of net and gross capital values.

Despite these difficulties, the indicated comparisons are undertaken without much additional comment or caveat. The necessary reservations

[39] See *Kaplan,* chap. 6.

apply throughout. My intention is to present first approximations; my hope is that the results, rough as they are, will prove more provocative than provoking.

Appended to this chapter are six tables, III.7 to III.12, with sources and notes. There, and in Table III.1, are the basic data that underlie the following comparisons.

Investment and capital. To obtain some notion of recent and prospective changes in the distribution of Russian capital by segments of the economy, I juxtapose investment and capital distributions in Table III.4. The under-

Table III.4
USSR: Distributions of Capital and Investment by Segment of the Economy
(percent)

Segment	1952–59 investment	January 1, 1960, capital	P 1960–65 investment
Total, excluding livestock	100	100	100
Industry and construction	42.7	30.2	42.4
Agriculture	15.8	9.9	14.3
Transport and communications	8.4	13.7	8.2
Other	33.1	46.1	35.0
Nonagricultural total	100	100	100
Industry and construction	50.7	33.6	49.5
Transport and communications	9.9	15.2	9.6
Other	39.3	51.2	40.9
Total industry and construction	100[a]	100	100[a]
Electric power stations	13.5	11.1	11.7
Coal	11.0	8.2	7.1
Petroleum and gas	13.0	6.8	15.6
Chemicals	3.6	4.6	9.5
Construction industry and building materials	11.1	11.3	10.1
Ferrous metallurgy	7.3	9.0	9.0
Timber, woodworking, and paper	4.6	5.5	5.4
Light industry ⎫		4.2	3.0
Textiles ⎬	7.2	3.0	1.9
Food industry ⎭		8.5	4.7
Other	28.8	30.7	23.9

[a] Refer to the 1952–58 and P 1959–65 investment distributions.
Note: The capital distributions are from Table III.1 with an estimated 138 billion rubles of livestock subtracted from the agricultural and total capital values. The investment distributions are from Table III.7 with adjustments as indicated in note 5 to that table. The capital distributions in Table III.1 specifically include machine-building and metalworking, and the investment distributions in Table III.7 only show machine-building separately; hence, for present purposes machine-building and metalworking appear in the item "Other" in the branch of industry distribution.

lying investment data are those for 1952–58 and P 1959–65 as stated in the Seven-Year Plan (see Table III.7 in the appendix). For P 1959–65, the investment data are ranges and I use the larger figures. In the sector distributions — but *not* in the distributions by branches of industry and construction — I have subtracted 1959 investment from the P 1959–65 figures and added it to 1952–58 investment. Other adjustments and estimates have been introduced to make the investment and capital data more comparable in scope.[40] The capital distributions refer to the capital values in Table III.1 except that livestock is subtracted from total and agricultural capital.[41]

Both the investment and capital data are in terms of July 1, 1955, prices and the unified cost estimates introduced in 1956. However, the use of some special valuation procedures for the capital revaluation might yield some incomparabilities between the investment and capital values.

There are also incomparabilities of another sort. Because of unfinished construction and capital retirements, the distribution of investment by segments of the economy may differ from the distribution of net increments to capital (net of retirements). There is evidence of sizeable increases in unfinished construction during the 1952–58 period and, for the prewar years, of a concentration of such increases in industrial construction.[42] Capital retirements, also, are likely to be heavily concentrated in industry and construction because so much of producers' durables falls in this sector and because temporary structures are used in construction. I have calculated the ratio of net capital increments to investment for industry and construction at 1955 prices for 1951–57 at 0.75.[43] If I assume

[40] See Table III.7, notes 4 and 5, for some details; others will appear in *Kaplan.*

[41] The basis for the livestock estimate will appear in *Kaplan,* Table C-5, note 5. The estimate involves the use of prerevaluation and postrevaluation capital indexes for the productive sectors and the derivation of livestock as the difference between agriculture including and excluding livestock. The pre- and postrevaluation indexes for the productive sectors are from *Narodnoe khoziaistvo 1959,* p. 66; *Narodnoe khoziaistvo 1958,* pp. 58–59; TSU, *Sel'skoe khoziaistvo SSSR,* p. 385.

[42] See *Kaplan,* Table C-6, note 2; *Tretii piatiletnii plan razvitiia narodnogo khoziaistva Soiuza SSR (1938–1942 gg.)* (Moscow, 1939), p. 225; *Itogi vypolneniia vtorogo piatiletnego plana razvitiia narodnogo khoziaistva Soiuza SSR* (Moscow, 1939), pp. 71, 72; A. Ferberg, "Vazhnoe uslovie vypolneniia plana kapital'nogo stroitel'stva," *Voprosy ekonomiki,* 1958, no. 12, p. 53; I. Sher and B. Savvin, "Nezavershennoe stroitel'stvo i puti ego sokrashcheniia," *Finansy SSSR,* 1959, no. 3, p. 29; B. Sokolov, "Sokrashchenie ob'emov nezavershennogo stroitel' stva — pervostepennaia narodnokhoziaistvennaia zadacha," *Voprosy ekonomiki,* 1958, no. 11, p. 38; N. Kachalov, "Krupnyi istochnik povysheniia effektivnosti kapital' nykh vlozhenii," *Voprosy ekonomiki,* 1959, no. 1, p. 49; V. Garbuzov, "Rol' finansov v razvitii sotsialisticheskogo sel'skogo khoziaistva," in *Finansy i sotsialisticheskoe stroitel'stvo* (Moscow, 1957), p. 168.

[43] See *Kaplan,* Table C-6, note 4. This comparison accepts the capital indexes in *Narodnoe khoziaistvo 1959,* p. 66, and *Narodnoe khoziaistvo 1958,* pp. 58–59, as reliable constant-price indexes for the given period (see *Kaplan,* chap. 6).

There are no independent data on capital retirements, but for petroleum and gas, January 1, 1960, capital is less than 1952–58 investment, and for coal, January 1, 1960,

that retirements and increases in unfinished construction occur only in industry and construction — an assumption contrary to fact — the 0.75 ratio applied to industry reduces the 1951–59 share of industry and construction to 36 percent. Extrapolation of the same ratio and assumption to the P 1960–65 investment data similarly reduces the share of industry and construction to 36 percent. Thus, the inequality between the industry shares in investment and capital is preserved.

I also show the investment and capital distributions in Table III.4 for the nonagricultural totals. I do this for two reasons: the adjustments of the investment and capital data to eliminate livestock are subject to possibly appreciable errors and I have doubts on other grounds of the comparability of the agricultural investment and capital data.[44]

The primary findings in regard to the sector distributions are: for industry and construction and for agriculture, the investment shares exceed the capital shares; and for the remaining sectors, the capital shares exceed the investment shares. In other words, if we assume fulfillment of the Seven-Year Plan investment goals and consider the capital distributions on January 1, 1952, 1960, and 1966, the shares of industry and agriculture are increasing and the shares of transport and other sectors are decreasing.

With respect to the branch of industry distributions in Table III.4, the following differences between the investment and capital distributions are noteworthy: the shares of fuels in 1952–58 and P 1959–65 investment — especially, of petroleum and gas — far exceed their share in capital; the share of chemicals in P 1959–65 investment far exceeds their share in capital which in turn exceeds somewhat their share in 1952–58 investment; the shares in investment of the light and food industries combined are appreciable less than their share in capital. I am reluctant to infer the suggested changes over time in the distribution of capital from these data because of the relative importance of capital retirements and unfinished construction in industry. It may be useful, however, to rank the industries in terms of the ratio of investment to capital. The rankings, implicit in Table III.4 are:[45]

---

capital is only 15 percent larger (Tables III.1 and III.7). I take these observations to be relevant because for both branches capital retirements should be relatively large as old wells and mines are exhausted and new ones are worked.

[44] See *Kaplan*, Table C-4, note 2, and Table C-6, note 4. The difficulties here refer primarily to the investment data.

[45] The underlying ruble data are in Tables III.1 and III.7. Only the larger P 1959–65 investment figures are used, but the ranking would be the same with the smaller figures. The rankings can also be obtained, of course, by ordering the quotients of the percentages in Table III.4.

It should be noted that other industries include the glass, china, and pottery industry with 0.6 percent of total capital; nonferrous metallurgy with 3.9 percent of total capital; and machine-building and metalworking with 19.0 percent of total capital. Machine-

Rank	Ratio of 1952–58 investment to 1960 capital	Ratio of P 1959–65 investment to 1960 capital
1	Petroleum and gas	Petroleum and gas
2	Coal	Chemicals
3	Electric power	Electric power
4	Building materials and construction	Ferrous metallurgy
5	Other industries	Timber, woodworking, and paper
6	Timber, woodworking, and paper	Building materials and construction
7	Ferrous metallurgy	Coal
8	Chemicals	Other industries
9	Light and food	Light and food

The horizontal lines indicate where the ratio for industry and construction falls: for example, in terms of the relation of 1952–58 investment to 1960 capital, the petroleum, coal, and electric power industries have higher ratios and the other industries, lower ratios, than industry and construction as a whole.

One final set of investment and capital comparisons seems useful. To obtain some notion of the rate at which additions to capital are planned, I determine the ratio of P 1960–65 investment to January 1, 1960, capital. From the data in Table III.1 in section 2,[46] and in Table III.7 and note 4 to Table III.7 in the appendix, the results are:

	Ratio of P 1960–65 investment to January 1, 1960, capital
Total, excluding livestock	0.88
Industry and construction	1.24
Agriculture	1.27
Transport and communications	0.53
Other	0.67
Nonagricultural total	0.84

Even if we assume that the Seven-Year Plan investment goal will be fulfilled, these ratios are only approximate measures of the rate of additions to capital. The ratios are too high because the numerators do not take account of capital retirements and increases in unfinished construction.[47] They are too low because the denominators include wear-and-tear

building alone (excluding metalworking) accounts for 11.8 percent of the total investment in 1952–58 and 10.7 to 10.9 percent in P 1959–65. In all cases, the total refers to industry and construction.

[46] As in Table III.4, 138 billion rubles are subtracted from total and agricultural capital to exclude livestock.

[47] If the ratio of 0.75 for the relationship of net increments to investment in industry

on existing capital. Each of these factors is large: (i) according to the capital inventory January 1, 1960, wear-and-tear is at least 500 billion rubles; (ii) extrapolation of 1951–57 relationships suggests that capital retirements and increases in unfinished construction in industry alone amount to some 250 billion rubles. On balance, the ratios for the totals appear to be too low and none of the ratios, except that for agriculture, is likely to be appreciably too high.[48] Thus, these calculations suggest quite rapid rates of *planned* capital formation.

The rapidity of these rates of capital formation can be judged by comparison with similar ratios for the United States. Tables III.8 and III.9 in the appendix show some data on capital net of depreciation at 1929 prices from recent studies of American capital formation. From the same studies, I obtain annual gross investment at 1929 prices. Beginning with capital at a specified date, I cumulate annual investment for the subsequent six years and express the sum as a ratio of beginning capital. These ratios are comparable with those for the USSR in that the periods are of approximately the same duration — six years. They are *not* comparable in one important respect: the denominators of the American ratios are net capital whereas the denominators of the Russian ratios are *gross* capital.[49] Since the numerators in both cases are gross investment, the appropriate American ratios are substantially *smaller* than the ratios I present. For selected periods, the American ratios of investment to capital are:[50] 1881–86 investment in relation to 1880 capital, 0.67; 1901–06 in-

---

(p. 118) is applied here, the ratios of investment to capital become: total, 0.79; industry and construction, 0.93; and nonagricultural total, 0.74. The totals, however, need to be reduced even further to reflect retirements and unfinished construction in sectors other than industry. The present calculation only suggests the proper minimum ratio for industry and its relationship, on extreme assumptions, to the ratios for other sectors.

[48] For industry and construction, the use of the wear-and-tear percentages in Table III.3 to reduce January 1, 1960, capital and of the 0.75 relationship to reduce P 1960–65 investment yield the same ratio as that calculated before the adjustments, that is, 1.24. For agriculture, comparisons between investment and capital in *Kaplan,* Tables C-4 and C-6, indicate that in the post-1956 period agricultural investment is substantially overstated relative to the corresponding capital increments; hence the agricultural ratio is appreciably too high.

[49] However, to the extent that American depreciation data reflect obsolescence and the Russian gross capital values take account of obsolescence in the valuations assigned (p. 100) this disparity is reduced.

[50] The capital data are from Table III.8. The investment data are from Simon Kuznets, *Capital in the American Economy: Its Formation and Financing* (Princeton, 1961), Tables R-5, R-7, R-30, and R-33, pp. 492, 497, 576–579, 596–597. Kuznets includes munitions in producers' durables; for present purposes, I subtract gross munitions. I obtain a 1954 figure by applying to the Kuznets 1953 figure (excluding munitions) the percentage increase in investment between 1953 and 1954 computed from U.S. Department of Commerce, *U.S. Income and Output* (Washington, 1958), Tables I-2 and V-4. In the latter computation, I add new public construction to private construction and producers' durables.

The substitution of the capital data in estimate B, Table III.8, for those in estimate A increases the ratios 0.02 to 0.03. The calculation for different periods yields essentially the

vestment in relation to 1900 capital, 0.61; 1923–28 investment in relation to 1922 capital, 0.59; and 1949–54 investment in relation to 1948 capital, 0.67. Thus, the American ratios of investment to *net* capital are appreciably below the Russian ratio of planned investment to *gross* capital. For capital of comparable scope, the disparity is even greater.[51]

Distribution of capital by segments of the economy. The Russian and American data on capital differ in at least one important respect: the former are gross, and the latter net, of depreciation. The Russian estimates of percentage wear-and-tear (Table III.3) do not cover all components of capital and, even if they did, it is far from clear that estimates of wear-and-tear derived from an inventory of assets are equivalent to accumulated depreciation derived from accounting data or estimates of service life. Thus, the conclusions from comparisons of Russian and American capital distributions are tenuous. The comparisons are made as first approximations and for those conclusions which appear to be independent of the differences between gross and net capital values.

In Table III.5, comparison is made of the Russian and American distributions of capital by sectors of the economy. The American distributions refer to capital at 1929 prices. Although for present purposes capital data

---

same results. The capital data in Table III.10, Panel I, and the investment data from Kuznets, *Capital in the American Economy,* yield the following ratios of investment to beginning capital:

1871–76	1880–85	1890–95	1900–05	1910–15	1920–25
0.57	0.65	0.72	0.60	0.49	0.48

Substitution of the capital data in Table III.10, Panel II, yields the following ratios of investment to beginning capital:

1899–1904	1909–14	1913–18	1919–24	1924–29	1948–53
0.62	0.55	0.46	0.47	0.61	0.68

[51] The Russian ratio is intended to suggest the rate of capital formation implied by investment data as projected in the Seven-Year Plan. Several components of the investment data may be subject to special reservations: collective farm investment and private housing construction may reflect outlays at prices above wholesale prices of July 1, 1955; and private and noncentralized investment may be unduly optimistic. Furthermore, in connection with the 1960 budget, concern was expressed in *Izvestiia,* October 28, 1959, p. 5, about the unduly large share of noncentralized in total investment; and more recently, a negative attitude has appeared toward private housing construction (see Anon., "Kto ne rabotaet tot ne est," *Kommunist,* 1960, no. 14, pp. 18–19).

Noncentralized investment and private housing in the Seven-Year Plan amount to something like 585 billion rubles, of which 66 billion rubles occurred in 1959 (see Table III.7, notes 4 and 5, and *Narodnoe khoziaistvo 1959,* pp. 542–543). If we subtract this amount — 585 minus 66 billion rubles — from P 1960–65 investment, the ratio of investment to capital is 0.70, still appreciably above the American ratios. It is very unlikely that correct accounts for all the reservations mentioned above would yield a ratio below this: (i) there is no indication of zero noncentralized investment; (ii) there are indications of a substitution of public or cooperative for private housing; (iii) the difference between zero noncentralized investment and private housing, on the one hand, and actual noncentralized investment plus increased public housing, on the other, seems adequate to allow for any overstatement involved in the collective farm investment data.

Table III.5

USSR and USA: Distributions of Capital by Sector (percent)

Sector	USSR capital, gross of depreciation	USA capital, net of depreciation, at 1929 prices			
	January 1, 1960	June 1, 1880	June 1, 1900	December 31, 1922	December 31, 1948
Total capital	100	100	100	100	100
Industry	28.3	6.3	10.2	17.4	19.6
Mining and manufacturing	24.9	6.3	9.5	15.2	15.5
Electric power production	3.4	0	0.7	2.2	4.1
Agriculture	9.9	18.4	9.5	8.5	7.2
Transport and communications	13.7	33.0	22.2	17.7	14.4
Housing	33.3	29.2	38.8	32.5	32.0
Other	14.7	13.1	19.3	24.0	26.8
Total capital, except "other"	100	100	100	100	100
Industry	33.2	7.2	12.6	22.8	26.7
Mining and manufacturing	29.2	7.2	11.8	20.0	21.2
Electric power production	4.0	0	0.8	2.8	5.5
Agriculture	11.7	21.1	11.8	11.2	9.8
Transport and communications	16.1	38.0	27.5	23.3	19.6
Housing	39.1	33.6	48.1	42.7	43.8
Total nonresidential capital	100	100	100	100	100
Industry	42.4	8.9	16.6	25.7	28.8
Mining and manufacturing	37.4	8.9	15.5	22.5	22.8
Electric power production	5.0	0	1.1	3.2	6.0
Agriculture	14.9	25.9	15.6	12.6	10.6
Transport and communications	20.5	46.5	36.2	26.2	21.2
Other	22.1	18.7	31.6	35.5	39.5

Note: USSR data are from Table III.1 with 138 billion rubles of livestock subtracted from agricultural and total capital. USA data are from Table III.8 with the A estimates for other and total capital employed throughout. Electric power production is the sum of lines 4a and 6 of Table III.8. Transportation and communications is the difference between "Public utilities" and "Privately owned electric light and power" in Table III.8. Housing is line 5 of Table III.8.

at current replacement costs are preferable, such distributions do not show mining and manufacturing separately, and, hence, will be employed only to indicate the difference resulting from the use of current rather than 1929 prices (see Table III.12 in the appendix and pp. 126–128).

Three separate distributions are distinguished in Table III.5 for different reasons. The distributions of total capital refer to Tables III.1 (in section 2) and III.8 (in the appendix) as they stand except for the elimination of livestock from the Russian data. Since "other capital" in Table III.8 is an estimate, the distributions of "total capital except other" are considered separately. Finally, because housing presents special problems, the distributions of total nonresidential capital are also considered.

A few words are necessary with respect to the comparability of the sector classifications. Industry in the Russian data includes fishing, the felling and hauling of timber, and certain specialized repair plants (see fn. 16), all of which appear to be excluded from American data. Fishing and timber, and possibly repair plants as well, account for no more than about 1 percentage point in the Russian industry share (see fn. 57). This relative overstatement is offset at least in part by the inclusion of force-account as well as contract construction in other capital in the Russian data whereas only contract construction is so included in the American data. The American housing data refer to nonfarm residential construction because of the difficulties in separating residential from all agricultural structures. Hence, relative to the Russian shares, the American housing shares are understated and agricultural shares are overstated. The American transport and communications data include steam railroads, street and electric railways, local bus lines, other transportation, the telephone and telegraph system, the radio and television industries, water supply, and irrigation.[52] Some of these, for example, water supply and irrigation, are not in Russian transport data but these are minor discrepancies.[53] However, a divergence in the opposite direction appears to be quantitatively important: the American data exclude, and the Russian data include, roads and the mail system. On balance, the American transport and communications shares appear to be understated relative to the Russian share.

The American data in Table III.5 are based on one of two estimates of total and other capital in Table III.8 (in the appendix). However, the

[52] See Melville J. Ulmer, *Capital in Transportation, Communications, and Public Utilities: Its Formation and Financing* (Princeton, 1960), appendix B.

[53] The Russian transport capital data apparently do include local bus lines and street railways (Bunich, pp. 51–52). However, even if such components were excluded from the transport data and included in municipal services, the difference would not be important. The capital in *all* municipal services is only 16 percent of that in transport and communications (see Table III.1).

alternative estimate yields only small differences in the relative distribution except for the share attributed to other capital.[54]

What conclusions are suggested by Table III.5? Consider, first, the sector shares in total capital. The Russian mining and manufacturing share substantially exceeds each corresponding American share; the Russian electric power share exceeds each American share except that for 1948; the Russian agriculture share exceeds each American share except that for 1880; the Russian transport and communications share is less than each American share; the Russian housing share is about the same as that of American housing in 1922 and 1948.

The observations regarding housing are puzzling. Of course, some American housing is included in agricultural capital; by 1948, however, the share of agriculture is only 7 percent, so that the addition of farm residences would not raise the American housing share much. Other American data at 1929 prices yield only slightly different estimates and, in one case, a lower one.[55] One possibility is that "other capital" is overstated. But in the distributions of total capital except other, the American shares of housing in 1922 and 1948 are still not much larger than the Russian share. Moreover, a larger American share of other capital seems plausible in terms of the components of other capital, and the previously noted inequalities in the shares of industry, agriculture, and transport and communications hold also for the 1922 and 1948 distributions of total capital except other.

It is also possible that the Russian share of housing in total capital is overstated. Such overstatement may arise from too high a valuation of private housing, which the capital revaluation indicates to be about 50 percent of total housing (see p. 113). Furthermore, private housing in the USSR tends to be older than socialized housing and inferior in quality, and net capital values or capital values net of wear-and-tear might show a housing share appreciably below that in Table III.5.

Because of the problems with respect to housing, I consider the distributions of total nonresidential capital in Table III.5. In the American

---

[54] The distributions of total capital in Table III.8 with estimate B substituted for estimate A are (in percentages of total): industry — for 1900, 10.7, 1922, 18.4, and 1948, 20.3; agriculture — for 1900, 10.0, 1922, 9.0, and 1948, 7.5; transport and communications — for 1900, 23.3, 1922, 18.7, and 1948, 14.9; housing — for 1900, 40.9, 1922, 34.4, and 1948, 33.3; and other — for 1900, 15.1, 1922, 19.5, and 1948, 23.9.

[55] As fn. 54 indicates, the alternative estimates in Table III.8 yield housing shares of 34.4 and 33.3 percent in 1922 and 1948, respectively. Goldsmith's data indicate housing shares on the same dates of 35.3 percent and, incorporating his alternative lower estimates of housing, 31.5 and 31.6 percent (see Raymond W. Goldsmith, *A Study of Saving in the United States* [Princeton, 1956], vol. III, Tables W-3 and W-4, pp. 20–21 and 23). These are the national wealth estimates, except for the housing component, that underlie estimate B in Table III.8.

distributions, agriculture includes farm residences and is, therefore, somewhat overstated relative to other sectors. If, in addition, we recall that American other capital includes some transport capital, the previous inequalities in the shares still hold: (i) Russian industry exceeds American industry; (ii) Russian agriculture exceeds American agriculture in 1922 and 1948; (iii) Russian transport and communications is exceeded by the corresponding American shares.

Suppose we assume that the Russian capital values net of wear-and-tear are more comparable with the American capital values, and consider the impact of the Russian wear-and-tear percentages in Table III.3 on the comparisons. Those percentages refer only to capital in organizations subject to the revaluation; but if residential capital and livestock are excluded from the Russian distribution, the omissions reduce to collective farms and budget organizations. I assume that the wear-and-tear percentage for collective farm capital is equal to or greater than that for state agriculture in Table III.3; that the wear-and-tear percentage for the capital of budget organizations — all, or virtually all, structures — is about the same as that for sectors whose assets are predominantly structures, that is, the nonproductive sectors; and that the exclusion of socialized housing from Table III.3 and the addition of the capital of budget organizations and collective farms leaves the wear-and-tear percentage for total capital essentially unchanged, that is, 25 percent. On this basis the Russian distribution of total nonresidential capital is affected by the subtraction of wear-and-tear as follows: the share of industry is unchanged; the shares of agriculture and of transport and communications are reduced; and the share of other capital is increased. If, furthermore, Russian housing is overvalued and/or has proportionately greater wear-and-tear than any other sector, the share in total capital of each sector except housing is further increased and that for housing is reduced.

As indicated above, these observations are based on American capital at 1929 prices. Since the relative dollar prices of capital goods may differ between 1929 and other years, the use of current prices may change the American capital distributions. In Table III.12 (in the appendix) I compare sector distributions of American capital at 1929 prices and at current replacement costs. The total capital figures are obtained in the same way as the estimate B totals in Table III.8 (in the appendix). However, the sector distributions differ between Tables III.12 and III.8 because mining and manufacturing capital at current replacement costs cannot be obtained for comparison with the 1929-price values. The data for the following sectors are obtained in the same way, from the same sources, as in Table III.8: agriculture, public utilities, electric light and power, nonfarm residential construction. One sector, which does not appear explicitly in Table III.8, is added in Table III.12: government and institutional structures. This leaves a residual, other capital, which consists largely — but substantially less than wholly — of manufacturing and mining capital.

For present purposes, the primary effects of the substitution of current for 1929 prices are: (i) a reduction in the 1900 and 1922 shares, and an increase in the 1948 share, of nonfarm residential construction in total capital; (ii) similar changes in the shares of total structures in total capital; (iii) opposite changes in the shares of other capital; and (iv) reduction in the 1948 shares of agriculture and of public utilities. Thus, in 1948 nonfarm residential construction is about 37 percent of total capital in the USA at replacement costs (Table III.12), and with farm residential construction the housing share approaches 40 percent; the Russian share of housing in gross capital is 32 percent (Table III.5) and in *net* capital probably less.

Since other capital consists largely of manufacturing and mining capital, Table III.12 suggests that the 1948 shares of industry and of the manufacturing and mining component in total capital are smaller in current than in 1929 prices.[56] Thus, the share of industry and, *a fortiori*, the share of mining and manufacturing in the Russian distribution substantially exceed the corresponding American shares. This inequality holds whether American capital is valued at 1929 or current prices, whatever the conclusion with respect to the valuation of Russian housing, and whether or not Russian wear-and-tear is subtracted from capital.

The findings with respect to the shares of agriculture and of transport and communications are not so clear. The Russian share of agriculture substantially exceeds the 1948 American share at current and at 1929 prices, and the excess would be larger if farm residential capital were excluded from the American agriculture data. However, this result depends in part upon my estimate for livestock and upon the accuracy of the collective farm capital figure, which is not a product of the capital inventory. Furthermore, wear-and-tear of collective farm capital is unknown, so that the agricultural share in *net* capital values is problematic.

The Russian share of transport and communications is between the 1948 American shares — public utilities less electric power — in 1929 and in current prices. The American data, however, exclude roads and the mail system. Moreover, the wear-and-tear percentages in Russian transport and communications are larger than the average for the economy as a whole. Therefore, unless the housing wear-and-tear percentages are appreciably larger than those for transport, it would seem that the Russian share in *net* capital is somewhat below the corresponding American share in 1948.

---

[56] The same suggestion emerges from the behavior of the 1948 shares of total structures and of housing, since producers' durables are heavily concentrated in manufacturing and mining and the shares of structures other than housing appear to be about the same or even smaller in current than in 1929 prices (Table III.12, lines 2, 3, and 5).

The Russian share is clearly less than the earlier American shares at 1929 or current prices.

Let me turn now to a comparison in Table III.6 of Russian and American capital distributions by branches of industry and by branches of manufacturing and mining. The American distributions are of capital values at 1929 prices; no corresponding distributions are available for capital at current replacement costs. The dates of the American distributions in Table III.6 differ from those in Table III.5 because the sources of the data are different: Table III.6 includes all dates for which the manufacturing and mining breakdowns are available.

The classifications for which both Russian and American capital values are available are less aggregative than the classifications employed in Table III.6. By aggregating the underlying data, I have attempted to achieve greater comparability. Some incomparabilities remain: Russian mining and manufacturing include some branches excluded from the American data — specialized repair shops in metals and metal products, the felling and hauling of timber in forest products, and fishing in foods. These branches appear to be insignificant in relation to total industrial capital, but their exclusion might make a perceptible difference in the share of foods.[57]

The major results of Table III.6 are as follows: (i) The American share of electric power in total industry has increased substantially over time and in 1929 and 1948 far exceeds the Russian share. (ii) Except for 1890, the American share of fuels in manufacturing and mining exceeds the Russian share. The relative importance of coal, on the one hand, and petroleum and gas, on the other, is strikingly reversed in the American as against the Russian distribution. (iii) Although the shares of chemicals, and stone, clay, and glass products are about equal in the Russian and American distributions of mining and manufacturing capital, less than one-half of the Russian capital is in chemicals.[58] (iv) The American share of metals and metal products in mining and manufacturing has increased considerably from 1890 to 1953, but in 1953 is still appreciably below the Russian share. It should be noted also that about 14 percent of post-1890 American capital in metals and metal products is accounted for by the motor vehicles industry: the shares of metals and metal products, excluding motor vehicles, are 23 percent in 1929, 26 percent in 1948, and

[57] Of 72.8 billion rubles of capital in the food industry, the fish industry accounts for 20.8 billion rubles (Table III.1). Not all of this should be excluded: fish processing, preserving, and canning should be included. If we assume that fishing accounts for 15 billion rubles, the share of foods is reduced from 10.3 to 8.4 percent. If repair shops and the felling and hauling of timber are assumed to account for 15 billion rubles and are also excluded, the resulting share of foods is 8.6 percent.

[58] See Table III.1; and Daniel Creamer, Sergei Dobrovolsky, and Israel Borenstein, *Capital in Manufacturing and Mining* (Princeton, 1960), Tables 23, A-9, A-15, and B-11, pp. 73–74, 248–251, 270–272, and 319.

Table III.6
USSR and USA: Distributions of Capital by Branch of Industry
(percent)

Branch	USSR capital, gross of depreciation	USA capital, net of depreciation, at 1929 prices			
	January 1, 1960	1890	1929	1948	1953
Total industry	100	100	100	100	—
Manufacturing	88.1	85.6	69.2	69.9	—
Mining	88.1	12.4	14.1	10.2	—
Electric power production	11.9	2.0	16.7	19.9	—
Total manufacturing and mining	100	100	100	100	100
Fuels	19.3	7.9	24.9	28.6	24.6
Coal	10.0	3.2	2.3	1.4	1.3
Petroleum and gas	8.3	4.7	22.6	27.2	23.3
Chemicals and stone, clay, and glass products	12.3	9.6	10.0	11.1	14.3
Metals and metal products	38.7	27.5	27.2	29.9	32.3
Forest products and paper, pulp, and products	6.7	13.7	9.7	7.5	7.0
Light and food industries	15.4	35.0	22.0	16.5	13.3
Textiles and products	4.2	15.8	9.0	5.7	4.7
Foods, beverages, and tobacco	10.3	16.7	12.2	10.4	8.3
Other	7.6	6.4	6.2	6.3	8.5

Notes: Data derived from Tables III.1 and III.9.
The dash (—) indicates that data are not available.

28 percent in 1953.[59] Unfortunately, the comparable Russian shares are unknown. (v) The American shares of the light and food industries — and of textiles and foods, separately — have declined markedly from 1890 to 1953. By 1953, the American share of the light and food industries is below the Russian share: textiles are a larger share and foods a smaller share in the American than in the Russian distribution, but foods are more important than textiles in both distributions. The Russian share of foods, and, therefore, of light and food industries combined, is overstated by the inclusion of the fishing industry, but adjustment for this overstatement is not likely to reverse the inequality (see fn. 57).

Would Russian capital values net of depreciation or wear-and-tear yield markedly different distributions by branches of industry? Unfortunately, there are no detailed or unambiguous data on this question. There is a statement that the ratio of revalued capital to capital at original cost on January 1, 1960, is 0.96 for ferrous metallurgy and machine-building, 1.14 for light industry, and 1.13 for the foods industry.[60] The corresponding ratio for industry as a whole is 0.98. Since these ratios are an indication of the average age of the assets involved — more precisely, the relative importance of assets acquired in 1955 or later — it appears that the assets in the light and food industries are older, and the assets of machine-building and ferrous metallurgy somewhat younger, than those for industry as a whole. If depreciation or wear-and-tear is proportional to age, these data suggest an appreciably smaller share of the light and food industries in *net* capital than in *gross* capital. The share of metals and metal products in *net* capital is probably about the same as its share in *gross* capital, although one cannot be sure because machine-building and ferrous metallurgy fail to exhaust metals and metal products and there are contrary indications below for machine-building and nonferrous metallurgy.

There is also a statement that the ratio of wear-and-tear to capital at replacement cost is 0.32 for the timber, woodworking, and paper industries (Table III.6); 0.18 for electric power stations; "somewhat larger" than the average for all industry in some branches of the light and food industries and in machine-building and nonferrous metallurgy.[61] Again, these data suggest a smaller share of the light and food industries in capital *net* of wear-and-tear than in *gross* capital. The uncertainty exists because of ignorance about the ratio for other branches of the light and food industries: is it more than "somewhat larger" or not larger at all? Uncertainty also exists in the case of metals and metal products because of the absence of a ratio for ferrous metallurgy and metalworking. If the

[59] See Creamer *et al.*, Tables A-9 and A-15.
[60] Beliakov, p. 7.
[61] Volodarskii, p. 11.

indicated ratios for electric power stations and for timber, woodworking, and paper are applied, the share of electric power stations in industrial capital *net* of wear-and-tear is 13 percent, compared with 12 percent in Table III.6; and the share of timber, woodworking, and paper in mining and manufacturing capital is 6.1 percent as against 6.7 percent. If the variation in wear-and-tear percentages by branches of industry is no greater than these scattered data indicate, the distribution of capital *net* of wear-and-tear will not differ appreciably from the distribution of gross capital.

The relative importance of structures. I assume that the Russian and American categories of structures and other capital are identical. Although I am sure there are marginal differences, my impression is that this is an approximately correct assumption. In any event, I am unable to find a discussion of this question in direct connection with the American capital data and I must proceed, if at all, as indicated.

To determine the relative importance of structures in Russian capital, I begin with data in Table III.2. Structures are intended to encompass the assets listed there as buildings, other structures, and transmission facilities. Again I subtract from total capital the estimate of 138 billion rubles for livestock. The ratio of structures to total capital excluding livestock is somewhat over 0.77 (see fn. 28). The ratio of nonresidential structures to nonresidential capital is somewhat over 0.66.[62]

For the comparable American ratios, I rely on data at current replacement costs since the relative prices of structures and other assets differ between 1929 and other years. Table III.11 in the appendix presents the American ratios of structures to total capital, including and excluding housing, for selected dates from January 1, 1899 to January 1, 1950. On January 1, 1950, the American ratios are about the same as those for the USSR: 0.79 for all structures and 0.67 for nonresidential structures. At earlier dates, the American ratios tend to be slightly higher; the largest observed in Table III.11 is 0.84 for all structures and 0.76 for nonresidential structures.[63]

---

[62] To obtain analogous ratios for total capital in organizations subject to the revaluation, I assume that of the 138 billion rubles of total livestock, 120 billion rubles belong to organizations not subject to the revaluation. Subtracting 18 billion rubles from total capital in "Buildings and structures," Table III.2, I obtain a ratio of 0.72 for structures to total capital excluding livestock. Subtracting 450 to 475 billion rubles of housing belonging to organizations subject to the revaluation (p. 111), I obtain a ratio of 0.64 for nonresidential structures to nonresidential capital.

[63] The data in Table III.11 are Goldsmith's for nonresidential capital and Grebler's for residential capital. The substitution of Goldsmith's data for residential capital does not affect the ratios materially. Depending upon which of Goldsmith's estimates for residential capital is employed, the ratios are: 0.84 on January 1, 1899, 0.82 to 0.83 on January 1, 1929, and 0.78 to 0.80 on January 1, 1950.

For the dates covered in Table III.11, the ratios at 1929 prices are higher than those

It is possible, of course, that the similarity of the Russian and American ratios of structures to capital is an accidental consequence of the use of net American values and gross Russian values. Though I cannot explore this possibility, it should be observed that the data in Table III.3 suggest little change in the Russian ratio of nonresidential structures to nonresidential capital as a consequence of subtracting wear-and-tear from the capital values. This conclusion, however, is subject to some reservations because of the absence of wear-and-tear percentages for the capital of collective farms and of budget organizations: the conclusion assumes that the percentage for collective farm capital is roughly like that for state agriculture and the percentage for the capital of budget organizations is roughly like those for buildings and other structures. Because of the absence of wear-and-tear percentages for private housing, the ratio of total structures to total capital net of wear-and-tear cannot be calculated.

The ratio of capital to gross national product. The final comparison attempted here is that between the Russian and American ratios of capital to gross national product. The absence of a 1960 gross national product figure for the USSR and, indeed, the absence of a recent figure for the USSR at July 1, 1955, prices make it necessary to indulge in some rather tenuous estimating. I begin with the 1955 figure at current prices obtained by Morris Bornstein: 961 billion rubles, adjusted for indirect taxes and subsidies.[64] To adjust for the difference between current and July 1, 1955, prices for the first half of 1955, I reduce the figure to 925 billion rubles.[65] On the basis of a consideration of sector indexes, Bornstein obtains an average annual rate of increase of gross national product in 1955–58 of 7 to 8 percent.[66] Elsewhere I have made a similar calculation with virtually the same results: an average annual rate of increase of 6.9 to 7.4 percent for 1955–58. Because agriculture did not maintain the 1955–58

at current replacement costs in the years before 1929 and lower in the years after 1929.

For the data underlying these statements, see Table III.12; Goldsmith, *A Study of Saving*, vol. III, Tables W-1, W-2, and W-3, pp. 14–15, 17, and 20–21; and Leo Grebler, David Blank, and Louis Winnick, *Capital Formation in Residential Real Estate* (Princeton, 1956), Table D-1, pp. 360–361.

[64] Morris Bornstein, "A Comparison of Soviet and United States National Product," in Joint Economic Committee, 86th Congress of the United States, 1st Session, *Comparisons of the United States and Soviet Economies* (Washington, 1959), part II, p. 380. As he observes, his results at established prices correspond closely with the results of other studies. His adjusted ruble figure also corresponds closely with a similar calculation of 975 billion rubles by Nancy Nimitz in an unpublished manuscript.

[65] The following price changes occurred in 1955: a substantial decrease in wholesale prices, including the prices of producers' durables and building materials, on July 1, 1955; scattered retail price reductions on individual items but no general changes in the centrally determined retail prices; and an increase in compulsory delivery prices, and a decrease in above-quota prices for grain. It should also be observed that the capital values are at the new unified cost estimates introduced in 1956 which amounted to an approximately 6 percent increase in the value of construction at July 1, 1955, price levels.

[66] Bornstein, p. 391.

rates of increase in 1958–60, the indicated rates of increase should be reduced. Accordingly, I assume an average annual rate of increase of from 5.5 to 6.5 percent for 1955–60 and obtain a 1960 gross national product at approximately July 1, 1955, prices of from 1,210 to 1,270 billion rubles.[67]

For present purposes, Russian capital figures of varying scope are related to gross national product: capital, including and excluding housing; capital gross and net of wear-and-tear. In all cases, the estimated 138 billion rubles of livestock are subtracted from the capital figure in Table III.1. In the case of capital exclusive of livestock and gross of wear-and-tear, the capital-output ratios are: total capital, 2.2 to 2.3 and nonresidential capital, 1.5 to 1.6.

Total wear-and-tear of capital in organizations subject to the revaluation is 502 billion rubles, of which about 100 billion rubles appear to refer to socialized housing.[68] Subtraction of these wear-and-tear estimates from capital yields the following ratios of capital net of wear-and-tear to gross national product: for total capital, $<(1.8$ to $1.9)$; for nonresidential capital, $<(1.4$ to $1.5)$. Since the wear-and-tear estimates do not cover all capital, these ratios exceed the "true" ratios; hence, the inequality signs above. Suppose that the wear-and-tear percentages for excluded capital are, alternatively, equal to or double those in Table III.3.[69] The resulting ratios of capital net of wear-and-tear to gross national product are:

	Wear-and-tear percentages in Table III.3	*Double the wear-and-tear percentages in Table III.3*
Total capital	1.7 to 1.8	1.5 to 1.6
Nonresidential capital	1.3 to 1.4	1.3

[67] The result is not very sensitive to small changes in the average annual rate of increase. A given proportionate change in the annual rate of increase yields a much less than proportionate change in the resulting gross national product figure. Thus, a 5 percent average annual rate of increase yields 1,180 billion rubles and a 7 percent rate of increase, 1,300 billion rubles.

[68] The ruble figure for total wear-and-tear is given in Beliakov, p. 8, and is approximately 25 percent of the 2,001.1 figure in Table III.2. Socialized housing is estimated above at 450 to 475 billion rubles (p. 111); application of the wear-and-tear percentage in Table III.3 yields about 100 billion rubles for housing wear-and-tear.

[69] The amounts of excluded capital — private capital, collective farm capital, and the capital of budget organizations — are: 826 billion rubles for all assets excluding livestock; and 826 less 467 to 492 billion rubles of private housing, or 335 to 360 billion rubles of nonresidential capital. On the indicated assumptions, the additional wear-and-tear to be subtracted is:

	Percentages in Table III.3	*Double the Percentages in Table III.3*
Total wear-and-tear	200	400
Nonresidential wear-and-tear	90	180

(See fn. 68)

The American ratios of capital to gross national product depend upon the prices used. At current prices, the ratios from the data in Table III.11 (in the appendix) are:

	Selected years in the 1899–1937 period	*1948*	*1950*
Total capital	1.9 to 2.1	1.6	1.7
Nonresidential capital	1.3 to 1.4	1.0	1.1

At 1929 prices, the ratios from the same sources as the data in Table III.11 are:[70]

	Selected years in the 1899–1937 period	*1948*	*1950*
Total capital	2.0 to 2.2	1.4	1.4
Nonresidential capital	1.3 to 1.4	0.9	0.9

Several additional observations need to be made with respect to the American data. The selected years are 1899, 1909, 1913, 1919, 1924, 1929, and 1937. In each case, I have attempted to select years in which output has not fallen below immediately preceding levels; hence, 1949 is eliminated. There is no discernible trend in the American ratios over the observed years in the 1899–1937 period (Tables III.10 and III.11 in the appendix). As the decade estimates in Table III.10 indicate, the absence of trend extends back to 1869–78 with, however, an 1879–88 ratio below the preceding and succeeding ratios. With respect to the annual estimates in Tables III.10 and III.11, the use of alternative data makes essentially no difference in the capital-output ratios.[71] I cannot explain the sharp reduction in the 1948 and 1950 capital-output ratios after so long a period of apparent stability. It is obviously *not* a relative price phenomenon: the downturn holds at 1929 and at current prices. It would be helpful to have later observations to determine whether the decline or the lower level persists.

Again, I compare the current-price ratios with the Russian ratios. Consider, first, the comparisons based on Russian capital net of wear-and-tear

---

[70] See Table III.10, panel II. The ratios for nonresidential capital are derived by subtracting the residential values, obtained from the source cited in note 2, Table III.10, from the total capital values.

[71] The substitution of Kuznets' Variant III for the Commerce concept of gross national product increases the capital-output ratios at most 0.1 at 1929 prices and 0.2 at current prices. The substitution of Goldsmith's residential construction data for Grebler's changes the capital-output ratios at most ±0.1. (See the sources to Tables III.10 and III.11.)

The decade estimates in Table III.10, however, yield capital-output ratios as high as 2.5 to 2.6 at 1929 prices in the 1909–18 decade and earlier. This reflects in part the substitution of Kuznets' Variant III for the Commerce concept of GNP. In any event, the decade estimates also indicate a sharp reduction in the capital-output ratio for the 1939–48 decade as against previous decades.

and American capital net of depreciation. For total capital the Russian ratio is somewhat below the American ratios in the 1899–1937 period and about the same as the American ratios in 1948 and 1950. For non-residential capital the Russian ratio is about the same as the American ratios in the 1899–1937 period and appreciably above the American ratios in 1948 and 1950.

As noted, it is far from clear that estimates of wear-and-tear derived from an inventory of assets are equivalent to accumulated depreciation derived from accounting data or from estimates of service life. An alternative comparison might be drawn in terms of capital gross of depreciation and wear-and-tear but net of retirements. If I understand Kuznets correctly, the addition of depreciation to the American capital values and the subtraction of capital retirements increase the American capital values at 1929 prices from 40 to 70 percent, with the larger figure applicable to the post-World War II data.[72] If this is so and if the same increases apply to current price data, the 1948 and 1950 American capital-output ratios are raised to something like 2.7 and the 1899–1937 ratios to 2.8 to 3.2. In this comparison, therefore, the Russian ratio for total capital is uniformly below the American ratios.

In his comments on the original version of this paper, Raymond Goldsmith called my attention to his unpublished national wealth estimates for the postwar years, which include capital at current prices gross of depreciation but net of retirements. These data and the official gross national product data yield the following capital-output ratios in selected postwar years:[73] total capital — for 1948, 3.4; 1950, 3.4; 1953, 3.4; 1956,

---

[72] See Table III.10, note 3. Kuznets' calculation refers to capital inclusive of elements other than structures and producers' durables. I assume that the difference between his capital figures, net of retirements and net of capital consumption, is the difference between retirements of fixed capital and capital consumption. On this basis, I add that difference to the fixed capital values net of capital consumption.

[73] The gross national product data are from *Survey of Current Business,* July 1961, p. 6. The capital data are from Raymond W. Goldsmith, *The National Wealth of the United States in the Post-War Period* (mimeographed), Table A-7.

Several observations should be made with respect to the capital data from this monograph and their implications:

Except for 1949 and 1954, when GNP dropped below prior levels, the capital-output ratios are essentially unchanged within the 1948–59 period.

Net capital data (Table A-5) yield the following ratios to GNP in the 1948–59 period (again excluding 1949 and 1954): for total capital, 1.9 to 2.0; for nonresidential capital, 1.0 to 1.2.

The ratios of gross to net capital at current prices fall from 1.82 in 1947 to 1.71 in 1958 (end-of-year values) and are essentially the same at constant — here, 1947/1949 — prices. (Tables A-5 through A-8.)

The net capital data incorporate revisions of the early postwar data from *A Study of Savings,* vol. III, Table W-1. The main change is a 20 to 25 percent increase in residential structures, part of which represents the inclusion of farm residences and public housing. (See Table A-35.) The revised Goldsmith data on residential structures exceed by 33 to 42 percent the 1947–53 data in Grebler *et al.,* Table D-1. (Part of this excess is

3.5; and 1959, 3.5; and nonresidential capital — for 1948, 2.0; 1950, 2.0; 1953, 2.0; 1956, 2.1; and 1959, 2.1. With these data it becomes clear that the Russian ratios for total and nonresidential capital are considerably below the corresponding postwar American ratios.

Although the inequality is marked in terms of gross capital, the absence of such inequality in terms of net capital should not be ignored. The Russian capital data point to substantial amounts of wear-and-tear; I would expect measures of wear-and-tear for the United States to be larger relative to capital net of retirements. Furthermore, the Russian capital values gross of wear-and-tear reflect an adjustment for obsolescence which in the American data is reflected, if at all, in depreciation. The two sets of results, therefore, should be coupled: the Russian ratios of *gross* capital to gross national product are considerably below the corresponding postwar American ratios; but the existing data[74] provide no evidence to support Russian ratios of net capital to gross national product that are markedly smaller than the corresponding postwar American ratios.

---

explained by Goldsmith's inclusion of farm residences.) Acceptance of the Goldsmith data implies that the share of residential structures is larger than observed on p. 127, above. Thus, the share of residential structures in net capital is 44 percent in 1948, 43 percent in 1950, 42 percent in 1955, and 40 percent in 1959; the corresponding shares in gross capital are 1 to 2 percentage points smaller. (See Tables A-5 and A-7.)

Acceptance of the Goldsmith data also implies somewhat larger shares of structures in total and total nonresidential capital than observed on p. 131, above. In terms of net capital, structures are 85 percent of total capital in 1948, 82 percent in 1950, and 81 percent in 1959; the corresponding shares of total nonresidential capital are 73, 69, and 68 percent respectively. In terms of gross capital, the respective shares are 1 to 3 percentage points larger. (See Tables A-5 and A-7.)

[74] Including the net capital data cited in the preceding footnote.

APPENDIX

The appendix consists of six tables, III.7 to III.12, with notes to each.

Table III.7 and Notes

Table III.7
USSR: Investment by Sector of the Socialized Economy, 1952–58 and P 1959–65
(in billions of rubles, at July 1, 1955, prices)

Sector	1952–58	P 1959–65	
	(1)	(2)	(3)
1. Industry	556	1,086	1,106
a. Electric power stations	75.1	125	129
b. Fuels	133.4	245	251
(1) Coal	61.2	75	78
(2) Petroleum and gas	72.2	170	173
c. Chemicals	19.9	100	105
d. Construction industry and building materials	61.5	110	112
e. Ferrous metallurgy	40.8	100	100
f. Machine-building	65.5	118	118
g. Timber, paper, and woodworking	25.3	58	60
h. Light and food industries	40	80	85
i. Other industries	94.5	150	146
2. Agriculture, excluding collective farm investment	119.6	150	150
3. Transport and communications	107.4	209	214
a. Railroad transport	59.3	110	115
4. Trade	22	40	40
5. Social-cultural services	260	455	460
a. Housing and municipal services	214	375	380
b. Other social-cultural services	46	80	80
6. Total investment, excluding collective farm investment	1,065	1,940	1,970
7. Collective farm investment	130.0	345	345
8. Total investment	1,195	2,285	2,315

1. Investment data for 1952–58 and P 1959–65 appear in three versions of the Seven-Year Plan: (i) the "draft theses" of Khrushchev's report in November 1958 to the 21st Party Congress, published in *Pravda,* November 14, 1958; (ii) the January 1959 report on the Seven-Year Plan by Khrushchev to the 21st Party Congress, published in *Pravda,* January 28, 1959; and (iii) the Seven-Year Plan as adopted in February 1959 by the 21st Party Congress, published in *Pravda,* February 8, 1959. Seven-Year Plan and 1952–58 data are also given in *Narodnoe khoziaistvo 1958* and in TSU, *SSSR v tsifrakh v 1959 godu* (Moscow, 1960) (hereafter cited as *Tsifrakh*). These sources differ in the quantity of investment data stated, but data given in more

than one source correspond exactly, with the following minor exceptions. For 1952–58 *Pravda,* November 14, 1958, p. 5, and January 28, 1959, p. 4, give 208 and 214, respectively, for housing and municipal services and 43 and 46, respectively, for other social-cultural services (in billions of rubles). Presumably, the figures in the earlier issue are preliminary, and I have used the data from the later issue. Similarly, for investment excluding collective farm investment, *Tsifrakh,* pp. 180–181, and *Narodnoe khoziaistvo 1958,* pp. 82–83, give 1,065 billion rubles, and *Pravda,* November 14, 1958, p. 5, gives 1,072 billion. I have used the former figure. The only difference in the P 1959–65 data is in other social-cultural services which in *Pravda,* November 14, 1958, p. 5, is 77 billion rubles, and in *Pravda,* January 28, 1959, p. 4, and February 8, 1959, p. 5, is 80 billion rubles; I use the latter figure on the assumption that the plan has been revised.

Thus, with exceptions to be specified in a moment, the data in Table III.7 are from *Pravda,* January 28, 1959, p. 4, and February 8, 1959, p. 5, and from *Tsifrakh,* pp. 180–181, 186–187. The exceptions are (i) the data for trade from A. Popov, "Torgovaia set' v semiletke," *Sovetskaia torgovlia,* 1959, no. 8, p. 4; (ii) the data for "other industries," obtained as a residual from total investment excluding collective farm investment; and (iii) the data for industry, fuels, social-cultural services, and total investment including collective farm investment, obtained in each case as the sum of components.

2. According to *Pravda,* February 8, 1959, p. 5, industrial investment in P 1959–65 is approximately double that in 1952–58. The industry data in Table III.7, obtained by adding to the specified industry components the residual from total investment, show a ratio of 1.95 to 1.99. I take this to be some support for identifying the residual with other industries, for the sums of specified industries yield ratios of 2.03 to 2.08 and these, in Soviet shorthand, would probably be described as "more than" rather than "approximately" double. Further support for this identification is the absence of some industry branches in the specified components — nonferrous metallurgy and metalworking, to mention the two most important omissions. The implication is that "other social-cultural services" include administration as well as education, public health, et cetera.

3. It is stated that P 1959–65 investment in light industry is 33 billion rubles, of which the textile industry accounts for 21 billion rubles (V. Kucherenko, *Plan velikikh rabot* [Moscow, 1959], p. 31). The light industry figure implies a maximum of 52 billion rubles for investment in the food industry.

4. According to *Pravda,* January 28, 1959, p. 5, P 1959–65 investment excluding collective farm investment is "about" 2,000 billion rubles and the addition of noncentralized investment, collective farm investment, and private housing construction brings the total "close" to 3,000 billion rubles. What are the implications?

a. If 1,940 to 1,970 billion rubles is "about" 2,000 billion rubles, I take the grand total, "close to" 3,000, to be about 2,900 billion rubles.

b. From *Narodnoe khoziaistvo 1958* (pp. 82, 619), *Sel'skoe khoziaistvo SSSR* (p. 387), and *Narodnoe khoziaistvo 1959* (p. 543), the ratios of collective farm and noncentralized investment to centralized investment are:

	1952–58	1951–55	1956	1957	1958	1959	P 1959–65
Collective farm investment	0.122	0.108	0.135	0.118	0.142	0.159	0.18
Noncentralized investment	0.112	0.063	0.120	0.140	0.203	0.216	—
Totals	0.234	0.171	0.255	0.258	0.345	0.375	—

My estimates of private housing construction (from *Kaplan,* Table D-8) as ratios of centralized investment (*Narodnoe khoziaistvo 1959,* p. 543) are: for 1951–55, 0.040; 1956, 0.057; 1957, 0.062; and 1958, 0.071. Thus, the ratios of collective farm investment, noncentralized investment, and private housing in the aggregate to centralized investment are: for 1951–55, 0.211; 1956, 0.312; 1957, 0.320; 1958, 0.416; 1959, 0.46; and P 1959–65, 0.47 to 0.49. (The 1959 ratio is obtained on the assumption that the 1959 ratio for private housing is 0.08 as against 0.071 in 1958.) The P 1959–65 ratio of total to centralized investment exceeds the corresponding 1952–58 ratio and each annual ratio within the 1952–58 period. However, most or all of the increase in that ratio between 1958 (and 1959), on the one hand, and P 1959–65, on the other, is accounted for by the increase in relative importance of collective farm investment.

c. On the basis of the foregoing indications, I divide the P 1959–65 figure for other than centralized investment, that is, 930 billion rubles, as follows: collective farm investment, 345 billion rubles; noncentralized investment, 430; and private housing, 155. I assume that the ratio of private housing to centralized investment has increased from 0.071 in 1958 to 0.08 in 1959 and that the relationship of P 1959–65 noncentralized investment and private housing is the same as in 1959 (that is, 0.216: 0.08), which is about the same as in 1958.

5. To make the investment data in Table III.7 more comparable with the January 1, 1960, capital values in Table III.1, private housing construction and noncentralized investment must be added to 1952–58 investment; livestock purchases and capital repairs must be subtracted from collective farm investment; P 1959–65 noncentralized investment must be distributed by sectors; and 1959 investment must be subtracted from P 1959–65 investment and added to 1952–58 investment. In each case, the available data are less than satisfactory. Nevertheless, I attempt the necessary estimates as follows. I confine attention here to the larger of the P 1959–65 sets of data.

a. In *Kaplan,* Table D-8, private housing construction at July 1, 1955, prices is estimated to be, for 1951–55, 24.4 billion rubles; 1956, 9.4; 1957, 11.4; and 1958, 14.1. I subtract 3 billion rubles for 1951 and obtain a figure for 1952–58 private housing construction of 56.3 billion rubles.

b. Since collective farm purchases of livestock and capital repairs are available only at current prices and information on price level changes is absent with respect to collective farm outlays, I use the current-price shares to obtain 1955-price outlays on capital repairs and livestock. The current-price shares in collective farm investment are: livestock purchases — for 1952–55, 15.8 percent; 1956, 14.3; 1957, 18.2; and 1958, 13; and capital repairs — for 1952–55, 11.9 percent; 1956, 10.8; 1957, 11.0; and 1958, 10. These total, for 1952–55, 27.7 percent; 1956, 25.1; 1957, 29.2; and 1958, 23. (The underlying data are from: Ia. Golev, *Sel'skokhoziaistvennyi kredit v SSSR* [Moscow, 1958], pp. 51, 76; A. Rumiantseva, *Obshchestvennye fondy kolkhozov* [Moscow, 1960], p. 19; S. Nosyrev, "Dolgosrochnyi kredit i ego znachenie v sozdanii osnovnykh fondov kolkhozov," *Uchet i finansy v kolkhozakh i sovkhozakh*, 1958, no. 3, p. 32; A. Zverev, "Gosudarstvennyi biudzhet pervogo goda semiletki," *Planovoe khoziaistvo*, 1959, no. 1, p. 11; V. Ushakov, "Finansirovanie i dolgosrochnoe kreditovanie Gosbankom sel'skogo i gorodskogo khoziaistva," *Den'gi i kredit*, 1959, no. 8, pp. 18, 19.) The application of these percentages to the 1952–58 collective farm investment data from *Narodnoe khoziaistvo 1958* (p. 619) yields 34.5 billion rubles, or 26.5 percent of total collective farm investment. For P 1959–65, there is no information on the share of livestock purchases and capital repairs in collective farm investment; hence, I assume the 1952–58 share of 26.5 percent and obtain 92 billion rubles.

c. Noncentralized investment in 1952–58, distributed by sector, is estimated to be: total, 120 billion rubles; industry, 22; agriculture, 0; transport and communications, 5; and others, 93. (See *Kaplan*, Table D-7, note 3. The procedure is: to estimate the 1951 distribution of investment including noncentralized investment; to subtract the 1951 data from corresponding 1951–58 data; and to obtain the difference between the resulting 1952–58 data, including noncentralized investment and the 1952–58 data in Table III.7 which exclude noncentralized investment. See TSU, *Sel'skoe khoziaistvo SSSR*, pp. 387–389, and *Narodnoe khoziaistvo 1958*, pp. 87, 618–619, and 622–623, for the underlying data; the 1951–55 percentage distributions are used to obtain 1951 investment including noncentralized investment in industry, transportation and communications, and other sectors.) For P 1959–65, noncentralized investment is estimated above at 430 billion rubles. On the assumption that the sector distribution is the same in P 1959–65 as in 1952–58, the results are (in billions of rubles): industry, 79 billion rubles; agriculture, 0; transport and communications, 18; and other, 333.

d. For 1959, and for earlier years as well, *Narodnoe khoziaistvo 1959* (pp. 542–543, 548–549) presents sector distributions of investment (including noncentralized and excluding collective farm investment) *including* project-making outlays. For the years before 1959, these distributions differ from those in *Narodnoe khoziaistvo 1958* (pp. 618–619, 622–623) only by the relatively small project-making outlays. Hence, for 1959, I obtain a distribution *excluding* project-making outlays on the assumption that the sector distribution of such outlays is the same in 1959 as in 1958 (see *Kaplan*, Table C-6, note 1). The results are: total investment, excluding collective farm investment, 268.0 billion rubles; industry, 126.4; agriculture, 19.2; transport and communications, 26.1; and other, 96.3. To these data must be added private housing construction, assumed above to be 8 per cent of 1959 *centralized* investment, or 17.6 billion rubles. (The centralized investment figure is from *Narodnoe khoziaistvo 1959*, p. 543.) Furthermore, from 1959 collective farm investment of 35.0 billion rubles (TSU, *Sel'skoe khoziaistvo SSSR*, p. 387) I subtract 9.3 billion rubles for capital repairs and livestock purchases, obtained on the assumption that the share of such outlays, 26.5 per-cent, is the same in 1959 as in 1952–58. The result, 25.7 billion rubles, must also be added to the 1959 data above.

e. For P 1959–65 data, the net results of the foregoing adjustments are (in billions of rubles):

	Total invest-ment	Industry	Agriculture Excluding collective farms	Collective farms	Transport and communi-cations	Other	Undistributed noncentralized investment
1. As in Table III.7 and note 4	2,900	1,106	150	345	214	655	430
2. Distribution of non-centralized investment	0	79	0	0	18	333	−430
3. Collective farm capital repairs and livestock purchases	92	0	0	92	0	0	0
4. Adjusted P 1959–65 investment (1 + 2 − 3)	2,808	1,185	150	253	232	988	0
5. 1959 investment	311.3	126.4	19.2	25.7	26.1	113.9	0
6. Adjusted P 1960–65 investment (4 − 5)	2,497	1,059	358		206	874	0

f. For 1952–59, the net results of the foregoing adjustments are (in billions of rubles):

	Total invest-ment	Industry	Agriculture Excluding collective farms	Collective farms	Transport and communi-cations	Other
1. 1952–58 investment in Table III.7	1,195	556	119.6	130.0	107.4	282
2. 1952–58 private housing	56.3	0	0	0	0	56.3
3. 1952–58 collective farm capital repairs and livestock purchases	34.5	0	0	34.5	0	0
4. 1952–58 noncentralized investment	120	22	0	0	5	93
5. Adjusted 1952–58 investment (1 + 2 − 3 + 4)	1,337	578	215		112	431
6. 1959 investment	311.3	126.4	45		26.1	113.9
7. Adjusted 1952–59 investment (5 + 6)	1,648	704	260		138	545

Table III.8 and Notes

The data in Table III.8 are obtained as follows:

Lines 1–4: From Simon Kuznets, *Capital in the American Economy,* Table 27, p. 198. The data in lines 2 and 4 correspond with those in Creamer *et al.,* Table B-11, p. 319, and Table 23, pp. 73–74; and Ulmer, Table B-1, pp. 235–236. However, the data in line 3 are somewhat below the figures in Creamer *et al.,* Table A-9, pp. 248–251 and Table A-15, pp. 270–272. Perhaps the explanation is, at least in part, that the latter data include site land and some mining capital (see Creamer *et al., pp.* 67, 205–206, 324–325). In line 3, the larger of the 1900 figures is comparable with earlier data and the smaller with later data.

Lines 4a and 6: From Ulmer, Table D-26, pp. 349–351.

Table III.8
USA: Capital by Sector of the Economy
(billions of 1929 dollars)

Sector	June 1, 1880	June 1, 1900	December 31, 1922	December 31, 1948
1. Agriculture	6.57	8.77	15.33	18.54
2. Mining	0.37	1.57	5.27	5.33
3. Manufacturing	1.88	7.64 7.16	22.04	34.78
4. Public utilities	11.80	20.98	35.39	45.29
a. Privately owned electric light and power	0	0.60	3.63	8.14
5. Nonfarm residential construction	10.45	35.72	58.32	82.79
6. Publicly owned electric light and power	0	0.03	0.25	2.33
7. Sum of above	31.07	74.71 74.23	136.60	189.06
8. Other capital				
a. Estimate A	4.7	17.8	43.1	69.3
b. Estimate B	—	13.21	33.13	59.53
9. Total capital				
a. Estimate A	35.8	92.5 92.0	179.7	258.4
b. Estimate B	—	87.44	169.73	248.59

Line 5: For 1900 and later years from Leo Grebler *et al.*, Table D-1, pp. 360–361. For 1880, the figure is derived from the June 1, 1890, figure in Grebler, and the net capital formation figure in Kuznets, *Capital in the American Economy,* Table R-35, note to line 4, p. 612.

Lines 8a and 9a: The 1880 figure for total capital (structures and equipment) is from Raymond W. Goldsmith, "The Growth of Reproducible Wealth of the United States of America from 1805 to 1950," in Simon Kuznets, ed., *Income and Wealth of the United States* (Cambridge, England, 1952), Table I, p. 307. Goldsmith's agricultural and residential components differ from those in Table III.8 but by approximately equal amounts with opposite signs. It should also be noted that although Kuznets makes no use of this total in connection with Table 27 in *Capital in the American Economy,* he does use the total as a base value for his calculation of the trend in total capital stock (see Table III.10).

The Goldsmith total minus line 7 yields line 8a for 1880. The data for subsequent dates are obtained as follows. From Kuznets, *Capital in the American Economy,* Table R-35, pp. 610–612, I obtain net capital formation for the periods June 1, 1880 to June 1, 1900, June 1, 1900 to December 31, 1922, and December 31, 1922 to December 31, 1948. Kuznets includes munitions in producers' durables and, for present purposes, I subtract net munitions, given in Kuznets, Table R-7, p. 497, from net capital formation. From the result, I subtract the increment in line 7 to obtain the increment to "other capital" as a residual. Line 8a is the sum of the 1880 value and the indicated increments. Line 9a is line 7 plus line 8a.

The calculation of increments is:

	June 1, 1880– June 1, 1900	June 1, 1900– Dec. 31, 1922	Dec. 31, 1922– Dec. 31, 1948
Total net capital formation	56.766	90.559	102.762
Less: Net munitions	0	2.88	24.13
Less: Increment in line 7	43.64	62.37	52.46
Increment in other capital	13.13	25.31	26.17

Lines 8b and 9b: I obtain total capital (structures and producers' durables) from Goldsmith, *A Study of Saving,* vol. III, Table W-3, pp. 20–21. From this total I subtract nonfarm residential capital and add the nonfarm residential capital data from Grebler, given in line 5. The adjusted total is entered in line 9b and line 8b is obtained as a residual.

The Grebler housing values are somewhat larger than Goldsmith's in 1900 but smaller in 1922 and 1948. In the latter years, the Grebler data still exceed the alternative lower estimates in Goldsmith, *A Study of Saving,* Table W-4, p. 23.

Table III.9 and Notes

Table III.9
USA: Capital by Branch of Industry
(billions of 1929 dollars)

Branch	1890	1929	1948	1953
Total industry	6.484	44.560	52.503	—
Manufacturing	5.553	30.853	36.685	45.258
Mining	0.803	6.262	5.340	5.421
Electric power production	0.128	7.445	10.478	—
Total manufacturing and mining	6.356	37.115	42.025	50.679
Fuels	0.503	9.250	12.013	12.453
Coal	0.206	0.869	0.598	0.646
Petroleum and gas	0.297	8.381	11.415	11.807
Chemicals; stone, clay, and glass products	0.607	3.700	4.660	7.229
Metals and metal products	1.745	10.096	12.579	16.348
Forest products; paper, pulp, and products	0.869	3.606	3.164	3.561
Light and food industries	2.226	8.178	6.952	6.758
Textiles and products	1.004	3.339	2.390	2.387
Foods, beverages, and tobacco	1.062	4.531	4.376	4.220
Other	0.406	2.294	2.657	4.330

Note: The dash (—) indicates that data are not available.

1. The manufacturing and mining data by branches are from Creamer *et al.,* Tables 23, A-9, A-15, and B-11, pp. 73–74, 248–251, 270–272, and 319.

For mining and its branches (excluding land and working capital), the data are calculated from capital values including working capital and stated relationships between capital-output ratios including and excluding working capital. For manufacturing, the data include site land but its value appears to be trivial (see Creamer *et al.*, pp. 205–206).

The post-1919 manufacturing data include some smelting and refining capital which also appears in mining. Hence, the sum of mining and manufacturing includes some unavoidable duplication. In terms of book value of capital including land and inventories, about 3 to 4 percent of manufacturing capital should be subtracted (Creamer *et al.*, Tables B-16, A-8, and A-15, pp. 241, 270, and 324–325).

The electric power data are from Ulmer, Table B-1, pp. 235–236, and Table D-26, pp. 349–351. The data represent end-of-year sums of capital in privately and publicly owned electric utilities. In addition, there are user-owned electric utilities with the following amounts of capital (in billions of dollars): 1890, 0.104; 1929, 2.283; and 1948, 1.351. These capital values represent electric utilities owned by hotels, electric railways, and manufacturing establishments and appear in segments of the economy other than electric power production. The decline in importance of user-owned facilities is a technological phenomenon (see Ulmer, pp. 313–314). Total industry is the sum of mining, manufacturing, and electric power production.

2. The branches of manufacturing and mining are aggregated from Creamer *et al.*, to provide categories approximately comparable to the classifications for which Russian data are available.

For 1948 and 1953, total manufacturing and mining and the metal products component, include shipbuilding; for the earlier years shipbuilding is excluded. For all years, apparently, manufactured gas, railroad repair shops, and several other minor branches are excluded (Creamer *et al.*, p. 196, fn. 4, and pp. 208–217).

Coal is the sum of anthracite and bituminous coal from Tables 23 and B-11. Petroleum is the sum of petroleum refining from Tables A-9 and A-15 and petroleum and natural gas from Tables 23 and B-11.

Chemicals and stone, clay, and glass products are the sum of: chemicals and allied products (Tables A-9 and A-15); stone, clay, and glass products (Tables A-9 and A-15); and other nonmetals mining (Tables 23 and B-11). In 1948 and 1953, but *not* in earlier years, chemicals account for the predominant portion of this category; for example, in 1953 chemicals account for 5.6 billion dollars.

In 1890 and 1929, metals and metal products are the sum of: iron and steel and products; nonferrous metals and products; machinery, excluding transportation equipment; transportation equipment; and metals mining (Tables A-9, 23, and B-11). In 1948 and 1953, metals and metal products are the sum of: primary metals; fabricated metals; machinery except electrical; electrical machinery; transportation equipment except motor vehicles (but including shipbuilding); motor vehicles and equipment; and metals mining (Tables A-15, 23, and B-11). Motor vehicles and equipment account for the following amounts in billions of dollars: 1890, 0.002; 1929, 1.419; 1948, 1,705; and 1953, 2.337.

Forest products and paper, pulp, and products include: in 1890 and 1929, forest products (Table A-9); in 1948 and 1953, lumber and basic timber products and furniture and finished lumber products (Table A-15); and in all years, paper, pulp, and products (Tables A-9 and A-15).

In 1890 and 1929, light and food industries are the sum of: food and kindred products; textiles and products; and leather and products (Table A-9). In 1948 and 1953, light and food industries are the sum of: textile mill products and apparel; leather and products; food and kindred products; beverages; and tobacco products (Table A-15). In the 1890 and 1929 classification, food and kindred products include beverages and tobacco (compare Tables A-9 and A-15).

Other industries, obtained as a residual, include: rubber products; printing, publishing, and allied products; professional, scientific, photographic, and optical equipment; and so-called miscellaneous manufacturing (Tables A-9 and A-15). It also includes a small statistical residual arising from the failure of specified components to exhaust the total in Tables A-9, A-15, B-11, and 23.

Table III.10 and Notes

1. The decade estimates follow a similar calculation in Kuznets, *Capital in the American Economy*, Tables 3 and 6, pp. 64–66 and 80–81. For closer comparability with the Russian data, I depart from Kuznets' calculations in the following respects: I use fixed capital only (structures and producers' durables); I exclude durable munitions from producers' durables; and I relate *net* capital to *gross* national product rather than to *net* national product.

With these departures, I follow Kuznets' procedures to obtain the *fixed* capital series in Table III.10. I begin with the 1880 figure for structures and equipment from Goldsmith, "The Growth of Reproducible Capital," Table I, p. 307, and reduce it somewhat to approximate an 1879 figure. I, then, cumulate by using Kuznets' decade averages (multiplied by 10) for net construction plus net producers' durables (*Capital in the American Economy*, Table R-15, p. 526). For the period after 1913, I subtract from net producers' durables corresponding averages for net munitions, calculated from Table R-7, p. 497.

For gross national product, I use Variant III from Kuznets, *Capital in the American Economy*, Table R-12, p. 512. Variants I and II differ from each other and from Variant III only in the measure of flows of goods to consumers; Variant III lies between Variants I and II which differ between themselves by 7 percent or less (Table R-12).

2. The annual estimates are obtained as follows. The capital data are the sum of: (i) producers' durables and structures other than residential from Goldsmith, *A Study of Saving*, vol. III, Table W-3, pp. 20–21; and (ii) non-farm residential construction from Leo Grebler *et al.*, Table D-1, pp. 360–361.

The gross national product data are from John Kendrick, *Productivity Trends in the United States* (Princeton, 1961), Table A-III, pp. 298–301. These data refer to the Department of Commerce concept and are derived from Kuznets' estimates for 1929 and before.

Table III.10
USA: Capital and Gross National Product
(billions of 1929 dollars)

I. Decade estimates

Year	Capital	Period	Geometric mean of terminal year capital values	Period	Annual average gross national product (Variant III)	Ratio of capital to gross national product
1869	23					
		1869–79	28	1869–78	10.7	2.5
1879	35					
		1879–89	44	1879–88	20.2	2.2
1889	56					
		1889–99	71	1889–98	27.9	2.5
1899	90					
		1899–1909	110	1899–1908	43.6	2.5
1909	134					
		1909–19	152	1909–18	59.1	2.6
1919	172					
		1919–29	198	1919–28	82.2	2.4
1929	229					
		1929–39	234	1929–38	87.3	2.7
1939	239					
		1939–49	249	1939–48	130.9	1.9
1949	260					

II. Annual estimates, selected years

Year	Capital at beginning of year	Gross national product (Commerce concept)	Ratio of capital to gross national product
1899	83.0	37.2	2.2
1909	124.2	55.9	2.2
1913	140.4	63.5	2.2
1919	161.1	74.2	2.2
1924	176.0	88.4	2.0
1929	215.5	104.4	2.1
1937	214.9	109.1	2.0
1948	237.7	173.0	1.4
1950	258.7	187.4	1.4

The capital data are those underlying line 9b of Table III.8. If the Goldsmith data on nonresidential structures are substituted for the Grebler data, the totals are somewhat smaller through 1919 and somewhat larger thereafter. The difference in the ratio of capital to gross national product, however, is 0.1 or less.

The Department of Commerce concept of gross national product yields a somewhat larger measure than Kuznets' Variant III, but use of the latter affects the annual ratios of capital to gross national product by 0.1 or less.

3. For comparability with the Russian data, the measure of capital should be the fixed capital component of Kuznets' total capital net of retirements (Kuznets, *Capital in the American Economy*, Table 3, column 2, p. 64). However, I am unable to reproduce directly the fixed capital component of that measure. I assume that the only difference between total capital net of retirements and net of capital consumption (*ibid.*, Table 3, columns 2 and 3; and for the 1949 difference, the mimeographed preliminary draft, page III-2) is the difference between retirements of fixed capital and capital consumption. I add that difference to the decade estimates in Table III.10 with the following results (in billions of 1929 dollars): fixed capital net of retirements for 1869, 32; 1879, 49; 1889, 77; 1899, 125; 1909, 193; 1919, 268; 1929, 363; 1939, 400; and 1949, 445. These values exceed those in Table III.10, Panel I, by 40 to 70 percent. In so far as retirements and capital consumption of munitions are unequal in Kuznets' calculations, my use of those calculations here is somewhat in error for 1919 and thereafter.

Table III.11 and Notes

Table III.11
USA: Capital, Structures, and Gross National Product, at Current Prices

Item	1899	1909	1913	1919	1924	1929	1937	1948	1950
1. Capital at beginning of the year (billions of dollars at current replacement costs)[a]	34.3	64.6	78.1	151.8	176.4	211.8	194.3	421.7	491.0
a. Producers' durables	5.6	11.0	13.8	34.6	32.8	37.2	31.2	79.9	104.2
b. Structures except non-farm residential	16.3	31.0	37.1	73.7	83.4	98.9	97.9	189.4	213.3
c. Nonfarm residential structures	12.4	22.6	27.3	43.6	60.2	75.7	65.2	152.4	173.6
2. Gross national product (Commerce concept; billions of dollars at current prices)	17.4	32.2	39.1	78.9	87.6	104.4	90.8	259.4	284.6
3. Ratio of capital to gross national product	2.0	2.0	2.0	1.9	2.0	2.0	2.1	1.6	1.7
4. Ratio of structures to total capital									
a. Including housing	0.84	0.83	0.82	0.77	0.81	0.82	0.84	0.81	0.79
b. Excluding housing	0.75	0.74	0.73	0.68	0.72	0.73	0.76	0.70	0.67

[a] Because of rounding, components need not add to totals.

1. The data in Table III.11 are obtained as follows:
Line 1: The sum of lines 1a, 1b, and 1c.
Lines 1a and 1b: From Goldsmith, *A Study of Saving*, vol. III, Table W-1, pp. 14–15.
Line 1c: From Leo Grebler *et al.*, Table D-1, pp. 360–361.
Line 2: For the pre-1929 period, from Kendrick, *Productivity Trends*, Table A-IIb, pp. 296–297. For 1929 and 1937, from U.S. Department of Commerce, *National Income: 1954 Edition* (Washington), 1954, Table 2, p. 162. For 1948 and 1950, from *U.S. Income and Output*, Table I-1, p. 119.
Line 3: Line 1 divided by line 2.
Line 4a: The sum of lines 1b and 1c, divided by line 1.

Line 4b: Line 1b divided by the difference between lines 1 and 1c.

2. The substitution of residential structures from Goldsmith, *A Study of Saving,* Table W-1, for the data in line 1c increases the ratios in lines 3 and 4a by at most 0.01. The substitution of Kuznets' Variant III of gross national product for the data in line 2 increases the ratios in line 3 for 1919 and later by 0.01 to 0.02 (see *Capital in the American Economy,* Table R-1, p. 486).

Table III.12 and Notes

1. The data in Table III.12 are obtained as follows:

Line 1: The 1929-price data are from Table III.8, line 1. The current-price data are from Alvin Tostlebe, *Capital in Agriculture: Its Formation and Financing since 1870* (Princeton, 1957), Table 7, p. 54. For 1922 and 1948, I have interpolated within Tostlebe's series.

Lines 2 and 3: The 1929-price data are from Table III.8 lines 4, 4a, and 6. The current-price data are from Ulmer, Tables B-1 and D-27, pp. 235–236 and 352–353.

Line 4: The 1929-price data are from Table III.8, line 5. The current-price data are from Grebler *et al.,* Table D-1, pp. 360–361.

Line 5: The 1929- and current-price data are the difference between: (a) government and institutional structures from Goldsmith, *A Study of Saving,* vol. III, Tables W-1 and W-3, pp. 14–15 and 20–21; and (b) publicly owned electric light and power from Ulmer, Tables D-26 and D-27, pp. 349–351 and 352–353. The June 1, 1900, figure for government and institutional structures is an interpolation between capital values for January 1, 1900 and 1901. The subtraction of all capital in publicly owned electric light and power yields a small error because some producers' durables are included.

Line 6: The 1929- and current-price data are obtained as residuals from line 7.

Line 7: The 1929-price data are from Table III.8, line 9b. The current-price data are the sum of: (a) producers' durables and nonresidential structures from Goldsmith, *A Study of Saving,* Table W-1, pp. 14–15; and (b) residential structures from Grebler *et al.,* Table D-1, pp. 360–361.

Line 7a: The 1929- and current-price data are the sum of: (a) nonresidential structures from Goldsmith, *A Study of Saving,* Table W-1, pp. 14–15; and (b) residential structures from Grebler *et al.,* Table D-1, pp. 360–361.

Essentially the same results are obtainable from data in Goldsmith, "The Growth of Reproducible Wealth," Table I, pp. 306–307. The percentage distributions of capital values at 1929 and at current prices are:

	1900		1922		1948	
	1929 prices	*Current prices*	*1929 prices*	*Current prices*	*1929 prices*	*Current prices*
Agriculture	10.4	10.8	9.0	9.5	7.8	7.9
Nonagriculture	42.7	43.5	44.1	44.1	39.3	36.7
Residences	38.5	38.0	35.6	34.5	35.6	39.2
Government	8.7	7.7	11.3	11.9	17.3	17.2
Total capital	100	100	100	100	100	100
Structures	84.5	84.2	81.7	81.4	76.8	80.8

Table III.12
USA: Sector Distributions of Capital at 1929 Prices and at Current Replacement Costs

| | 1900 | | | | December 31, 1922 | | | | December 31, 1948 | | | |
| | June 1, capital 1929 prices | | January 1, capital current prices | | 1929 prices | | Current prices | | 1929 prices | | Current prices | |
Sector	Billions of dollars	Percent of total	Billions of dollars	Percent of total	Billions of dollars	Percent of total	Billions of dollars	Percent of total	Billions of dollars	Percent of total	Billions of dollars	Percent of total
1. Agriculture	8.77	10.0	4.307	11.4	15.33	9.0	14.6	9.1	18.54	7.5	32.0	6.8
2. Public utilities, except electric light and power	20.38	23.3	8.787	23.3	31.76	18.7	30.620	19.2	37.15	14.9	62.347	13.2
3. Private and public electric light and power	0.63	0.7	0.245	0.6	3.88	2.3	3.548	2.2	10.47	4.2	19.384	4.1
4. Nonfarm residential construction	35.72	40.9	13.677	36.3	58.32	34.4	51.143	32.0	82.79	33.3	174.273	37.0
5. Government and institutional structures except public electric power	7.11	8.1	2.874	7.6	19.14	11.3	19.348	12.1	39.20	15.8	74.796	15.9
6. Other capital (residual)	14.83	17.0	7.824	20.7	41.30	24.3	40.6	25.4	60.44	24.3	107.7	22.9
7. Total capital	87.44	100	37.714	100	169.73	100	159.827	100	248.59	100	470.545	100
a. Total structures	74.39	85.1	31.620	83.9	137.92	81.3	129.041	80.7	188.95	76.0	376.851	80.1

IV

INDUSTRIAL PRODUCTION

RAYMOND P. POWELL

---

1. INTRODUCTION

In inquiring into Soviet industrial production I propose to address myself to the question of the <u>sources</u> of growth rather than to that of the relative merits of the several indexes of industrial production now available. Some of the data bear on the latter question, but the fact that they do so is a by-product of the inquiry. My principal concern is with the manner in which the Soviet Union industrialized, not with precision in measuring its rate of industrial growth.

Growth is viewed here in the usual fashion — as the combined result of increases in the quantity of productive resources employed, improvements in technology, and, what may be of exceptional importance in some periods of Soviet development, improvements in the efficiency with which resources are used at given levels of technology. Whatever its formal adequacy, this approach is admittedly rather mechanical and a-historical. It does, however, provide an access of sorts to the central problem which Soviet industrial accomplishments pose: To what extent are those accomplishments explainable by the prosaic process of funneling into industry increasing quantities of inputs — inputs which are tangible, measurable, and, ultimately if not initially, costly? To what extent, alternatively, are they the consequence of the release of human aspirations and ingenuity, the contriving of improved organizational forms and allocative devices, the adoption of advanced techniques available from abroad or invented at home, that is, of forces which are intangible, unmeasurable, and, if costly, only incidentally so?

I proceed from the familiar supposition that the contribution of increased inputs to recorded growth can be approximated by estimating the output which would have resulted had the same inputs been used with a given production function and unvarying technology. The difficulties which this procedure encounters — problems of aggregation, of disequilibrium observations, of unmeasured changes in the quality of inputs, of interdependence between inputs and technological change — are well known, and no solution of them is attempted. One issue concerning the procedure does require comment, not because it can be settled here, but because my choice of statistical series may otherwise appear arbitrary. This is the issue of the conceptually proper measures of inputs and outputs.

Conceptual Problems

The logic of the procedure requires that, so far as possible, inputs and outputs be measured in a way appropriate to the underlying analytic concept, the production function. If the assumption of a functional relation between inputs and outputs is plausible, it is so only with respect to physical inputs and outputs. The relation is a technological one. The function derives logically from the "law of the uniformity of nature." It specifies nothing about the relation of inputs to outputs in value terms.

Ideally, then, one should measure inputs and outputs in such terms as man-hours, machine-hours, and tons produced, each measure relating to inputs or outputs which are perfectly homogeneous, at least over the range of substitutions relevant to the problem at hand. In fact, the retention of completely homogeneous categories is not feasible; aggregation of unlike inputs or outputs becomes unavoidable; beyond some low level of aggregation, the relative values of unlike inputs or outputs appear a better approximation to the possibilities of their physical substitution than any common physical unit of measurement. But, and this is my point, the use of value weights in combining unlike inputs or outputs provides no license for netting the value of some inputs out of the value of outputs and attributing the remaining output to the remaining inputs.

Once we depart from the simple technological function there is no guide to choice but analogy, and the validity of analogies is not demonstrable. But there is no apparent analogue in the technological function to the subtraction, for example, of current purchases from other sectors or capital consumption from the value of outputs, since inputs and outputs are commensurable only in value terms. Nor, if the netting out in physical terms were conceivable, is there anything in the production function which justifies imputing a part of total output to a part of inputs. While, because of its welfare connotations, we might wish to explain changes in net value added within a sector, the production function is not suited to the purpose: two identical physical production processes can yield different behaviors of net value added if the price weights attached to inputs and outputs differ between the two. If the production function is our explanatory vehicle, we are committed to explaining the behavior of output gross of all inputs. The appropriate statistical measures are, therefore, gross output in the sense indicated and all identifiable inputs.

The point at issue is more than a conceptual nicety. Soviet industry was predominantly in its earlier years and in significant degree thereafter a processor of agricultural raw materials. Only on extreme assumptions could it be supposed that the flow of such materials into industry had no consequences for industrial output, whatever the measure of output. If, because of the concentration of investment in industry, it can be argued that the rapid growth of that sector was at the expense of agricultural growth, it can be argued equally well that the slow growth of agriculture was itself a restraint on industry. Indeed, in some periods at least, a shift of investment from industry to agriculture might have accelerated the increase of industrial output. The contribution of agriculture to the performance of industry ultimately proves difficult to analyze, but it cannot be accounted for simply by subtraction of agricultural inputs from industrial output.

A more pointed illustration of the dependence of industry on other sectors is provided by the behavior of industry during the transportation crisis of the early 1930's.[1] Virtually all indexes of Soviet industrial output, gross or net, show a distinct sag from 1931 or 1932 to 1934, followed by a spurt of growth in the next two or three years. Although the causes of this wide swing in growth rates were numerous, a primary cause was undoubtedly the deterioration and then rapid improvement of transportation services supplied to industry by the railroads. To deduct transportation inputs from industrial output is to risk attributing to industry inefficiencies which in fact arose in another sector.

A somewhat different illustration of the effects of netting inputs from outputs can be observed with capital inputs. In the course of Soviet industrialization, a large shift occurred in the composition of capital, from inventories to fixed capital and, within the latter, from structures to

---

[1] See Holland Hunter, *Soviet Transportation Policy* (Cambridge, Mass., 1957), chaps. 3 and 4.

equipment. Consequently, the flow of capital consumption rose more rapidly than the flow of net capital services. That output is invariant to the inputs reflected in capital consumption is as implausible as that it should be invariant to current purchases from nonindustrial sectors. That its effects can be eliminated by netting capital consumption from both inputs and outputs has, again, no evident sanction in the concept of a production function.[2]

With some unavoidable exceptions to be noted, I include all identifiable physical inputs in inputs, deducting the value of none from computed outputs. This choice of statistical measures is by no means novel. It is essentially the one made in input-output calculations.[3] It is also one commonly made in studies of agricultural production.

Statistical Problems

The kinds of statistical series required are more easily described than obtained. For a number, no careful independent estimates have yet been compiled, and the present inquiry is for that reason premature. Lacking firm estimates, I have improvised approximations to the required series if at all possible and, if necessary, by devices cruder than scrupulous scholarship would normally permit. This procedure can be defended only on the grounds that the conclusion sought is a best guess, based on data that are readily available. I have drawn heavily on the researches of others[4] and have in some instances put burdens on their findings which they did not intend them to bear. It is hoped that rashness in the compilation of the statistics is matched by reserve in the drawing of infer-

[2] I have avoided describing the change in the composition of the capital stock in terms of average service lives, because of the peculiarities of inventory accounting. Although inventories are defined as short-lived assets, they are treated in conventional accounting as perpetual (but depletable) assets, and the charge for their services is therefore interest costs only. The explanation of this apparent paradox is that we charge as current costs and treat as noncapital inputs the labor, materials, et cetera, which produce the flow through the inventory stock and capitalize those outlays only when they are associated with a net increase in the stock. It would be equally logical to capitalize the costs of gross additions to inventories and to charge capital consumption as inventories are used up. However, the conventional practice is followed here.

The same accounting convention implies that a net reduction in inventories should be counted as an input. Such a reduction occurs only once in the inventory series used here, in 1929, and in that instance is small. For simplicity, net inventory consumption is omitted from the input series.

[3] Intrasector transactions, usually recorded in input-output tabulations, are excluded here from both inputs and outputs as endogenous to the sector's production processes and principally an expression of integration within the sector.

[4] I am especially indebted to Abram Bergson and to Richard H. Moorsteen, whose unpublished researches provide the basis of much of this paper. I am also indebted to Janet Chapman, James Blackman, and Jerzy Karcz. I have relied heavily on a published study by Norman M. Kaplan and Richard H. Moorsteen, *Indexes of Soviet Industrial Output,* The RAND Corporation, Research Memorandum RM-2495, May 13, 1960.

ences. In any case, the inquiry must be regarded as a reconnaissance and its findings as tentative.

The data are meant to cover the actual territory of the USSR, including the acquisitions of 1939 and 1940 from the dates of their occurrence. In general, the portions of subsequent increases in inputs or outputs attributable to the added territories cannot be identified. At the time of their acquisition, they evidently accounted for both inputs and outputs on the order of 10 percent of those in the pre-1939 Soviet territories.

Industry includes manufacturing, mining, electric power generation, lumbering, and fishing. Force-account construction is not meant to be included but may not be fully excluded in all series. The production of munitions is included, and this fact should be kept in mind if the estimates are compared with others relating to the output of civilian products only. The inclusion of munitions presumably reduces the statistical reliability of the output series. Resources employed in munitions, however, cannot be excluded from the input series, and, in any event, Soviet industrialization cannot well be accounted for if a major final product is disregarded.

The unavoidable consolidation into one sector of industries likely to have extremely diverse production functions is unfortunate. It would be desirable at least to segregate manufacturing, but the data do not permit it. Moreover, the inclusion of extractive industries means that output can be affected by changes in the supply of natural resources, for which, it should be noted, no measure is attempted.[5] The latter is one of the more serious deficiencies of the inquiry.

As far as possible, all output and input series have been computed with alternative ruble price weights, of 1937, 1928, and 1950. The conversions to 1928 and 1950 prices are incomplete at a number of points, and the 1937 price series should be regarded as the basic estimates. Prices of all three years are meant to correspond to Abram Bergson's factor cost valuations, that is, prevailing prices adjusted for turnover taxes and subsidies. The adjustments are often rough and partial.

As will appear, the results of the calculations differ substantially depending on the price weights used. The interpretation of these differences is a familiar problem in the analysis of Soviet development. Since no conclusive solution is apparent, I record the estimates in all three sets of prices and attempt to interpret the differences when I come to consider the relation of inputs to outputs. I have not composed series with variable price weights, partly for reasons of expositional simplicity and partly because series weighted with prices other than those of the three years referred to are unavailable.

For all the statistical series presented, annual estimates have been made for 1928 to 1958, with the exception of the war years. The annual estimates,

[5] Site land is also omitted but probably with no significant consequence.

some of which are of especially questionable reliability, may give an unjustified appearance of precision. However, they provide a check of the reliability of estimates spanning several years by testing whether similar procedures yield plausible estimates for intermediate years. In addition, they indicate the representativeness of benchmark observations. The annual data are set forth in the appendix, and the notes to the appendix tables contain extended explanations of their derivation. Because the estimates for year-to-year changes are unreliable, rates of change between selected benchmark years have been computed and are shown in the text. The choice of benchmarks is guided partly by historical events — such as terminal years of five-year plans — and partly by data availability.

2. INDUSTRIAL OUTPUT

To repeat, industrial output encompasses the entire flow of products from industry to other sectors, including the flow to final uses in the GNP sense. It is valued at prices received by industry, adjusted for turnover taxes and subsidies. Since the measure is gross of purchases from other sectors and of depreciation charges but net of intermediate transactions within the industrial sector, it cannot be described as either gross or net. It is referred to here as final industrial product, since it is final from the viewpoint of industry, although in part intermediate for the economy as a whole. For output so defined, as estimated here, annual rates of change between selected years are shown in Table IV.1.

Table IV.1
USSR: Final Industrial Product, Annual Rate of Change,
Selected Periods, 1928–58
(percent)

Period	1937 Prices	1928 Prices	1950 Prices
1928–32	7.1	18.1	7.1
1932–37	12.6	17.7	10.9
1937–40	8.8	10.8	6.1
1940–45	−3.8	−2.5	−10.5
1945–50	9.2	9.3	16.6
1950–55	9.7	9.6	9.9
1955–58	11.0	11.0	11.4
1928–40	9.8	16.1	8.4
1950–58	10.2	10.1	10.5
1928–58	7.4	10.1	7.0

Note: Data derived from Table IV.9 in the appendix. Here and for later tables, where sources and methods are not given, see appendix.

Since the output concept used is unlike that employed for most indexes of industrial production, series for value added (gross of depreciation) have also been derived — by deducting from final product the value of industrial purchases of agricultural raw materials and transportation services (see Table IV.10 in the appendix).[6] For the thirty years from 1928 to 1958, the annual growth rates of the value added series are 8.1 percent in 1937 prices, 11.3 percent in 1928 prices, and 7.2 percent in 1950 prices, all somewhat higher than the rates of the final product series. Within shorter periods, differences between the two sets of series are sometimes quite large.

Derivation of the Production Series

The final product estimates can with essential accuracy be described as the industrial production series implicit in Abram Bergson's estimates of Soviet GNP by use.[7] From the components of Bergson's estimates I have, in fact or in effect, extracted that portion which can be identified as of industrial origin, made a rough correction for transportation and distribution costs incurred in delivering the product to the final user, and treated the sum of the resulting component estimates as the measure of industrial output.[8]

Two components, deliveries of equipment to investment and of building materials to construction, are drawn from the original estimates which underlie Bergson's. The equipment series are Richard H. Moorsteen's estimates of investment in machinery, computed by deflating investment data in current prices. The construction materials series are my estimates of materials consumed in construction, computed by aggregating physical quantity data. Both series include allocations of materials and spare parts to capital repairs, as that term is defined in Soviet practice. They do not include, as they should, allocations to current repairs in nonindustrial sectors.

A third component, investment of industrial products in inventories, comes from a capital stock study which Moorsteen and I have under way, but both the procedures and the results closely resemble Bergson's. Total inventories are derived, for several separate sectors and for goods on hand and goods in transit separately, largely by deflating current values of

---

[6] It is not relevant here whether this is the ideal method for computing value added. It is peculiar in that it can conceivably yield a negative figure, which, however, would not be a nonsense result. It would reflect the fact that in the prices of another year the value of purchases from other sectors in a given year could well exceed the value of final product. The relation of this value added index to indexes aggregated with value added weights is discussed below.

[7] *The Real National Income of Soviet Russia Since 1928* (Cambridge, Mass., 1961); hereafter cited as *Real SNIP*.

[8] A more detailed statement of sources is given in the notes to Table IV.9 in the appendix.

inventories on January 1 of each year. Soviet sources report a substantial amount of data on current values of inventories; missing figures can be estimated from reported liabilities which, as a result of Soviet financial procedures, are tied rather closely to real short-term assets. The deflators are Bergson's or extensions of his price indexes. I isolate the industrial component on the basis of the sector in which the inventories are held and on the basis of information, principally for the weight years, on the composition of inventories in individual sectors.

For all other components, the estimates in 1937 and 1950 prices are taken directly from Bergson, in the years covered by him: 1928, 1937, 1940, 1944, and 1948–55. These include retail purchases by households, munitions purchases by government, military subsistence, and a sundry category consisting largely of other government purchases (for education, health, administration, and internal security) but including also household purchases of electric power. With minor exceptions, Bergson's estimates are deflations of current-price magnitudes. The identification of the industrial share of each component is mine, but most of the data are from Bergson.

Bergson estimates GNP in 1928 prices for 1928 and 1937 only, and bears no responsibility for the series nominally in 1928 prices for other years. Strictly speaking, only equipment and construction are in 1928 prices throughout; other components are generally interpolated or extrapolated on the basis of their 1937 price counterparts. By 1937, however, equipment and construction account for 41 percent of final industrial product in 1928 prices, and their share probably remained high in the following years, except for the immediate postwar years.

For the noninvestment components in years not covered by Bergson, in all three sets of prices, the procedures are much the same as Bergson's, the deflation of current price series by price indexes, but they are extremely crude. The production series for these years are, therefore, also crude.

The components referred to thus far are the whole of those covered in the production estimates. Among deliveries to GNP uses, the principal omissions — for lack of data — are military procurements other than munitions and subsistence, and outlays for state stockpiles. Neither of these is likely to have been typically a large share of the total, but in particular years their omission may significantly affect the series. Among intermediate sales to other sectors, only one is included, sales of materials to construction. The others — sales to transportation, communications, trade, and agriculture — are omitted not primarily because of lack of data but because they are quite small.[9]

The size of the omitted outputs can be approximated. Total costs of final industrial product in 1937, including profits and depreciation but

[9] See the notes to Table IV.9 in the appendix.

omitting costs paid to the trade sector, amounted to 91.0 billion rubles. The final product accounted for in my component estimates is 84.9 billion. The difference of 6 billion appears to be a plausible magnitude for the omitted sales to GNP uses and to other sectors. While it is not a trivial amount, it does not suggest a gross undercoverage.

A further problem of coverage arises in connection with imports and exports. Logically, exports of industrial products should be included in output, imports of materials consumed by industry should be counted as inputs, and imports of industrial products delivered directly to final uses should be excluded. Because of data limitations, this logic is only partially followed. Exports of industrial products are omitted from the output estimates, and, with two exceptions, imports going directly to final uses are included, since they are included in the final use components from which output is estimated. To some extent, these two errors must be offsetting. The exceptions in the treatment of imports are the exclusion of investment in imported equipment in 1928–33, when it was sizeable, and the exclusion of receipts from Lend-Lease, reparations, and war booty, in 1944–53. To the extent that the latter consisted of goods delivered directly to final uses, their subtraction from total output is proper. To the extent that they consisted of raw materials subsequently processed by domestic industry, their exclusion represents precisely the kind of netting of inputs from outputs against which I argued above. The composition of these receipts is only partly known and, in any case, the estimates are probably too rough to justify any elaborate treatment. Nevertheless, the failure to include among inputs receipts of industrial raw materials from external sources is likely to obscure an important factor in the recovery of Soviet industrial production in the years immediately following the war.

The price indexes used in deflating current-price series also depart from the specifications. In particular, the indexes of consumer prices, which enter into the deflation not only of household purchases at retail but also of government purchases and inventories, are indexes of retail prices, unadjusted for turnover taxes. The adjustment to a factor cost valuation is made only for each expenditure category as a whole. How far the estimates may diverge from those which would result if individual products were valued at factor cost is impossible to say, but the difference may not be trivial.[10]

A final defect in the output estimates is the treatment of distribution

---

[10] Bergson, *Real SNIP,* p. 135, describes a calculation of retail sales to households in 1937 prices, in which adjustments for turnover taxes are made separately for 22 commodity categories. In this calculation, the increase of sales from 1928 to 1937 is *smaller* than that obtained with unadjusted 1937 retail price weights. Kaplan and Moorsteen, pp. 92–93, provide evidence that for 1950–55 the structures of retail and wholesale prices for consumer goods were not sufficiently different to produce appreciable differences in quantity indexes weighted by them.

costs, including transportation from producer to final user. To obtain output at prices received by the seller, distribution costs have been deducted from each component estimate. For the weight years, such costs in current prices can be determined with fair accuracy. For other years, it is assumed that the share of distribution costs in the value of output, in weight-year prices, remained constant over time. This is not a particularly plausible assumption. It has not, moreover, been reconciled with the assumptions made in estimating transportation inputs into industry.

Reliability of the Production Series

The presumptive reliability of the output series, clearly, is not high. For year-to-year changes and for periods not covered by Bergson, especially, substantial errors are possible.[11] It would be unwise to insist, for example, that output rose as much as 37 percent from 1934 to 1935 (although the increase was probably large), that output fell absolutely from 1939 to 1940, or that there was virtually no increase from 1953 to 1954. It would be tempting to smooth out some of the more erratic variations by interpolating between benchmark years with physical quantity indexes. Since, however, other estimates of Soviet industrial production have been derived from quantity data, consistent reliance upon deflation (construction materials aside) permits a useful check on the reliability of the results.

How closely the results of deflation correspond to those of aggregation of physical quantities is tested in Table IV.2. The Kaplan-Moorsteen series is their index of all industrial products in 1950 prices.[12] It is composed by aggregating physical output series with 1950 value weights. In principle, the weights are value added in industry. In fact, the weights for subcomponents are generally retail prices for consumer goods and wholesale prices for producer goods. In my series for value added in 1950 prices, which is also shown in Table IV.2, I too calculate subcomponents in terms of price weights. Hence the comparison is in this respect unrevealing. Kaplan and Moorsteen combine their components with wage bill weights; my weights implicitly include profits and depreciation. Kaplan and Moorsteen omit munitions and additions to goods in process. For comparison with the Kaplan-Moorsteen index, therefore, I have in Table IV.2 deducted from

[11] In addition to the usual difficulties with Soviet statistics, the procedures used here are particularly sensitive to errors in the dating of price changes. A given percentage error in the price index used in deflating inventories operates not on the annual investment in inventories but on the total stock of inventories. If a change in prices is slightly misplaced in time, which can easily occur with the Soviet data, capital gains on inventories actually occurring in one year can be mistakenly attributed to a contiguous year, and the change in investments in inventories in successive years thereby be grossly misrepresented.

[12] The Kaplan-Moorsteen index shown here is less akin conceptually to my basic series than their index of final products of industry (p. 260), but the method of computation of the latter makes comparison difficult.

Table IV.2

USSR: Value Added in Production of Finished Civilian Goods,
in 1950 Prices, 1927/28–1958

(1950 = 100)

Year	Present estimates[a]	Kaplan and Moorsteen[b]
1927/28	—	27.1
1928	29.7	—
1932	39.3	41.6
1937	64.0	67.4
1940	73.9	71.2
1945	35.4	36.6
1946	45.8	45.4
1947	57.0	55.7
1948	69.2	71.7
1949	88.7	87.2
1950	100	100.0
1951	112	111.5
1952	119	118.9
1953	136	130.3
1954	143	143.6
1955	161	158.1
1956	185	171.7
1957	200	188.4
1958	228	202.3

[a] Data derived from Table IV.10 in the appendix.
[b] Kaplan and Moorsteen, p. 235.
Note: The dash (—) indicates that data are not available.

my series for value added in 1950 prices the estimated amounts of value added in munitions production and in additions to goods in process.[13]

On the whole, the two series move fairly closely together. My estimate for 1928 exceeds the Kaplan-Moorsteen figure for 1927/28 by close to 10 percent, a difference which appears explainable by the difference in time periods and by the evident omission from the Kaplan-Moorsteen index of some output of small-scale industry.[14] From 1932 through 1955, my

[13] Total value added in 1950 prices is given in Table IV.10 in the appendix, the gross value of munitions purchases in Table IV.9, also in the appendix. Scattered data for various time periods suggest that value added in munitions production accounts for roughly 50 percent of the gross value, in current prices. On this, see Bergson, *Real SNIP,* appendix E; Norman M. Kaplan *et al., A Tentative Input-Output Table for the USSR, 1941 Plan,* The RAND Corporation, Research Memorandum RM-924, September 2, 1952, p. 7; Kaplan and Moorsteen, pp. 219 and 266; and Richard Moorsteen, *Prices and Production of Machinery in the Soviet Union, 1928–1958* (Cambridge, Mass., 1962). I assume a 50 percent share in all years in 1950 prices. Value added in goods in process is estimated from data for inventories by sectors and by components, contained in the Moorsteen-Powell study.

[14] Kaplan and Moorsteen, pp. 8–9.

index remains within about 5 percent of the Kaplan-Moorsteen index, although the relation between the two exhibits some quite drastic short-run changes. From 1955 to 1958, the two diverge rapidly, and by 1958 mine exceeds the other by 13 percent.

Even if both indexes were entirely free of statistical error, they would not necessarily coincide. The Kaplan-Moorsteen index is a value-added-weighted index, mine is a value added index. They would coincide only if the share of value added in the gross value of individual products, in weight-year prices, remained constant over time.[15] If, as seems plausible, the value added share in individual products has risen, that is, materials requirements have fallen, the index of value added should rise more rapidly than the index with value added weights. In fact, my index does rise somewhat more rapidly than the Kaplan-Moorsteen index between the benchmark years from 1932 on, except from 1940 to 1945. The differences, however, are generally small and could be explained by a variety of factors.

The divergence between the two indexes from 1955 to 1958 is evidently due to errors in both. My estimates for these years are exceptionally unreliable. However, the rate of increase shown by my final product series in 1950 prices, 11.4 percent, exceeds only moderately the rate of increase of the Soviet official index in 1955 prices, 10.3 percent.[16] Since these two indexes are rather similar conceptually, it may be reasonable to retain my estimates as upper limits for the growth rates of the last three years covered.[17]

On the other hand, Kaplan and Moorsteen (pp. 54 and 126) emphasize that their post-1950 growth rates are likely to be understated because of unmeasured improvements in the quality of machinery, and they express particular reservations on their machinery output index for 1958. Their estimates can then be taken as the basis for a lower limit for the change in final product by reversing the calculation by which I derive value

---

[15] See *ibid.*, p. 21.

[16] See TSU, *Narodnoe khoziaistvo SSSR v 1959 godu* (Moscow, 1960), p. 141; hereafter cited as *Narodnoe khoziaistvo 1959*. Other issues of the handbook are similarly cited.

[17] Both indexes are gross of purchases from other sectors and include munitions production and additions to goods in process. The price weights in both are prevailing prices adjusted for turnover taxes. Besides the 5-year difference in their weight years, the two differ chiefly in that the official index includes intermediate transactions within industry and the operations of repair shops.

I do not compare here my final product estimates with the official index for the period since 1928 generally, since the reliability of the latter is too questionable to provide a helpful test of the accuracy of my estimates. The interested reader can establish for himself that the final product series in 1928 prices moves rather closely with the official index, nominally in 1926/27 prices, over the prewar years; it drops below the official index in the postwar years to 1950. From 1950 to 1955, the final product index in 1950 prices rises less rapidly than the official index, which in those years was weighted with 1952 prices.

added in the production of finished civilian goods.[18] So estimated, 1958 final product in 1950 prices is reduced from 707 to 653 billion rubles. Annual rates of increase in 1950 prices are reduced to 8.4 percent for 1955–58, 9.4 percent for 1950–58, and 6.7 percent for 1928–58. These alternative estimates will be useful for subsequent reference.

The 1955–58 period aside, the broad correspondence of my estimates with the Kaplan-Moorsteen series is reassuring, although it bears directly on the estimates in only one set of prices. Except for 1950 prices, the two estimates derive from almost entirely separate data. Their mutual consistency lends considerable credibility to both. It provides evidence, as well, of consistency between the Bergson GNP estimates and the Kaplan-Moorsteen index of industrial production and, moreover, of the internal consistency of the basic Soviet data on which all the estimates rest.

3. Industrial Inputs

In comparison with the production estimates, the input measures are defective beyond adequate expression. To my knowledge, labor and inventories are the only industrial inputs which have been the subject of independent inquiries in the West. The available measures of the first are unsatisfactory in important respects; the second is a relatively small share of total inputs.

Labor

I take as the index of labor inputs the unweighted number of wage earners (*rabochie*) employed in industry, roughly adjusted for variations in hours worked. Rates of change between benchmark years are shown in Table IV.3. Although the series does not cover all labor employed in industry, it will be treated as if it did and given ruble values in the weight years equal to total expenditures on labor, including wage supplements (see Table IV.11).

The employment series underlying the labor index is essentially that composed by Kaplan and Moorsteen, and its characteristics are discussed in their study (pp. 153ff.). It is meant to cover wage earners in state industry, cooperative artisans, and workers in industrial subsidiaries of nonindustrial enterprises; it does not include penal labor. The estimates for 1928 and 1932 — the increase between these two years is particularly difficult to establish — are based on a careful study of reported employment data. Employment figures for all other years are derived from the official indexes of industrial output and productivity in industry. The adjustment of employment to man-hours, for which information is limited,

---

[18] That is, I extrapolate value added in production of finished civilian goods from 1955 to 1958 on the Kaplan-Moorsteen index and add value added in munitions and goods in process and the value of purchases from agriculture and transportation.

Table IV.3
USSR: Labor Inputs in Industry (Man-hours),
Annual Rate of Change, Selected Periods, 1928–58
(percent)

Period	Annual rate of change
1928–32	10.1
1932–37	4.2
1937–40	6.0
1940–45	0.7
1945–50	5.8
1950–55	5.1
1955–58	1.7
1928–40	6.6
1950–58	3.8
1928–58	4.7

Note: Data derived from Table IV.11 in the appendix.

is also largely Kaplan and Moorsteen's. For the years not covered by them, I have interpolated from data similar to those which they use.[19]

The principal deficiency of the labor series is that it does not allow for quality changes. Improvements in the average quality of labor must have been a major contributing force to the growth of the Soviet economy as a whole. Although the presumption is less strong that a marked improvement has occurred within industry alone (much of the change in the economy came from the conversion of peasant into relatively skilled urban labor), improvement over the period from 1928 to 1958 appears likely. Within shorter periods, especially from 1928 to 1932 and possibly from 1940 to 1945, quality probably deteriorated. The use of price weights would not necessarily record all such changes, but it would come nearer to doing so than the unweighted index. The assumption that changes in hours represent a proportionate change in labor inputs may produce further inaccuracy in the index.

The failure to weight the labor index also means that any aggregate input measure reflects imperfectly the effects of shifting the weight year. It would be difficult to assert confidently that a labor index weighted with early year wage rates would rise more rapidly than one with late year rates, although that is not unlikely; a difference in growth rates with different weights is virtually certain. My input and output measures are on this account not fully comparable; since labor weighs heavily in the input measures, the incomparability may be large.

[19] For the prewar years, the interpolations are based on Donald R. Hodgman, *Soviet Industrial Production, 1928–1951* (Cambridge, Mass., 1954).

Capital

Estimated rates of change of capital inputs in industry are shown in Table IV.4. These are measures of gross capital services, not of the capital stock. Annual estimates of the stock are, however, shown in the appendix, and it is from these that the service estimates are computed.

The inventory figures pose no particular statistical problem. They are from the Moorsteen-Powell study, with annual averages computed from figures for January 1. Estimates are made separately for producers' and consumers' goods industries. Inventories include raw materials, goods in process, finished products, and, in accordance with Soviet accounting practice, short-lived and small-valued tools. Goods in transit to which title is held by industrial enterprises are omitted on the ground that they are more appropriately treated as inputs to transportation. It is worth noting that inventories are a substantial component of the total capital stock, amounting in current prices to 40 percent of the (net) stock in 1928, 39 percent in 1937, and 34 percent in 1950.

In view of repeated Soviet complaints of the "hoarding" of inventories, it could be questioned whether all recorded inventories should be regarded as engaged in the production process. The predominant motive for hoarding is evidently the need to hold reserves against contingencies arising from erratic and unreliable deliveries of supplies (stocks held for speculation on price rises cannot be of much consequence). Over some range, the size of such reserves is likely to be a significant determinant of the volume of output, and their treatment as productive inputs therefore appears appropriate. Since truly unemployed inventories cannot be identified, I include the services of the entire stock in capital inputs. The services of inventories are measured by interest charges only (see fn. 2); services, therefore, move with the stock and their rate of change is invariant to the interest rate.

The absence of independent estimates of the stock of fixed capital in Soviet industry is the most critical lack in this inquiry. I undertake to cope with it by splicing, so to speak, the estimates compiled by Moorsteen and me of the fixed capital stock in the economy as a whole with data reported in official sources. The details of this operation are involved and are best relegated in their entirety to the appendix (see notes to Table IV.12 in the appendix). In substance, they come to the deflation of reported current values of industrial equipment and structures in the terminal years of the period and the interpolation — effectively free-hand — of intermediate years on official indexes which are purportedly in constant prices. How tenuous the inferences are on which the resulting estimates hang can be appreciated by reference to the appended discussion.

Fixed capital services are computed from the stock estimates as the

Table IV.4
USSR: Capital Inputs in Industry, Annual Rate of Change,
Selected Periods, 1928–58
(percent)

Period	Fixed capital			Total	
	i = 8%	i = 20%	Inventories	i = 8%	i = 20%
1937 Prices					
1928–32	24.8	24.9	8.5	18.4	17.5
1932–37	13.3	13.1	10.6	12.5	12.2
1937–40	12.6	12.1	11.3	12.2	11.9
1940–45	−0.9	−1.0	−7.3	−2.5	−2.9
1945–50	10.3	10.5	13.0	10.9	11.2
1950–55	12.1	12.2	9.2	11.4	11.4
1955–58	11.0	11.1	7.7	10.3	10.2
1928–40	16.8	16.7	10.1	14.3	13.9
1950–58	11.7	11.8	8.6	11.0	10.9
1928–58	11.3	11.2	7.2	9.9	9.7
1928 Prices					
1928–32	25.5	25.7	13.2	22.3	21.8
1932–37	13.7	13.4	12.6	13.4	13.2
1937–40	13.0	12.5	11.4	12.6	12.2
1940–45	−1.3	−1.3	−6.7	−2.2	−2.5
1945–50	10.7	10.9	12.8	11.1	11.3
1950–55	12.3	12.4	9.5	11.8	11.8
1955–58	11.4	11.5	7.3	10.8	10.7
1928–40	17.3	17.1	12.5	16.1	15.7
1950–58	12.0	12.1	8.7	11.5	11.4
1928–58	11.5	11.5	8.2	10.8	10.6
1950 Prices					
1928–32	24.0	24.2	10.0	19.0	18.3
1932–37	12.6	12.4	11.2	12.2	12.0
1937–40	11.9	11.6	11.5	11.8	11.6
1940–45	−1.0	−1.0	−7.1	−2.5	−2.8
1945–50	9.6	9.7	12.8	10.3	10.6
1950–55	11.6	11.7	9.4	11.1	11.1
1955–58	10.0	10.1	7.5	9.4	9.4
1928–40	16.1	16.0	10.9	14.3	14.0
1950–58	11.0	11.1	8.7	10.4	10.4
1928–58	10.7	10.6	7.5	9.7	9.5

Note: Data derived from Table IV.12 in the appendix.

sum of depreciation on gross assets and interest charges on net assets.[20] Depreciation is computed on a straight line at 4 percent for equipment and 2 percent for structures. Alternative calculations are made with interest rates of 8 and 20 percent. Because of the unreliability of the division between equipment and structures for most years, the two are treated in combination.

Except that the depreciation rates rest on some information on service lives in the Soviet economy,[21] these calculations have virtually no foundation in fact. Straight-line depreciation is an accurate measure of the annual decline in capital values only on special assumptions about the time-shape of the service streams rendered by assets and about the rate of interest. It is particularly indefensible to assume that it remains accurate at interest rates of both 8 percent and 20 percent. I have no data on the actual shape of service streams, and the stock estimates are too poor to justify experimentation with alternative depreciation formulas. The choice of interest rates is discussed below.

In addition to their other shortcomings, the fixed capital estimates take no account of changes in the intensity with which assets are used. A varying part of the total may have been held in stand-by reserves. Obsolete and inoperative assets may have accounted for a varying share of the total. Changes in the number of shifts worked and in operating rates undoubtedly occurred. It is scarcely conceivable that accurate measures of such changes could be had, but disregarding them further impairs the reliability of the service series.

Purchases from Other Sectors

Current purchases by industry from other producing sectors are estimated only for agricultural raw materials and transportation services. The latter series is allowed to represent also communications inputs into industry and its weight is increased accordingly, an arbitrary but small imputation. The principal remaining sector is trade, which is probably of minor significance. The coverage of current purchases by industry may, therefore, be regarded as quite complete. Computed rates of change for such inputs are shown in Table IV.5. Single series are shown for the two components because alternative price weights are not employed; weight-year values are given in Table IV.14 in the appendix.

The derivation of the series for agriculture is among the oddest used here, but its results may be among the most reliable. Essentially, the series is the Kaplan-Moorsteen index, in 1950 prices, of industrial production of finished consumers' goods, with a minor adjustment for agricultural

---

[20] Since they are easily reproduced, the capital service series in absolute values are not shown.

[21] Assembled in the Moorsteen-Powell study.

Table IV.5
Industrial Purchases from Other Sectors, Annual Rate
of Change, Selected Periods, 1928–58
(percent)

Period	From agriculture	From transportation	Combined total		
			1937 Prices	1928 Prices	1950 Prices
1928–32	0.5	16.4	3.4	6.0	5.2
1932–37	8.6	14.9	10.2	11.4	11.2
1937–40	2.6	3.5	2.8	3.2	3.0
1940–45	−19.3	−5.6	−14.1	−11.1	−11.9
1945–50	20.4	14.1	17.9	16.4	16.8
1950–55	11.1	10.3	10.8	10.4	10.6
1955–58	6.5	11.3	8.3	9.4	9.1
1928–40	4.3	12.4	6.0	7.5	7.1
1950–58	9.3	10.7	9.9	10.0	10.1
1928–58	4.3	9.1	5.5	6.4	6.2

Note: Data derived from Table IV.14 in the appendix.

raw materials absorbed in increases in goods in process.[22] There are several grounds for thinking that the production index is a good surrogate for industrial purchases from agriculture. Goods consisting of processed agricultural raw materials account for nearly the whole of consumers' goods produced by Soviet industry.[23] Bread and bakery products and sewn goods are represented in the Kaplan-Moorsteen index by flour and fabrics although the processing within industry of the latter materials presumably increased over time.[24] And, what is most convincing, the Kaplan-Moorsteen index, for years from 1937 on, moves quite closely with the volume of procurements from agriculture of products processed by industry.[25] Divergences do appear within short periods, but, in view of possible changes in state stockpiles and other diversions of procured materials from industrial consumption, the Kaplan-Moorsteen index appears superior to one composed directly from procurement data. For years before 1937, similar comparisons cannot be made, but the production index behaves plausibly relative to agricultural output when account is taken of known changes in procurement policies and in imports (notably of cotton) and exports of unprocessed agricultural products.

[22] The production index for 1927/28 is adjusted upward slightly to correct for its apparent understatement of small-scale production. Figures for years not covered in the production index are interpolated on data obtained from my output indexes.
[23] See Kaplan and Moorsteen, pp. 203 and 209.
[24] *Ibid.*, p. 19.
[25] See notes to Table IV.14 in the appendix.

Nor is the fact that the agricultural series is weighted with only one set of prices a serious deficiency. Unpublished calculations made by Jerzy F. Karcz indicate that price indexes for agricultural procurements are highly insensitive to the quantity weights used. It follows that quantity indexes would be insensitive to the price weights used.[26]

Unlike the agricultural series, that for industrial purchases from transportation (*cum* communications) is an unmitigated makeshift. It is simply an index of total ton-kilometers of freight moved by all forms of Soviet transportation.[27] Calculations relating to the 1941 Plan[28] indicate that transportation services to industry accounted before the war for less than half of total freight revenues. The share of industry in the physical quantity of freight hauled may have been larger, but the index can scarcely be an accurate measure of inputs to industry alone. The assumption that it is invariant to price weights has no defense.

4. The Relation of Inputs to Outputs

The Production Function

I commenced with the question of how much of Soviet industrial growth could be accounted for by increases in productive inputs, utilized with given production functions and unvarying technology. I now have approximations to the statistical series required, but the problem remains of what production function should be used as the basis of the comparison. To this I have no satisfactory solution.

The fitting of production functions to quantity data alone encounters familiar and disabling statistical difficulties. The alternative procedure, which I shall follow, is to read rates of substitution between inputs from relative input prices as reflected in factor shares. The rationality of Soviet factor pricing is doubtless more questionable even than that of product pricing, and a thorough revamping of factor prices is not feasible. An adjustment for the lack of interest charges in Soviet costing, however, is obviously required.

Capital services were computed above with assumed interest rates of 8 percent and 20 percent in each weight year. These rates are meant to bound the range within which the true interest rate is likely to have fallen, although common observation is about all that suggests they do so. There is nothing symmetrical in the use of the same rates in all three years, and

---

[26] It may appear puzzling that an index of the quantity of agricultural procurements should be unaffected by price weights whereas indexes of retail sales of consumer goods, which are the basis of my output indexes, are, for 1928–37, highly sensitive to price weights. However, the share of agricultural materials in the total cost of consumer goods, excluding turnover taxes, is relatively small, amounting to about 32 percent in 1937.

[27] See Hunter, p. 344.

[28] Kaplan *et al.*, p. 7.

it might be supposed that the interest rate has declined over time. Against any possible fall in the marginal physical productivity of capital, however, must be set the fall in the supply price of capital relative to output prices in general. In strict logic, the introduction of a positive interest rate requires appropriate adjustments in the prices with which outputs are weighted, but this refinement also must be foregone.

Given the assumed interest rates, the share of each input in total costs can be computed (Table IV.6). Costs attributed to labor, agriculture, and

Table IV.6
USSR: Shares of Inputs in Total Industrial Costs, 1928, 1937, and 1950
(percent)

Input	1937		1928		1950	
	$i = 8\%$	$i = 20\%$	$i = 8\%$	$i = 20\%$	$i = 8\%$	$i = 20\%$
Labor	62.4	55.0	45.1	38.6	68.3	58.6
Fixed capital	8.2	14.4	10.5	17.7	11.0	18.8
Inventories	3.4	7.6	4.4	9.5	3.7	8.0
Agriculture	18.5	16.3	28.6	24.5	7.9	6.8
Transportation	7.5	6.7	11.4	9.7	9.1	7.8
Totals	100.0	100.0	100.0	100.0	100.0	100.0

Note: See text for derivation.

transportation are those actually paid. Capital charges are those implied by the assumed depreciation and interest rates. In all three years the computed capital shares at 8 percent interest lie below, and those at 20 percent above, the shares of profits and depreciation in costs actually recorded in Soviet industry. It turns out also that the capital shares at each of the assumed interest rates are of roughly the same order of magnitude in all three years. The shares of other inputs vary widely.[29]

Assuming that the indicated factor shares are meaningful, one can still make a wide variety of assumptions about the substitutability of inputs and about the sign and size of returns to scale. With respect to the latter, I assume in the calculations following that returns to scale are constant and make such allowance as I can for variable returns in interpreting the results. With respect to factor substitutabilities, it may be worth while to consider three possible alternatives.

At one extreme, it could be assumed that all inputs are perfect substitutes for one another. The input series would then properly be added arithmetically, with weights equal to their shares in total costs. Such

[29] Reported data on factor shares, including nominal profits and depreciation, are given in the notes to Table IV.9 in the appendix.

arithmetic summations are shown in Table IV.16 in the appendix. The assumption of perfect substitutability, however, although it has implicitly been made in the computation of the component input series, is rather implausible for substitutions among major categories of inputs.

It could be assumed at the other extreme that there is no substitutability among inputs, that coefficients are fixed. If this had been the case in Soviet industry, output attributable to increased inputs would have grown from 1928 to 1958 at the rate of the most slowly growing input, agricultural raw materials. Fixed coefficients for a sector as comprehensive as industry appear absurd. However, as has been previously remarked, agricultural inputs evidently have moved with the output of consumer goods, and the effects of agricultural inputs on this part of output probably resembled those of a nonsubstitutable input. It appears advisable, nevertheless, to disregard this fixity, because of a deficiency in the input series, namely, the omission of inputs of natural resources. One would suppose that the upward pull on output of the latter inputs was typically strongest when the restraint on output from agricultural inputs was most severe. On these — clearly inadequate — grounds, I assume that agricultural raw materials are as easily substituted for other inputs as they are for one another and that there is some positive substitutability among all.

If neither perfect nor zero substitutability is reasonable, an intermediate assumption is called for. Because it is simple and familiar, not out of conviction that it fits reality, I assume that the elasticity of substitution is unitary, that is, I assume a Cobb-Douglas function, although I apply it to measures of inputs and outputs different from those with which it has been associated historically.

The Contribution of Aggregate Inputs

Given the general shape of the production function, six different sets of possible coefficients for a Cobb-Douglas function are provided in Table IV.6, one for each weight year and interest rate. Although this is a large number of alternatives, to reduce it would require additional assumptions even less acceptable than those previously made. I therefore compute from each set of coefficients separately (adding the input series in the logs, with weights equal to the coefficients) the outputs which would have resulted from the given inputs. The component input series in each case are those with prices or interest rates corresponding to those of the coefficients. For projected outputs so computed for benchmark years, rates of change are shown in Table IV.7. The logarithmic additions of the input series differ significantly from arithmetic additions only for the calculations in 1928 prices.

If the assumptions made in computing projected outputs are adhered to and shortcomings in the statistics are disregarded, the relation between

Table IV.7
USSR: Projected Final Industrial Product from Given Inputs,
Annual Rate of Change, Selected Periods, 1928–58
(percent)

Period	1937 Prices		1928 Prices		1950 Prices	
	i = 8%	i = 20%	i = 8%	i = 20%	i = 8%	i = 20%
1928–32	9.9	10.7	9.6	11.1	11.3	12.5
1932–37	6.7	7.3	7.9	8.6	6.7	7.3
1937–40	5.9	6.4	5.6	6.6	6.1	6.9
1940–45	−3.7	−3.6	−5.9	−5.6	−1.7	−1.9
1945–50	9.6	9.7	11.5	11.6	8.2	8.6
1950–55	7.3	7.7	8.3	8.8	6.9	7.5
1955–58	4.4	5.0	5.4	6.0	4.0	4.8
1928–40	7.5	8.2	7.9	8.9	8.1	8.9
1950–58	6.2	6.7	7.2	7.7	5.8	6.4
1928–58	5.6	6.0	5.9	6.5	5.8	6.3

Note: Data derived from Table IV.17 in the appendix.

actual and projected rates of change in output (Tables IV.1 and IV.7)
provides a measure of the time rate of change in technology and efficiency.[30] Such rates are shown in Table IV.8. Improved efficiency is to
be understood as improved utilization of inputs apart from changes in the
technology employed.

The ratios of projected to actual rates of change in output, and hence
the presumed contribution of increased inputs to output, vary widely with
the prices used. Since the projected output series differ only moderately
from one another, the principal source of the divergences lies in the series
for actual outputs. The differences among the latter arise from differences
in the product prices with which outputs are weighted.

It is a well known feature of Soviet development that changes over
time in product prices and quantities have been markedly and inversely
correlated: those products whose output has increased most rapidly have
shown the largest relative decline in prices. This can be observed with
respect to industrial products in Table IV.9 in the appendix. Its most
notable illustration is in the changes in machinery prices and production
between 1928 and 1937. Another is in the changes in munitions prices and
quantities from 1937 to 1950, and probably more marked, if the comparison could be made, from 1937 to the late war years.

In principle and disregarding the deficiencies of Soviet prices, the

[30] The rate of change in technology and efficiency equals (1 plus the rate of change in
actual output) divided by (1 plus the rate of change in projected output) minus 1.

Table IV.8
USSR: Implied Annual Rate of Change in Technology and
Efficiency, Selected Periods, 1928–58
(percent)

Period	1937 Prices		1928 Prices		1950 Prices	
	i = 8%	i = 20%	i = 8%	i = 20%	i = 8%	i = 20%
1928–32	−2.5	−3.3	7.8	6.3	−3.8	−4.8
1932–37	5.5	4.9	9.1	8.4	3.9	3.4
1937–40	2.7	2.3	4.9	3.9	0	−0.7
1940–45	−0.1	−0.2	3.6	3.3	−9.0	−8.8
1945–50	−0.4	−0.5	−2.0	−2.1	7.8	7.4
1950–55	2.2	1.9	1.2	0.7	2.8	2.2
1955–58	6.3	5.7	5.3	4.7	7.1	6.3
1928–40	2.1	1.5	7.6	6.6	0.3	−0.5
1950–58	3.8	3.3	2.7	2.2	4.4	3.9
1928–58	1.7	1.3	4.0	3.4	1.1	0.7

Note: See text for derivation.

changes in relative product prices must have been due to the combined effects of changes in relative input prices, changes in technology and efficiency, and economies or diseconomies of scale. Disproportionate effects upon product prices doubtless were caused by changes in input prices, but these should not necessarily have worked solely or strongly in the observed direction. Changes in technology and economies of scale, on the other hand, were almost certainly concentrated heavily in those industries in which output expanded most rapidly. For this reason, the differences among the three series for actual output can be interpreted as due chiefly to the heavier weight given by earlier year prices to industries in which technological change and scale effects were large. The differences among the calculations are therefore neither surprising nor without meaning: they are a consequence of the aggregation of component industries within which the relative importance of the several sources of growth was not uniform.

This is not to say that measures in all three price weights are equally valid for present purposes. Gains in output from increasing returns to scale are properly attributed to increased inputs. The calculations in Tables IV.7 and IV.8 therefore understate the contribution to output of increased inputs and overstate the contribution of improved technology and efficiency. The errors are in the same direction in the calculations in all three prices, but they are probably particularly large in the calculations in 1928 prices, because of the exceptionally heavy weight given by prices of that year to products for which economies of scale had not yet been exploited. While the 1928 price calculations need not be ruled out altogether — they are of special interest for the 1928–37 period — they should be treated with exceptional caution.

If some intuitive allowance is made for the distortion due to scale effects, the answer to my original question for the thirty years from 1928 to 1958 is reasonably clear. The rate of increase in projected relative to actual outputs is no lower than 58 to 64 percent in 1928 prices; it is as high as 76 to 81 percent in 1937 prices, and 83 to 90 percent in 1950 prices. The rate of increase in technology and efficiency relative to that in actual output is no higher than 40 percent, in 1928 prices at an 8 percent interest rate, and as low as 10 percent, in 1950 prices at a 20 percent interest rate. Although the contribution of technology and efficiency is not necessarily trivial, Soviet industrial growth appears explicable in large measure by the increase in productive resources employed.

In subperiods, the sharply disparate results can plausibly be accounted for as the consequence of opposing forces differently weighted. From 1928 to 1932, the effects of new techniques and economies of scale presumably were large in the rapidly expanding sectors (heavily weighted by 1928 prices). At the same time, the average skill and discipline of labor in industry as a whole declined. Elasticities of substitution between inputs, in the short run and for such extreme changes in factor proportions as occurred, were probably lower than those I assume. Organizational inefficiencies probably increased with the enormous increase in total inputs, early experimentation with central planning, and the general disorder with which the First Five-Year Plan came to an end. The spurt in measured improvement in technology and efficiency from 1932 to 1937 can be explained by the resolution of the difficulties of the preceding period and by continuing technological change.

The differences among the measures in the three intervals from 1937 to 1950 are due principally to differences in the relative weights attached to munitions. Technological improvements in this sector presumably were large; economies of scale may have been large also, although these may be transferable between munitions and machinery production. For 1937–40, all the calculations indicate a decline in the rate of technological and efficiency gains relative to 1932–37, perhaps because the recovery from the disequilibrium of the early 1930's was largely accomplished in the earlier period, perhaps because of the depressing effects of the purges. From 1940 to 1945, the quality of labor may have declined again, large shifts occurred in the composition of output and in input proportions, and various organizational dislocations may have resulted from the war. The period from 1945 to 1950 is again one of recovery. However, this period differs from the 1930's in that the sector which had probably experienced the largest technological gains in the preceding period, munitions production, was sharply contracted. By all of the measures, little or no gain in technology and efficiency was recorded over the ten years from 1940 to 1950.

From 1950 to 1955, measured improvements are substantial and from 1955 to 1958 spectacular. Indeed, what is perhaps most startling and least plausible in the calculations is the distribution of technological and efficiency gains, measured in prices other than those of 1928, between the years preceding and those following 1950. In 1937 prices, the annual rate of improvement was 0.6 to 0.9 percent from 1928 to 1950 and 3.3 to 3.8 percent from 1950 to 1958. In 1950 prices, the rate was −0.5 to 0 in the earlier period and 3.9 to 4.4 percent in the later. This difference may be due in part, however, to statistical error.

I have described my final product estimate for 1958 as an upper limit. If my figure for 1958 in 1950 prices is replaced by that computed from the Kaplan-Moorsteen index, the rate of improvement in technology and efficiency is reduced to 3.4 to 4.2 percent in 1955–58 and 2.8 to 3.4 percent in 1950–58 (and to 0.4 to 0.9 percent in 1928–58). These are considerably lower rates of gain than those initially calculated, and they may still be too high because of errors in the input estimates.[31] On the other hand, the Kaplan-Moorsteen index probably understates the rate of output growth. Unless the input estimates are greatly in error, the gains in the recent past remain remarkably high relative to those of earlier years.

This apparent difference is not easily explained by technological change. Soviet borrowings of Western techniques in the early years of industrialization were deliberate, extensive, and certainly consequential. That their effects do not register clearly in the calculations, except when outputs are weighted with very early prices, must be due to offsetting inefficiencies arising from other sources or to more adverse changes in the quality and composition of factor inputs than I allow for. By 1950, on the other hand, the gains to be had from further technological borrowings, though still significant, would appear reduced relative to those available earlier. One can speculate that the rapid and accelerating gains of the 1950's are attributable instead to the absence of severe and pervasive disturbances like those of the early 1930's and the war, to the organizational innovations and increased rationality of the post-Stalin regime, or to the mastering of reasonably efficient techniques of centralized planning and administration. Also, there is evidence that in the economy as a whole during the 1950's the introduction of new types of equipment was accelerated and the average age of both equipment and structures in operation

---

[31] The estimated growth of the fixed capital stock is puzzlingly low in 1958. The reduction in hours worked may not have meant a proportionate decline in labor input.

was greatly reduced.[32] If these changes occurred also in the industrial capital stock and if, as is plausible, fixed capital is in some degree the "carrier" of new technology, a rapid increase in technological change in this period may be credible. But, in the absence of firmer data, it is risky to press *ad hoc* explanations too far.

5. COMPARISON WITH U.S. INDUSTRIAL GROWTH

I cannot attempt a serious comparison of the growth of Soviet and U.S. industry, because data conceptually similar to those for the USSR are not readily accessible for the U.S. There is no reasonable doubt that the rate of growth in Soviet industry from 1928 to 1958 was high relative to that of the U.S. in the same period and in earlier periods as well.[33] The difference varies with the price weights used for Soviet output and would no doubt also vary with alternative weightings of U.S. output. Whether there are significant differences in the sources of growth in the two economies remains to be established by further inquiries.

It may be of interest, nevertheless, to consider rates of change in the "productivity" or "efficiency" of total inputs which have been estimated for U.S. industry: Kendrick finds a 2 percent annual increase from 1899 to 1953 for both manufacturing and mining, Schmookler a 1.41 percent increase in manufacturing and a 2.49 percent increase in mining from 1869–78 to 1919–28.[34] These calculations differ somewhat from one another, but they can be most nearly matched for Soviet industry by comparing value added with the arithmetic sum of labor and net capital inputs. Rates of improvement so calculated for 1928–58 are 2.0 to 2.6 percent in 1937 prices, 3.1 to 4.2 percent in 1928 prices, and 1.2 to 1.8 percent in 1950 prices. The 1928 price figures aside, the Soviet rates are about the same as those for U.S. industry.

This conclusion, if it were sustainable, would be remarkable. That Soviet industry, with the advantages of a late start, with a higher rate of growth in output, and with a particularly rapid increase in equipment and other capital, should show a rate of improvement in technology and related factors no greater than that attained by U.S. industry would suggest some significant inefficiency in a broader sense of the term than I have given it. It would suggest also that the dominance of increased inputs in Soviet

[32] See Moorsteen, and Moorsteen and Powell.

[33] Compare, for example, G. Warren Nutter, "The Structure and Growth of Soviet Industry: A Comparison with the United States," in Joint Economic Committee, 86th Congress of the United States, 1st Session, *Comparisons of the United States and Soviet Economies* (Washington, 1959), part I, p. 105.

[34] See John W. Kendrick, "Productivity Trends: Capital and Labor," *Review of Economics and Statistics,* August 1956, p. 251; and Jacob Schmookler, "The Changing Efficiency of the American Economy, 1869–1938," *ibid.,* August 1952, p. 230.

growth was great not only relative to other sources of growth but in comparison with U.S. experience. I suspect that there was a difference in this direction in the industrialization processes of the two countries. However, I have stated previously my objections to calculations based on net outputs and inputs. And, before a reliable comparison can be made, the statistics for both Soviet and U.S. industry require extensive reworking.

APPENDIX

The appendix consists of nine tables, IV.9 to IV.17, with notes to each.
Table IV.9 and Notes

In the space available it is impossible to present a sufficiently detailed explanation of the final product estimates (and of other estimates) to permit the reader to reproduce the calculations. To give some basis for independent judgment, I show in Table IV.9 the components as well as the totals. However, the component series cannot safely be read as measures of the output of particular kinds of products. Some products appear in several final product categories, for example, consumer goods in retail sales, inventories, military subsistence, and other deliveries to GNP uses. Products with both intermediate and final uses are included only in proportion to the latter. The product composition of receipts from external sources, except for machinery and munitions, is not estimated. Finally, the aggregates are estimated on the assumption that certain errors in the components are offsetting, notably those arising from imports and exports for which no allowance has been made, but also, if I understand Bergson's procedures rightly, those occurring in component estimates of sales for military uses.

The derivation of the estimates is most easily explained by grouping together those series with more or less common sources: the three investment components; all other components in 1928, 1937, 1940, 1944, and 1948–55; and all other components in the remaining years.

The three investment components derive in all years and for all price weights from finished estimates for investment. Those for equipment are from Richard Moorsteen, *Prices and Production of Machinery in the Soviet Union, 1928–1958* (Cambridge, Mass., 1962), with extensions to additional years and conversions to alternative price weights from the Moorsteen-Powell study. Those for structures are from Raymond P. Powell, *A Materials-Input Index of Soviet Construction, Revised and Extended,* The RAND Corporation, Research Memorandum RM-2454, September 28, 1959, with extensions from Moorsteen-Powell. Those for inventories are computed from stock estimates made in Moorsteen-Powell.

The equipment estimates are those Moorsteen derives by deflating investment in current prices, not his aggregated domestic output series. I assume that 90 percent of his estimates of investment in new equipment and 60 percent of his investment in capital repairs constituted industrial product at price to the seller (the percentages are suggested by data given in Moorsteen). Equipment from external sources (such as commercial imports, receipts on Lend-Lease account) is excluded in the years in which it is thought to have been of consequence, 1928–33 and 1944–48. Part of this adjustment has been made by Moorsteen; the remainder is made here by simple extrapolation

Table IV.9
USSR: Final Industrial Product, by Components, 1928–58
(billions of rubles)

Category	1928	1929	1930	1931	1932	1933	1934	1935	1936	1937	1938	1939	1940
1937 Prices													
Retail sales	27.6	32.6	30.8	30.1	29.0	27.5	28.8	29.6	33.2	39.6	45.0	52.6	45.6
Equipment	1.5	2.3	3.7	4.6	5.5	5.5	5.9	7.6	10.6	10.7	12.1	11.5	11.3
Construction	2.9	3.5	4.6	5.0	5.0	4.5	5.4	6.7	9.0	7.8	7.7	7.9	7.9
Inventories	0.9	−1.1	0.3	3.8	2.0	1.8	1.0	9.0	5.4	5.5	4.0	5.9	2.6
Munitions	0.4	0.5	0.7	0.8	0.8	0.9	2.9	4.8	8.2	9.5	12.3	19.9	26.8
Military subsistence	0.5	0.5	0.6	0.6	0.6	0.7	0.9	1.1	1.4	1.7	2.0	2.9	3.4
Other to GNP uses	1.8	2.3	2.9	3.5	4.0	4.2	4.9	6.6	8.5	10.1	11.4	12.0	11.6
Unallocated external receipts	0	0	0	0	0	0	0	0	0	0	0	0	0
Sum of above	35.6	40.6	43.6	48.4	46.9	45.1	49.8	65.4	76.3	84.9	94.5	112.7	109.2
Adjusted total	38.2	43.5	46.7	51.9	50.3	48.3	53.4	70.1	81.8	91.0	101	121	117
1928 Prices													
Retail sales	5.4	6.6	6.5	6.6	6.6	6.5	7.2	7.7	9.1	11.4	13.0	15.1	13.1
Equipment	1.0	1.7	2.9	4.1	5.9	6.5	7.3	9.4	13.9	14.4	17.1	16.2	16.5
Construction	1.7	2.2	2.9	3.1	3.1	2.7	3.3	4.1	5.6	4.9	4.8	4.9	4.8
Inventories	0.7	0.4	1.2	2.5	1.4	0.8	0.9	4.2	2.4	2.1	1.8	2.4	2.3
Munitions	0.2	0.3	0.4	0.4	0.4	0.5	1.7	2.8	4.8	5.7	7.4	11.9	16.1
Military subsistence	0.2	0.2	0.2	0.2	0.2	0.3	0.4	0.4	0.6	0.8	0.8	1.2	1.4
Other to GNP uses	0.8	1.0	1.3	1.6	1.8	1.9	2.3	3.0	3.9	4.7	5.4	5.7	5.6
Unallocated external receipts	0	0	0	0	0	0	0	0	0	0	0	0	0
Sum of above	10.0	12.4	15.4	18.5	19.4	19.2	23.1	31.6	40.3	43.9	50.3	57.4	59.8
Adjusted total	10.7	13.3	16.5	19.8	20.8	20.5	24.7	33.8	43.1	47.0	53.8	61.4	64.0
1950 Prices													
Retail sales	65.1	77.0	72.8	71.2	68.7	65.2	68.3	70.3	78.9	94.2	105.7	122.1	104.5
Equipment	4.2	6.4	9.8	11.1	12.3	11.6	12.4	16.0	22.0	21.3	23.6	22.0	23.8
Construction	9.2	11.6	15.1	16.2	16.3	14.5	17.3	21.2	28.5	25.0	24.1	25.0	24.7
Inventories	2.0	−1.7	1.5	9.0	4.9	4.0	2.6	19.4	11.6	11.7	8.6	12.8	7.2
Munitions	0.7	0.7	1.0	1.2	1.1	1.3	3.9	6.3	10.7	12.1	15.6	25.3	34.0
Military subsistence	1.1	1.1	1.3	1.3	1.3	1.5	2.0	2.4	3.1	3.7	4.4	6.4	7.5
Other to GNP uses	4.0	5.1	6.5	7.8	8.9	9.4	11.0	14.8	19.1	22.7	25.7	26.9	26.0
Unallocated external receipts	0	0	0	0	0	0	0	0	0	0	0	0	0
Sum of above	86.3	100.2	108.0	117.8	113.5	107.5	117.5	150.4	173.9	190.7	207.7	240.5	227.7
Adjusted total	92.5	107	116	126	122	115	126	161	186	204	223	258	244

	1944	1945	1946	1947	1948	1949	1950	1951	1952	1953	1954	1955	1956	1957	1958
1937 Prices															
Retail sales	24.5	30.4	33.3	30.7	33.8	41.2	53.4	59.4	63.7	76.4	90.3	93.4	101.5	115.9	123.0
Equipment	4.8	7.9	10.2	12.7	15.4	18.4	24.6	26.1	26.4	29.5	34.8	42.0	52.2	58.4	65.3
Construction	3.1	3.3	5.0	6.2	8.3	10.5	12.1	13.7	15.3	16.9	18.6	20.6	21.6	23.6	25.8
Inventories	1.3	1.9	1.1	9.1	7.5	21.8	10.7	16.4	15.1	15.3	-2.6	6.3	17.6	10.5	29.9
Munitions	64.1	57.6	31.8	27.4	25.9	25.9	25.3	27.8	36.2	36.1	30.3	39.4	37.6	37.5	36.2
Military subsistence	11.8	9.4	4.6	3.4	2.8	3.0	4.1	5.2	6.4	6.6	6.7	6.6	6.3	6.3	6.1
Other to GNP uses	9.7	11.6	12.9	14.0	16.5	13.6	13.7	13.7	13.8	13.5	15.6	16.3	17.6	19.0	20.2
Unallocated external receipts	-18.2	-31.5	-17.4	-11.1	-4.7	-4.4	-2.7	-2.8	-2.7	-2.1	0	0	0	0	0
Sum of above	101.1	90.6	81.5	92.4	105.5	130.0	141.2	159.5	174.2	192.2	193.7	224.6	254.4	271.2	306.5
Adjusted total	108	97.1	87.4	99.1	113	139	151	171	187	206	208	241	273	291	329
1928 Prices															
Retail sales	7.1	8.7	9.6	8.8	9.7	11.9	15.4	17.1	18.3	22.0	26.0	26.9	29.2	33.4	35.4
Equipment	6.6	10.9	13.2	16.2	20.2	24.6	32.3	32.1	32.4	36.6	44.2	53.7	66.3	72.0	79.4
Construction	1.9	2.1	3.2	3.9	5.3	6.6	7.6	8.7	9.7	10.7	11.8	13.2	13.8	15.2	16.7
Inventories	0.3	0.5	1.7	3.5	1.5	9.2	4.8	7.0	6.1	7.6	-0.9	1.9	6.9	4.6	11.5
Munitions	38.4	34.6	19.1	16.4	15.5	15.5	15.2	16.7	21.7	21.7	18.2	23.6	22.6	22.5	21.7
Military subsistence	4.7	3.8	1.8	1.4	1.1	1.2	1.6	2.1	2.6	2.6	2.7	2.6	2.5	2.5	2.4
Other to GNP uses	4.5	5.4	6.1	6.7	8.0	6.7	6.7	6.7	7.0	6.9	7.8	8.4	9.1	9.8	10.4
Unallocated external receipts	-7.5	-13.0	-7.2	-4.6	-1.9	-1.8	-1.1	-1.2	-1.1	-0.9	0	0	0	0	0
Sum of above	56.0	53.0	47.5	52.3	59.4	73.9	82.5	89.2	96.7	107.2	109.8	130.3	150.4	160.0	177.5
Adjusted total	59.9	56.7	50.8	56.0	63.6	79.1	88.3	95.4	103	115	117	139	161	171	190
1950 Prices															
Retail sales	55.8	69.9	77.2	71.8	79.8	96.5	124.6	138.7	147.8	179.7	215.4	222.2	241.5	275.7	292.6
Equipment	8.0	13.1	18.3	23.2	28.8	35.2	47.6	50.7	50.6	55.9	65.3	79.4	99.1	111.3	123.2
Construction	9.6	10.5	15.5	19.1	25.7	32.5	37.2	42.4	47.4	52.2	57.4	63.4	66.2	72.7	79.4
Inventories	2.3	3.3	4.1	18.3	12.8	45.7	23.2	34.3	30.8	34.5	-4.9	11.8	35.1	22.4	60.6
Munitions	81.4	73.2	40.4	34.8	32.9	32.9	32.1	35.3	46.0	45.8	38.5	50.0	47.8	47.6	46.0
Military subsistence	25.9	20.6	10.1	7.5	6.1	6.6	9.0	11.4	14.0	14.5	14.7	14.5	13.8	13.8	13.4
Other to GNP uses	21.5	26.0	29.0	31.8	37.8	30.7	30.8	30.5	30.7	29.8	34.3	36.0	38.9	42.0	44.6
Unallocated external receipts	-45.3	-78.4	-43.3	-27.6	-11.7	-11.0	-6.7	-7.0	-6.7	-5.2	0	0	0	0	0
Sum of above	159.2	138.2	151.3	178.9	212.2	269.1	297.8	336.3	360.6	407.2	420.7	477.3	542.4	585.5	659.8
Adjusted total	171	148	162	192	227	288	319	360	386	436	451	512	581	628	707

from Moorsteen's estimates. Price weights are wholesale prices received by the seller; no adjustment is thought to be necessary for correspondence to factor cost valuation.

The original estimates of investment in construction are indexes of materials consumed in construction. On the reasonable assumption that all such materials are of industrial origin, the same indexes are used to measure deliveries to construction of industrial materials. Since the original estimates are meant to measure materials of a given degree of fabrication, the indexes fail to record any increase in fabrication within the industrial sector. The value of materials at origin and in current prices in 1937 is estimated from Raymond P. Powell, *A Materials-Input Index of Soviet Construction, 1927/28 to 1955*, The RAND Corporation, Research Memoranda RM-1872 and RM-1873, February 14, 1957, part II, p. 482, and *A Materials-Input Index, Revised and Extended*, p. 86. Figures for 1928 and 1950 are estimated from the 1937 figure and from indexes of physical quantities and prices of materials given in the same sources. The weights are prevailing wholesale prices received by the seller. No adjustment is made for materials of nondomestic origin.

The original estimates of total inventories on January 1 of each year are aggregates of separate estimates for component sectors and for each sector of inventories on hand and goods in transit. Annual investment is the difference between beginning and end-of-year values (figures for the unenlarged territory are used for 1939 and 1940). Inventories of industrial origin in each sector are estimated as follows. All inventories in producers' goods industries, transportation and communications, and trade are assumed to be of industrial origin. A fraction of inventories, determined from data given in Moorsteen and Powell, on the composition of inventories in the weight years, in consumers' goods industries and procurement, is assumed to be of industrial origin. No inventories in agriculture, contract construction, and "other" sectors are attributed to industry, either because total inventories are negligible or because (in the case of agriculture) the industrial share in the total is negligible. The price indexes used in deflating inventories are too numerous for description but are substantially those used in the Bergson GNP estimates. Adjustments from market to factor cost valuations are made only for consumers' goods industries and trade, but are thought to be necessary only there. The distribution costs of inventories appear small and are not corrected for. No adjustment is made for inventories acquired from nondomestic sources.

The second group of estimates, those for deliveries to GNP uses other than investment in 1928, 1937, 1940, 1944, and 1948–55, derive entirely from Bergson, *Real SNIP*.

(i) The industrial component in private consumption outlays is based on Bergson's estimates of retail sales to households in state and cooperative shops and restaurants, valued at factor cost. All sales in collective farm markets are excluded. Except for 1928, which is discussed separately below, figures in 1937 factor cost valuations are given by Bergson. For 1928 and 1950 valuations, Bergson shows the adjustment from market prices to factor costs for total retail purchases only; I assume that the same percentage adjustment can be made for state and cooperative trade alone. Bergson's estimates, in 1928 prices, are for 1928 and 1937 only; I extrapolate his series from 1937 on the series in 1937 prices.

For 1928, in all prices, Bergson gives only total household purchases in all retail markets. Following Kaplan and Moorsteen, p. 152 fn., "extra-village" sales, included in the 1928 total, are assumed to be the counterpart of collective farm market sales and are deducted. On the basis of Oleg Hoeffding, *Soviet National Income and Product in 1928* (New York, 1954), p. 101, such sales in 1928 are estimated to be 3.28 billion rubles in current prices, or 27.1 percent of Bergson's total for retail purchases. Extra-village sales are assumed to account for the same share of the 1928 total in factor costs of all three weight years.

From TSU, *Sovetskaia torgovlia* (Moscow, 1956), pp. 48–49, the share of unprocessed agricultural products (eggs, potatoes, vegetables, fruits, berries, and melons) in state and cooperative trade in current market prices can be computed as 1.6 percent in 1928, 3.0 percent in 1937, and 2.3 percent in 1950. Total household purchases, including those in restaurants, in factor costs of each weight year, are reduced by the percentage indicated for the weight year.

From data in Bergson, *Real SNIP*, the distribution costs of goods sold at retail are assumed to have accounted for 15 percent of the value of sales at prevailing *retail* prices in both 1928 and 1937 and for 10.8 percent in 1950; an equivalent absolute amount is deducted from the value of sales at factor cost. The share of distribution costs in all years other than the weight year is assumed the same as in the weight year. No adjustment is made for retail sales of consumer goods of nondomestic origin.

(ii) Munitions purchases by government are taken directly from Bergson or computed from data given by him, with minor adjustments and one extension.

Bergson combines munitions with other military procurements in 1928, 1937, and 1949. The share of munitions in the total in 1928 and 1937 is here assumed the same as in 1940, that in 1949 the same as in 1948. Bergson makes the adjustment from market prices to factor costs for total military procurements only, but the adjustment is small and I use his data for munitions in market prices. Bergson's figures for munitions procurements are at sellers' prices, excluding distribution costs, and I make no adjustment for distribution costs. Bergson does not estimate munitions in 1928 prices beyond 1937; I extrapolate his series on that in 1937 prices.

For 1944, Bergson's estimate of munitions received on account of Lend-Lease is 6.5 billion rubles in 1937 prices. I deduct this amount from the 1944 total in 1937 prices, and a proportionate amount from totals in the prices of the other two years. Separate corrections for munitions from nondomestic sources are not made in the other years covered by Bergson.

(iii) Figures for military subsistence, in 1937 and 1950 prices, are Bergson's estimates at factor cost, reduced, rather arbitrarily, 10 percent to allow for distribution costs and for nonindustrial products.

The logic of this procedure may be questionable. If I follow Bergson, his estimates of military subsistence (and pay) are meant to measure the "real" value of military services rendered, not necessarily the actual subsistence provided to the armed forces. However, since he generally computes munitions outlays as a residual, his combined estimates of munitions and subsistence would seem reasonably appropriate for present purposes even if the component estimates are somewhat inappropriate. The same logic would call for the inclusion here of part of Bergson's estimate of "other" procurements by the military, but I cannot identify the industrial component in these.

Subsistence in 1928, in 1928 prices, is Bergson's, but I extrapolate 1937 as well as subsequent years on his series in 1937 prices, which is the procedure by which Bergson converts from 1937 to 1950 prices (his 1937 figure, in 1928 prices, is deflated). No adjustment is made for supplies from nondomestic sources.

(iv) Other deliveries to GNP uses consist principally of government purchases for education, health, administration, and internal security, but include also sales of electric power to households.

Bergson gives directly, in 1937 *market* prices, nonlabor outlays for health care and for education and electricity purchased by households (a few missing years in the last series are interpolated or extrapolated). His series for government administration and internal security combine labor and nonlabor outlays, but his deflators suggest a nonlabor share of about 30 percent. To reduce market price valuations to factor cost, I assume the two were identical for electricity and, for the other components, that the whole of the adjustments made by Bergson are attributable to nonlabor outlays. I deduct an amount equal to 10 percent of the market value of materials purchased to allow for distribution costs.

Series in 1928 and 1950 prices are derived, essentially, by establishing weight-year values for the several components from data provided by Bergson (and, for electricity prices, in Janet G. Chapman, *Real Wages in the Soviet Union Since 1928,* forthcoming) and extrapolating on the 1937 price series. No adjustment is made for purchases of products of nondomestic origin.

(v) "Unallocated external receipts" covers receipts from Lend-Lease, reparations, and war booty, which have not been allowed for in other components. Since equipment and munitions have been adjusted separately, the category includes receipts of finished consumer goods and intermediate industrial products. These cannot be attributed to any single final use component. The estimated combined sum of these receipts, in 1944–53, is therefore deducted from the total of deliveries of industrial products previously estimated.

For 1944, Bergson estimates Lend-Lease receipts of products (which seem to be largely of industrial origin) other than equipment and munitions to have been 23.5 billion rubles in 1937 market prices (excluding trade margins and extra processing costs on consumer goods). By adjusting the consumer goods component to factor costs by the ratio applied to all consumer goods, the total is reduced to 18.2 billion, the figure used in the 1937 price estimates.

I convert the same total to 1928 and 1950 prices with price indexes for consumer goods, for the consumer goods part of the total, and for basic industrial products for the remainder. The consumer price indexes are those implied in the estimates of retail sales to households in prices of the three weight years. The basic industrial price index, including products, is from Abram Bergson, Roman Bernaut, and Lynn Turgeon, *Basic Industrial Prices in the USSR, 1928–1950: Twenty-five Branch Series and Their Aggregation,* The RAND Corporation, Research Memorandum RM-1522, August 1, 1955, p. 69a.

For 1948 to 1953, Bergson provides estimates of reparations in 1937 rubles. I use his figures without adjustment for the 1937 price series. For the 1928 and 1950 price series, I extrapolate from 1944 on the 1937 price series (a highly questionable procedure).

For components other than investment and for years other than those covered by Bergson (1929–36, 1938–39, 1945–47, and 1956–58), I derive estimates by procedures which are basically similar to Bergson's but which, in comparison with his, are extremely casual. In all cases, my estimates are calculated in 1937 prices only. I then use the same series to interpolate between, or extrapolate from, Bergson's estimates in all three sets of prices.

(i) The interpolating series for private consumption for 1929–36 and 1938–39 is computed by deflating retail sales in state and cooperative shops and restaurants, without adjustment for coverage, by retail price indexes. The current price data are given in *Sovetskaia torgovlia,* p. 20. The price indexes are adaptations of indexes composed in Moorsteen and Powell, for deflation of trade inventories. The latter are based on official price indexes for 1929 and 1932, on information provided by Janet Chapman on the relation of 1936 to 1937 prices, and on crude interpolations.

The interpolating series for 1945–47 is based on estimates in Moorsteen and Powell of retail sales in ration trade and restaurants, in commercial trade, and in special rural trade, and price indexes for these components provided by Janet Chapman. The handling of these data parallels that in the Moorsteen-Powell study.

Figures for 1956–58 are extrapolated from 1955 on the official index for retail trade in constant prices, given in *Narodnoe khoziaistvo 1959,* p. 633. The official retail price index for years after 1948 moves quite closely with the Chapman estimates; no general price revision has occurred since 1954.

(ii) Interpolating and extrapolating series for munitions are composed by deflating *total* reported budget outlays for military purposes. The necessary budget data are obtained from TSU, *Narodnoe khoziaistvo SSSR* (Moscow-Leningrad, 1932), p. 577; K. N. Plotnikov, *Biudzhet sotsialisticheskogo gosudarstva* (Leningrad, 1948), pp. 70, 142, 216, and 303; and, for years after 1945, various official sources, including the annual messages of the Minister of Finance as published in *Pravda.* The deflator is one derived by Moorsteen and Powell for deflation of inventories in producers' goods industries, from the Moorsteen index of machinery prices, the Bergson-Bernaut-Turgeon index of basic industrial prices, and a rough index of wage costs in industry.

For 1945–47, munitions obtained from nondomestic sources are assumed to have changed linearly, as a fraction of total munitions, from 1944 to 1948, and to have been zero in the latter year. The estimates of deliveries of munitions, together with those of military subsistence, are a likely source of significant error.

(iii) Military subsistence is interpolated and extrapolated on the basis of the series for munitions (including in 1945–47 munitions from nondomestic sources).

(iv) For other deliveries to GNP, I omit electricity sold to households. Budget outlays for education, health, administration, and internal security, are taken from substantially the same sources as those for military outlays. For 1929–36 and 1938–39, these are deflated by the average of the indexes used to deflate munitions and retail trade. Estimates for 1956–58 are extrapolated from 1955 on the current price data, since no major price changes occurred.

(v) The adjustment for receipts from nondomestic sources, other than equipment and munitions, is made for 1945–47 only. Moorsteen cities data for *planned* budgetary receipts from customs and reparations in 1944 of 24 billion rubles, in 1945 — but including some unrelated items — of 51.7 billion, and in 1946 of 19.1 billion. I deduct 17.8 billion, the amount of the same unrelated items planned for 1944, from the 1945 total. Total receipts from nondomestic sources are then extrapolated from 1944 on the current price figures. From the resulting totals, I deduct receipts already attributed to equipment and munitions. For 1947 I use the average of 1946 and 1948. Even rough accuracy in these estimates is highly improbable.

The preceding calculations yield totals for final industrial product in the current prices (factor costs) of the weight years of 84.9 billion rubles in 1937, 10.0 billion in 1928, and 297.8 billion in 1950. These totals are not comprehensive because they omit some deliveries to GNP uses ("other" military procurements, purchases for state stockpiles) and deliveries to other sectors excepting construction. That the omitted deliveries to other sectors are probably small can be seen from data for the 1941 Plan composed in Norman Kaplan *et al.*, Table 1, p. 7. These indicate sales by industry to transportation, communications, trade, and agriculture, of 12.2 billion rubles, at a price level which was already considerably above that of 1937. Of this total, 7.6 billion represents sales of petroleum products, chiefly to agriculture but in considerable quantities to transportation. Of the 7.6 billion, however, approximately 50 percent was accounted for by turnover taxes (*ibid.*, Table 1 and p. 127), and other peculiarities in the pricing of petroleum might justify a further reduction in the petroleum figure. The next largest transactions are sales of 1.5 billion rubles of coal to transportation and 0.7 billion of chemical products to agriculture. Considerable physical quantity data for these transactions are available, but their small weight makes their omission relatively insignificant if not entirely justified.

I estimate the total costs of final product rather than the value of the omitted outputs. The totals and their division among components are (in billions of rubles): wages and supplements — for 1937, 53.0; for 1928, 4.79; for 1950, 204.8; agricultural materials — for 1937, 15.7; for 1928, 3.04; for

1950, 23.7; transportation services — for 1937, 6.4; for 1928, 1.21; for 1950, 27.4; and nominal profits and depreciation — for 1937, 15.9; for 1928, 1.66; for 1950, 63.3. These total — for 1937, 91.0; for 1928, 10.70; and for 1950, 310.2 billion rubles.

The 1937 price figures are derived as follows:

(i) The net product of (value added in) industry and construction is given as 75.9 billion in Abram Bergson, Hans Heymann, Jr., and Oleg Hoeffding, *Soviet National Income and Product, 1928–48: Revised Data*, The RAND Corporation, Research Memorandum RM-2544, November 15, 1960, p. 33.

(ii) I estimate that net product of construction was 10.0 billion, which leaves 65.9 for industry alone. The construction figure is based on Powell, *A Materials-Input Index, Revised and Extended*, pp. 64 and 86.

(iii) I add nominal depreciation charges of 3.0 billion, as given on p. 2 of the unpublished Statistical Appendix to Robert W. Campbell, "A Comparison of Soviet and American Inventory-Output Ratios," *American Economic Review*, September 1958.

(iv) I add purchases from agriculture, 15.7 billion, and from transportation, 6.4 billion (see Table IV.14 on p. 199). The resulting total for final product gross of depreciation is 91.0 billion rubles.

(v) Wages and supplements in industry and construction were 61.8 billion according to Abram Bergson, *Soviet National Income and Product in 1937* (New York, 1953), p. 123. Those in construction can be estimated as 8.8 billion (see Powell, *A Materials-Input Index, Revised and Extended*, p. 86). The residual attributable to industry is 53.0 billion rubles.

(vi) Subtracting wages from net product leaves nominal profits and related charges of 12.9 or the same, gross of depreciation, of 15.9 billion.

The cost calculations for 1937 omit no component of apparent consequence with the possible exception of purchases of services from trade. Disregarding the latter, I take 91.0 billion as the true value of final industrial product and raise the sums of the estimated components in 1937 prices in all years by the ratio 91.0/84.9.

The 1928 figures are derived by similar procedures.

(i) Net product in industry and construction, but omitting lumbering and fishing, is given as 7.95 billion in Bergson, Heymann, and Hoeffding, p. 33.

(ii) From Powell, *A Materials-Input Index, Revised and Extended*, pp. 64 and 88, I estimate net product in construction as 2.00.

(iii) I make a crude estimate of net product in lumbering and fishing of 0.38, on the basis of wage and net product data in Hoeffding, pp. 141 and 143, and more detailed wage data, for 1929, given in TSUNKHU, *Sotsialisticheskoe stroitel'stvo SSSR* (Moscow, 1934), p. 319. Net product in all industry is then 6.33 billion.

(iv) Depreciation in sectors identifiable as industrial was 0.49 billion (*Narodnoe khoziaistvo SSSR*, p. xxvi).

(v) As explained in the notes to Table IV.14 on p. 199, price and quantity data imply purchases from agriculture of 3.21 billion, from transportation of 1.28 billion.

(vi) The cost of final product implied by the above estimates is 11.31

billion. However, because of the crudity of the cost estimates, I doubt that the difference between 11.31 and the sum of the component product estimates, 10.0 billion, represents solely undercoverage in the latter. I therefore assume that the ratio of actual to computed product in 1928 was the same as in 1937 and take the actual value of final product as 10.7 billion. For consistency, I reduce the cost components proportionately: net product to 5.99, depreciation to 0.46, agriculture to 3.04, and transportation to 1.21.

(vii) Hoeffding, p. 142, calculates wages and supplements in industry of his coverage and in construction as 6.27. From this I deduct 1.80 for wages in construction and add 0.32 for wages in lumbering and fishing (sources are those cited in the discussion of net product). Total industrial wages are then 4.79.

(viii) The net product of 5.99 minus wages of 4.79 leaves nominal profits of 1.20. Profits plus depreciation are 1.66. I raise the computed output series in 1928 prices by the ratio 10.7/10.0.

For the series in 1950 prices, I proceed somewhat differently.

(i) No independent net product estimate appears to be available. I assume that my computed output figure in 1950 is understated by the same percentage as that for 1937 and take the actual 1950 total to be 319.2.

(ii) Purchases from agriculture are 23.7, those from transportation 27.4 (see Table IV.14). Deducting these from the output total implies a net product plus depreciation of 268.1.

(iii) Wage data compiled in Moorsteen and Powell indicate a rise in average industrial wages from 1937 to 1950 of 180 percent. In Table IV.11 on p. 188, I estimate that employment rose 38 percent over the same period. Taking the 1937 wage and supplements figure as base, and without adjusting for possible changes in the relative size of supplements, the figure for 1950 is estimated as 204.8 billion. This leaves a total of nominal profits and depreciation of 63.3 billion.

Again, I raise the computed output total by the ratio 319.2/297.8.

Table IV.10 and Notes

All figures given in Table IV.10 are computed by deducting industrial purchases from agriculture and transportation (Table IV.14 on p. 199) from final industrial product (Table IV.9).

Table IV.11 and Notes

Employment: The employment series is not of direct use in the discussion in the text but provides the basis for the man-hour estimates.

In Table IV.11, figures for 1928, 1932, 1937, 1940, 1950, and 1955–58 are from Kaplan and Moorsteen, p. 264, with 1937 equal to 100. The 1928 figure omits fishing. The 1933 and 1935 figures are interpolated between 1932 and 1937 on the basis of reported employment totals cited by Kaplan and Moorsteen.

For 1929–31, 1934, 1936, and 1938–39, the estimates are derived from Hodgman, p. 112. For 1929–31 and 1934 they are interpolated on the basis

Table IV.10
USSR: Value Added in Industry, 1928–58
(billions of rubles)

Year	1937 Prices	1928 Prices	1950 Prices
1928	26.3	6.5	74.4
1929	30.2	8.5	87.0
1930	33.7	11.6	95.2
1931	38.5	14.7	105
1932	36.7	15.5	99.5
1933	34.8	15.2	93.0
1934	39.0	18.9	102
1935	53.6	26.9	133
1936	62.4	35.0	153
1937	68.9	37.9	167
1938	77.6	44.1	183
1939	93.8	50.6	213
1940	93.1	54.0	203
1944	97.1	54.6	149
1945	84.7	50.8	125
1946	73.1	44.3	136
1947	82.0	48.5	161
1948	91.6	54.1	189
1949	114	68.0	243
1950	123	75.7	268
1951	138	81.0	302
1952	151	87.9	323
1953	167	97.6	367
1954	165	98.9	375
1955	194	119	427
1956	221	138	488
1957	235	146	525
1958	269	163	597

of reported data for workers in large-scale industry, cited by Hodgman. The 1936 figure is the average of those obtained by extrapolating from 1935 to 1936 on the reported data cited by Hodgman and from 1937 to 1936 on the figures computed by Hodgman from the official productivity index. For 1938–39 the figures are interpolated on data of the latter sort computed by Hodgman.

The 1945 figure is interpolated between 1940 and 1950 on the basis of total industrial employment figures for these three years given in TSU, *SSSR v tsifrakh* (Moscow, 1958), p. 313, and TSU, *Promyshlennost' SSSR* (Moscow, 1957), p. 23.

All other postwar years are derived by the procedure used in Kaplan and Moorsteen, namely, by dividing the official index of industrial production by the official index of labor productivity. The production index is given in

Table IV.11
USSR: Labor Inputs in Industry, 1928–58
(1937 = 100)[a]

Year	Employment	Man-hours
1928	51.7	55.5
1929	56.0	58.8
1930	64.8	66.5
1931	75.3	75.5
1932	83.3	81.5
1933	77.0	75.6
1934	83.7	82.6
1935	92.1	91.3
1936	96.5	96.1
1937	100	100
1938	105	105
1939	106	106
1940	109	119
1945	93.7	123
1946	101	119
1947	108	127
1948	119	140
1949	126	149
1950	138	163
1951	145	171
1952	153	181
1953	160	189
1954	171	202
1955	177	209
1956	182	215
1957	189	218
1958	196	220

[a] Weight-year values are 53.0 billion rubles in 1937,
4.79 billion in 1928, and 204.8 billion in 1950.

Promyshlennost' SSR, p. 33. Productivity indexes are obtained from *ibid.,* p. 25, and from the annual plan-fulfillment reports.

Man-hours: Figures for 1928, 1932, 1937, 1940, 1950, 1955, and 1956, are from Kaplan and Moorsteen, pp. 268 and 272, with 1937 equal to 100.

On the basis of the discussion in *ibid.,* p. 161, I obtain figures for 1929–31, 1933–36, and 1938–39, assuming that hours worked per year changed linearly from 1928 to 1932 and from 1932 to 1937, and that they remained at the 1937 level in 1938 and 1939.

For 1945, I make the arbitrary assumption that hours worked lay midway between the 1944 and 1946 figures. Bergson, *Real SNIP,* appendix H, estimates the 1944 figure to be 44 percent above the 1937 level.

Hours in 1946–48 and 1951–54 are assumed to be the same as in 1950 and 1955. No general change is known to have occurred from 1946 to 1956.

For 1957 and 1958, data given in *Narodnoe khoziaistvo 1958*, p. 665, indicate a change in the average working day from 7.96 hours during 1956 to 7.4 hours at the beginning of 1959, or a decline of 7 percent. According to Kaplan and Moorsteen, p. 161, the decline in hours was slow in 1957 but accelerated during 1958. Interpolating crudely, I assume average hours in 1957 to be 98 percent and in 1958, 95 percent of the 1956 level.

Weight-year values: See the notes to Table IV.9.

Tables IV.12 and IV.13 and Notes

Inventories

All figures given in Table IV.12 are from Moorsteen and Powell. Entries are average of figures for January 1. For 1939, figures are for the unenlarged territory; for 1940, they are for the enlarged territory.

Fixed Capital

I undertake here not only to explain the derivation of the fixed capital estimates but also to give the reasons for thinking that the results approximate the behavior of industrial capital. These reasons are essentially the correspondence, in certain respects, of official data with estimates compiled by Moorsteen and me for the fixed capital stock in the economy as a whole. The results, therefore, can best be interpreted as industrial capital series which are conceptually consistent with the Moorsteen-Powell aggregate estimates, and some explanation of the latter is called for.

I pass over the issue of the ultimate meaning and measurability of capital. In the estimates referred to, capital is a stock of physical assets aggregated with domestic prices of the weight years. The problem of establishing prices for assets in a year in which they were not produced (the problem of "new products" or quality change) is handled somewhat differently for equipment and structures. For a full discussion of the procedures used in compiling equipment prices, reference should be made to Moorsteen's *Prices and Production of Machinery*. In general, the new products problem for equipment appears fairly modest up to the 1950's; thereafter it may be of considerable consequence. For structures, values are assumed to vary with the quantity of materials (in weight-year prices) consumed in their construction. The case for a materials-input index of construction is argued in Powell, *A Materials-Input Index, 1927/28 to 1955*, part I, pp. 33ff. Care should be taken, however, in comparing these estimates with U.S. series obtained by deflating current values with prices of materials and labor. A rough check suggests that deflated and materials-inputs series for the U.S. behave very much alike, but application to Soviet construction of the standard U.S. estimating procedure (input-price deflation) yields series which differ greatly from those cited here. On the U.S. data, see *ibid.*, pp. 37ff.; on alternative Soviet indexes, see Powell, *A Materials-Input Index, Revised and Extended*, pp. 3 and 9.

The point of departure for the capital stock estimates is official data on the value of equipment and structures, by sectors, in current prices in 1928.

Table IV.12
USSR: Industrial Capital Stock, 1928–58
(billions of rubles; annual averages)

	Equipment		Structures			Total	
Year	Gross	Net	Gross	Net	Inventories	Gross	Net
				1937 Prices			
1928	7.2	4.8	11.8	8.0	15.8	34.8	28.6
1929	8.4	5.6	13.6	9.2	15.5	37.5	30.3
1930	11.0	7.3	16.4	11.3	16.0	43.4	34.6
1931	14.3	10.2	20.8	14.3	18.9	54.0	43.4
1932	18.5	13.7	25.5	17.7	21.9	65.9	53.3
1933	23.1	16.8	29.4	20.6	23.2	75.7	60.6
1934	27.1	19.3	33.0	23.0	23.8	83.9	66.1
1935	31.0	21.6	36.1	25.5	27.0	94.1	74.1
1936	35.7	24.5	39.2	27.8	32.3	107	84.6
1937	40.3	27.2	42.0	30.1	36.3	119	93.6
1938	46.7	30.8	45.8	32.8	40.5	133	104
1939	54.3	34.6	50.9	36.5	45.1	150	116
1940	62.6	39.0	57.1	40.9	50.1	170	130
1945	58.2	34.3	59.3	41.4	35.3	153	111
1946	63.0	37.5	61.9	42.5	36.4	161	116
1947	69.4	42.3	66.0	44.9	39.9	175	127
1948	77.8	48.6	72.5	49.5	43.7	194	142
1949	86.3	55.7	80.0	54.9	52.8	219	163
1950	95.9	64.3	88.3	61.2	65.0	249	191
1951	107	74.1	97.1	67.7	74.6	279	216
1952	119	83.7	107	75.4	83.9	310	243
1953	134	94.6	118	85.0	94.0	346	274
1954	153	106	129	94.7	100	382	301
1955	174	121	141	104	101	416	326
1956	197	138	151	114	107	455	359
1957	225	159	164	126	115	504	400
1958	246	176	172	133	126	544	435
				1928 Prices			
1928	6.4	4.3	6.9	4.7	5.9	19.2	14.9
1929	7.5	5.0	8.0	5.4	6.1	21.6	16.5
1930	9.8	6.5	9.6	6.6	6.6	26.0	19.7
1931	12.8	9.1	12.2	8.4	8.2	33.2	25.7
1932	16.6	12.3	14.9	10.4	9.7	41.2	32.4
1933	20.7	15.1	17.2	12.0	10.6	48.5	37.7
1934	24.2	17.3	19.3	13.5	11.1	54.6	41.9
1935	27.7	19.3	21.2	15.0	12.9	61.8	47.2
1936	31.9	21.9	23.0	16.3	15.6	70.5	53.8
1937	36.0	24.3	24.6	17.6	17.6	78.2	59.5
1938	41.7	27.5	26.8	19.2	19.6	88.1	66.3
1939	48.5	30.9	29.8	21.4	21.7	100	74.0
1940	55.9	34.8	33.5	24.0	24.3	114	83 1

Table IV.12 (Contd.)

Year	Equipment		Structures		Inventories	Total	
	Gross	Net	Gross	Net		Gross	Net
1928 Prices (Contd.)							
1945	52.0	30.6	34.7	24.2	17.6	104	72.4
1946	56.3	33.6	36.2	24.9	18.4	111	76.9
1947	61.9	37.7	38.6	26.3	20.2	121	84.2
1948	69.4	43.4	42.4	29.0	21.9	134	94.3
1949	77.0	49.7	46.8	32.1	26.2	150	108
1950	85.5	57.3	51.7	35.8	32.2	169	125
1951	95.8	66.1	56.8	39.6	36.9	189	143
1952	106	74.6	62.7	44.1	41.6	210	160
1953	120	84.3	69.1	49.8	47.0	236	181
1954	136	94.7	75.6	55.4	50.2	262	200
1955	155	107	82.1	60.8	50.6	288	218
1956	176	123	88.0	66.5	53.4	317	243
1957	200	142	95.6	73.3	57.4	353	273
1958	219	156	101	77.5	62.6	383	296
1950 Prices							
1928	13.6	9.1	31.8	21.6	30.9	76.3	61.6
1929	15.8	10.4	36.7	24.8	30.8	83.3	66.0
1930	20.6	13.7	44.2	30.3	32.3	97.1	76.3
1931	26.7	19.0	56.1	38.7	38.4	121	96.1
1932	34.3	25.5	68.8	47.8	45.3	148	119
1933	42.6	31.1	79.3	55.4	48.4	170	135
1934	49.7	35.4	89.0	62.1	50.0	189	147
1935	56.6	39.4	97.4	68.8	57.4	211	166
1936	64.8	44.4	106	74.8	68.6	239	188
1937	72.7	49.1	113	81.1	77.1	263	207
1938	83.8	55.2	123	88.5	85.8	293	229
1939	96.9	61.8	137	98.5	95.3	329	256
1940	111	69.2	154	110	107	372	286
1945	100	59.0	160	112	76.1	336	247
1946	108	64.2	167	115	79.0	354	258
1947	118	71.9	178	121	87.1	383	280
1948	132	82.3	195	133	94.5	421	310
1949	145	93.6	216	148	113	474	355
1950	160	107	238	165	139	537	411
1951	178	123	262	183	160	600	466
1952	197	138	289	203	180	666	521
1953	220	155	319	229	203	742	587
1954	249	173	349	255	214	812	642
1955	282	195	380	281	218	880	694
1956	317	222	407	308	230	954	760
1957	360	255	442	339	248	1050	842
1958	391	279	465	358	271	1127	908

That the official current-price valuations are consistent with our valuation procedures is doubtful. Nevertheless, these figures, deflated to weight-year prices, are taken as the initial capital stock. Thereafter our procedure is essentially a perpetual inventory, with annual gross investments added and retirements subtracted from the stock in existence at the beginning of each year. Rough corrections are made for territorial acquisitions and war losses. The value of the net (depreciated) capital stock is computed on the basis of sundry data on the service lives of various kinds of assets in the Soviet economy. The reference here is to series described in the Moorsteen-Powell study as the "basic estimates," which are computed from investment data exclusive of capital repairs and on the assumption of straight line depreciation.

Industrial fixed capital on January 1, 1928, and 1960: The first point of apparent correspondence between the Moorsteen-Powell estimates of the aggregate stock and official Soviet data relates to the size of the stock in current prices. As noted, our estimates commence with official data in current prices for January 1, 1928. They yield figures, which can be only slightly dependent upon the 1928 data, for the aggregate stock in current prices on January 1, 1959, the latest date to which the estimates are carried. These figures (gross of depreciation) are 1,790 billion rubles for structures, 500 billion for equipment, and 100 billion for the capitalized costs of installing equipment, or a combined total of 2,390 billion rubles. The official census of the capital stock for January 1, 1960 (see *Narodnoe khoziaistvo 1959,* pp. 65ff.), in approximately current prices, arrives at 2,185 billion for total structures, and 527 billion for equipment, subject to revaluation only and presumably inclusive of installation costs, or a combined sum of 2,712 billion rubles. The amount of equipment not subject to revaluation can be read from the reported data to have been less than 214 billion, but it is unlikely to have been more than a fraction of that figure. According to our estimates, the total stock was growing at approximately 11 percent annually in the immediately preceding years, which suggests a January 1, 1960, total from our estimates of about 2,650 billion.

The restricted coverage of the census equipment figure makes the comparison inexact. The official data probably exclude unfinished structures, which are included in our estimates. It is unlikely that the census figures are revalued in current prices by procedures consistent with ours (for structures, especially) or, for that matter, by the procedures used for the official current price valuations in 1928. Nevertheless, there is a correspondence of rough orders of magnitude, although better for the total than for the components, between the official and the independent estimates of the gross stock.

Two further similarities are relevant. The revaluation of the stock from acquisition to current prices in the census is indicated to have raised the value of the stock (subject to revaluation) 12.4 percent; our estimates of the total stock (January 1, 1959) at current prices exceed those at acquisition costs by 11.9 percent. According to the census, the depreciated value of the stock subject to revaluation was 75 percent of its gross value; our estimates imply a ratio for all assets of 73 percent. The census data are based on an appraisal of physical wear-and-tear rather than on bookkeeping depreciation charges and therefore are probably closer to our figures than they otherwise would be.

On the basis of the foregoing, I make this inferential leap: because the census figures in current prices for the aggregate stock appear consistent with our estimates, I assume that the census figures for industry alone are also consistent with our estimates. I then deflate the census data (gross and net and for structures and equipment separately) to prices of the three weight years. Since deflated values for the industrial stock in 1928 have been similarly derived, I have figures for the industrial capital stock, in constant prices, for both ends of the time period. These are independent estimates in that the deflation is independently performed. They are entirely dependent, however, upon the official data in current prices.

The results of the calculations are (in billions of rubles):

	Equipment		Structures	
	Gross	Net	Gross	Net
January 1, 1928				
1937 Prices	6.7	4.5	10.9	7.4
1928 Prices	6.0	4.1	6.4	4.3
1950 Prices	12.7	8.7	29.4	20.1
January 1, 1960				
1937 Prices	274	196	192	148
1928 Prices	244	174	112	86
1950 Prices	436	311	518	399

In detail, the estimates are derived as follows:

(i) For the 1928 stock, all figures are from Moorsteen and Powell, except that electric power is here included with industry.

(ii) In the 1960 census (*Narodnoe khoziaistvo 1959*, pp. 67 and 69), total gross assets in industry on January 1, 1960, in approximately current prices, are given as 800.1 billion, of which 490.6 are structures. Revalued equipment is 300.4, revalued "other" assets 5.8. I assume the remaining 3.3 of un-revalued assets is equipment, and I arrive at a total for equipment of 303.7. On the basis of data given in Moorsteen and Powell, I assume that 39.5 billion of the equipment total represents installation costs.

(iii) 1960 structures I deflate to weight-year prices with the price index of construction outputs, given-year weights, shown in Powell, *A Materials-Input Index, Revised and Extended*, p. 85. Prices are assumed unchanged from 1956 to 1960.

The equipment deflators I compute from detailed data in Moorsteen, by procedures used in Moorsteen and Powell to deflate the 1928 industrial equipment figure. This involves aggregating indexes for 13 categories of equipment known to be used by industry. The calculation is actually for 1958, the latest year covered by Moorsteen's data, but no significant change is thought to have occurred from 1958 to 1960. The weights employed are all 1958 weights, except that the internal weights for the 13 components, for the indexes on 1928 and 1950 bases, are 1955 weights.

Installation is deflated to the prices of all three weight years with the arithmetic average of the construction and equipment indexes. In the following operations, installation is again combined with equipment.

(iv) The 1960 census (*Narodnoe khoziaistvo 1959*, p. 75) gives the ratio of net to gross assets in industry as 75 percent. Using data from the census for the net/gross ratio by kind of assets and data on the distribution by kind of industrial assets (*ibid.*, pp. 74 and 69), I estimate that the ratio for structures was 77.1 percent and for equipment 71.4 percent. Application of these percentages to gross assets yields 1960 net assets in all three prices.

Industrial fixed capital in intermediate years: To obtain estimates for the years between 1928 and 1960, I again proceed from a comparison of our estimates with official data. The Soviet statistical handbooks published from 1956 through 1959 give an index of the total stock of fixed capital (together with indexes for component sectors), which is stated to be gross of depreciation, exclusive of livestock, and valued in "comparable" prices. What the comparable prices are is not explained, nor is there any indication that the annual figures are for the beginning or end of each year or averages. I assume that they are annual averages, although for my purposes it makes little difference. The official index compares as follows with our independent index, annual averages, in *1937* prices, and with 1950 equal to 100 for both series: for 1928, official, 26.0 and Moorsteen-Powell, 27.4; for 1940, official, 81.2 and Moorsteen-Powell, 88.6; for 1950, official, 100 and Moorsteen-Powell, 100; for 1954, official, 139 and Moorsteen-Powell, 142; for 1955, official, 153 and Moorsteen-Powell, 158; for 1956, official, 168 and Moorsteen-Powell, 174; and for 1957, official, 185 and Moorsteen-Powell, 192.

I restrict the comparison to the series in 1937 prices chiefly for simplicity. Our series in 1928 prices rises more rapidly than the official series; that in 1950 prices is further from the official series than the 1937 price series for 1928–50, and closer to it for 1950–57, but the difference is small in the latter period. The change in weight years has relatively small effects on the capital index.

The inference I draw from the close resemblance of the official and independent indexes is a limited one: that the official index for the total stock, and hence the official indexes for component sectors, are truly in constant (noncurrent) prices in some meaningful sense of the term. That is to say, they are not mislabeled as are official series, published in the same sources, for annual investment in fixed capital. The latter are purportedly in 1955 prices; for the prewar years, they are almost certainly in current prices (see Powell, *A Materials-Input Index, 1927/28 to 1955*, part II, pp. 505ff.).

The correspondence is probably a coincidence. It is extremely unlikely that the compilers of the official index have reduced the value of assets, especially of structures, to constant prices by procedures at all like ours. It is much more likely, judging from past Soviet practice, that the official index is a chained index, linking, for example, series in prices of 1933, 1936, 1945, et cetera. The fact that the result is nevertheless close to ours could be explained by the following hypothesis, which is the one on which I proceed: The use of chained indexes for the component sectors (especially if they included, as one of their links, earlier reported indexes in 1933 prices) would probably yield higher increases over the whole period for each component than would be obtained by application of the Moorsteen-Powell procedures. But, if the component series were combined by weights from a late year, say 1955, when the weights of components which grew relatively slowly over time might well be relatively large, then the aggregate index could nevertheless approximate the Moorsteen-Powell index. This explanation must remain almost pure supposition, but some evidence lends it credibility.

The official index of fixed capital in industry, shown in the sources as a component of the total stock, is available for more years than the total (the industry index, which has slightly different versions, is reproduced below). For the early years (1928, 1932, and 1937), the official industry series, as Kaplan and Moorsteen, p. 272, have pointed out, looks very much like the earlier reported series in 1933 prices (references to this series are based on an unpublished memorandum by Norman Kaplan). The official aggregate series for the prewar years looks not at all like the 1933 price series. The latter, with 1928 equal to 100, is 165 in 1932, 295 in 1936, and in the neighborhood of 400 in 1938 (all for January 1). The official aggregate series in 1940 is only 312 percent of its 1928 level. The official series for "productive" capital (see *Narodnoe khoziaistvo 1958*, pp. 52–53), which excludes principally housing and public buildings, both of which have probably grown slowly, rises from a 1928 base to only 157 in 1932, 298 in 1937, and 443 in 1940.

Furthermore, the increase in the official industrial index is considerably greater over the entire period than that indicated by the estimates previously arrived at for January 1, 1928, and 1960. These, in 1937 prices and crudely extended to 1928 and 1958 averages (see below), imply a gross stock at the later date 22.0 times the 1928 level. The official series implies a figure about 28.7 times the 1928 level.

Comparison of the official series for industry with the Moorsteen-Powell series for total assets suggests that the discrepancy between the terminal values of the official and estimated industry indexes does not arise continuously over time. From 1928 to 1932 and 1937, the official industry index rises very rapidly relative to our total index; from 1937 it rises quite gradually and consistently. While it would be hard to say how large a relative rise in industrial capital from 1928 to 1937 would be implausible, the relative rise from 1937 on could not be much smaller than that indicated by the comparison. Hence the inflation in the official industrial index probably occurs in the interval from 1928 to 1937, that is, in the period in which it evidently is the old 1933 price series.

My second inferential leap, therefore, is to assume that values for the (gross) industrial capital stock can be interpolated between the terminal years on the official index, sufficient adjustments being made within the interval 1928–37 to absorb the entire apparent inflation in the official index.

The discussion thus far of the official indexes has disregarded the revisions published in 1960 (see *Narodnoe khoziaistvo 1959,* p. 66). The changes made in the individual sector indexes were limited. However, the new version included livestock in the total — presumably not the whole of livestock but that part which in Soviet practice is counted as fixed capital. The Moorsteen-Powell estimates include a series for all livestock. If, disregarding this discrepancy, our estimates for fixed capital plus livestock are compared with the new official series, the correspondence is no longer so close: the principal difference is that, with 1950 equal to 100, the official index for 1928 is 36.6, whereas ours is 33.0 in 1937 prices and 33.3 in 1950 prices. I suspect, however, that this divergence is further evidence that the components of the official index are combined with weights from a year as late as 1955. From 1950 to 1955, the price of livestock approximately doubled, while prices of fixed capital declined. If the weight of livestock in our index is doubled, the 1928 value is raised to 38.1 in 1937 prices and 36.3 in 1950 prices.

In detail, the interpolation of gross fixed capital in intermediate years is based on the data given in Table IV.13.

The first official series is for industry alone. Through 1955 it is from *Promyshlennost' SSSR,* p. 16, and for 1956 from TSU, *SSSR v tsifrakh,* p. 50.

The second and third official series are for industry and construction. The second is from *Narodnoe khoziaistvo 1956,* p. 38, and *Narodnoe khoziaistvo 1958,* p. 58. The third is the revised official index, published in *Narodnoe khoziaistvo 1959,* p. 66. As is evident, the revisions are modest.

The interpolating index is calculated as follows:

For 1932, 1937–40, and 1945–56, the entries are the first official index. It is inferred, from comparison with the Moorsteen-Powell aggregate index, that this series includes the acquired territories in 1939 and 1940.

The 1928 and 1957 figures are extrapolated from 1940 and 1956, respectively, on the second official index.

The 1959 figure is extrapolated from 1957 on the third official index; and that for 1958 is interpolated on a straight percentage line. The rate of increase in these two years is inexplicably small relative to that of the preceding years, and an error may occur at this point.

For 1929–31 and 1934–36 the figures are interpolated on the basis of the official index in 1933 prices (annual averages). The latter are from the Kaplan unpublished memorandum and from Kaplan and Moorsteen, p. 272, except that 1936 is interpolated from figures for January 1, 1936, and the 1937 average.

January 1, 1960, is linked to 1959 on the assumption that January 1, 1959, equaled the average of 1958 and 1959 and that 1959 equaled the average of its two termini.

The January 1, 1928, figure is extrapolated from average 1928 on the official 1933 price series.

Total gross assets in 1937 prices are then estimated for all years from 1937 to 1958 by extrapolating from the January 1, 1960, absolute figure on the interpolating index. The 1928 and 1929 figures are similarly estimated from the January 1, 1928, total (the inflation in the 1933 price series does

Table IV.13
Data Used in Interpolating Gross Fixed Capital
(1950 = 100)

	Official indexes			Interpolating index
January 1, 1928	—	—	—	7.34
Average 1928	—	7.71	7.45	7.92
Average 1929	—	—	—	9.19
Average 1930	—	—	—	11.8
Average 1931	—	—	—	15.6
Average 1932	20.2	—	—	20.2
Average 1933	—	—	—	24.9
Average 1934	—	—	—	29.3
Average 1935	—	—	—	33.9
Average 1936	—	—	—	39.2
Average 1937	44.7	—	—	44.7
Average 1938	50.2	—	—	50.2
Average 1939	57.1	—	—	57.1
Average 1940	65.0	63.3	63.4	65.0
Average 1945	63.8	—	—	63.8
Average 1946	67.8	—	—	67.8
Average 1947	73.5	—	—	73.5
Average 1948	81.6	—	—	81.6
Average 1949	90.3	—	—	90.3
Average 1950	100	100	100	100
Average 1951	111	—	—	111
Average 1952	123	—	—	123
Average 1953	137	—	—	137
Average 1954	153	154	—	153
Average 1955	171	172	172	171
Average 1956	189	190	—	189
Average 1957	—	212	—	211
Average 1958	—	—	—	227
Average 1959	—	—	245	244
January 1, 1960	—	—	—	253

Note: The dash (—) indicates that data are not available.

not appear to begin before 1930). For years between 1929 and 1937, the figures are estimated on the interpolating index, on the assumption that the discrepancy between it and the values for 1929 and 1937 previously established arose linearly over time.

To divide the total series in 1937 prices between equipment and structures, I assume for simplicity that the distribution in 1928 and 1958 was the same as on January 1, 1928, and January 1, 1960. I then interpolate series for each component for the intermediate years from the Moorsteen-Powell aggregate estimates and adjust the resulting figures equiproportionately to the known totals of industrial capital in each year.

The estimates in 1928 and 1950 prices are straight line interpolations for each component between the terminal years on the basis of the 1937 price series.

To derive net capital from gross, I assume 1928 and 1958 ratios of net to gross the same as January 1, 1928, and 1960, and interpolate ratios for the two components separately on the Moorsteen-Powell aggregate series. This is one of the weakest links in the estimating procedure. No effort is made to reconcile it with the service lives assumed in estimating depreciation rates. However, no suitable procedure for determining annual retirements could be devised.

Tables IV.14 and IV.15 and Notes

Purchases from Agriculture

In Table IV.14, for all years except 1929–31, 1933–36, 1938–39, and 1944, I use the Kaplan-Moorsteen index (p. 235) of industrial production of finished consumers' goods, adjusted slightly for agricultural raw materials used in increases in goods in process. The latter adjustment is based on Moorsteen and Powell. The Kaplan-Moorsteen index for 1927/28 is raised 8 percent to allow for the difference between 1927/28 and 1928 and for the possible undercoverage of the production index. The authors (p. 9) suggest 8 percent as an upper limit for the effects of undercoverage alone.

As explained in the text, this procedure yields a fair approximation to the consumption of agricultural raw materials by industry: the resulting index corresponds rather closely to changes in procurements of products processed by industry, as shown in Table IV.15.

The consumers' goods output index is the Kaplan-Moorsteen series, adjusted as described. The first procurement series is derived from data in an unpublished memorandum by Jerzy F. Karcz for the volume of centralized and decentralized procurements of grain, sugar beets, raw cotton, potatoes, milk, and meat and livestock, weighted with average *1937* prices realized in the same procurements, which are also provided by Karcz. The second procurement series is computed similarly, except that flax is also included and the quantity data other than for animal products refer to harvest rather than calendar years. The procurement data are from *Narodnoe khoziaistvo 1958*, p. 357, and *Narodnoe khoziaistvo 1959*, pp. 322–323.

For the years not covered by Kaplan and Moorsteen, I compose an interpolating index from the sum of my final product estimates, in 1937 prices for retail sales to households, changes in inventories of consumers' goods, military subsistence, and 50 percent of "other" deliveries to GNP. An index similarly composed for 1928, 1932, 1937, and 1940, moves closely with the Kaplan-Moorsteen index; one for 1945 does not, presumably because external supplies of consumer goods were important in that year.

Table IV.14
USSR: Industrial Purchases from Other Sectors, 1928–58

Year	From agriculture (1937 = 100)[a]	From transportation (1937 = 100)[b]	Combined totals		
			1937 Prices	1928 Prices	1950 Prices
			(billions of rubles)		
1928	65.0	27.2	11.9	4.2	18.1
1929	71.3	32.7	13.3	4.8	20.4
1930	66.9	39.6	13.0	4.9	20.6
1931	66.9	45.5	13.4	5.1	21.6
1932	66.2	49.9	13.6	5.3	22.2
1933	65.0	51.5	13.5	5.3	22.2
1934	66.9	61.6	14.4	5.8	24.3
1935	73.9	76.4	16.5	6.9	28.2
1936	85.3	93.4	19.4	8.1	33.5
1937	100	100	22.1	9.1	37.7
1938	109	103	23.7	9.7	40.1
1939	128	107	27.0	10.8	44.8
1940	108	111	24.0	10.0	41.2
1944	39.5	79.9	11.3	5.3	21.7
1945	44.6	84.4	12.4	5.9	23.5
1946	54.1	90.4	14.3	6.5	26.5
1947	69.4	97.3	17.1	7.5	30.8
1948	87.3	122	21.5	9.5	38.7
1949	102	143	25.1	11.1	45.2
1950	113	163	28.2	12.6	51.1
1951	134	183	32.7	14.4	58.7
1952	143	201	35.3	15.6	63.6
1953	161	216	39.0	17.1	69.8
1954	176	234	42.6	18.6	76.1
1955	191	266	47.1	20.7	84.6
1956	207	298	51.6	22.9	93.3
1957	219	337	56.0	25.3	102
1958	231	367	59.8	27.1	110

[a] Weight-year values are 15.7 billion rubles in 1937, 3.04 billion in 1928, and 23.7 billion in 1950.

[b] Weight-year values are 6.4 billion rubles in 1937, 1.21 billion in 1928, and 27.4 billion in 1950.

Purchases from Transportation

As explained in the text, the index is for ton-kilometers of freight hauled by all forms of transportation. Data for 1928–55, except 1944, are from Hunter, p. 344. Those for 1956–58 are from *Narodnoe khoziaistvo 1959*, p. 487. The figure for 1944 is extrapolated from 1945 on the basis of data for freight carried by railroads only, given in Hunter, p. 331. Combined totals

Table IV.15
Consumers' Goods Production and Industrial
Procurement of Agricultural Products
(1937 = 100)

Year	Output of consumers' goods	Procurement	
1937	100	100	100
1940	108	113	106
1945	45	—	54
1948	87	95	—
1950	113	—	127
1952	143	146	—
1953	161	—	146
1954	176	159	159
1955	191	—	167
1956	207	—	200
1957	219	—	197
1958	231	—	229

Note: The dash (—) indicates that data are not available.

are the sums of the component indexes, each multiplied by its absolute values in the weight years.

Weight-Year Values

For 1937, purchases from agriculture are taken to equal the total reported value of procurements in that year, given in Bergson, *Soviet National Income and Product in 1937*, p. 105. The figure is too large by the amount of procurements not transmitted to industry; it is too small, for factor cost valuations, to the extent that procurement prices were lowered by subsidies in agriculture. The two errors are assumed to be roughly offsetting.

For transportation and communications in 1937, I commence with data for the 1941 Plan given in Kaplan *et al.*, p. 7. The value of transportation services to industry is there given as 10.6 billion. Rather arbitrarily, I include also the value of communications services, 1.7 billion, for a combined total of 12.3 billion. I assume that the physical quantity of these services rose from 1937 to the 1941 Plan in proportion to ton-kilometers of freight hauled (the necessary data are given in *Gosudarstvennyi plan razvitiia narodnogo khoziaistva SSSR na 1941 god*, American Council of Learned Societies Reprint, p. 5; *Narodnoe khoziaistvo 1959*, p. 487; and Hunter, p. 331) and that their prices rose over the same interval in proportion to average revenues per ton-kilometer in rail transport (the latter from an unpublished memorandum by James Blackman).

For 1928 and 1950, absolute values are computed from the 1937 values with physical quantity and price indexes. The quantity indexes are those entered in Table IV.4. The price index for agricultural procurements is from the unpublished memorandum by Karcz; that for transportation is again Blackman's index of average revenues per ton-kilometer in rail transportation.

For 1928, these procedures yield figures of 3.21 for agriculture and 1.28 for transportation. For reasons given in the notes to Table IV.9, total estimated costs for 1928 appear high, and these figures are reduced to 3.04 and 1.21, respectively.

Table IV.16 and Notes

The series are the arithmetic sums of inputs of labor, capital services, and purchases from other sectors. All the data are from Tables IV.11, IV.12, and IV.14 except that capital services have been computed from Table IV.12 on the assumption of 4 percent and 2 percent straight line depreciation rates for equipment and structures respectively, and the 8 percent and 20 percent interest rates.

Table IV.16
USSR: Total Inputs in Industry, 1928–58
(billions of rubles)

Year	1937 Prices		1928 Prices		1950 Prices	
	$i = 8\%$	$i = 20\%$	$i = 8\%$	$i = 20\%$	$i = 8\%$	$i = 20\%$
1928	44.1	47.5	10.6	12.4	93.8	101
1929	47.5	51.2	11.7	13.7	101	109
1930	51.7	55.8	12.8	15.1	112	121
1931	57.9	63.1	14.4	17.4	126	138
1932	62.3	68.7	15.9	19.8	137	151
1933	59.9	67.2	15.9	20.4	131	147
1934	65.3	73.2	17.7	22.7	144	161
1935	72.7	81.6	20.1	25.7	160	180
1936	79.3	89.4	22.5	29.0	174	197
1937	85.0	96.2	24.4	31.5	185	210
1938	90.5	103	26.3	34.3	196	224
1939	95.7	110	28.3	37.2	205	236
1940	101	117	29.8	39.8	221	255
1945	90.0	103	25.1	33.8	205	235
1946	90.4	104	26.0	35.2	204	235
1947	98.7	114	28.4	38.5	221	255
1948	112	129	32.7	44.1	249	286
1949	122	142	36.6	49.6	271	313
1950	135	158	41.1	56.1	300	349
1951	147	173	45.5	62.7	323	379
1952	157	187	49.6	68.8	346	409
1953	169	202	54.1	75.8	369	440
1954	183	219	58.9	82.9	398	475
1955	194	233	63.9	90.1	422	505
1956	205	248	69.7	98.9	445	536
1957	216	264	75.8	109	467	568
1958	224	277	80.6	116	484	593

Table IV.17 and Notes

Data are the same as those used in Table IV.16 except that component series have been added logarithmically.

Table IV.17
USSR: Projected Final Industrial Product from Given Inputs, 1928–58
(billions of rubles)

Year	1937 Prices		1928 Prices		1950 Prices	
	$i = 8\%$	$i = 20\%$	$i = 8\%$	$i = 20\%$	$i = 8\%$	$i = 20\%$
1928	42.2	45.0	10.6	12.4	86.6	91.2
1932	61.6	67.6	15.3	18.9	133	146
1937	85.0	96.2	22.4	28.6	184	208
1940	101	116	26.4	34.6	220	254
1945	84.3	97.4	19.8	26.3	202	231
1950	133	155	34.2	45.6	300	349
1955	189	225	51.0	69.4	419	500
1958	215	260	59.7	82.7	471	575

V

AGRICULTURAL PRODUCTION

D. Gale Johnson *

The emphasis of this chapter is on Soviet agricultural output and the analysis and measurement of factors associated with changes in output. My effort to explain agricultural output is directed primarily toward the resources used in agricultural production, for two reasons. First, I believe that the major objectives of Soviet planners have been to increase agricultural output to provide a growing food and fiber supply for an expanding industrial labor force, while at the same time releasing labor for industrial employment. Second, comparisons of U.S. and Soviet agriculture, which I have been asked to make, are most meaningful when related to the common elements of the two agricultures. These common elements are output and the resources required in production.

While there is new material in this paper, it draws heavily on an article by Arcadius Kahan and me in the Joint Economic Committee's

* I am indebted to Arcadius Kahan and Douglas Diamond for their contributions to the research program which has served as a base for this chapter.

Comparisons of the United States and Soviet Economies. Among the topics explored further here are the impact of territorial change on agricultural output, the feed supply situation, and the consistency of certain official serial data.

In section 1, I present estimates of agricultural output, showing the effect of territorial expansion upon output, and make some observations on the consistency of official Soviet data. Section 2 sets forth estimates of input changes, indexes of total inputs, and measures of productivity with comparisons with the United States. A final section (3) explores some of the factors associated with the changes in output. At this point I attempt to assess the possible effects on output of specific changes or programs such as the substitution of mechanical for animal power, the corn program, and the new lands program.

1. Total Agricultural Output

In 1959 an official Soviet index of gross agricultural output was published for most years from 1913 through 1958. This index has at least one interesting feature (Table V.1). Although published originally as a single index series, the geographic or area base varies. From 1917 through 1939, the 1913 base refers to the geographic area of September 17, 1939. For 1940 and later years, the base is the volume of production in 1913 on the territory now included in the Soviet Union. It was not until 1960 that the dual base was revealed.[1]

The technique used to reflect the impact of territorial change upon agricultural output is not without some merit; however, it has the disadvantage of attributing the increases in output realized between 1913 and 1940 in acquired territories to Soviet agriculture when, in fact, the increases were achieved while the territories were outside the Soviet Union. Because of the considerable interest in the effect of the territorial expansion, I present the published official information as well as estimates where official data are lacking on the output of the different territories in 1940 (Table V.2). The estimates, based on prices paid to collective farmers in 1958, indicate that in 1940, the output on the acquired territories was 16.6 percent as large as the 1940 output on the territory on September 17, 1939; of the output in 1940 on current territory, 14.3 percent was produced on the acquired territory.

We found that the choice of price weights has relatively little impact on the index of gross output. We experimented with several sets of weights: average market prices for 1926–27 and 1925–29, average realized prices for 1955, the average of free market and purchase prices for 1955, prices paid

---

[1] See TSU, *Sel'skoe khoziaistvo SSSR* (Moscow, 1960), p. 21; hereafter cited as *Selkhoz 1960.*

Table V.1
USSR: Official Index of Gross Agricultural Output, 1913–59
(1913 = 100)

Year	Total	Crops	Livestock
1913	100	100	100
1917	88	81	100
1920	67	64	72
1921	60	55	67
1926	118	114	127
1927	121	113	134
1928	124	117	137
1929	121	116	129
1930	117	126	100
1931	114	126	93
1932	107	125	75
1933	101	121	65
1934	106	125	72
1935	119	138	86
1936	109	118	96
1937	134	150	109
1938	120	120	120
1939	121	125	119
1940	141	155	114
1945	86	93	72
1946	95	100	87
1947	122	140	89
1948	136	158	96
1949	140	156	109
1950	140	151	118
1951	130	133	126
1952	142	148	129
1953	146	148	141
1954	153	153	153
1955	170	175	160
1956	193	201	177
1957	197	198	196
1958	218	227	205
1959	218	217	218

Note: Entries for 1913–57 are from TSU, *Narodnoe khoziaistvo SSSR v 1958 godu* (Moscow, 1959), p. 350; hereafter cited as *Narodnoe khoziaistvo 1958*. Entries for 1958 and 1959 are from *Selkhoz 1960*, p. 21.

Table V.2

USSR: Agricultural Output on Territory of September 17, 1939, and
Present Territory, 1913 and 1940

	1940		1913	
Product	Territory Sept. 17, 1939	Present territory	Territory Sept. 17, 1939	Present territory
	Quantity output			
Grain (mill. tons)	85.0ᵃ	95.5	76.5	86.0
Sugar beets (mill. tons)	17.0ᵇ	18.0	10.9	11.3
Potatoes (mill. tons)	63.4ᶜ	75.9	23.3	31.9
Vegetables (mill. tons)	11.9ᵉ	13.7	4.4ᵈ	5.45
Flax (mill. tons)	0.28ᶠ	0.35	0.33	0.40
Seed cotton (mill. tons)	2.24	2.24	0.74	0.74
Sunflower (mill. tons)	2.50ᵍ	2.64	0.74	0.75
Meat, live weight (mill. tons)ʰ	6 3	7.5	6.61	7.93
Milk (mill. tons)	26.6	33.6	24.8	29.4
Wool (mill. tons)	0.15	0.16	0.18	0.192
Eggs (bill.)	10.2	12.2	10.2	11.9
	Gross value (billion rubles, 1958 prices)			
Crops	121.3	137.8	83.8	97.0
Livestock	84.4	102.1	85.3	101.0
Total	205.7	239.9	169.1	198.0
Output of acquired territory	34.2		28.9	
Output on acquired territory as percent of total output on early 1939 territory and on present territory	16.6	14.3	17.1	14.6

ᵃ Average output for 1938–40 on 1939 territory is given at 77.9 million tons. Grain area in acquired territory is at least 9.8 million hectares in 1940; average yield in 1940 on present territory, 8.6 centners. Assumed average yield on acquired territory is 10.5 centners, based on average yield of 10.8 centners on private plots and private farms in 1940. Of total private grain area of 10.9 million hectares, 9.9 million were on private farms and thus almost all on acquired territory since 99.9 percent of all sown area was socialized in 1940 on territory of September 17, 1939. Private plots of collective members and workers and employees are included in socialized or collectivized area (see *Selkhoz 1960*, pp. 9, 128, 196, 202, 204, 206).

ᵇ In 1940 (present territory) private sugar beet area was 60,000 hectares, of which 55,000 were assumed on acquired territories, since in 1950 only 4,000 were in private hands and in 1956 none. Average yield on private lands in 1940 was 187.5 centners per hectare.

ᶜ Subject to some uncertainty. Area of potatoes, vegetables, and melons on acquired territory (area on private farms in 1940) was 1.5 million hectares. Assumed 1.25 million hectares in potatoes and average yield of 100 centners, compared with 107 centners for all private production.

ᵈ *Narodnoe khoziaistvo 1958*, p. 418.

ᵉ Assumed equal to 87 percent of 1940 production on present territory. Area on private farms estimated at 200,000 hectares out of total area of 1.5 million hectares. Estimate may be low since all private yields were 112 centners per hectare compared with 78 centners in socialized sector.

ᶠ Total private flax area 82,000 hectares in 1940 and 41,000 in 1950. Assumed 40,000 hectares on private farms on acquired territory in 1940. Yield in 1940 on all production, 4.2 centners, was assumed for acquired territories.

ᵍ Total private sunflower area was 288,000 in 1940 on present territory; private area in 1950 was 80,000 hectares. However, only 125,000 hectares are assumed on acquired territory and estimate may be on low side. Yield in 1940 of 11.2 centners on all private production was assumed.

ʰ Excludes change in inventories, which was 200,000 tons in 1940 and zero in 1913 on both territories.

Note: All output data, unless otherwise indicated, are from *Selkhoz 1960*, pp. 131–141, 196–206, and 328–329.

to collective farmers in 1958, and U.S. farm prices.[2] The largest discrepancy seldom exceeded 10 percent.[3] Consequently, I have used only one

[2] For some of the indexes see D. Gale Johnson and Arcadius Kahan, "Soviet Agriculture: Structure and Growth," in Joint Economic Committee, 86th Congress of the United States, 1st Session, *Comparisons of the United States and Soviet Economies* (Washington, 1959), part I, p. 204.

[3] V. Starovskii, "On the Methodology of Comparing Economic Indices of the USSR and the USA," *Problems of Economics,* July 1960, p. 22, makes much the same point: "If we compare the value of gross production of Soviet and American agriculture in

set of output data, weighted by the 1958 collective farm purchase price.

In Table V.3 we compare the official agricultural output index with our index, based on eleven commodity groups. We do not know the price weights used in compiling the official data, but there is some evidence that for recent years reference was made to average prices for 1956.[4] The coverage of the official index is broader than ours; it includes unfinished production, land preparation for the following year's crop, hay and feed crops, and some fish.[5] Thus, one should not expect exact correspondence between the two. However, some of the differences, especially for the early years, seem to be too large to be explained by the difference in coverage.

The calculated index is based upon official Soviet output data except for vegetable output for some years in the thirties and the output of grain, flax, sunflowers, vegetables, and sugar beets for 1940 on the territory of September 17, 1939.[6] For the present calculations, the low official estimates of 65.2 million tons of grain for 1909–13 and 72.5 million tons in 1913 on the 1939 territory and 76.5 and 86 million tons on present territory for 1909–13 and 1913 have been accepted.[7]

Some of the differences in the two indexes and their components are puzzling. I think it safe to assume that the official index, like ours, includes changes in livestock inventories. However, the calculated livestock index is also shown excluding changes in inventories. The official index of output increases 24 percent between 1913 and 1928; contemporary sources indi-

1959 in comparable prices, we find that in rubles Soviet output is 77% and in dollars it is 80% of American output." The same viewpoint is expressed by I. A. Ioffe in "The Level of Labor Productivity in the USSR and the USA," in the same periodical (p. 28). It is quite clear that Soviet calculations are based on less aggregated data than I have used.

The 1958 price weights yield a smaller increase in output between 1928 and 1959 than 1926/27 prices because of the lower relative prices (in 1958) of cotton. The lower indexes in the thirties obtained by using 1958 weights instead of 1926/27 or 1925–29 weights is due to the increase in livestock prices relative to crop prices (especially grains, potatoes, vegetables, and cotton) and the low level of livestock output during that period. In 1937, for example, livestock output was more than 30 percent below 1928 output, while crop output was 35 percent greater.

[4] Indexes were compared with estimates of total value of gross agricultural output, stated to be in 1956 prices (*Selkhoz 1960,* pp. 21 and 22).

[5] A. Vikhliaev, "O metodakh ischisleniia valovoi produktsii sel'skogo khoziaistva v sopostavimykh tsenakh," *Vestnik statistiki,* 1960, no. 10, pp. 54–61.

[6] The basis of the estimates for 1940 is given in Table V.2.

[7] For an exhaustive discussion of grain statistics see Naum Jasny, *The Socialized Agriculture of the USSR* (Stanford, 1949), pp. 725–760. Jasny estimates the 1909–13 grain crops at 81.6 million tons. On the assumption that the Central Statistical Committee underestimated production 10 percent, grain production in 1913 was 91 million tons. The Gosplan accepted this figure until about 1930. Current official Soviet statistics for 1909–13 and 1913 are the estimates of the Central Statistical Committee for all crops. In *Economic Statistics of the Soviet Union,* issued by Amtorg Trading Corporation (New York, 1928), p. 3, the 1913 grain production is given as 96.6 million tons. Reasonable estimates of grain production for 1909–13 and 1913 on 1939 territory are 77 and 91 million tons, respectively, and on current territory 86 and 102 million tons.

Table V.3

USSR: Indexes of Gross Agricultural Output, Official and Calculated, 1913–59

	Total		Crops		Livestock		
						Calculated	
Year	Official[a]	Calculated[b]	Official	Calculated	Official	A[d]	B[e]
Territory of 1939, 1913 = 100							
1913	100	100	100	100	100	100	100
1928	124	116	117	117	137	115	120
1928–32	117	106	122	122	106	90	106
1933	101		121		65		
1933–37[c]	122	105	140	129	87	81	71
1937	134	127	150	161	109	95	108
1938–40	132	118	139	130	118	107	107
1940	(156)	122	(172)	145	(116)	101	99
Present territory, 1940 = 100							
1913	71	82	65	70	88	98	99
1940	100	100	100	100	100	100	100
1945	60		57		64		
1949–53	99	99	95	92	109	109	107
1950	99	97	97	91	104	105	106
1951	92	95	86	84	111	110	105
1952	101	101	95	96	113	109	112
1953	104	105	96	93	124	122	121
1954	109	110	99	98	134	125	127
1955	121	124	113	113	140	139	135
1956	137	142	130	136	155	151	146
1957	141	141	128	119	172	171	161
1958	156	161	147	144	180	184	172
1959	156	161	140	131	191	198	190

[a] *Selkhoz 1960*, p. 21, except for 1940; base shifted from 1909–13 to 1913. Estimate for 1940 was based on indexes for 1938 and 1939 in *Narodnoe khoziaistvo 1958*, p. 350 and average index for 1938–40. I do not believe the estimates for total and crop output for 1940 on 1939 territory are reasonable. See fn. c, below.

[b] All output data, except for vegetables during the 1930's are from *Selkhoz 1960*, pp. 196–204 and 328–329, or Table V.2, above. Vegetable output is from Johnson and Kahan, p. 231 for 1928–40 on pre-1940 territory. Includes changes in livestock inventories. Weights are 1958 prices paid to collective farms.

[c] The averages of the annual indexes for 1933–37, given in *Narodnoe khoziaistvo 1958*, were 114 for total output, 130 for crops, and 88 for livestock. The difference for livestock is probably due to rounding; the other two differences imply revisions in output data or price weights. Similar comparisons for 1928–32 and 1949–53 revealed no differences. There is no official output index for 1940 (1939 territory) and the indexes, calculated as indicated in fn. a, are probably affected by differences of the type found for 1933–37.

[d] Includes changes in livestock inventories, measured in terms of live weight.

[e] Excludes changes in livestock inventories.

cated an increase of 6 to 10 percent.[8] If we had used more reasonable grain figures, the estimated increase would have been 10 percent. The difference is due to the livestock component, since the 1928 crop indexes are identical. Interestingly enough, the largest increase in the four major livestock products between 1913 and 1928 was 25 percent for milk. Wool production declined, meat production, including changes in inventory, increased only 13 percent, and eggs 6 percent.[9] Yet the official index of livestock output increases 37 percent.

For the period since 1940, on current territory, the correspondence is close. The total indexes are almost identical, but they conceal offsetting differences in the crop and livestock components. The latter are probably due to weighting and to the inclusion of feed other than grains in the official index. The increase in output between 1913 and 1940 on present territory is certainly exaggerated: the official index for 1959 on a 1913 base is 218; if more reasonable estimates were used for 1913, it would probably be less than 190.

The official indexes for 1940 for the 1939 territory were derived from the 1938–40 averages given in *Selkhoz 1960* and the annual figures for 1938 and 1939 given in *Narodnoe khoziaistvo 1958*.[10] The derived figures for 1940 seem quite unreasonable, although the procedure followed should give a reasonable answer.

In Table V.4 the indexes of gross agricultural output are adjusted for changes in territory. Part A is calculated with 1940 as a base; the 1940 territory used varies with the year being compared to it, for example, the index for 1928 is based on the pre-1939 territory, while the index for 1959 is based on current territory. Part B has a 1913 base, and the 1913 territory covered is comparable with that in the specific year for which the index is calculated. This part is comparable with the official estimates in Table V.1 in terms of the method used. Part C, with 1928 as base, is derived from part A. The 1959 index is 169; whereas the index is 196 when no adjustment is made for territorial expansion.

An index of farm output is given for the United States. As noted below, although the indexes are not strictly comparable — the index for the U.S. eliminates farm production uses from gross farm output — the results are not significantly affected by the differences. The increase in output from 1928 to 1959 is almost identical in the two countries. Between 1940 and 1950 for obvious reasons, farm output increased much more in the U.S. than in the USSR. Between 1950 and 1959 farm output increased 66 per-

[8] Jasny, p. 219.
[9] *Selkhoz 1960*, p. 328.
[10] The indexes in *Selkhoz 1960*, given with 1909–13 as base, were readily converted to a 1913 base since an index for 1913 was also given. The territory included in the 1913 index was not given, but available data indicate that the output index for 1913 should be almost the same as that for 1909–13, for 1939 or present territory.

Table V.4
USSR: Gross Agricultural Output Index; and USA: Farm Output;
Selected Years, 1913–59

		USSR			USA[d]
			Livestock		
Year	Total[a]	Crops[a]	A[b]	B[c]	Farm output
A. 1940 = 100					
1913 (Present territory)	82	70	98	99	73
1913 (1939 territory)	82	69	99	101	
1928	95	81	115	121	92
1928–32	87	85	90	107	92
1933–37	86	89	81	72	85
1937	104	111	95	83	100
1938–40	97	90	106	109	98
1940	100	100	100	100	100
1949–53	99	92	109	107	128
1950	97	91	105	106	123
1951	95	84	110	105	127
1952	101	96	109	112	132
1953	105	93	122	121	133
1954	110	98	125	125	133
1955	124	113	139	135	138
1956	142	136	151	146	139
1957	141	119	171	161	139
1958	161	144	184	172	151
1959	161	131	198	190	153
B. 1913 = 100					
1928	116	117	115	120	
1940	122	145	100	98	
1953	128	133	124	122	
1959	196	187	202	192	
C. 1928 = 100					
1938–40	102	111	92	88	
1940	105	123	87	82	
1949–53	104	114	95	88	
1953	110	115	106	99	
1954	116	121	109	105	
1955	130	139	121	111	
1956	149	168	131	120	
1957	148	147	149	133	
1958	169	178	160	142	
1959	169	162	172	156	

[a] Calculated from Table V.3.
[b] Including changes in livestock inventories.
[c] Excluding changes in livestock inventories.
[d] U.S. Department of Agriculture, *Changes in Farm Production and Efficiency*, Statistical Bulletin no. 233, revised, July 1960, p. 48.

cent in the USSR and 24 percent in the USA. The U.S. did not attempt to expand farm output during the fifties; in fact, the effort was in the opposite direction. However, it must be said that the output expansion in the USSR since 1950 has been a dramatic one.

For comparison with inputs, gross agricultural output is not appropriate, since it includes agricultural products used in producing other agricultural products, for example, feed for livestock. The proper measure should exclude all intra-agricultural uses of farm products. We constructed such an index based upon eleven major groups of farm products.[11] The only farm products of any significance not included are fruits, berries, and oil crops other than sunflowers. We believe that this index includes at least 95 percent of the total amount of agricultural products available for sale or home consumption.

Table V.5 presents our index of farm output available for sale and home consumption, including livestock output that may be retained for

Table V.5
USSR: Indexes of Agricultural Output Available for Sale or
Home Consumption and Gross Output, Selected Years, 1928–59
(1928 = 100)

Year	Sale or home consumption[a]	Gross output[b]
1928	100	100
1937	113	110
1938	104	
1940 (present territory)	117	122
1950	125	119
1953	133	129
1954	138	134
1955	154	152
1956	172	174
1957	172	173
1958	194	197
1959	193	196

[a] Weights are 1958 prices paid to collective farms. For output estimates, see Johnson and Kahan, pp. 234–237.
[b] Calculated from Table V.3.

[11] The data underlying the index and the price weights used are given in Johnson and Kahan, appendix 4 and p. 204. The estimates of flax and potatoes are probably too high for the 1930's and the estimates of grain and sunflowers are probably somewhat too high for 1950 to date. Revisions, however, are unlikely to affect the output index more than 2 or 3 percent. In any given year the error in the estimates of grains, potatoes, and milk used as feed may be significant, but averages for three to five years reduce it considerably.

investment. Our estimated gross agricultural output is included for comparison.[12] There is very little difference between the two indexes for several reasons. First, for the period studied crop and livestock outputs have not changed much in relation to each other. The value of the crops included in our gross agricultural output index was about 48 percent of the total in 1928 and 1953 and 47 percent in 1959. There were some exceptions to this relative constancy: in 1937 and 1940 the crop output accounted for more than 60 percent of the total. Second, seed use is a major deduction from gross output and there has been little change in the output-seed ratio for grains and potatoes, the two crops for which seed use is important. Third, a major factor in the growth of agricultural output has been the increase in the output of industrial crops; and for these commodities gross output and the amount available for sale and home consumption are almost identical. Calculations made for the United States also reveal no significant difference between the two output measures.

Except for certain adjustments made in calculating net agricultural output, we have accepted throughout official estimates of output for individual commodities.[13] When Khrushchev stated that the use of the biological yield concept by Malenkov, and presumably by Stalin and himself, was dishonest, we believed that output data made available subsequently would approximately reflect the output of farm products available for sale, home consumption, or further use in production.[14] It is now quite clear that this assumption was unjustified: the so-called barn yields of such crops as grain or sunflowers do not represent the amount of useful product of appropriate moisture content.[15] While the official meat output series, in

[12] No adjustment is made here for territorial change since our input index relates to the territory of the given year.

[13] See Johnson and Kahan, appendix Table 3, for assumptions made in deriving net agricultural output, defined there to exclude farm productive use of agricultural output.

[14] *Ibid.,* p. 203 for the attack by Khrushchev upon Malenkov.

[15] According to V. Suslov, "Proizoodstvo maslichnykh Kul'tur v 1959–1965 godakh," *Ekonomika sel'skogo khoziaistva,* 1959, no. 6, p. 32, the barn yield of sunflower seed in 1958 was 8 to 8.5 percent below the reported yield. A. I. Gozulov, *Statistika sel'skogo khoziaistva* (Moscow, 1959), pp. 148 and 451, states that the grain harvest is almost certainly reported in terms of "bunker weight" or the weight at the combine. Examples of excess moisture and waste ranging (for 3 oblasts) from 6.8 to 22.6 percent in grain for 1955 and 1956 are given in K. P. Obolenskii, ed., *Metody opredeleniia ekonomicheskoi effektivnosti sel'skokhoziaistvennogo proizvodstva* (Moscow, 1959), p. 74. The volume of moist and wet grain, especially in the Urals, Western Siberia, and Eastern Siberia and northern Kazakhstan, is apparently very great. Newly harvested grain is reported often to have a moisture content of 18 to 20 percent and in "particular years moisture amounts to 30–35 percent." Storable grain has a moisture content of 14 percent or less. Of the grain procured in 1956 in the new lands area (six oblasts), a large fraction had 19 percent or more moisture content. The percentage varied from 13 to 44 percent by oblasts. It was also reported that in 1956, 6.5 million tons of wet and moist grain were transported from the new lands area to other regions; this grain had 400,000 tons of excess moisture, an excess moisture content of more than 6 percent. The problem of excess moisture in delivered grain did not seem to be greater in 1956 than in 1950–55, according to V. T.

terms of slaughter weight, appears to be consistent over time, it is not comparable with U.S. data on meat output and should not be so treated.[16]

In two published series, estimates for *recent* years have been revised upward, while those for earlier years have been left unchanged. One, the milk output series, has been adequately discussed by Nancy Nimitz.[17] The other instance is provided by the data on hay. A comparison of the recent data on hay production with the previous estimates of hay stored for winter feed on collective and/or state farms indicates upward revision of recent estimates. In 1957 it was reported that the hay prepared or cut on collective farms was 56.2 million tons in 1953 and 46 million tons in 1956.[18] The *Selkhoz 1960* data on total hay production on collective farms, presumably a more inclusive concept, are 55.7 million tons for 1953, or slightly smaller than the earlier figure, and 53.8 million tons for 1956, or almost 8 million tons larger than the earlier figure. Hay prepared in the socialized sector was reported to be 58 million tons by November 1, 1958.[19] Hay production on collective and state farms in 1958 was reported as 84.2 million tons out of a total of 85.2 million tons.[20] Presumably the difference between hay prepared or stored and hay production represents hay harvested by collective farm members, hay distributed to collective farm members, and hay fed before the winter feeding period. But since in 1953 hay stored slightly exceeded hay production and in recent years the difference has been positive and increasing significantly, the hay production series is probably not comparable over time.

The reliability of current estimates of output before the revolution is certainly open to question. The probable underestimate of grain production has already been referred to. Strumilin, apparently unwilling to accept the present official estimate of flax-fiber output for 1913 (present territory) of 401,000 tons, has estimated the output for that year at 460,000 tons, a difference of 15 percent.[21]

Tevosian, ed., *Khlebooborot i elevatornoskladskoe khoziaistvo SSSR za 40 let, 1917–1957, gg.* (Moscow, 1957), pp. 111, 74, and 112.

[16] See Johnson and Kahan, pp. 203 and 221–223. V. Starovskii (pp. 9 and 10) compares the slaughter weight of meat in the Soviet Union with that in the USA, although the concept of meat output in the Soviet Union is much more inclusive. It is not always easy to compare output estimates of different countries; several American writers, myself included, have implied that Soviet milk output includes milk sucked by calves, but Starovskii (p. 15) states that this is not correct.

[17] Nancy Nimitz, *Soviet Statistics of Meat and Milk Output: A Note on Their Comparability Over Time,* The RAND Corporation, Research Memorandum RM-2326, February 6, 1959, pp. 18–24. In section 3 I discuss the relationship between changes in the feed supply and livestock production. I believe that the exaggeration of milk output relative to earlier data started in 1945.

[18] *Mashino-Traktornaia,* 1957, no. 5, p. 4, and *Selkhoz 1960,* pp. 203, 205, and 207.

[19] "Novye uspekhi sovetskoi ekonomiki," *Vestnik Statistiki,* 1958, no. 11, p. 6.

[20] *Selkhoz 1960,* pp. 203, 205, and 207.

[21] G. S. Strumilin, *Statistiko-ekonomicheskie ocherki* (Moscow, 1958), pp. 238–243. Jasny (p. 727) notes that Strumilin was head of one office of the Gosplan that approved

While Western students of Soviet agriculture have had doubts about the accuracy of the gross output data for the late fifties, it was not until recent months that confidence in the procurement data was shaken. I certainly believed that they were rather reliable, since they were reported by a monolithic procurement agency that I assumed maintained accurate records. Recent revelations in the Soviet press concerning statistical malpractices have included procurement as well as output data. Specific references have been made to exaggeration of cotton and makhorka procurements; the practice of certain collective farms of purchasing dairy products in state stores and delivering the purchased products to the procurement agency has also been described.[22] Meat, wool, and egg deliveries have been reported to be falsified.[23]

There is still so much uncertainty concerning the degree and timing of exaggerations that an accurate output index cannot be constructed. I believe that exaggeration increased substantially with the abolition of the machine tractor stations in 1958 and with the greater pressure upon collective and state farms to accept and achieve impossible output and delivery goals as a result of campaigns, for example, to overtake the U.S. in per capita meat and milk output. I think that the official and calculated indexes probably overestimate output in the late fifties compared with 1950 about 10 to 15 percent. Thus, gross output may have increased about 45 percent between 1950 and 1959 instead of approximately 55 to 60 percent. However, no matter what reasonable downward adjustment is made in the output estimates, significant increases have been achieved since 1953.

2. INPUTS AND PRODUCTIVITY

Our efforts to construct long-term aggregate measures of inputs used in agriculture have not yet been completely successful. We have not been

---

the upward revision in Czarist production data made by D. N. Ivantsov. These revisions have been discarded and are no longer reported in official Soviet compendia.

[22] The *Current Digest of the Soviet Press* for the first six months of 1961 contains numerous indications of padding and falsification of procurement data as well as output data. Khrushchev stated (*Pravda,* January 11, 1961, *Current Digest,* 1961, no. 1, p. 22): "It must be said, comrades, that it is an incredible thing when a collective farm buys butter in the stores, includes this butter in the fulfillment of its plan and pledges, and delivers it to the state." Falsification of cotton procurement data is described in detail in *Pravda,* April 16, 1961 and *Kommunist Tadzhikistana,* April 14, 1961, *Current Digest,* 1961, no. 15, p. 9 and no. 12, p. 10. In the case of grain, the quantities procured and available for disposition by the state may be exaggerated by a process described by Khrushchev (*Pravda,* January 21, 1961, *Current Digest,* 1961, no. 8): "A Union republic or province reports fulfillment of the grain procurement plan, and the next day asks the state for seed and for feed grain for the livestock." In 1959, he reported, the RSFSR delivered 1,643 million poods of grain but returned to the farms 361 million poods, or 22 percent.

[23] *Pravda,* March 28, 1961, p. 2; March 29, 1961, p. 2.

able satisfactorily to surmount three main difficulties. First, there are major problems in obtaining consistent estimates of certain inputs for successive periods as farm organization was radically changed. The labor input is especially troublesome, particularly in terms of comparability of measures for recent years and the twenties. Our knowledge of current labor input in the private sector is very meager; Ioffe (p. 28) has estimated that private farming activities utilized almost a third of all labor inputs in Soviet agriculture in 1955.[24] Second, the bases for changes in current purchases, in the value of buildings and investment other than machinery, and in the land input are quite limited or subject to analytical problems. Third, the weights or coefficients for the input indexes are based upon meager information; furthermore, because of large changes in relative prices reasonable weights for current purchases and machinery vary substantially during the period. Because of the several-fold increase in current purchases from the nonfarm sector, the various reasonable weights given to such purchases yield quite different estimates of aggregate inputs.

We hope eventually to construct a series of chain-linked indexes for the several input categories that are made up of many subcategories. We also hope to derive suitable weights for many different years for aggregating the major input categories into a single input index. For the present we can offer nothing more than a set of what we hope are reasonable approximations.

Table V.6 summarizes our estimates of the major inputs. A detailed exposition of the derivation is impossible within the limits of this paper, but a general explanation of the content of each series is presented.

Because of the large weight attached to the labor input, we give two series. One is based upon our estimate of the number of man-days of farm employment; the other is based upon the number of able-bodied individuals principally engaged in agriculture. The series differ, and substantially, because the number of days worked per year has increased substantially since 1928, from about 120 to 170 or 180 days per year.[25]

It can be argued that the increase in number of days worked per year

[24] According to the estimates published by the Central Statistical Administration in connection with the 1959 Population Census total, annual average employment in agriculture was 33 million in 1959, of whom 6.2 million were engaged in individual auxiliary employment. On this basis, 23.1 percent of total farm labor was employed in private agriculture (TSU, "Distribution of USSR Population by Social Groups, Branches of the Economy and Occupations . . . ," *Problems of Economics,* 1960, no. 11, p. 5). This estimate is not necessarily inconsistent with Ioffe's, since the concept of average annual employment probably rests on major activity and excludes some work done on private plots by workers and employees and collective farm members.

[25] Arcadius Kahan, "Changes in Labor Inputs in Soviet Agriculture," *Journal of Political Economy,* October 1959, p. 457. The estimate of man-days worked is based on Kahan's work.

Table V.6
USSR: Indexes of Input in Agriculture, Selected Years, 1928–59

Year	Current purchases	Live-stock	Capital	Land	Labor Man-days A	Labor Numbers B	Total inputs Aa	Total inputs Bb
				1928 = 100				
1928	100	100	100	100	100	100	100	100
1938c	590	76	97	125	112	85	141	126
1938d	590	76	97	125	112	85	122	106
				1938 = 100				
1938	100	100	100	100	100	100	100	100
1950	137	112	98	108	108	91	109	100
				1950 = 100				
1950	100	100	100	100	100	100	100	100
1955	149	108	155	122	94	100	108	112
1959	193	141	194	129	93	99	115	118

a Based on man-days.
b Based on numbers engaged in agriculture.
c Based on 1955 weights.
d Based on weights adjusted for importance of current purchases in 1928; see text for discussion.
Note: Full documentation will be provided in a publication of the National Bureau of Economic Research.

is a consequence of improved organization and therefore the appropriate measure is the number of workers principally engaged in agriculture. However, the increase in the number of days worked may have been attained at the expense of other activities, such as handicrafts and work at nonfarm jobs as well as leisure. Since there is no clear reason for using one measure or the other, I present alternative estimates of aggregate inputs.

The estimates of current purchases are very rough. The only continuous series available are for purchases of fertilizer and petroleum products. It has been assumed that for the period since 1938 changes in current purchases can be approximated by the changes in these two items, which in 1955 amounted to about 40 percent of all current purchases from nonagriculture. Another component, spare parts and repair materials, which should be closely related to petroleum products, perhaps accounted for another fifth in 1955. The estimates of current purchases for 1928–38 are derived from Jasny (p. 767).

Livestock, excluding workstock, is represented by inventory, valued at 1955 prices, and an interest rate of 8 percent. The capital stock, which includes primarily machinery and workstock, was converted to a flow by the use of the same interest rate and a 10 percent depreciation rate, except for workstock.

Land has been measured by the sown area, weighted regionally by average grain yields during 1900–15. Because regional differences in grain yields are not large in the Soviet Union the resulting measure is only slightly different from the simple changes in total sown area.

The weights were derived by estimating the value of agricultural output (net of interfarm transfers and use), and the annual expenditure or service flow for each category of inputs. The total value of agricultural output is the value of marketings plus the value of income in kind. Income in kind was valued at the average price realized by all farm sellers. This was done for consistency with the estimates presented by Bergson in Chapter I.

The weights are for the year 1955. The coefficient for land was assumed to be 0.30, and is very close to the residual after the values for all other inputs are deducted from the value of output. The other weights are: labor, 0.5764; current expenditures, 0.0564; capital, 0.0379, and livestock, 0.0293.[26] While I believe that it is more appropriate to weight the inputs by means of a logarithmic function, arithmetic weights have been used for consistency with the procedure used for aggregate inputs in the United States.

The determination of the weight for current purchases is difficult because of the changes in the prices of such inputs. Their prices relative to product prices increased substantially after 1928 until the price reforms of the late forties and the early fifties, but in recent years farm products have increased substantially compared with these input prices. The estimated share of current expenses in agricultural output was approximately 1.5 percent in 1928, then increased to more than 8 percent in 1938, and declined to less than 6 percent in 1955. Since the increase in current purchases after 1938 was substantially greater than the increase in agricultural output, the decline in relative expenditure was due to a substantial shift in relative prices.

No attempt has been made to adjust for territorial change; but the inputs are compared with measures of output which also refer to the terri-

---

[26] The 1955 weights yield aggregate input indexes for 1928–38 that seem to be too high (see Table V.6). The enormous increase in current purchases, to an index of 590 in 1938, combined with the 1955 weight of 0.0564, raises the total input index about 28 points. In *A Study of the Growth Potential of Agriculture in the USSR,* The RAND Corporation, Research Memorandum RM-1561, October 3, 1955, p. 13, I found, on the basis of evidence presented by Jasny, that current purchases from the nonfarm sector amounted to about 1.6 percent of gross agricultural income in 1928 and 8.2 percent in 1938. Consequently, we made an alternative calculation, reducing the weight for current purchases to 0.0157, leaving the other weights unchanged, and dividing the resulting 1938 weighted total by the sum of the weights (0.9593).

tory of the specific year. Because our estimates of the individual inputs and weights are tentative, the total time span between 1928 and 1959 has been divided into three periods.

The input estimates are probably more reliable for the period after 1938 than before. The comparability of the labor input data for the period of private farming in the late twenties with those for the period of socialized farming in the late thirties is subject to question. Furthermore, the radical changes in relative proportions of the various inputs apparently occurred before 1938. Consequently, separate input indexes for periods of approximately a decade are probably more accurate than a single index for the entire period.

Table V.7 presents the indexes of farm output and inputs for both the

Table V.7

USSR, 1928–59 and USA, 1910–59: Agricultural Output and Input, and Ratio of Output to Input, Selected Periods

Period	Output relative, final ÷ initial year	Input relative, final ÷ initial year		Ratio: output to input	
		A[a]	B[b]	A	B
USSR					
1928–38	104	141[c]	126[c]	0.74	0.83
1928–38	104	119[d]	107[d]	0.87	0.97
1938–50	120	109	100	1.10	1.20
1950–55	123	108	112	1.14	1.10
1950–59	154	115	118	1.34	1.30
USA					
1910–28	123	118		1.04	
1928–38	105	94		1.12	
1938–50	128	110		1.16	
1950–55	112	101		1.11	
1950–59	125	102		1.23	

[a] Labor measured by man-days.
[b] Labor measured by numbers engaged.
[c] Based on 1955 weights.
[d] Weight for current purchases reduced to 0.0157 from 0.0564.
Note: Data for USSR derived from Tables V.5 and V.6; for USA, output data were derived from Table V.4 or source cited in notes to Table V.4 and input data from U.S. Department of Agriculture, *Changes in Farm Production and Efficiency*, Statistical Bulletin no. 233, revised July 1960, p. 48.

USSR and the USA. Between 1928 and 1938 inputs increased more than output in the USSR. Between 1938 and 1950 the ratio of output to input increased 10 to 20 percent, depending upon whether labor is measured in terms of man-days or numbers employed. Between 1950 and 1959 the increase in the ratio of output to input was of the order of 30 percent, if one accepts official output data; the actual increase may have been nearer 15 to 20 percent.

For the USA data are presented for 1910 and 1928 as well as for the periods used for the USSR. During the period of transition from animal to mechanical power, there was very little input savings in American agriculture. The ratio of output to input increased 12 percent between 1928 and 1938, and 16 percent between 1938 and 1950.

Would the product of input indexes for the three periods (using the input index for 1928–38 based on the smaller weight for current purchases) yield a meaningful input index for 1959 compared with 1928? As a rough check, an input index was calculated based on logarithmic weights. Using the 1955 weights, the logarithmic weighted indexes for 1959 compared with 1928 were 152, with labor measured by man-days, and 122, with labor measured by numbers. The corresponding indexes obtained by multiplying the designated indexes in Table V.7 are 149 and 126. As an approximation, it may be said that the increase in aggregate inputs between 1928 and 1959 was about a fourth with labor measured by numbers, and a half with labor measured by man-days. However, other not unreasonable sets of weights (say for the late thirties) give quite different results.

It is worth noting that climatic factors played some role in the rather favorable ratio of output to input in 1959 compared with 1928. The unusually favorable weather in 1958 yielded larger feed supplies in 1959 than would have been the case if 1958 weather had been nearer the long-term average. Under the conditions prevailing in the Soviet Union, favorable weather in one year has a positive effect on output in the subsequent year. And, as has been noted earlier, the output estimates for 1959 are probably not comparable with the 1928 estimates, representing a substantial degree of exaggeration.

3. Factors Associated with Increased Agricultural Output

Available knowledge does not permit us to separate the contributions to the growth of output of the three major forces: (i) improvements in technology and knowledge, (ii) improvements in the efficiency with which resources are combined and utilized, and (iii) changes in the quality of inputs, especially labor. However, I shall consider in turn certain changes in quantity of inputs, input substitutions, and changes in output combinations that have had or were expected to have a favorable influence upon total agricultural output and presumably upon output per unit of input.

It is important to know what changes have been associated with increased output. If crop output has increased mainly because of an increase in sown area and only secondarily because of higher yields, attention is focused upon the possibilities of further increases in sown area, and the reasons why yields have not increased. If the substitution of mechanical for animal power has been a major factor in increased output, we can infer, since the substitution is now almost two-thirds completed, that future output gains from this source are likely to be quite small. These and similar questions are not apparent from comparisons of output and input indexes, at least not from the broad input indexes I have had to use.

Increase in Sown Area

In 1928 the total sown area was 113 million hectares, 8 million hectares greater than the 1913 area on comparable territory.[27] By 1938 the sown area had increased to 137 million hectares. The new territory acquired had approximately 14 million hectares of sown area.[28] The 1950 area was 4 million hectares below 1940. As a result of the new and idle land campaign, inaugurated in 1954, the total sown area increased approximately 40 million hectares between 1953 and 1958. Thus between 1928 and 1958 the total sown area increased almost 86 million hectares, or slightly more than 76 percent. Excluding the sown area resulting from territorial acquisition, the increase amounts to 64 percent. As indicated in Table V.5, the increase in output available for sale or home consumption between 1928 and 1958 was 93 percent; the increase in output per unit of sown area was about 10 percent.

It is generally presumed that the recent increase in sown area should have resulted in a significant reduction in average national yields, since the regions where sown area, and especially grain area, expanded were assumed to have low yields. This presumption is valid to a surprisingly limited degree. Two estimates of the yield effect of the expansion of the grain area have been made. In the first, the acreage distributions, which were available for all republics and 12 regions in the RSFSR for 1913, 1938, 1953, and 1956, were weighted by regional yields for 1900–15. The area distributions produced the following yields (in centners): for 1913, 8.02; 1938, 7.79; 1953, 8.62; and 1956, 7.62. Until 1953 the expansion of grain area was in the higher yielding areas, but the new lands program reversed this. However, the 1956 area distribution implies an average yield of only 0.4 centner below the 1913 area distribution. The second test, which involved a comparison of 1913 and 1958 with 1955–58 yields, suggests about the same reduction in average yield due to the shift in grain area. The 1913 area distribution of grain indicated an average yield of 9.43 centners; the 1958 distribution a yield of 8.93

[27] *Selkhoz 1960*, p. 127. According to Jasny (p. 219) Soviet estimates made during the late twenties indicated that total cropland in 1928 was 3 percent less than in 1913.
[28] Based on the 1940 sown area of private farmers given in *Selkhoz 1960*, p. 128.

centners. This is a small change and is due as much to the contraction of grain area in high-yielding regions as to the expansion of grain in low-yielding areas. The republics plus the regions within the RSFSR that had lower grain areas in 1958 than in 1913 had an average yield of 10.24 centners when weighted by 1913 area and 10.35 when weighted by 1958 area. These regions had 70.2 million hectares of grain in 1913 and only 54.2 million in 1958. The regions or republics with larger grain areas in 1958 than in 1913 had an average yield in 1955–58 of about 7.8 centners, whether weighted by 1913 or 1958 areas. If the expansion of grain area had been achieved by holding the grain area at the 1913 level in the areas where sowings were reduced and by expansion in the new areas to bring the grain area up to the 1958 level, the average yield in 1958 would have been 9.18 centners per hectare.

The expansion of the sown area, accompanied by increases in complementary inputs, has been a major factor in the increased agricultural output. The expansion of grain production in the virgin and idle land program has permitted a retrenchment of the grain area in those regions where the yield of feed crops is relatively high, primarily in the Ukraine, Northern Caucasus, and the Central Black Soil Zone.

Through 1960 the new lands program seems to have been a success, even if one discounts the yields in these areas for their apparently high moisture content. An estimate of the grain output gained from the expansion of sown area in the new lands area can be made on the following assumptions: (i) the average yields for 1955–59 represent the long-run average yields that can be maintained on a grain area expansion of 32.7 million hectares, and (ii) the 1955–59 grain yields represent the yields that would have been realized had the 1953 grain area been maintained. The yield assumptions probably somewhat overstate the gain from expansion since some of the new land was undoubtedly inferior to that previously sown.

The 1953 grain area, if 1955–59 yields are assumed, would have produced 34.9 million tons of grain; the 1958 area (the largest for the years 1955–59) would have produced 53.8 million tons. The increase would have been 18.9 million tons. Of this increase, if a seeding norm of 1.5 centners per hectare is assumed, 3.6 million tons would have been required for seed, leaving a net increase in output of 15.3 million tons.[29]

In 1955 I estimated that the new lands program, which was then assumed to involve 30 million hectares, might increase grain output 16

[29] Area and yield data are from *Selkhoz 1960,* pp. 147, 214, and *Narodnoe khoziaistvo 1958,* pp. 399 and 421. The regions — Western Siberia, Far East, Urals, and Volga — include some oblasts not in the new lands area. Furthermore, 1959 yield data are not quite comparable with data for 1955–58 because of changes in the boundaries of Western Siberia, the Urals, and the Volga regions, but the error should be small. *Selkhoz 1960* (pp. 223–229) presents considerable information for the new lands oblasts but does not give data on total grain area.

million tons, from which seed requirements on 18 million hectares (2.4 million tons) should be deducted to arrive at the net output.[30] At that time I assumed that approximately 40 percent of the land would have to be fallowed; this practice has not been followed although I still believe that it would be economical to do so. Some output is also obtained from the 8.6 million hectares of the new land area that is not sown to grain. However, the yields of the other crops grown in these areas are very low, perhaps about 2 to 3 centners of feed units per hectare. If grain is assumed to have a feed unit value of unity, the total annual production of the new lands program measured in feed units may be estimated as about 17 million tons, net of seed. If the grain output in this region is reduced 12 percent because of the high moisture content, spoilage, and inclusion of waste material, the net production of grain might amount to 13 million tons and the total, in feed units, to 15 million tons.

The criterion of success in the above discussion of the new lands program is increased grain output. I believe that under the circumstances prevailing in 1953, the fourth year with no significant increase in agricultural output, any program that gave promise of increased output would have been considered a potential success. But the program has been a success on two other counts. First, the new lands program was the lowest cost alternative for achieving rather rapid increases in grain output. Significant increases in grain output in other areas of the Soviet Union would have required large increases in fertilizer output, which, because of the capital investment required, could not have been achieved in less than three or four years and then only at the expense of other investment programs. Second, the increased grain has been relatively low cost grain measured in terms of resources engaged in agriculture. Output per unit of labor and machinery, including variable inputs associated with machinery, has been high in the new lands area compared with the rest of the Soviet Union. Of course, if agricultural output in the area had to be reduced to about the 1953 level because of the development of dust bowl conditions, the loss of the capital invested in transportation and marketing could offset or more than offset the cost savings in agriculture achieved since 1955. However, even if the grain area had to be reduced materially, the adoption of the farming methods of the Prairie Provinces of Canada which involve, among other things, extensive use of clean fallow, could yield a gross grain output approximately equal to the average for the past seven years.

---

[30] I mention the 1955 projection not to prove that I was approximately right and that Khrushchev was most optimistic in assuming that yields in the new lands area would be 10 centners per hectare, but simply to indicate that under the climatic conditions in most of the grain areas of the Soviet Union reasonably accurate estimates can be made on the basis of performance in North America under similar conditions. For my estimate of the new lands program, see "Observations on the Economy of the USSR," *Journal of Political Economy,* June 1956, pp. 209–210.

Substitution of Mechanical for Animal Power

In 1928 approximately 32 percent of all feed was required for farm horses; if the feed for oxen is added, the requirement may have been 35 percent of all feed. In 1959 approximately 10 percent of all feed was required for animal power. The reduction in feed for power animals was 40 million tons between 1928 and 1959.[31] This was enough feed to produce about 6 million tons of pork (live weight) or 35 to 40 million tons of milk. The gross value of either of these amounts of livestock products, in 1958 collective farm prices, was approximately 12 to 13 percent of the value of farm products available for sale or home consumption. This source of increased output has now been rather largely exhausted, although some further gain in the quantity of products available for sale or use will occur as horse numbers continue to decline.

Increased Crop Yields

An increase in the output per unit of cultivated land can reflect an increase in the yield of individual crops, or a change in the mix of crops toward crops with a higher yield value per unit of land. The latter type of shift requires more resources, particularly labor, and we designate it as a shift toward labor intensive crops. First, we consider the increase in yields per hectare of individual crops.

Table V.8 presents the average yields of the six major farm crops in the

Table V.8
USSR: Gross Crop Yields, 1925–59

Period	Grain	Cotton	Sugar beets	Sunflowers	Potatoes	Flax fiber
			Centners per hectare			
1925–29	7.9	8.8	132.0	6.24	79.3	2.1
1930–34	6.8	6.3	95.3	5.31	80.0	1.8
1935–38	7.1	11.4	147.3	5.50	78.5	1.9
1950–54	7.8	16.5	150.8	5.47	86.2	1.3
1955–59	9.7	20.2	180.6	9.04	91.0	2.6
			Indexes, 1925–29 = 100			
1925–29	100	100	100	100	100	100
1930–34	86	72	72	85	101	86
1935–38	90	130	112	88	99	90
1950–54	99	187	114	88	109	62
1955–59	122	230	137	145	115	124

Note: Data derived from Johnson and Kahan, p. 211, except those for 1955–59, which are from *Selkhoz 1960*, p. 209.

[31] The number of horses, more than 32 million in 1928, dropped to 11 million in 1959.

Soviet Union. Except for cotton, yields increased only moderately between 1925–29 and the first half of the fifties. However, the official yields of all crops during 1955–59 exceeded the 1925–29 levels. The increase in cotton yields was substantial, namely, 130 percent; and the increases for sugar beets (37 percent) and sunflowers (45 percent) were also sizeable, although the sunflower yield should perhaps be discounted 10 percent. The 22 percent increase in grain yields, which may represent a true increase of 12 percent, although not large, has been a major factor in the recent growth of Soviet agricultural output.

Average crop yields for the United States, with corresponding indexes, are given in Table V.9. Grain yields are much higher in the U.S. than

Table V.9
USA: Crop Yields, 1925–59

Period	Grain	Cotton	Sugar beets	Potatoes
Centners per hectare				
1925–29	13.0	5.8	244	76.4
1950–54	17.0	10.1	347	169.2
1955–59	21.0	14.6	387	193.7
Indexes, 1925–29 = 100				
1925–29	100	100	100	100
1950–54	122	175	142	222
1955–59	151	252	159	254

From U.S. Department of Agriculture, *Agricultural Statistics*, 1952 (Washington, 1952), pp. 2, 19, 26, 33, 35, 47–48, 56, 75–76, 97, and 296 for 1925–50; and U.S. Department of Agriculture, *Crop Production, 1960 Annual Summary*, December 16, 1960, pp. 41–43 and 46–48 for 1951–60.

in the Soviet Union and the increase in grain yields of 51 percent greatly exceeds the increase in the Soviet Union. In 1925–29 potato yields were approximately the same in the two countries; since then the U.S. average yield has increased about 150 percent while there has been little increase in the Soviet Union. The higher cotton yields in the Soviet Union are explained by the fact that during 1925–29 and 1955–59 virtually all cotton was grown on irrigated land.[32] The yield of cotton on irrigated land in the United States is currently about 33 centners per hectare. A significant part of the higher absolute yields of sugar beets in the United States is due to the higher proportion grown on irrigated land.

In themselves, differences in national average yields of various crops or

[32] If the effect on yield of the shift from unirrigated to irrigated land in the United States were eliminated, the increase in cotton yield since 1925–29 would be about the same in the two countries.

trends in national yields, do not indicate either comparative performances of the two agricultures or the potentialities for yield increases of the lower yielding areas. Climatic and soil conditions are dramatically different in certain instances, especially for grains, and cotton and sugar beets are grown under quite different conditions in the two countries. Because of the importance of grain in both agricultures, it is pertinent to compare yields in the USSR with yields in reasonably similar areas in the United States.

In an earlier study, I made a detailed analysis of the climatic and soil conditions of the Soviet Union and of North America to determine areas in North America with conditions similar to those prevailing in each major grain-producing area of the Soviet Union.[33] Five states (North Dakota, South Dakota, Nebraska, Montana, and Wyoming) and the Prairie Provinces of Canada include most of the climatically comparable areas. The average yields of this area, when calculated on the basis of sown or harvested area, are probably greater than can be achieved in the grain-growing areas of the Soviet Union. The use of summer fallow is much greater; in the Prairie Provinces the area of summer fallow during 1945–54 was equal to 50 percent of the sown area of wheat, barley, and oats. For the area as a whole, the summer fallow area was about a third of the total grain area, including corn. Furthermore, in some instances, the comparable area was only a part of the province or state; for example, in Alberta the comparable crop districts were the two lowest yielding districts.

Three states — North Dakota, South Dakota, and Nebraska — provide quite close climatic analogies for about half of the total Soviet grain area. The areas in the Soviet Union not included in these analogies are the relatively low-yielding areas of Rostov, lower Volga, part of the Urals, and the western areas of the RSFSR. The latter areas, while low-yielding at present, have a considerable potential for increased yields. The major areas not included are Western Siberia, Eastern Siberia, Alma Ata Oblast, and Central Asia. The major difference between the three states and the comparable areas in the Soviet Union is that the eastern parts of Nebraska and South Dakota are reasonably hospitable to corn, and the corn area represents about 30 percent of the combined area of wheat, oats, barley, and corn.

The absolute and relative yields, compared with the U.S. averages, for certain combinations of areas in the United States and Canada (for 1945–54) are as shown in Table V.10.

The grain yields in the comparable areas range from 57 to 78 percent

[33] D. Gale Johnson, *Climatic and Crop Analogies for the Soviet Union: A Study of the Possibilities of Increasing Grain Yields,* The University of Chicago Office of Agricultural Economics, Research Paper no. 5716, December 16, 1957.

Table V.10
Grain Yields of USA and Canada, 1945–54

Area and grains	Grain yields (centners per hectare)	Percent of comparable U.S. average[a]
Five states and prairie provinces		
Wheat, oats, and barley	11.2	69
Wheat, oats, barley, and corn	12.2	75
Prairie provinces		
Wheat, oats, and barley	12.7	78
Wheat, oats, and barley plus summer fallow area	8.4	57
Three states		
Wheat, oats, and barley	9.8	60
Wheat, oats, barley, and corn	12.2	75
Wheat, oats, barley, and corn, including summer fallow area	10.7	73
United States		
Wheat, oats, barley, corn, and grain sorghum	16.3	
As above, but including summer fallow	14.7	

[a] Comparable U.S. average depends on inclusion of summer fallow area in calculation of yield.

of the relevant U.S. average. The tabulation indicates the importance of corn as a factor responsible for the high average yields in the U.S., since the U.S. average for wheat, oats, and barley for 1945–54 was 12.0 centners per hectare. It also indicates the effect of including the total cultivated area devoted to grains upon the yield level.

A comparison of the above yields with recent yields in the Soviet Union indicates that grain yields in that country are at reasonable levels. According to *Selkhoz 1960* (p. 196), average yields for various periods and years have been (in centners per hectare) : for 1949–53, 7.7 ; 1950–56, 8.2 ; 1954–58, 8.2 ; 1958, 11.3 ; and 1959, 10.5. Even if recent yields are discounted 8 to 10 percent for comparability with the U.S. and Canadian yields, the average levels are not far below the average for the three states for wheat, oats, and barley, and approximately the same as in the Prairie Provinces, if cultivated summer fallow is included in the area used to calculate yields.

Furthermore, there have been no significant yield increases in the specified North American areas if periods of time with reasonably similar climatic conditions are considered. Climatic conditions during 1920–29 and 1945–54 were approximately the same for the northern plains area in the

United States and the Prairie Provinces in Canada. Yields in 1957–60 have been significantly higher than during 1945–54, but much of the increase can probably be explained by weather variations. Between 1920–29 and 1945–54, the average yield of five grains increased 10 percent. If the area of fallow is included in the calculation of yields, there was a decline in yields.

Increases in Labor Intensive Crops

While the proportion of the sown area devoted to the four major industrial crops (cotton, sunflowers, sugar beets, and flax) has remained unchanged at approximately 6.5 to 7 percent since 1928, an increasing proportion of the technical crops has been grown on irrigated land. Consequently, if the value of the land were considered, the proportion of the land devoted to technical crops would have risen. Between 1928 and 1955–59 the percentage of the gross output of six major crops contributed by the technical crops increased from 9 to almost 18 percent. Thus the major factor in the relative increase of the output of technical crops was increased output per unit of cultivated land (Table V.11).

Table V.11
USSR: Sown Area, Total Value, and Value per Hectare of Crops,
1928, 1955–57, and 1955–59

Item	1928	1955–57	1955–59
Total			
Area of included crops (mil. ha.)	105.6	147.1	145.6
Total output of included crops (bil. rubles)	6.5	11.3	11.9
Output per hectare (rubles)	62.5	76.8	81.7
Index, output per hectare	100.0	122.9	130.7
Grain, potatoes, and vegetables			
Area (mil. ha.)	98.6	137.3	135.6
Output (bil. rubles)	5.9	9.3	9.8
Output per hectare (rubles)	59.8	67.7	72.2
Index, output per hectare	100.0	113.2	120.7
Industrial crops			
Area (mil. ha.)	7.0	9.8	10.0
Output (bil. rubles)	0.6	2.0	2.1
Output per hectare (rubles)	85.7	204.1	210.0
Index, output per hectare	100.0	238.1	245.0

Notes: Weights used were 1926–27 prices.

Sown area and output data are from *Selkhoz 1960*, pp. 132–133 and 202–203, and *Narodnoe khoziaistvo 1958*, pp. 386–387 and 420–421. Prices are from Johnson and Kahan, p. 204,

The output per hectare of the crops included increased 31 percent between 1928 and 1955–59.[34] The increase in output per hectare for grains, potatoes, and vegetables was only 21 percent, while the increase for industrial crops was 145 percent. Although much of the increase in the output of industrial crops per hectare was due to the increased importance of irrigation, a significant part of the increase in total output of crops was due to the greater emphasis given to industrial crops which use a relatively small part of the total sown area.

The Corn Program and the Feed Supply

With the output and area data in *Selkhoz 1960* we can approximate the impact of the corn program upon the feed supply. The data are for 1955–59.

During the five-year period, the total area sown to corn was 102.2 million hectares. The output of dry grain was 42.0 million tons, and the dry grain equivalent of corn in the milk-wax stage was 20.0 million tons, a total of 62.0 million tons of grain. The total production of green feed, including silage, was 462.3 million tons. Assuming a feed unit value of 1 for grain and 0.13 for the green feed, the total production in terms of feed units was 123 million tons.[35] This was an average yield of 12 centners of feed units per hectare.

The grain yield from mature grain was 17.5 centners; the yield of corn in the milk-wax stage was 12.3 centners; and the average for all corn grain was 15.3. The average national yield for all grain for the same years was 9.7 centners. At first glance the corn program contributed a substantial quantity of grain. However, if oblast or republic wheat yields are weighted by the relative importance of corn grain for six areas that include 90 percent of all corn harvested for grain, the average yield of wheat was 15.2 centners in these areas for 1955–59.[36] Thus compared to wheat in

[34] A similar measure for the United States indicates an increase in crop yields per acre of 72 percent for the same years (see U.S. Department of Agriculture, *Major Statistical Series of the U.S. Department of Agriculture, Annual Summary,* December 17, 1958, p. 49). The index of yields per harvested acre for 18 field crops was used. The estimates for the Soviet Union are based on official Soviet data, which we believe are somewhat too high for most crops for the years 1955–59.

[35] The feed unit value of 0.13 is based on I. S. Popov, *Kormovye normy i kormovye tablitsy* (Moscow, 1955), and represents corn silage without cobs or grain. The grain content of silage made with corn in the milk-wax stage is included in grain output. Our interpretation of the data on corn given in *Selkhoz 1960* (pp. 156–157) is that only corn that does *not* reach the milk-wax stage is included in the silage area. Part or all of the stalks from the corn harvested in the milk-wax stage are undoubtedly put in silage. If the corn silage yield is multiplied by the corn silage sown area, the total does not equal the amount of corn silage.

[36] The areas were the Central Black Soil Zone, Povolzhe, Northern Caucasus, Urals, Ukraine, and Moldavia. The first two were assumed to have the same yield for wheat, namely, 10.7 centners (see *Selkhoz 1960,* p. 221 and TSU, *Posevnye ploshchadi SSSR* (Moscow, 1957), I, 362–366).

the same general area, there was little or no grain yield advantage for corn, except for the seed saving of about one centner per hectare.

If the production of grain was the major objective of the corn program, not much has been accomplished. During the five years 1949–53, total corn grain production was 26.5 million tons on a total of 21 million hectares. Thus the increase in grain was 36.5 million tons or an average of about 7.1 million tons per year; of this increase only 15.5 million tons (3.1 million tons per year) was in the form of dry grain.

However, the most appropriate assessment of the corn program is in terms of the total feed output or of the yield of feed per hectare. As noted above, the yield of feed units was 12 centners, composed of grain and green feed. In addition, several tons of corn stover were probably available for use.[37] Assuming that the quantity of feed in the stover equals 40 percent of the value of the mature grain harvested, the feeding value of the total quantity of stover produced would have been about 17 million tons of feed units; and the total yield of feed would have been about 14 centners of feed units per hectare.[38]

A rough analysis made of the grain areas displaced by corn and the yields of the combination of wheat and other grains involved indicated that the probable yield of the grains displaced was about 85 percent of the average yield of wheat. This would imply that the average yield of the other grains, including wheat, displaced by corn was about 13 centners per hectare for 1955–59. If a differential of one centner per hectare of seed is assumed, the gain in net grain from the transfer may have been a little more than 2 centners per hectare.

Does a feed unit yield of 14 centners per hectare represent an improvement over the alternative uses of the land? If all the expansion of corn for all purposes had been at the expense of grain, this would not have been

---

[37] The upward revision of the hay figures may represent the counting of corn stover as hay; the corn stover would be derived from the corn harvested at the mature stage. The feed value of stover is approximately a quarter to a third of the total value of the mature corn plant or a third to a half of the feeding value of the grain.

[38] The above estimates of feed derived from corn probably exclude some corn harvested as green feed; namely, the corn area included in annual grasses. The area involved has been about 6 million hectares in recent years. We do not believe that the feed harvested from this area involves a significant quantity. Khrushchev described it as follows:

"What is green fodder? Actually it is spoiled corn. The corn was planted, but not cultivated, and it became overgrown with weeds and thistles." (*Pravda,* December 21, 1958)

We are mystified by the data that indicate that almost 40 million tons of the silage output of corn was not stored in silos, but was apparently fed to livestock directly from the field, yet some part of the output of corn which does not reach even the milk-wax stage of maturity is included in sown annual grasses. We conclude that the corn classified as green feed in the sown area data is not included in the corn silage output, since the combined area of corn silage and corn harvested in the milk-wax stage multiplied by the reported silage yield is almost exactly equal to the corn silage actually harvested, except for 1959 when the output figure is 7 to 10 million tons smaller than the product of area and yield (*Selkhoz 1960,* pp. 247–249).

the case. The straw that is harvested with the small grains has a feed value equal to at least a third of the value of the grain. However, some of the corn area must have displaced low-yielding pastures and meadows, although realistic planning would presumably attempt to determine if the small grains, including wheat, could not also have replaced them. The corn program has been too large in the sense that it extends into areas where corn has a comparative disadvantage. Real gains have been achieved in the Ukraine, Northern Caucasus, and probably the Central Black Soil Zone, but some of these gains have been offset by expansion into areas either too dry or too cold.

Perhaps the most important contribution of the corn program has been the improvement in the quality of the feed supply and the change in its seasonal distribution.[39] Improvement could have been achieved in other ways, such as by expansion of legume hays.

Increased Feeding Efficiency and Changes in the Feed Supply

While there has probably been some increase in output of livestock products per unit of feed, it is difficult to say how important this factor has been. Undoubtedly livestock are better housed today than they were during the thirties or in the years immediately after the last war. Whether they are better housed than during the twenties is a moot point. As noted earlier, the corn program has probably meant an improvement in the quality of the feed supply as well as a better seasonal distribution; both of these factors could result in additional output per unit of feed as ordinarily measured. But other changes, such as an increase in the protein content of rations and in relative importance of concentrates in the ration, do not seem to have occurred. Without these changes, significant improvements in feeding efficiency are not likely. The higher milk output per cow has resulted in an increased ratio of output per unit of feed since a high-yielding cow requires no more feed for maintenance than a low-yielding cow. If a cow produces only 1,000 kilograms per year, about three-fourths of the feed consumed is required for maintenance; but if output increases to 1,500 kilograms, only two-thirds of the feed goes for maintenance. *Selkhoz 1960* contains considerable data on the quantities of various feeds produced since 1940. While some of the series, especially those for hay and silage crops, may not be consistent over time, we compare the changes in the output of such feeds and the feed requirements for the livestock output as officially estimated (Table V.12). The feed output estimate assumes that all of the traditional feed grains — corn, oats, and barley — net of seed requirements are fed to livestock. It is assumed that the grains used for food and industrial purposes are offset by by-products from flour milling.

[39] For a brief discussion, see Johnson and Kahan, pp. 219–220.

Table V.12
USSR: Feed Unit Value of Production of Certain Feeds and
Estimated Feed Requirements of Livestock Output,
Including Feed for Horses, Selected Years, 1940–59
(million tons of feed units)

Year	Feed output[a]	Feed requirements[b]	Difference
1940	64	151	87
1945		108	
1950	54	141	87
1953	58	161	103
1955	73	172	99
1956	76	186	110
1957	71	197	126
1958	105	204	99
1959	97	222	125

[a] Based on *Selkhoz 1960*, pp. 202–203. Feed values used were: concentrates, 1.0; hay, 0.45; silage crops, 0.15; and root crops, 0.12. Rough adjustments were made to include silage from natural sources. Feed output of a given year is used in the latter half of the same year and the first half of the following year.
[b] For method of estimation, see Johnson and Kahan, p. 225. The one difference is that official gross milk output has been used to estimate feed requirements for milk cows.

The major sources of feed not included in Table V.12 are pasture, straw, and potatoes. The increase in the difference in recent years implies either an improvement in feeding efficiency or some exaggeration in output estimates for livestock products. Potato output has increased only moderately since 1940, and in some years in the early fifties was below the 1940 level. The feed value of straw actually utilized might have increased, but the dependence upon straw as a feed has always been heavy. Pastures might have been somewhat underutilized, but in the last several years millions of hectares of pastures have been plowed up and sown to crops.

The data on feed output and feed requirements cast some doubt on the consistency of the livestock output figures over time. These doubts are reinforced by Nancy Nimitz's study of milk output data referred to earlier. One of the dramatic successes claimed for the Khrushchev agricultural program has been the increase in total milk output and especially the increase in average milk output per cow.

Table V.13 gives data on average milk output per cow since 1928. Most of the yields for state and collective farms and for the socialized sector and average yields for all sectors are from official sources; those that I have estimated are indicated.

Some of the features of the pattern of milk yields are surprising. First, collective farm milk yields were stable, except for a small decline in 1945,

Table V.13
USSR: Average Annual Milk Production per Cow by Sectors,
Selected Years, 1928–59
(kilograms)

Year	All sectors	Socialized	Collectives	State farms	Private[b]
1928	1,040[a]				
1932			931		
1934		962		908	
1937	1,152[a]	1,128	1,027		
1938	1,223[a]				
1940	1,185	1,124	1,017	1,803	1,205
1945	1,125[a]		945	1,424	1,220
1950	1,370	1,137	1,027	2,256	1,490
1953	1,389	1,157	1,016	2,577	1,553
1954	1,414[a]				
1955	1,524[a]				
1956	1,682	1,693	1,611	2,413	1,673
1957	1,720	1,930	1,858	2,314	1,570
1958	1,755	1,994	1,937	2,256	1,570
1959	1,818	2,067	2,004	2,315	1,600

[a] Based on average number of cows at beginning and end of year and total output of cow milk, not total milk.
[b] Based on distribution of cows between socialized and private sectors.
Note: Data derived from TSU, *Forty Years of Soviet Power, in Facts and Figures* (Moscow, 1958), pp. 149 and 170; *Selkhoz 1960*, pp. 263, 368–370, 328–329, and 333; and *Narodnoe khoziaistvo 1958*, pp. 447 and 479–480.

between 1937 and 1953, yet the yields of private livestock increased 350 kilograms or almost 30 percent between 1940 and 1953. Second, the average milk yield and the private milk yield for 1945 are not consistent with the probable feed situation at that time. Between 1940, when the feed supply situation was quite good, and 1945 the milk yield declined only 60 kilograms. Between those two years the total sown area, on comparable territory, declined 37 million hectares, or 25 percent. The grain sown area decreased from 110 to 85 million hectares, and the estimated grain crop from 95.5 to about 57 million tons; the potato crop decreased from 76 to 58 million tons, and the area of sown fodder crops from 18 to 10 million hectares.[40] Third, the continued increase in private milk yields up to 1953

[40] *Selkhoz 1960*, pp. 132–133 and 202–203; *Forty Years of Soviet Power*, p. 159; Jasny, p. 231. In addition, grain procurements declined only 15 million tons compared with a decrease in output of 38 million tons; and potato procurements decreased very little, from 12.9 to 11.8 million tons. The procurement of milk and dairy products fell 50 percent (from 10.8 to 5.4 million tons) although milk output supposedly decreased only 7.2 million tons from 33.6 million tons in 1940 (data on procurements from *Forty Years of Soviet Power*, p. 142).

and between 1953 and 1956 implies the availability of substantial feed from the state sector; we have no evidence that such additional amounts of feed were made available.[41]

The above comparisons and comments are not conclusive. The most one can say is that a decline in average milk per cow of 300 to 400 kilograms between 1940 and 1945 would not be surprising. If there had been, in fact, no increase in the milk yield of privately owned cows since 1940 and if the yield in the socialized sector is now being overestimated by about 250 kilograms, as implied by Nancy Nimitz (p. 23), the present total milk output is being overestimated by 11 million tons compared with 1940 and earlier years.[42] The average milk yield for 1959 might have been 1,500 kilograms instead of 1,818.

4. SUMMARY

Although there has been a considerable increase in official data on Soviet agricultural output, there is some evidence that recent official output data overstate significantly actual output available for use. Any attempt to adjust the official data must be based largely on conjecture, but we would judge that aggregate output data for the years since 1958 are 10 to 15 percent too high compared with the early fifties.

Estimates of the output of the acquired territories in 1940 for eleven commodity groups indicate that about 14 percent of 1940 output on present territory was produced on acquired territory. According to the calculated output index, agricultural output increased 60 percent between 1928 and 1959, after adjustment is made for the expansion of territory.

A comparison of changes in total inputs with changes in output reveals a decline in the output-input ratio between 1928 and 1938, an increase of 10 to 20 percent between 1938 and 1950, and an increase of about 30 percent between 1950 and 1959 if official output data are accepted.

The increase in total sown area and the substitution of mechanical for animal power have been the two most important factors in the increase in gross agricultural output since 1928; increases in crop yields were the next most important factor; while increases in feeding efficiency played

[41] There were substantial declines in the production of meat (28 percent in live weight) and eggs (60 percent) between 1940 and 1945. The number of horses decreased by one-half.

[42] The view that the 1940 milk output of 33.6 million tons was also an overestimate rests upon the published estimate of cow numbers for January 1, 1940, 22.8 million. See *Selkhoz 1960,* p. 263. It is fairly certain that this number refers to the territory of September 17, 1939 and not to current territory. The official milk yield of 1,185 kilograms for 1940 implies 27.7 million cows for 1940. The number of cows on January 1941 is given as 27.8 million. For cow milk produced in 1940, *Selkhoz 1960* (p. 333) gives 32.8 million tons out of a total of 33.6 million tons.

only a minor role. The corn program has had little effect on total feed output, but probably resulted in a significant improvement in the quality of the feed supply as well as a favorable change in the seasonal availability of feed.

VI

CONSUMPTION

Janet G. Chapman*

The task of this chapter is to compare the level and pattern of consumption in the Soviet Union with present and past levels and patterns of consumption in the United States and to analyze the major similarities and differences. The changes in consumption levels in the Soviet Union since the eve of the First Five-Year Plan are traced in some detail in section 1. To trace in similar detail the entire history of consumption in the United States seems less necessary and, in any case, is too large a task for this paper. For the major aggregative measures of consumption — real per capita consumer income and real wages — annual data are shown for the United States since the Civil War. These provide the basis for the historical comparisons in section 2 concerning the rate of growth of consumption and real wages. The more detailed comparison in section 3 is limited to the Soviet Union today and the United States at two

* This chapter was originally prepared as a report for The RAND Corporation; however, any views expressed in it are those of the author and should not be interpreted as reflecting the views of The RAND Corporation or the official opinion or policy of any of its sponsors.

periods — today and in 1890 — and is concerned with differences in the pattern as well as the level of consumption. Section 4 is devoted to discussion of the factors responsible for the similarities or differences found. Considering Soviet development as a case of general economic growth, we attempt to pick out those aspects of Soviet consumption which appear to be primarily related to the stage and level of economic growth. However, as will be seen, the explanation is often found in the particular time and place of Soviet economic development and in the policies of the rulers of the Soviet planned economy.

1. Changes in Soviet Consumption Levels Since 1928

Changes in the level and pattern of Soviet consumption during the period of the five-year plans are given in Table VI.1. The planned goals for 1965 are also shown for many items but the discussion will be limited for the most part to performance up to 1958. The first five items are aggregative measures valued at 1937 Soviet prices. Item 1 is an index of per capita consumer income or household consumption valued at adjusted market prices of 1937. Item 2 is also an index of real per capita household consumption but it includes communal services. The index of real per capita consumption of communal services alone is item 3. Communal services are the free educational, health, and physical culture services provided by the government and other public institutions. All educational and health services are treated as consumption, although it is clear that some or all such services might usefully be considered investment. In this connection, it should be noted that education includes scientific research, which accounts for a sharply rising share of the total over the period. These measures are based on Abram Bergson's calculations through 1955 with a rough extension to 1958.[1] The adjusted market prices involve the revaluation of farm income in kind at retail prices (less transport and trade margins not incurred) rather than at average realized farm prices, and the revaluation of housing and services to correspond more closely to the United States price structure. Item 4 is an index of per capita purchases of consumer goods valued at 1937 market prices. It is computed from retail sales of goods to households for consumption and my index of average prices in all Soviet retail markets computed on the basis of given-year weights with 1937 as base year. Item 5 is my index of average annual wages of all nonagricultural wage earners and salaried employees, net of direct taxes and purchases of government bonds, valued at 1937 market prices. It is computed by deflating the index of money wages (based on official figures) by my cost of living index computed

---

[1] More complete references and explanations of the measures are given in the notes to Table VI.1 in the appendix.

on the basis of given-year weights with 1937 as base year.[2] For simplicity, I show in Table VI.1 only indexes based on the measures valued in terms of 1937 prices. Alternative computations based on Soviet prices of other years, however, generally make a significant difference in these indexes for the period 1928 to 1937, relatively little difference for the period since 1937, but again a significant difference for the comparison of 1928 with 1958 (or other post-1937 years).

Before proceeding, it seems in order to indicate the results obtained with different valuation procedures. When per capita household consumption is valued at adjusted market prices of 1950 there is a rise of 1 percent instead of a fall of 3 percent between 1928 and 1937 but the over-all change between 1928 and 1958 is about the same as when 1937 prices are used. When valued at adjusted market prices of 1928, however, per capita household consumption increases between 1928 and 1937 by 22 percent; and if this index is linked to the index number for 1937–58 based on 1950 prices, the increase between 1928 and 1958 is 126 percent. Net real wages in 1928, when valued in terms of 1928 prices, are 120 percent of the 1937 level; and when this index is linked to the index for 1937–58 valued at 1958 prices, the rise in net real wages over the entire period 1928–58 is 29 percent, compared with the fall of 7 percent when wages are valued throughout at 1937 prices.[3] Similar differences are obtained for household consumption including communal services and for real per capita purchases of goods; and the relationships among these measures are not significantly affected by the choice of valuation procedure. The following discussion deals with the index numbers in terms of 1937 prices shown in Table VI.1. There are good reasons for using the 1937 price structure for valuation purposes but it should be kept in mind that for some periods — 1928–37 in particular — alternative and theoretically equally valid measures give significantly different results.[4]

Per capita consumption declined slightly between 1928 and 1937; but the large rise in per capita consumption of communal services meant that per capita consumption including communal services increased almost 10 percent. The same increase is shown in per capita purchases of consumer goods. Real wages, however, dropped sharply between 1928 and 1937. In all these cases the 1937 figures undoubtedly represent a recovery from a much lower point in 1932 or thereabouts. Recovery apparently continued

[2] My detailed price and cost of living indexes extend only to 1954 and the projections to 1958 are based on Soviet indexes.

[3] Actually, the detailed computations are made for 1954 using 1954 prices, and the 1958 index number of real wages is a projection from that for 1954.

[4] These valuation problems are discussed more fully in Abram Bergson, *The Real National Income of Soviet Russia Since 1928* (Cambridge, Mass., 1961), chaps. 3, 10, 12, 13, and in my forthcoming *Real Wages in Soviet Russia Since 1928,* chaps. iii, v, ix; hereafter cited as *Real SNIP* and *Real Wages.*

Table VI.1

USSR: Selected Indicators of Consumption, 1928–58 and Plan 1965

Indicator	1928	1932	1937	1940	1944	1950	1955	1958	P 1965	1958 as per-cent of 1928
1. Per capita consumption in 1937 adjusted market prices[a] (1937 = 100)	103	—	100	96	66	114	159	191	—	185
2. Per capita consumption and communal services in 1937 adjusted market prices (1937 = 100)	91	—	100	96	69	116	157	185	—	203
3. Per capita consumption of communal services at 1937 factor cost (1937 = 100)	29	—	100	101	86	131	150	154	—	531
4. Per capita purchases of goods at 1937 prices[b] (1937 = 100)	91	—	100	95	56	120	189	233	341	256
5. Net average annual wage, nonagricultural wage earners and salaried employees, in 1937 prices (1937 = 100[c])	175	—	100	94	65	101	141	164	221	93
6. Hours actually worked per week in industry	37.3	—	36.1	39.3	52	42	42	39	34	105
7. Per capita industrial output of consumer goods (1937 = 100)										
a. Foods	70	69	100	88	45[d]	87	126	143	—	204
b. Nonfoods	64	68	100	97	41[d]	114	189	218	—	341
c. All consumer goods	68	69	100	92	43[d]	97	150	172	250	253
8. Per capita output of selected foods										
a. Flour (kilograms)	158	—	169	149	86[d]	121	162	159	—	101
b. Potatoes (kilograms)	110	116	200	191		243	138	150	225	136
c. Meat, poultry, lard (kilograms)	32	17	18	24	15[d]	27	32	38	68	119
d. Milk (kilograms)	178	113	141	141	108[d]	145	169	224	391	126
e. Eggs (number)	65	25	45	56		59	87	105	144	162
f. Fish (catch) (kilograms)	5.5	8.4	9.7	7.2	6.4[d]	9.6	13.9	14.2	20	258
g. Sugar (kilograms)	8.5	5.2	14.7	11.1	2.7[d]	13.8	17.4	26.2	41–44	308
h. Vegetable oil (kilograms)	3.0	3.1	3.3	4.1	1.7[d]	4.5	5.9	7.0	—	233
i. Vegetables (kilograms)	53	58	66	53	—	41	57	55	—	104
j. Vodka (liters)	3.7	4.6	5.4	4.7	2.5[d]	3.4	5.9	7.0	—	189
k. Beer (liters)	2.6	2.7	5.4	6.2	2.3[d]	7.2	9.4	9.6	—	369
9. Per capita output of selected nonfoods										
a. Cotton fabrics (meters)	17.7	17.0	20.9	20.3	9.2[d]	21.4	30.0	28.0	34.2	158
b. Wool fabrics (meters)	0.6	0.6	0.6	0.6	0.3[d]	0.9	1.3	1.5	2.1	250
c. Silk and synthetic fabrics (meters)	0.1	0.1	0.4	0.4	0.2[d]	0.7	2.7	4.1	6.4	410
d. Linen fabrics (meters)	1.2	0.8	1.7	1.5	0.6[d]	1.5	1.6	2.3	2.7	192
e. Hosiery (pairs)	0.4	1.3	2.5	2.5	0.5[d]	2.6	3.9	4.3	5.3	1075
f. Shoes (pairs)	0.5	0.5	1.1	1.1	0.4[d]	1.1	1.4	1.7	2.2	340
g. Soap (kilograms)	2.0	2.3	3.0	3.6	1.3[d]	4.5	5.5	6.6	—	330
h. Cigarettes (number)	327	366	540	515	143[d]	686	1006	1120	—	343

10. Consumer durables, output or sales per 1,000 population (physical units)

										Index
a. Radios										
i. Receiving sets	—	—	0.2	1.2	0.8	—	5.4	17.6	17.8	—
ii. Loudspeakers	—	—	0.4	4.1	9.1	—	10.6	42.1	16.9	—
b. Gramophones	—	—	···	3.1	1.6	—	2.0	4.3	—	—
c. Refrigerators	1.9	···	···	—	···	—	2.8	0.7	1.6	721
d. Sewing machines	—	2.0	—	0.9	—	—	7.5	8.4	13.7	—
e. Kerosene stoves	—	—	—	0.3	—	—	25.0	28.1	—	—
f. Electric hotplates	—	—	—	3.7	—	9.3	23.3	17.0[e]	—	—
g. Clocks and watches	5.9	19.6	20.6	12.8	—	45.1	97.4	112.8	—	1912
h. Bicycles	0.2	0.7	3.0	1.0	—	3.8	14.2	16.0	—	8000
11. Urban housing space, square meters per capita	5.8	4.9	4.6	4.5	3.9	5.0	5.1	5.5	8.7	95
12. Publications per capita per year										
a. Newspapers	13	—	41	—	23[d]	38	51	63	—	485
b. Periodicals	2.0	1.5	1.3	—	0.44[d]	1.0	1.8	3.1	—	155
c. Books and pamphlets	1.8	4.1	2.4	—	1.74[d]	4.5	5.2	5.3	—	294
13. Movies attended per capita per year	—	—	—	4.5	—	—	6.3	16.4	—	—
14. School enrollment per 1,000 total population										
a. Grades 1 to 4	65	114	128	110	116[d]	110	69	86	—	132
b. Grades 5 through university	15	31[f]	64[f]	85	47[d,f]	100	109	90	—	600
15. Medical care and health										
a. Doctors per 10,000 population	4	5	6	7	—	14	16	17	—	425
b. Hospital beds per 10,000 population	16	26	36	40	—	56	65	73	92	456
c. Crude death rate per 1,000 population	24.2	17.8[g]	18.1	—	—	9.7	8.2	7.2	—	30
d. Infant mortality, deaths under 1 per year per 1,000 births	187[h]	—	184	—	—	81	60	41	—	22

[a] At adjusted market prices of 1928, the 1928 index is 82. At adjusted market prices of 1950, the 1928 index is 99 and the 1958 index is 185. Linking the 1928 index valued at 1928 prices to that for 1958 valued at 1950 prices results in a 1958 index of 226 percent of 1928.

[b] At 1928 prices, the 1928 index is 62.

[c] At 1928 prices, the 1928 index is 120. At 1954 prices, the 1958 index is 155. If these two indexes are linked, the 1958 index is 129 percent of 1928.

[d] 1945.

[e] 1957.

[f] Excluding students in Labor Reserve and FZU (Factory Training) schools.

[g] 1938.

[h] 1926/27, European USSR.

Notes: The Soviet population figures used in computing the per capita data are shown in the appendix.
The dash (—) indicates that data are not available; the symbol ... that the quantities are zero or negligible.
Here and for later tables, where sources and methods are not given, see appendix.

through 1939 but then all these measures except communal services show a moderate decline in 1940, when preparations for war were well under way, and all show a substantial further decline during the war.[5] By 1950, the prewar level had been regained or surpassed and all measures show rapid increases after 1950. Compared with the 1937 level, 1958 real per capita consumption, excluding communal services, was more than 90 percent higher and, including communal services, was 85 percent higher; real per capita purchases of goods were well over twice as large, and real net wages were 64 percent higher.[6] The gain by 1958 over 1928 was 85 percent in real per capita consumption excluding communal services and over 100 percent including communal services. Per capita consumption of communal services had increased 5.3 times. But net real wages had still not quite regained the 1928 level.[7] This is true also of real hourly wages for, although hours are currently being reduced, the work week in 1958 was still somewhat longer than in 1928 (see item 6).

The relationship among these aggregative measures of income, purchases, and wages is interesting. If real wages had not quite regained the 1928 level by 1958, how could real per capita consumer income approximately double and real per capita purchases of consumer goods increase even more? The main explanation is that by 1958 many more people were working in nonagricultural occupations at wages which, although not at the 1928 level, were considerably above earnings in agriculture in 1928. In 1928, real per capita income was about 1.7 times larger in urban households than in rural households.[8] The number of nonagricultural wage earners and salaried employees increased from some 9 million in 1928 to over 48 million in 1958, while the total population increased only 37 percent.[9] Most of the increase in the nonagricultural labor force was due to the migration from the farms, but it is also true that more family members, particularly wives, have entered the industrial labor force. These structural shifts were concentrated in the 1928–37 period when the dis-

---

[5] The wartime measures are less reliable than those for other years owing both to inadequacies of data and to difficulties of valuation. Because price indexes cannot adequately take into account wartime scarcities and quality deterioration, the measures probably understate the decline.

[6] As Bergson pointed out, the 1958 per capita purchases of goods for consumption may be on the high side. Reports in the Soviet press suggest that state and collective farms have been making unauthorized purchases in the retail shops in order to fulfill their delivery targets. The underlying retail sales data take account of Soviet information on the extent of institutional purchases at retail, but it seems unlikely that such information covers unauthorized purchases by institutions.

[7] As already noted, a gain of 29 percent is obtained with alternative valuation procedures.

[8] Oleg Hoeffding, *Soviet National Income and Product in 1928* (New York, 1954), pp. 63–70.

[9] TSU, *Narodnoe khoziaistvo SSSR V 1958 godu* (Moscow, 1959), p. 658 (hereafter cited as *Narodnoe khoziaistvo 1958*). Estimates of the total and urban Soviet population are shown in the appendix.

parity in movement between real wages and per capita consumer income was most pronounced. Thus, it is hardly astonishing that per capita consumption rose while wages fell between 1928 and 1937 and that over the whole period per capita consumption rose substantially although wages did not. Another reason for the difference in movement is that measures of real consumer income tend to exaggerate the increase in consumption since they reflect more than do measures of real wages the shift of processing from the household to the market that accompanies rapid industrialization and urbanization. This shift is reflected in the greater rise in per capita purchases of consumer goods than in real per capita consumer income.

For similar reasons the per capita industrial output of consumer goods also rose more than real per capita consumer income (Table VI.1, item 7). The increase in the per capita industrial output of consumer goods from 1928 to 1958 was about the same as that in per capita purchases of consumer goods, although the former increased more rapidly between 1928 and 1937 and more slowly during the postwar years than the latter.[10] Industrial output and consumer purchases of goods both exclude consumer goods which are not sold (mainly farm consumption in kind but also such items as homemade clothing) and industrial output also excludes farm products sold without further processing directly to consumers mainly on the peasant market, and these together were a considerably larger share of total consumption in 1928 than in 1958.[11]

Increases in the degree of fabrication should also make the index of industrial output of consumer goods rise faster than real per capita consumer income.[12] It is understood that per capita consumption of industrial consumer goods may differ from per capita output because of such factors as industrial uses, imports or exports, and stockpiling.

To turn now to per capita output of individual consumer goods on a

[10] Industrial output of consumer goods is valued at 1950 retail prices and is not entirely comparable with the per capita purchase figures valued at 1937 retail prices. However, the prices used for the industrial output of consumer goods may not make much difference. G. Warren Nutter, in "Industrial Growth in the Soviet Union," *American Economic Review*, May 1958, no. 2, p. 404, calculates two indexes of industrial output, one based on 1928 price weights and one based on 1955 price weights, but the results do not differ much in the case of consumer goods, except for consumer durables.

[11] See Norman Kaplan and Richard Moorsteen, *Indexes of Soviet Industrial Output*, II, The RAND Corporation, Research Memorandum RM-2495, May 13, 1960, pp. 150–152, for estimates of the changing share in total consumption, consumption in kind, and sales of agricultural produce directly to consumers.

[12] This tendency may be rather weak in the present case as Kaplan and Moorsteen found it necessary to represent two highly fabricated commodity groups (bread and bakery products, and garments) by less highly fabricated commodities (flour and fabrics). On the other hand, their index probably somewhat overstates the rise in output from 1928, since the output of small-scale industry, which was fairly important in 1928, could not be included for all commodities.

physical basis, the products under item 8 in Table VI.1 represent the basic foods plus alcoholic beverages. For flour, sugar, vegetable oil, vodka, and beer, the figures refer to industrial output and for potatoes, meat, milk, eggs, and vegetables they refer to net agricultural output after allowances for feed, seed, and other production uses and losses. These series are the closest to actual per capita consumption possible; they probably reflect consumption fairly well, except in the case of potatoes and vegetable oil where industrial uses may account for significant quantities. The figures illustrate the drastic decline in the consumption of meat and other animal products of the early 1930's and the compensatory increase in the consumption of bread and potatoes; the further substitutions during the war; and, finally, the rapid improvement in the consumption of animal products and a beginning of a decline in the consumption of the cheap starchy foods in the past few years. Until recently, the only significant advances were in fish, sugar, vegetable oil, and beer; and these are the only foods listed which show an increase as large as, or larger than, that of the industrial output of food, which doubled over the 30 years 1928–58. Obviously, per capita consumption of food increased only moderately between 1928 and 1958.

In manufactured consumer goods, the Soviet performance has been more impressive. The increase in the per capita output of fabrics was modest during the prewar years but has been more substantial since the war. Cotton fabrics, still by far the most important clothing material, increased almost 60 percent over the entire 30-year period and larger increases are shown for wool and, especially, for silks and synthetics. The per capita output of hosiery, although still modest, has increased over ten times, and probably reflects a considerable shift from home knitting to factory output. Per capita output of garments, if adequate data were available, would probably also show a large rise. The increase in the per capita output of shoes appears to be substantial.[13] Substantial increases are shown also in the output of soap and cigarettes. Consumer durables are treated separately under item 10 and for the most part refer to retail sales. Production has been increasing rapidly in the postwar years and is enormously higher than in the prewar years. But consumer durables are still so scarce that consumption is expressed, not on a per capita basis, but per 1,000 persons.

Housing in the Soviet Union is an acute problem and, as item 11 shows, the 1928 per capita urban housing space has still not been regained. Even the 1965 goal will not quite provide the meager nine square meters per capita long considered in the Soviet Union as the minimum health standard. The Soviet urban family characteristically lives in one room of an apart-

---

[13] The 1928 shoe output figure is believed to be comprehensive; if it is not, the increase is overstated.

ment, sharing kitchen and toilet facilities with several families. The Soviet peasant family usually lives in a separate house but must be even more crowded than the urban family. In terms of total floor space, the current rural average is four square meters per capita or only half the urban average of 8 square meters.[14] Household utilities and other types of consumer services, for which measures are not available, may have increased more or less as did household purchases of consumer goods but standards for these are still very low.

The remainder of Table VI.1 deals with areas where considerable gains have been achieved. The per capita output of newspapers and books (items 12a and 12c) and movie attendance (item 13) have increased greatly. School enrollment in the first four grades for children aged 7 to 11 (item 14a) has not shown much gain, as most children received a four-year education in 1928; but there has been a sixfold gain in secondary and college enrollment (item 14b). The decline in the latter in recent years is probably the result of a decline in the proportion of the population which is of the secondary school and college age level rather than a decline in the proportion of this age group attending school or college. The numbers of doctors and hospital beds (items 15a and 15b) have increased over four times on a per capita basis and the qualitative advances in medical care have been much greater. The crude death rate (item 15c) and the infant mortality rate (item 15d) have been greatly reduced and the average life expectancy has been extended from some 44 years in 1926 to 68 years in 1958.[15] Reduction in mortality and increase in life expectancy — or, in broader terms, the general health of the population — reflect, of course, changes in many aspects of living besides medical care. But in the USSR there has been a substantial effort to improve the health of the population.

Social security is an important aspect of the Soviet worker's level of consumption. Many provisions for social security were established soon after the Revolution and considerable advances have been made since, although improvements have not been altogether steady. In 1930, it was officially announced that unemployment, which had been a problem in 1928, was abolished. The Soviet worker need have no fear of being without a job. By 1928, provisions had already been made for unemployment insurance (abolished in 1930), for temporary disability (illness, accident,

[14] S. G. Strumilin, "What Communism Is: Thoughts About the Future," *Current Digest of the Soviet Press,* 1960, no. 15, p. 12. The figures in Table VI.1 are in terms of dwelling space and exclude such items as kitchens, corridors, and stairways.

[15] USSR Council of Ministers' Central Statistical Administration, "On the Level of Education, Nationality Composition and Age Structure of the Population of the USSR According to Data of the 1959 All-Union Population Census," *Current Digest,* 1960, no. 5, p. 7. Adjusted for changes in the age distribution of the population, the reduction in the death rate and the increase in life expectancy would probably be smaller.

pregnancy, and childbirth) compensation, for permanent disability insurance, and for insurance for the dependent survivors of deceased insured workers. Old-age insurance was established more slowly but by 1932 most wage earners and salaried employees were covered and in mid-1937 coverage was extended to all wage earners and salaried employees. Benefit payments have as a rule compensated for the entire pay lost because of temporary disability, but the period of employment required for eligibility for such benefits has from time to time been lengthened. In the case of disability, survivors', and old-age pensions, the size of the pension, as a percentage of former earnings, tended to decline throughout the period up to the new pension law of 1956.[16] Nevertheless, the increasing number of workers covered by social insurance and the widespread grants and pensions have meant an increasing share of pensions and allowances in total household income over the period. As a percentage of household outlays for consumption, pensions and allowances were 3.2 in 1928, 3.5 in 1937, 2.8 in 1940, 9.9 in 1944, 6.5 in 1950, 6.7 in 1955, and 10.4 in 1958.[17]

2. Trends in Real Consumer Income and Real Wages in the Soviet Union and the United States

Annual data for the United States on real per capita consumption and real wages since 1869, expressed in 1954 dollars, are shown in Table VI.2. The series on real per capita consumption is Simon Kuznets' revised series on the flow of goods to consumers. In concept, it is closely comparable with the Soviet real per capita consumption including communal services (Table VI.1, item 2) in that at least a rough approximation to final services of government to consumers is included. The U.S. series for real annual wages of all nonfarm employees in Table VI.2 is comparable with the Soviet series for real annual wages of all nonagricultural wage earners and salaried employees, except that the U.S. figures are gross earnings and the Soviet figures are net of taxes and bond purchases. Since this U.S. series extends back only to 1890, Table VI.2 also shows real wages of production workers in manufacturing, both annual and per hour actually worked, from 1860 to 1958. The 1860–90 figures are Clarence Long's and the 1890–1913 figures are those of Albert Rees.

To repeat, in the Soviet Union, real per capita consumption including communal services more than doubled over the thirty years 1928–58. This is a faster rate than occurred in the United States over the same

---

[16] See Chapman, *Real Wages.*

[17] Abram Bergson, Hans Heymann, Jr., and Oleg Hoeffding, *Soviet National Income and Product, 1928–48: Revised Data,* The RAND Corporation, Research Memorandum RM-2444, November 15, 1960, pp. 6–7; Oleg Hoeffding and Nancy Nimitz, *Soviet National Income, 1949–55,* The RAND Corporation, Research Memorandum RM-2101, April 6, 1959, pp. 4–5; and Nancy Nimitz, *Soviet National Income and Product, 1956–58,* The RAND Corporation, Research Memorandum RM-3112-PR, June 1962, pp. 2–3.

period but is similar to the rate that prevailed in the United States from the end of the Civil War to about 1929. In the United States the gain in real per capita consumption between 1928 and 1958 was 52 percent and it has taken more nearly the past fifty years to double real per capita consumption. But U.S. real per capita consumption approximately doubled in the 26 years from 1869 to 1895 and again approximately doubled in the 34 years from 1895 to 1929. In terms of the American experience the Soviet achievement looks quite respectable, particularly since the American progress was achieved in a peaceful world — not even World War I touched native land — while the 1928–58 period for the Soviet Union was characterized by the upheavals of the revolution in agriculture and the devastation of a major war fought largely on Russia's own soil.

In view of recent trends, one should perhaps say that consumer satisfactions have been postponed in the Soviet Union. Real consumption declined under the First Five-Year Plan and increased only modestly during the prewar planning period as a whole when rapid advances in industry were scored and, understandably, declined drastically during the war. It is only in the 1950's that real gains have been made by Soviet consumers. The increase in real per capita consumption of some 68 percent since 1950 is indeed a rapid growth — over 6.5 percent a year.[18] In recent years consumer income has been increasing commensurately with gross national product[19] and the industrial output of consumer goods has been increasing as rapidly as total industrial output.[20] For the time being at least, Soviet consumers are sharing the fruits of the general rate of progress of the economy.

In the United States the economy is subject to cyclical fluctuations and when GNP falls consumer income also falls. But it is difficult to find in the United States experience any parallel to the sharp reduction in Soviet standards that occurred in the early period of the Plans. At least, this is so with the possible exception of our Great Depression, and even here it should be observed that the reduction in standards that occurred was from a far higher level than the one which prevailed in the USSR in 1928.

If trends in per capita consumption diverge in the two countries, those in real wages do so far more. For the USSR, as we have seen, real wages for long fluctuated below and only now have re-attained the initial level.

[18] Such a rate of growth seems to have been sustained in the United States only in the 1870's (see Table VI.2).

[19] Household consumption plus communal services remained a virtually constant share of GNP, valued at current ruble factor cost, between 1954 and 1958, according to Bergson, *Real SNIP*, p. 245, and Nimitz, *Soviet National Income and Product, 1956–58.* The significance in this connection of the relatively large part that "productive consumption" — education and health care — plays in Soviet consumption was pointed out by Herbert Levine in his discussion of this chapter.

[20] N. Kaplan and R. Moorsteen, "An Index of Soviet Industrial Output," *American Economic Review,* June 1960, pp. 296, 312.

Table VI.2
USA: Per Capita Consumer Income and Wages, 1860–1958
(in 1954 dollars)

Year	Per capita consumer income	Wages, nonfarm employees, annual	Wages, production workers in manufacturing	
			Annual	Hourly
1860	—	—	855	0.27
1865	—	—	—	0.22
1869	238	—	—	0.28
1870	232	—	769	0.30
1871	233	—	—	0.31
1872	276	—	—	0.31
1873	280	—	—	0.32
1874	285	—	—	0.32
1875	285	—	—	0.33
1876	301	—	—	0.33
1877	327	—	—	0.32
1878	340	—	—	0.33
1879	376	—	—	0.34
1880	429	—	907	0.34
1881	412	—	—	0.36
1882	438	—	—	0.36
1883	429	—	—	0.38
1884	434	—	—	0.39
1885	440	—	—	0.39
1886	438	—	—	0.41
1887	440	—	—	0.42
1888	432	—	—	0.42
1889	438	—	1,216	0.44
1890	429	1,644	1,250	0.43
1891	451	1,647	1,262	0.43
1892	460	1,668	1,268	0.43
1893	454	1,646	1,220	0.45
1894	432	1,632	1,171	0.44
1895	478	1,726	1,248	0.44
1896	468	1,710	1,252	0.47
1897	498	1,732	1,274	0.45
1898	498	1,748	1,271	0.45
1899	548	1,784	1,355	0.47
1900	542	1,787	1,371	0.48
1901	600	1,821	1,403	0.49
1902	594	1,835	1,477	0.51
1903	617	1,857	1,462	0.52
1904	611	1,829	1,414	0.52
1905	631	1,888	1,480	0.52
1906	684	1,890	1,565	0.55
1907	683	1,877	1,533	0.54
1908	628	1,831	1,401	0.54
1909	683	1,935	1,506	0.55
1910	681	1,930	1,515	0.56
1911	702	1,907	1,535	0.57
1912	708	1,950	1,558	0.57
1913	717	1,981	1,581	0.60
1914	694	1,872	1,535	0.59

Table VI.2 (Contd.)

Year	Per capita consumer income	Wages, nonfarm employees, annual	Wages, production workers in manufacturing	
			Annual	Hourly
1915	672	1,929	1,561	0.60
1916	723	2,034	1,635	0.64
1917	709	2,004	1,650	0.66
1918	708	1,977	1,795	0.74
1919	736	1,953	1,780	0.74
1920	749	1,941	1,834	0.72
1921	775	2,026	1,734	0.70
1922	799	2,131	1,793	0.70
1923	850	2,225	1,951	0.75
1924	891	2,234	1,953	0.78
1925	861	2,221	1,940	0.76
1926	916	2,248	1,948	0.76
1927	927	2,303	1,991	0.80
1928	940	2,362	1,973	0.80
1929	985	2,371	2,041	0.82
1930	949	2,370	1,944	0.85
1931	868	2,452	1,917	0.89
1932	775	2,413	1,743	0.88
1933	774	2,378	1,805	0.92
1934	803	2,369	1,922	1.06
1935	808	2,395	2,049	1.06
1936	872	2,451	2,191	1.07
1937	924	2,503	2,338	1.18
1938	921	2,491	2,210	1.21
1939	968	2,590	2,400	1.23
1940	1,010	2,623	2,510	1.29
1941	1,070	2,752	2,807	1.35
1942	1,040	2,196	3,140	1.42
1943	1,051	3,107	3,478	1.51
1944	1,073	3,292	3,658	1.60
1945	1,131	3,336	3,445	1.59
1946	1,251	3,326	3,139	1.56
1947	1,250	3,195	3,123	1.57
1948	1,253	3,210	3,145	1.58
1949	1,262	3,306	3,220	1.64
1950	1,315	3,449	3,447	1.73
1951	1,301	3,417	3,480	1.79
1952	1,320	3,528	3,573	1.85
1953	1,355	3,679	3,739	1.95
1954	1,353	3,757	3,737	1.97
1955	1,422	3,947	3,991	2.05
1956	1,439	4,082	4,110	2.12
1957	1,449	4,109	4,092	2.14
1958	1,423	4,138	4,035	—

Note: The dash (—) indicates that the data are unavailable.

In the USA, real wages throughout have fluctuated about a systematically rising trend.

The courses of real wages in the Soviet Union and in the United States before 1929, however, show some interesting similarities. As has been said, over the entire period 1928–58 Soviet real wages made no gain while real per capita consumption more than doubled. In the United States there has been no comparable decline or stagnation in real wages, but real wages rose less rapidly than real per capita consumption from 1870 to 1929: real per capita consumption increased over four times while real annual wages in manufacturing increased 2.6 times between 1870 and 1929, and between 1890 and 1929 the former increased 2.3 times while real annual wages of all nonfarm employees increased 1.4 times. Since 1929 the tendency has been for real wages to rise faster than real per capita consumption. The faster rise of real per capita consumption than of real wages in the Soviet Union was explained above primarily in terms of the rapid shift of workers from low-income agricultural occupations to higher paying industrial jobs. In the United States, too, during the period of industrialization there was a great increase in the proportion of the labor force engaged in industry, where productivity and earnings were higher than in agriculture. Here, of course, immigration from abroad was an important source of new industrial workers in addition to migration from the farms. Also, the process took place more slowly than in the Soviet Union.

The relatively slow gain in real wages shown in both countries may be an inevitable feature of industrialization. The very process of industrialization means large additions both to the industrial labor force and to capital. The rapid increase in the labor force can only be achieved by increasing the number of inexperienced and unskilled workers — from the farms, ordinarily, but in the United States also from abroad — which tends to lower (at least initially) the average quality of the labor force. Also, although wages must be high enough to attract the new workers, if their previous standard of living was lower than that of the industrial workers, as was true of the Soviet peasant and even of the American immigrant, they may be willing to work for a lower real wage. At certain periods also in both countries — in the Soviet Union from 1928 to 1930 when there was unemployment in the cities as well as agricultural underemployment and in the United States during the height of immigration from 1890 to 1913 — the supply of workers was plentiful relative to the ability of industry to absorb them efficiently.

At the same time, and probably more basic, capital cannot be increased, the machines cannot be provided for the growing labor force if the increase in output is all spent on increasing real wages. Much of the increment in output must be devoted to increasing capital, whether by the captains of industry of 19th century America or by the dictators of 20th century Russia, if industrialization is to be initiated and sustained. How high the rate of investment is in relation to available resources and how much consumption is sacrificed in order to achieve and maintain the rate of growth is, of course, subject to variation. Not hampered by the restraints imposed by a free enterprise economy, Stalin carried the rate of investment to a height which involved a serious curtailment of consumption.[21]

3. Levels and Patterns of Consumption in the Soviet Union and the United States

In this section the level and pattern of consumption in the Soviet Union today are compared with those in the United States today and in 1890. The year 1890 is taken to represent for present purposes a period in some respects comparable with the current stage of Soviet development.[22] By the 1890's, after rapid industrial development, the American continent had been settled and the railroads and heavy industries established. Although 43 percent of the labor force was still engaged in agriculture and only 35 percent of the population was classified as urban, the country had been transformed from an essentially agricultural to an essentially industrial and urban economy. Much the same kind of transformation was achieved under the Soviet five-year plans. The percentage of the labor force in agriculture in the Soviet Union in 1958 was about the same as in the United States in 1890, although by 1958 48 percent of the population of the Soviet Union was classified as urban, a level of urbanization not reached in the United States until 1910. Also, real per capita consumer income was roughly the same in the Soviet Union in 1958 as it had been in the United States in 1890 and in both countries it had approximately doubled during the preceding thirty years.[23] These are interesting and pertinent points of comparability which appear to justify the choice of periods. The differences between the United States of the 1890's and the Soviet Union of today are large and significant. One might consider the comparison also as a contrast between the achievements under the virtu-

[21] At the Princeton conference, Herbert Levine pointed out that the rate of investment in the Soviet Union was already high in 1928 so the problem of building it up from a very low level did not exist. For this and other reasons the forced industrialization drive of the 1930's was not as painful as it might have been. This is so only if the rate of investment is measured in current prices. When (as I believe is more appropriate here) the measurement is made instead in constant prices, the rate of investment sharply increased after 1928, though, as Franklyn Holzman suggested, it may not have remained after the early 1930's at the peak levels reached in those years. See Bergson, *Real SNIP*, chap. 13.

[22] Needless to say, in other areas the Soviet economy of today is more advanced than the American economy of 1890.

[23] For the United States this is true of the 26 years, 1869 to 1895 (see Tables VI.1 and VI.2).

ally unrestrained capitalism of the United States before the "age of reform" and under the completely planned economy of the Soviet Union.
The year 1958 represents "today" simply as the latest year for which most
of the data are available. In some cases, rough projections had to be made
to bring the measures even up to this date. As 1958 was a recession year
for the United States, it was not a peak consumption year in all respects.

A number of aspects of consumption in the Soviet Union in 1958 and in
the United States in 1890 and 1958 are assembled in Table VI.3. The first
is an over-all measure of real per capita household consumption including
communal services, expressed in 1954 dollars. Such a measure is fraught
with difficulties, particularly when patterns of consumption are as different as those of the United States and the Soviet Union today and of
the United States of 1890, but if other measures are considered as well,
such over-all measures can be useful. For purposes of comparing levels of
consumption, two viewpoints should be kept in mind in considering possible biases in aggregative measures. The first might be termed the "subsistence" approach, in which the concern is with basic human needs —
food in terms of calories, proteins, vitamins; clothing in its function of
covering and protecting; housing as shelter. From this point of view the
shift of processing from the household and the increasing degree of
fabrication which accompany industrialization as well as the increasing
costs of consumption due to urbanization mean that the per capita income
of the more advanced country is exaggerated, and probably substantially,
in relation to that of the less advanced country.[24] But from the second
viewpoint — it might be called the "complete consumption" approach —
the availabilities, the range of choice, the quality improvements, the style,
the convenience, the wrappings, and the luxury frills are real benefits.
From this point of view the consumption level of the more advanced
country will be much less overstated and may at times be understated
relatively to that of the less advanced country. On balance, aggregative
measures of real consumer income and real wages tend to overstate the
current American consumption level in relation to that of 1890 and to
the Soviet consumption level of today by a considerable amount in terms
of subsistence, but by a lesser amount, or perhaps not at all, in terms of
complete consumption. Many of the other comparisons in Table VI.3 are
of consumption in physical terms, usually at early stages of production,
and are most appropriate to the subsistence approach. Qualitative differences are ignored although in almost every case, current American

[24] This, at least, is true so long as the less advanced country is not below the margin
of subsistence. In terms of welfare and ill-fare, as Simon Kuznets says, "A national
income of X units which means starvation of a goodly part of the population is not
one-half, but a much smaller proportion, of an income of 2X which permits fair
living." (*Economic Change, Selected Essays in Business Cycles, National Income, and
Economic Growth* [New York, 1953], p. 207).

products are superior, often immensely so, to Soviet products and to old-fashioned American products.

The measures of Soviet real per capita consumption, real wages, and pensions are expressed in terms of 1954 dollars by translating the Soviet magnitudes in 1954 rubles into 1954 dollars at the rate of 10 rubles per dollar. This is the ratio found by Norman Kaplan and Eleanor Wainstein between Soviet and American retail prices of goods and services when Soviet consumption weights are used.[25] Any such comparison is subject to many difficulties and not much weight can be put on the exact dollar figures. The comparability of the 1954 dollar figures for the United States at such widely different dates as 1890 and 1958 is also subject to question.

The measures of real per capita consumption, including communal services, suggest that the Soviet consumer enjoys a real per capita consumption perhaps a tenth higher than that of the 1890 American and only one-third of that of the American of today (item 1). The Soviet gross real wage is less than 60 percent of that of the American of 1890 on an annual basis, but because of the much shorter work week on an hourly basis, the Soviet wage is almost 80 percent of the 1890 American wage (item 2). The Soviet real wage is well under a quarter of the current American wage, either gross or net of taxes, and both annually and hourly. The average wage figures refer to average earnings of all nonfarm wage earners and salaried employees.[26]

The Soviet industrial worker now works 39 hours a week or only about one hour longer than the American worker in manufacturing of today, and this extra hour is currently being cut off. The current work week in both countries is much shorter than the 1890 American work week of some 54 hours.[27] But more family members, particularly women, are working

[25] If, alternatively, the American magnitudes were translated into 1954 rubles, the appropriate rate would be 14.3 rubles per dollar, obtained by Norman Kaplan and Eleanor S. Wainstein, *An Addendum to Previous USSR-US Price Comparisons,* The RAND Corporation, Research Memorandum RM-1906, May 13, 1957, when American consumption weights are used. U.S. real per capita consumer income including communal services in 1958 is 300 percent of the Soviet when both are valued in 1954 dollars (at 10 rubles per dollar) and 428 percent of the Soviet when both are valued in 1954 rubles (at 14.3 rubles per dollar). Similarly, the U.S. gross annual real wage in 1958 is 439 percent of the Soviet when both are valued in 1954 dollars and 628 percent of the Soviet when both are valued in 1954 rubles. Both valuation procedures are equally valid. That showing the smaller U.S. superiority is used here, since it may provide the more meaningful comparison from the subsistence point of view.

Full references and more detailed explanations of the measures are given in the notes to Table VI.3 in the appendix.

[26] Interestingly, the Soviet hourly wage for this group is about the same as the 1890 American hourly wage of production workers in manufacturing, and the planned 1965 average annual wage of all Soviet nonagricultural wage earners and salaried employees — about a third higher than in 1958 or about 1,250 1954 dollars — is what the American production worker in manufacturing earned in 1890 (see Table VI.2).

[27] Albert Rees, "Pattern of Wages, Prices and Productivity," in American Assembly,

Table VI.3
USSR, 1958 and USA, 1890 and 1958: Selected Indicators of Consumption

Indicator	USSR 1958	United States 1890	United States 1958	USA 1958 as percent of USSR 1958
1. Per capita consumer income and communal services, in 1954 dollars	475	429	1,423	300
2. Average wage, nonfarm employees, in 1954 dollars				
a. Annual, gross	943	1,644	4,138	439
b. Annual, net, 3 dependents	875	1,644	3,750	429
c. Hourly, gross	0.46	0.59	2.09	454
3. Annual old-age pension for worker earning average wage, in 1954 dollars				
a. Individual	613 to 660	. . .	1,283	194 to 209
b. Maximum family	766 to 825	. . .	2,814	341 to 367
4. Per capita consumption or output of major foods				
a. Flour (kilograms)	159	102	58	36
b. Potatoes (kilograms)	150	85[a]	48	32
c. Meat, poultry, lard (kilograms)	38	89	91	239
d. Milk (kilograms)	224	350[a]	314	140
e. Eggs (number)	105	293[a]	358	341
f. Fish (catch) (kilograms)	14	12	12	86
g. Sugar (kilograms)	26	24	44	169
5. Per capita output of clothing				
a. Cotton fabrics (meters)	28.0	42.9	47.1	168
b. Wool fabrics (meters)	1.5	6.4	1.4	93
c. Other fabrics (meters)	6.4	—	12.4	194
d. Hosiery (pairs)	4.3	—	10.3	240
e. Shoes (pairs)	1.7	2.3[b]	3.3	194
6. Consumer durables, output or sales per 1,000 population (physical units)				
a. Radios	35	. . .	84[c]	240
b. TV sets	4.4	. . .	31	705
c. Washing machines	2.4	. . .	21	875
d. Refrigerators	1.6	. . .	18	1,125
e. Vacuum cleaners	1.1	. . .	19	1,727
f. Electric irons	10	. . .	32	311
g. Sewing machines	14	—	13[d]	93
h. Automobiles	0.3	. . .	25	8,333
i. Bicycles	16	—	18[d]	113
j. Motorcycles	1.7	. . .	0.2[d]	12
7. Consumer durables, stocks per 1,000 population, physical units				
a. Radios	177	. . .	734[e]	415
b. TV sets	12	. . .	254	2,117
c. Washing machines	5[f]	. . .	259	5,180
d. Refrigerators	—[g]	. . .	278	—
e. Automobiles	—	. . .	234[e]	—
8. Urban housing space				
a. Stock (square meters per capita)	5.5	—	15 to 32	273 to 582
b. Rooms per capita	0.3	1.0	1.2[h]	400

Table VI.3 (Contd.)

Indicator	USSR 1958	United States		USA 1958 as percent of USSR 1958
		1890	1958	
9. Utilities				
a. Percentage of housing with electricity				
i. Urban	85 to 95	. . .	99[e]	104 to 116
ii. Farm	39[e]	. . .	96[e]	246
b. Percentage of urban housing with central heating	4[e]	. . .	59[h]	1,475
c. Telephones per 1,000 population	11.5	3.7	379	3,296
10. Publications per capita per year				
a. Newspapers	63	42	134[i]	213
b. Periodicals	3	—	46[i]	1,533
c. Books and pamphlets	5	—	6[i]	120
11. Movies attended per capita	16	. . .	15[d]	94
12. Higher education				
a. Enrollment in college, percent of college-age population	8 to 12	3	25	208 to 312
b. Number graduating from college, percent of population 20 to 24	1.4	0.3	3.3	236
c. College graduates, percent of population over 24	3.4[j]	—	7.6[k]	224
13. Medical care and health				
a. Doctors per 10,000 population	17	16	13[e]	76
b. Dentists per 10,000 population	1.3	2.8	5.9[e]	454
c. Hospital beds per 10,000 population	73	47[a]	92[e]	126
d. Crude death rate per 1,000 population	7.2	19.4	9.5	132
e. Infant mortality (deaths under 1 year), per 1,000 births	40.6	163	26.9	66

[a] 1909.
[b] 1900.
[c] 1956.
[d] 1955.
[e] 1957.
[f] Urban RSFSR. Maximum possible stock in 1965 estimated at 69 per 1,000 population by Marshall I. Goldman, "The Soviet Standard of Living, and Ours," *Foreign Affairs*, July 1960, p. 636.
[g] Maximum possible stock in 1965 estimated at 43 per 1,000 population by Goldman, p. 636.
[h] 1950.
[i] 1954.
[j] 1959.
[k] 1960.
Note: The dash (—) indicates that data are not available; the symbol . . . that the quantities are zero or negligible.

in the Soviet Union than in the United States today or in 1890. Fifty-seven percent of the total population of the Soviet Union is in the labor force as contrasted with 42 percent in the United States today and only 37 percent in 1890.[28] This reflects in part the fact that the working age groups form a larger part of total population in the USSR than in the USA in either period, but it is also true that a larger proportion of the persons of working age is in the labor force in the Soviet Union. This is markedly true of women. Thus, 63 percent of the women 16 and over are in the labor force in the Soviet Union while 18 percent of the women 14 and over (perhaps something over 20 percent of the women aged 16 and over) worked in the United States in 1890 and only 35 percent of the women 14 and over work in the United States today.[29] Child labor, an evil of the 1890's, no longer exists in either country. The number of hours of work per family may not differ much from the number of hours put in by the American family of 1890 and is greater than the number of hours put in by the American family of today. The earnings of each Soviet worker need support fewer persons than the earnings of the American worker. With 57 of each 100 persons in the labor force in the Soviet Union, each breadwinner must support about 1.8 persons, him or herself and less than one dependent. In the United States, each member of the labor force had to support 2.7 persons in 1890 and 2.4 persons in 1955.

On matters of social security the Soviet worker is much better off than the American worker of 1890, who had to rely on his savings or earnings of other family members in illness and old age, with possibly sporadic charity or the poorhouse. Extensive provisions for social security were introduced in the Soviet Union before they were introduced here; and even today in relation to earnings the benefits available to the Soviet worker compare well with those available to the American. A detailed comparison cannot be made here but as an illustration the old-age pension to which a worker earning the average wage would be entitled is shown in Table VI.3, item 3. The Soviet worker's old-age pension is smaller than the American's but it is a much larger percentage of his wage. Thus, retirement on pension means a relatively smaller reduction in consumption for the Russian worker than would be experienced by an American worker retiring on his social security pension. The American, however, is more likely to have

---

Wages, Prices, Profits and Productivity (New York, 1959), p. 20. The figures refer to hours actually worked and exclude vacations and holidays paid for but not worked.

[28] The Soviet figure for 1955 is from Warren W. Eason, "The Labor Force" in Joint Economic Committee, 86th Congress of the United States, 1st Session, *Comparisons of the United States and Soviet Economies* (Washington, 1959), part I, p. 75. Those for the United States are from U.S. Department of Commerce, *Historical Statistics of the U.S., Colonial Times to 1957* (Washington, 1960), pp. 71–72. The 1890 labor force refers to persons 10 years and older and is from census data. The current labor force figure, for 1955, refers to persons 14 and older, and is from current population reports.

[29] Eason, p. 79; *Historical Statistics*, 1960 ed., p. 71. The current figures for both countries refer to 1955.

additional provisions for income in old age and some savings. Finally, the standard retirement age in the United States is 65 for men and 62 to 65 for women while Soviet men may retire at 60 and women at 55, or earlier if they were engaged in underground, dangerous, or hot jobs.

To turn now to per capita consumption in physical terms, the food and clothing products compared (Table VI.3, items 4 and 5) are basic commodities, for the most part at an early stage of production. Qualitative differences are not taken into account. For all food products but fish the United States data are estimates of consumption while the Soviet data refer to output and probably overstate consumption. For both countries the figures for textiles and clothing refer to output, and consumption may differ because of foreign trade or uses of fabrics in industry. The current American consumption of food had already been attained by 1890, or by 1909 at the latest. The American of 1890 ate much more bread and potatoes than the American of today, and less sugar but about the same quantities of meat, milk, and eggs. As Americans have grown richer and more sedentary they have cut calories and substituted some sweets for bread and potatoes while maintaining their consumption of the high protein foods and probably increasing their consumption of the "vitamin" foods — vegetables and fruits, especially citrus. The Russian undoubtedly consumes sufficient calories — probably more than the American — but a very high proportion is still supplied by bread and potatoes.[30] Despite substantial improvements in supplies of animal products in the past few years, he still eats less than half the meat, less than one-third of the eggs, and less milk also than the American of either period. He partially compensates for this by a larger consumption of fish. He consumes less sugar than the American of today but somewhat more than the American of 1890.

With respect to fabrics for such items as clothing and bedding, hosiery, and shoes, the Soviet consumer seems to be considerably worse off than the American of either period (item 5). In comparison with the American of today, the Russian consumes only about 60 percent as much material, less than half the number of socks and stockings, and not much over half the number of shoes. The Soviet consumption of clothing, however, is considerably closer to the present American level than the Soviet consumption of consumer durables (see item 6). The American consumer of 1890 had none of the currently important consumer durables for the simple reason that most of them were not made then.[31] The American consumer of today buys over twice as many radios, 7 times as many TV sets, almost

---

[30] As already suggested, the potato figure may exaggerate consumption.

[31] It would be interesting to compare the American household of 1890 with the present Soviet household in the simple consumer durables and household equipment in common use in 1890 and still in many cases in common use in the Soviet Union, but unfortunately the relevant data are not available.

9 times as many washing machines, 11 times as many refrigerators, 17 times as many vacuum cleaners, and 83 times as many cars as the Soviet consumer. The Soviet consumer, on the other hand, buys more motorcycles and sewing machines than the American. As most modern consumer durables have only recently become available to the private Soviet household, the Soviet household lags even further behind the American in stocks of consumer durables owned.[32] Americans, for example, own over 4 times as many radios, 21 times as many TV sets, and almost 52 times as many washing machines as Russians (item 7). When quality differences are taken into account, the disparity is even larger. Thus, Soviet room loudspeakers are included with radio receiving sets in Table VI.3; Soviet washing machines typically handle 3.75 to 5 pounds of dry wash compared with the American capacity of 8 or more pounds and the clothes have to be hand wrung;[33] Soviet sewing machines are usually operated by hand or by foot treadle while almost all American sewing machines are electric.

It is perhaps in housing that the difference between Soviet and American consumption is most striking. No precise comparisons of available living space can be made since the Russians measure housing space in square meters and we measure ours in rooms. The figures in Table VI.3, item 8, although offering a wide range for American per capita square meters, suggest the possible difference. As is customary with Soviet living space figures, the American figures for both living space and persons per room exclude kitchens, although this adjustment does not necessarily make the figures more comparable, since American kitchens are private and often serve as dining areas. Soviet occupancy of 3.2 persons per room is four times American occupancy of today. In 1950, less than 16 percent of American dwelling units had an occupancy of over 1 person per room and only 2 percent of nonfarm dwellings had over 2 persons per room, counting

---

[32] As Alexander Erlich brought out in the discussion (at the Princeton conference), the question of stocks of consumer goods is more important than I suggest here. If stocks of all consumer semidurables and durables were taken into account, the Soviet consumer's position would appear even worse in comparison with that of the present and also that of the 1890 American consumer. Similarly, the Soviet gain between 1928 and 1958 might be smaller. The declines in Soviet consumer income in the early 1930's and the war years and the war losses must have seriously depleted stocks of consumer goods; and the possibilities of replenishing them must, at least until recently, have been very limited at the still low level of income of the better periods. The American consumer of either 1890 or 1958, on the other hand, experienced a fairly steady gain in income, which permits the gradual building up of a houseful of consumer goods. Particularly when current income is low, an accumulated stock of furniture, bedding, dishes, and utensils, and an adequate supply of clothing are a distinct advantage.

[33] Also, the water must be separately heated because there is no running hot water; but it is planned in the future to produce machines which will heat the water, according to Kriazhev i Markovich in *Sotsialisticheskii Trud,* 1959, no. 6, as translated in *Problems of Economics,* II, no. 8, December 1959, p. 52.

kitchens.[34] Americans appear to have had almost as much living space in 1890 as today, although there is little information on this point. But the total housing space which according to Winnick (p. 8) now is remarkably evenly distributed was likely to have been less evenly distributed in 1890. The urban worker of the 1890's, except in the large cities and some mill towns, generally lived in a separate house, although it must have been more crowded and of poorer quality than middle and upper class housing. But in the slums of New York, Boston, and Cincinnati he lived in a tenement house with accommodations that were probably similar to those of the average Soviet urban resident of today. In 1893 in the slums of New York, where the tenement problem was considered the worst in the world, occupancy was 1.9 persons per room. The typical dumbbell apartments of the common old-law tenement houses consisted of three or four rooms and the plans indicate they provided, at that occupancy rate, about 4.5 square meters per person.[35] This is less space than the Soviet average; but it was a separate apartment with its own cooking area and (usually) sink, although toilets were shared with other families. Many slum families undoubtedly doubled up or took in lodgers but, in principle, and probably often in fact, the individual family occupied a private apartment. The Russians have only recently begun to build self-contained apartments for separate families (aside from the luxury flats for the upper ranks of the intelligentsia). These are very modest, consisting of two rooms providing, at the present occupancy rate of 4 or 5 persons, about 7 square meters of living space plus a kitchen and bathroom (which together with foyer and closets add 15 square meters of total space), or a total floor space of 10 to 11 square meters per person.[36] In contrast, the typical new single family house being built in the U.S. today has 3 bedrooms in addition to at least living room, kitchen, bath, and garage, with an average floor space of about 114 square meters, or almost 23 square meters per person if occupied by 5 persons, or 28.5 square meters per person if occupied by 4 persons.[37]

With regard to household utilities, the comparisons in Table VI.3, item 9, are limited to electricity, central heating, and telephones, for lack of

[34] U.S. Department of Commerce, *Statistical Abstract of the U.S., 1959,* (Washington, 1959), p. 767. Counting kitchens, the 1950 average occupancy was 0.69 persons per room, according to Louis Winnick, *American Housing and Its Use* (New York, 1957), pp. 1, 8.

[35] U.S. Dept. of Labor, *How American Buying Habits Change* (Washington, 1959), pp. 62–64; Robert W. Deforest and Lawrence Veiller, eds., *The Tenement House Problem* (New York, 1903), I, 4, 8–9, 101. These figures include kitchen space; apparently cooking was done in part of a room used for several purposes.

[36] V. Lagutenko, I. Loveiko *et al.,* "Prisoners of Abstraction," *Current Digest,* 1960, no. 13, pp. 26-27. In the future, these apartments will be occupied by two or three persons, according to the same source.

[37] *Statistical Abstract, 1959,* p. 762. The data refer to 1956. Floor space is computed from outside dimensions and includes all space on first and higher floors but excludes all basement space, garages, unfinished attic space, and open or screened porches.

adequate data on other items, but some scattered additional information will help round out the picture. The utilities we rely on so heavily today have been developed largely since 1890. At that time some of the finer American houses and many of the tenements in the larger cities were equipped with cold running water, flush toilets, and sometimes with gas for lighting and, rarely, for cooking; but the typical American family made do with the pump, the privy, the kerosene lamp, and wood, coal, or kerosene stoves for cooking and, along with fireplaces, for heating. Today virtually all dwellings in the United States and a large share of urban dwellings in the Soviet Union have electricity. The Soviet Union has three times as many telephones per capita as the U.S. in 1890 but the U.S. today has 33 times as many as the Soviet Union.[38] So far as the availability of other utilities is concerned, Moscow and Leningrad appear to be approaching current American urban standards. In Moscow government-owned housing, 86 percent of the dwelling space is now equipped with running water (usually cold only) and 83 percent with flush toilets, compared with 99 percent with running water (usually including hot) and 96 percent with flush toilets in American urban housing in 1950. But even in Moscow, only 39 percent of the housing space is equipped with baths. In Moscow also, 67 percent of the government-owned housing is centrally heated compared with 4 percent for the entire urban USSR, and 96 percent of the Moscow government-owned housing is piped for gas compared with 25 percent for the urban USSR.[39] Except in the matter of electricity, the other Soviet cities must be well behind Moscow and Leningrad and, of course, American cities. The rural population of both countries is less well equipped with water and plumbing. Most American farm houses have electricity but in 1950 only 43 percent had inside running water and only 28 percent had inside flush toilets.[40] But the Soviet peasant lives largely in a pre-utility world. Table VI.3 shows that 39 percent of Soviet farms have electricity but the figure refers to collective farms and the number of collective farmers' houses with electricity must be much smaller. It seems safe to assume that few peasant houses have running water and flush toilets, and not all villages have public hydrants. Presumably none have anything which would be classified as modern central heating but the old peasant stove may provide efficient heating. Soviet per capita consumption of electricity and water is undoubtedly very much

[38] The difference would be greater if only private phones were considered. Only about one-third of all Soviet urban phones are in private apartments, while about 70 percent of all American phones are residential. The Soviet figure, for 1960, is computed from N. Psurtsev, "Everyone Needs a Telephone," *Current Digest,* 1961, no. 9, p. 28 and TSU *Narodnoe khoziaistvo SSSR v 1959 godu* (Moscow, 1960), p. 532. The U.S. figure, for 1957, is from the *Statistical Abstract, 1959,* p. 514.

[39] Timothy Sosnovy, "The Soviet Housing Situation Today," *Soviet Studies,* XI, July 1959, pp. 8–9.

[40] *Statistical Abstract, 1959,* p. 768.

lower than modern American consumption not only because a smaller percentage of the Soviet population enjoys the use of these utilities and the USSR limits the amount of current and water supplied to consumers but also because Americans consume huge amounts with their baths and showers, garbage disposals, washing machines and other household machinery, and gadgets.

Several items in Table VI.3 concern cultural matters and education. The comparisons are of necessity primarily quantitative. Clearly, content and quality are of prime importance in these areas but it is beyond the scope of this paper to attempt such an evaluation. In the matter of publications (item 10), the Soviet Union may be ahead of the United States of the 1890's and is considerably closer to current U.S. levels than in many other areas of consumption. Although they still publish less than half the number of newspapers per capita (and those much smaller) and fewer periodicals, they publish almost as many books and pamphlets per capita as the United States today. Soviet movie attendance is higher than American (item 11). American attendance has declined about half since the 1940's, presumably because of television.

In regard to education, we can only consider data on the numbers receiving education at different levels as proportions of the relevant age groups. At the elementary and secondary school level even such comparisons are not precise because comparable data on the age distribution of the population are not available and because the American and Soviet school systems differ. In contrast to the American system, where children begin first grade at age 6 and twelve grades of school are offered, in the Soviet Union children start first grade at age 7 and are offered seven to ten grades. The number of hours of attendance in the Soviet ten-year school is close to that in the American twelve-year school.[41] The first seven grades of school are compulsory in the Soviet Union and it can be assumed that virtually all children receive a seven-year education. This was probably largely true of the United States in 1890 and is certainly true of the United States today. Soviet enrollment in the secondary schools, both general and vocational, has increased phenomenally during the five-year plans and the proportion of the Soviet population of secondary-school age in school is probably much larger than in the United States in 1890 but smaller than in the United States today. The proportion of persons of college age receiving a college education in the Soviet Union is much larger than in the United States in 1890 but under half the proportion in the United States today (item 12).

Provisions for medical care are compared in Table VI.3, items 13a, 13b, and 13c. Currently there are more doctors per capita in the Soviet Union

[41] U.S. Department of Health, Education and Welfare, *Education in the USSR,* Bulletin 1957, no. 14 (Washington, 1957), p. 60.

than in the United States but there were more in the United States in 1890 than in either country today.[42] The Soviet Union has less than half the number of dentists per capita in America in 1890 and less than a quarter the number in America today. In hospital facilities, the Soviet Union is not far behind the United States and by 1965 plans to have as many hospital beds per capita as the United States has today. The advance in medical knowledge, in prevention as well as cure, and the development of "wonder" drugs mean the quality and effectiveness of medical care today in either country are far superior to that in the United States in 1890. The quality of the services of the Soviet doctors and dentists is apparently below current American standards.[43]

The Soviet crude death rate today is lower than the American but these figures reflect differences in the age composition of the two populations (item 13d). Adjusted for age, the Soviet death rate is probably higher than the American. The infant mortality rate in the Soviet Union is very much lower than in the United States in 1890 but still markedly higher than in the United States today (item 13e).

Two significant questions bearing on consumption which cannot be adequately treated quantitatively should be discussed. The first is the question of fluctuations in income and employment. The Soviet Union is not subject to the cyclical fluctuations of the free enterprise economy. The Soviet worker, therefore, need have no fear of cyclical unemployment though he is subject to temporary interjob unemployment.[44] The American worker of the 1890's was much less secure. He could lose his job if times got worse, usually lost several weeks' pay through lay-offs even if he didn't actually lose his job, and his wages were subject to fluctuations with the business cycle. In 1890, time lost in unemployment was something over 6 percent, but this was a boom year; four years later time lost in unemployment was 18 percent, and in the depression of the 1930's unemployment reached a peak of over 36 percent in 1933.[45] Since then we have learned much more about controlling the economy, and fluctuations of this magnitude are unlikely in the future. Unemployment, nevertheless, remains a problem and in 1958 almost 7 percent of the civilian labor force

[42] This curious finding appears to be true even if allowance is made for a somewhat broader classification of doctors in 1890 than in the American 1957 figure. The explanation is not clear, but one factor may be that in the "horse and buggy" era more doctors were needed to take care of a given population than since the development of the automobile.

[43] U.S. Department of Health, Education and Welfare, *The Report of the U.S. Public Health Mission to the USSR, August 13 to September 14, 1957* (Washington, 1959).

[44] At the Princeton conference Walter Galenson suggested that the Soviet automation program may be giving rise to problems of technological unemployment.

[45] Stanley Lebergott, "Earnings of Nonfarm Employees in the U.S., 1890–1946," *Journal of the American Statistical Association,* March 1948, pp. 76–77. These figures apparently include time lost by the partially unemployed as well as by those completely unemployed. On a narrower definition, 25 percent of the civilian labor force was unemployed in 1933 (see *Historical Statistics,* 1960 ed., p. 73).

was unemployed.[46] And for the American worker it was not until the 1930's that any real provision was made for social security, for maintaining at least some income in periods of unemployment, of inability to work, and in old age.

The second question is that of the distribution of income, a matter on which per capita averages throw little light. The distribution of consumer income in the Soviet Union, although by no means equal, may be less unequal than the distribution in the United States in the 1890's because of the absence of private ownership of the means of production in the Soviet Union, probably narrower differentials in earned income, and the extensive social security benefits and free services. With the rapid expansion in industry in the United States up to 1890, the number and wealth of the upper and middle classes had greatly increased. So had the size of the industrial labor force and, while wages were rising, great numbers of the workers were unskilled, many of them immigrants, who were paid at very low wages and had no security of employment or income. The extremes of wealth and poverty were most conspicuous in the big cities but there were undoubtedly wide variations in real income in the rest of the country as well. When distribution is considered, the comparisons of average per capita consumption in Table VI.3 are seen in a rather different light. With an average real consumer income of almost the same size but with a more unequal distribution of income, there may have been more Americans in 1890 suffering from extremely low incomes than there are Russians today.

Distribution of income in the United States today is considerably less unequal than in 1890 but may still be more unequal than in the Soviet Union. When consumer income is at such a high level, however, inequalities in distribution may not be so serious and do not necessarily mean anyone really suffers from a subsistence point of view. In 1957 the fifth of the American consumer units (families and unattached individuals) receiving the lowest personal income (under $790 per capita at 1954 prices) had an average personal income of $446 per capita at 1954 prices. These figures are before taxes but taxes are low at this level and the after-tax figures would not differ much. This is only about one-quarter of the average for all American consumer units of $1,873 before taxes or $1,686 after taxes per capita at 1954 prices and provides a meager living by American standards.[47] But it is significant that the average personal income (not counting communal services) of the poorest fifth of American consumers is close to the average consumer income (including communal services) estimated at $475 in 1954 prices for all Soviet consumers.

[46] *Statistical Abstract, 1959*, p. 206.

[47] Computed from the distribution of income and the number and average size of families and consumer units in *Historical Statistics*, pp. 163–166 and the BLS consumer price index in *Statistical Abstract, 1959*, p. 333.

In summary, the comparison of the United States of 1890 with the Soviet Union brings out some striking differences in the pattern of consumption while suggesting that per capita real consumer income was at about the same level. The Soviet real wage seems lower but more people work fewer hours. Soviet income is more equally distributed and steadier. The work is probably on the whole less arduous and factory conditions are certainly superior in the Soviet Union than in the United States in 1890. The Soviet consumer seems somewhat worse off in terms of the basic food and clothing needs than the 1890 American with a diet adequate in calories but low in proteins and worse off in housing space although necessarily better off in those items — utilities and consumer durables — that were not available for technological reasons in the 1890's. He is better off in terms of cultural and communication media — radio and TV, books and newspapers, and the movies; in terms of educational opportunities available to him quantitatively and qualitatively; and in matters of medical care and health than the American of 1890. Clearly, with such differences in pattern of consumption, it depends very much on tastes whether one concludes that the comparative advantages and disadvantages of the Soviet consumer add up to a real income that is approximately equal to, inferior to, or superior to that of the American of 1890. In comparison with the American of today, the Soviet consumer is considerably worse off in most areas, especially in the quantity of goods and services available for his private personal consumption. In certain areas — the length of the industrial work week, social security, books, movies, education, and health care — the disparity is smaller. In these areas, however, quantitative comparisons fall short of a full and meaningful basis for evaluation.

4. Analysis of the Differences in Levels and Patterns of Consumption

Why is Soviet consumption so much lower than American consumption today? The major factor here, of course, is that Soviet gross national product is much smaller than American. Why this is so is the subject of other chapters. Secondly, the share of consumption is smaller in the USSR than in the United States. Valued at current factor cost, the share of household consumption plus communal services in the Soviet GNP was 70 percent in 1928; it fell to 63 percent in 1937, 61 percent in 1940, and 45 percent in 1944. It has increased from the wartime low but not to the 1928 level, and has been around 60 percent since 1954.[48] According to Kuznets, in the USA the flow of goods to consumers, at current prices, and including an approximation to the services of government to final

[48] Bergson, *Real SNIP*, pp. 237, 245; and Nimitz, *Soviet National Income and Product, 1956–58*, p. 16.

consumers, was 74 percent of GNP in 1890 and 75 percent in 1955.[49] The Department of Commerce series, which are more comparable with Bergson's, suggest a lower percentage — something under 70 percent for recent years.[50] In our consumption-oriented capitalist economy, consumption is a large and fairly constant share of GNP. In the Soviet economy, consumption has been held down in order to achieve rapid industrialization and military power. As the Soviet Union with a much smaller GNP has attained enough military strength to be a cause of serious concern, it is hardly surprising that consumption is at a much lower level.

We shall now explore the factors responsible for the unique features of the Soviet pattern of consumption. The stage of economic development and the level of consumer income appear to be primarily responsible for one outstanding feature of the Soviet consumption pattern — the importance of the basic necessities. Aside from this, the explanation generally seems to lie either in the nature of the Soviet economy and the policies of its leaders or, especially in contrast to the U.S. of 1890, in the timing of Soviet industrial development. The technological advances since 1890 explain several of the differences between the consumption patterns of the USSR today and the U.S. in 1890. On social questions such as hours of work and social security, advances in international standards formed a framework for Soviet policy very different from that prevailing in 1890.

In the Soviet Union the government plans not only the amount of total consumption but also the kinds, qualities, and quantities of specific consumer goods. Distribution of consumer income is also largely a matter of government policy. Incentive wages are an important tool in attaining the goals, and the operating principle of income distribution is "to each according to his contribution," although it is tempered by the Communist ideal of egalitarianism and the necessity to care for the young and the old and to ensure that no one starves. Distribution of the consumer goods is for the most part left to the operation of the market where freedom of consumer choice prevails. But the government also plays a larger role than in most countries in the direct distribution of consumer goods and services. Thus, in 1958, about 15 percent of total household consumption

[49] The 1955 figure is derived from the Variant I series given in Simon Kuznets, *Capital in the American Economy: Its Formation and Financing* (Princeton, 1961), Table R-1, p. 486; the 1890 figure is based on unpublished revisions of earlier series kindly supplied by Simon Kuznets.

[50] According to the Department of Commerce, in 1956 personal consumption expenditure was 64.3 percent of GNP (*U.S. Income and Output* [Washington, 1958], pp. 118–119). If we add public expenditures on education and on health and medical care, including vocational rehabilitation, institutional care, school lunch program, and child welfare (*Historical Statistics,* 1960 ed., p. 193) net of public construction of schools and hospitals (*U.S. Income and Output,* p. 190), household consumption plus public education and health services come to 67.6 percent of GNP in 1956.

including communal services (valued at current factor cost) was directly distributed in the form of free education and health services. In addition, income payments made by the government directly — pensions and allowances, stipends, and scholarships — amounted to 11 percent of household consumption expenditures or to about 9.7 percent of household consumption plus communal services.[51] Thus, beyond its general control over the economy, the Soviet government directly allocates one-quarter of all consumption. In contrast, in the United States in 1890, government expenditures on health and education probably amounted to less than 2 percent of household consumption plus the communal services, and transfer payments must have been very small. Today, government expenditures on health and education amount to about 5 percent of household consumption plus communal services, and government transfer payments to another 4 percent.[52] In the Soviet Union the welfare of the population is determined to a great extent by government actions and hence government priorities and attitudes. This is in contrast to the situation in a market economy where the consumer is sovereign and is able to a larger or smaller degree at different periods to determine his own welfare. Many of the special features of the Soviet consumption pattern must be understood in this light.

A fundamental feature of the Soviet consumption pattern is the large role of basic necessities, a manifestation of Engel's law. In this respect the Soviet consumption pattern somewhat resembles the American pattern of 1890 but differs strikingly from the American consumption pattern of today. Although Soviet consumption of the protein foods and of clothing is still well below the American level today and even in 1890, consumption of these basic necessities is closer to the current American level than consumption of less essential goods, services, and housing. Food alone takes some 58 percent of the Soviet worker family's budget while it took something over 40 percent of the budget of American worker families in the 1890's and only 32 percent in 1950.[53] And, as has been said, the Soviet diet

[51] See Nimitz, *Soviet National Income and Product, 1956–58.*

[52] These are rough estimates and undoubtedly could be considerably refined. In 1890, public expenditures on education were $146 million and on health and medical programs $18 million, according to *Historical Statistics,* p. 193. Together, these expenditures amount to 1.8 percent of Kuznets' revised estimate of the flow of goods to consumers (component series, variant I) of $9,350 million. The current U.S. figures are computed from the 1956 Department of Commerce personal consumption expenditures and government transfer payments (less personal contributions for social insurance) in *U.S. Income and Output,* pp. 118–19, 134–35, 144–45, and public expenditures on (i) education, (ii) health and medical programs, including health and medical care of veterans, and (iii) vocational rehabilitation, institutional care, school lunch programs, and child welfare, given in *Historical Statistics,* 1960 ed., p. 193. From the public expenditures on education, health, and related welfare services are deducted public construction of schools and hospitals (*U.S. Income and Output,* p. 190). Soviet communal service is net of construction.

[53] In the USSR, according to *Current Digest of the Soviet Press,* 1960, no. 12, p. 10,

is very heavy on bread and potatoes and light on meat and milk. Basic needs must, of course, be met first and in a poor country this means there is relatively little left for other purposes. It has been a Soviet policy, born of necessity, to attempt to satisfy first the basic needs of all. In the matter of housing, a third traditional basic need, the Russians have managed little more than to maintain a roof over the head. They have, however, provided electricity and running water in most urban housing. Water, of course, is a basic necessity but piped water becomes a necessity only in congested urban areas or where there are no other sources of supply. Electricity, just coming into use in the 1890's, is virtually a basic necessity today and it is probably cheaper under present technological conditions, as well as safer, than kerosene. What constitutes the basic necessities may be affected by economic and technological developments. Also, this question is to some extent a matter of values and to this extent may be the subject of policy. And, of course, what types of consumer goods and services are provided beyond the basic necessities, however defined, is a matter for policy in a planned economy.

Basic necessities are, after all, whatever is necessary to maintain the health and working efficiency of the population and the reproduction of the race. As a matter of Soviet policy, health care has been furnished on a considerable scale. Medical care is provided almost entirely as a public good and the government is currently devoting to health care goods and services amounting to 5.5 percent of household consumption including health care. In the United States, although public concern for health is increasing, medical care has been considered largely a private matter and today less than a quarter of total expenditures on health and medical care are financed by the government. Health and medical care, public and private, accounted for not quite 7 percent of total U.S. household consumption including communal services in 1956.[54] This is a larger share of a larger total than in the USSR. These comparative totals of expenditures in the two countries cannot be taken as a meaningful measure of the difference in the real value of the health care available to the Soviet and American populations, although it is undoubtedly true that Americans receive more

---

among worker families with an average per capita income up to 6,000 rubles a year, food accounted for 66 percent of their expenditures on goods. This would be 58 percent of their total expenditures for consumption if services account for about 12.5 percent of their expenditures, as I estimate for 1954 in *Real Wages.*

In the USA, food accounted for 41 percent of the budgets of normal families of workers in 9 basic industries in 1889–91 and for 43 percent of the budgets of city wage and clerical workers in 1901. The 1950 figure relates to city wage and clerical worker families of two or more persons (see *Historical Statistics,* 1960 ed., pp. 179–181). Alcoholic beverages are included with foods in the 1950 American figure but it is not clear whether they are included in the earlier American figures or in the Soviet figure.

[54] Personal consumption expenditures on medical care and health expenses (*U.S. Income and Output,* pp. 150–151) are added to the figure on public expenditures on health and medical care and related welfare services, described in footnote 52.

and better health care than the Russians. The Russians, however, have made substantial gains in the field of health. Because of the advanced stage of medical knowledge, the Soviet Union has been able, in a way not possible for 19th century America, to make large strides in health with a direct, and relatively small, investment in medical care and public health. To some extent, investment in health programs has been an effective substitute for investment in more and better housing space.[55] Although housing is more congested in the USSR than in Czarist Russia or in the industrial slums of 19th century America, the high infant mortality rate, the frequent and widespread epidemics, and relatively constant state of ill health associated with poor housing conditions in earlier times appear, except for tuberculosis, to have been conquered.[56]

Education, too, has been a matter of high priority for the Soviet regime. A larger share of a much smaller total consumption is devoted to education in the Soviet Union than in the United States. Currently, of total household consumption including communal services, some 10 percent goes to education in the Soviet Union, compared with 4.5 percent, including both public and private expenditures, in the United States.[57] Education is entirely a public matter in the Soviet Union and largely a public matter in the United States. About three-quarters of current American expenditure on education is governmental, but in the United States the demand for public education has come largely from the people themselves, who have increasingly expressed their desire to share in the advance of knowledge, for preparation for responsible citizenship, and for more equality of opportunity, culturally and socially as well as in the matter of occupation and income. At the same time, the people are reluctant to pay higher taxes, and thus limit public expenditure on education. Moreover, an alternative to public education has often been sought in private education. In the Soviet Union the government made large allocations for many reasons, but not least because of the needs of industrialization. On the eve of the five-year plans, the educational level of the population was still very low. In 1926 almost 45 percent of the population was illiterate.[58] Moreover

---

[55] Winnick, *American Housing,* p. 2.

[56] Frank Lorimer, *The Population of the Soviet Union* (Geneva, 1946), pp. 120–121; U.S. Department of Health, Education and Welfare, *Report of the U.S. Public Health Mission to the USSR,* p. v.

[57] Personal consumption expenditures in 1956 on private education and research (*U.S. Income and Output,* pp. 150–151) are added to the figure on public expenditure on education described in footnote 52.

[58] In 1959, 1.5 percent of the population was illiterate. USSR Council of Ministers, "On the Level of Education," p. 5. The figures refer to the population between 9 and 49 years of age. Presumably if the older people, born before the Revolution, were included, current illiteracy would be somewhat higher.

In the United States in 1890, 13.3 percent of the population 10 years and older was illiterate and in 1952, 2.5 percent of the population 14 years and over was illiterate (*Historical Statistics,* 1960 ed., p. 214).

given the advanced level of knowledge and technology that was available when the industrialization drive was begun, even the simplest jobs in modern factories required a minimum of education and much more advanced education and research was crucial if full advantage was to be taken of the technological possibilities. While the initiative was the rulers', the great advances in education could hardly have been achieved without the active support of the population. In the Soviet Union, perhaps even more than in the United States, education is the path to advancement in income and status. Beyond this, the Soviet, like the American people, place a high value on education in itself.

The importance of education and of mass communication explains also the great increase in publications, the relatively widespread availability of radios and TV sets, and, in part, the high movie attendance.

Once the basic necessities and the high educational requirements are met, there is relatively little left over. Consumer durables, pleasant housing, adequate utilities, and many services are for the most part luxuries in the Soviet Union. Some luxuries must be made available as incentives and to make differentials in earnings effective. Thus, even food and clothing are made in different qualities and styles and may include luxury elements. The output of cigarettes and alcoholic beverages has increased, although the regime's preference for sobriety is reflected in the larger increase in the output of beer than of vodka. The provision of effective incentives is probably also a large factor in the small but rapidly increasing supply of consumer durables. Other factors are involved here also, among which is the increase in resources which can be devoted to consumption. Among the durables, the relatively generous supply of radios and TV sets can be explained by the importance of mass communication. Sewing machines and bicycles, also in relatively wide use, are almost necessities and the simple types produced do not compete seriously for resources. Other household machinery is undoubtedly viewed as useful in freeing time from housework for more productive labor, but if it is to be efficient, its production and operation will compete much more seriously for the resources currently devoted to investment and defense. And automobiles are the ultimate in this respect. But cars, household machinery, and other durables have become so much a part of the world image of the American standard of living that it presumably was deemed important to prove to the world that the Soviet Union could also produce them.

In the Soviet Union housing has been neglected because of its heavy demands on resources and its "unproductive" nature, despite the rapid growth of urban population. But it is now recognized that a fairly determined attack on the housing problem cannot be longer delayed. The current Seven-Year Plan will provide almost the minimum health standard of 9 square meters per capita and by 1980 it is planned to have three times the 1958 per capita dwelling space.[59] But the fully mechanized private house and yard and private automobile which symbolize the American level of living is an expensive complex far beyond the resources of the Soviet Union now, or for a long time to come. The very thought of it appears to terrify Khrushchev — all that steel, oil, rubber, and gas for cars, houses for cars, when there aren't enough for people. The Soviet planners appear to be searching for some alternative, less expensive complex. Khrushchev rejects widespread private ownership of cars but promises better public transportation, more taxis, and more cars for rent. Low buildings for housing, not to mention separate houses, are too expensive to construct and provide with utilities. The ideal (which is probably still being formulated) appears to be blocks of large buildings or "apartment hotels" containing small private apartments (mainly for sleeping) and many areas for communal use — dining rooms, nurseries and kindergartens, club and recreation rooms, workshops and photo labs — with neighborhood shopping and cultural centers containing besides schools, shops, and other more traditional facilities, a kitchen factory to serve all the dining rooms, and a car-rental store.[60] Such an ideal clearly reflects the desire to devote resources to other higher priority goals but it also reflects a different concept of housing and a desire to avoid the parking problems, congested streets, and other nuisances of the private car economy. The American taste for the separate single family house is, after all, somewhat unique with historical origins in the isolated farm house, but it has grown with our increasing ability to cater to it and has been fostered, unconsciously, by the advent of the automobile. The taste for separate and private family life, however, is by no means unique and from this standpoint the Soviet ideal must seem rather grim to the individual Soviet citizen. But to the Soviet leaders, reducing family life to a minimum and greatly enlarging the public areas of living make for the easier control of the population.

One striking contrast between the United States of the 1890's and the Soviet Union brought out above relates to hours of work and participation in the labor force. Why does the Soviet Union have so many people at work for such short hours? In the first place, participation in the labor force was high for both sexes even before the Revolution.[61] To maintain a high labor force participation was surely in the interests of the regime, as well as in accord with the Communist slogan "from each according to

---

[59] Strumilin, *Current Digest,* 1960, no. 15, p. 12.

[60] See G. Gradov, "The City and Everyday Life," *Current Digest,* 1960, no. 2, pp. 36–37.

[61] W. W. Eason, in Joint Economic Committee, *Comparisons of the United States and Soviet Economies,* 1959, part I, p. 79.

his ability." [62] The short hours are to be explained primarily as a Communist ideal, a promise of the Revolution. This promise reflected international ideals and was directed to workers not only at home but throughout the world. The 8-hour day had long been the goal of workers — in the United States since the Civil War. Here many workers secured the 8-hour day during World War I, although it was not until the 1930's that federal legislation made the 40-hour week the standard for all. Immediately after the Russian Revolution the new government promulgated the 8-hour day and a 2- to 4-week paid vacation. In 1929 and 1930 the work day was reduced to 7 hours for 5 working days out of a 6-day week (equal to about 41 hours per 7-day week), with a 6-hour day for the more dangerous occupations. Despite the increasing demands of the industrialization drive, hours were not increased until the onset of the war. In mid-1940 the standard week was set at 48 hours, six 8-hour working days in a 7-day week. This remained the standard, although there was extensive overtime during the war, until March 1956 when two hours were lopped off on Saturdays and days preceding holidays. Currently, hours are being further reduced with the goal a 35-hour week by 1968. It is somewhat puzzling that the Soviet Union, facing as it does a shortage of labor due to the low birth rate of the war years, is promising the shortest work week in the world. Is this a fulfillment of the revolutionary promise, combined with a desire to show the world that in at least one aspect of the worker's welfare the Soviet Union can surpass the United States? Perhaps some more practical aspects are involved; for example, a shorter work week may be an inducement for more wives to enter the labor force and for more to remain in it even when income is rising and the wife's earnings are less of a necessity.

The Soviet social security program is also primarily implementation of an international ideal and a promise of the Revolution. It, too, was outlined in legislation immediately following the Revolution and was implemented more effectively in the Labor Code of 1922. However, the drive for industrialization has led to modifications of the social security system as originally outlined. For example, social security provisions have been a means of discouraging labor turnover by periodic increases in the length of time a worker must have been employed in the same enterprise to be eligible for the maximum temporary disability benefits, from 2 years in 1931 to 12 years in 1955. Also, while benefits to workers temporarily absent from the labor force have, subject to the stiffened eligibility provisions, compensated for almost all earnings lost, benefits to the dis-

---

[62] Also, as Levine pointed out at the Princeton conference, the increased participation of wives in the industrial labor force tended to lessen the pressure on the stock of urban housing.

abled and the old were allowed to decline as a percentage of former earnings up to the reforms of the pension law of 1956.[63] The 1956 improvements in pensions were probably provided to permit the recipients to support themselves, but substantial further improvements in pensions are promised in the current Seven-Year Plan.

[63] See Chapman, *Real Wages.*

APPENDIX

Soviet Population

The data on Soviet population used in this study are shown, in millions, in the accompanying tabulation.

July 1	Total	Urban
1928	151.5	28.2
1932	158.1	—
1937	165.2	49.0
1940[a]	195.1	61.8
1945	175.0	55.0
1950	182.3	69.7
1955	197.0	85.6
1958	207.1	97.7
P 1965	233.7[b]	115

[a] Postwar boundaries.
[b] January 1966.
Note: The dash (—) indicates that data are not available.

The figures are obtained as follows:

Total population:

1928–1955 (except 1932) and January 1966: Foreign Manpower Research Office, U.S. Bureau of the Census.

1932: Frank Lorimer, *The Population of the Soviet Union* (Geneva, 1946), p. 135.

1958: Interpolated between the 1955 figure and that for January 1959, from the Soviet census.

Urban population: Based largely on estimates by John F. Kantner of the Foreign Manpower Research Office, U.S. Bureau of the Census. The P 1965 figure is an estimate from Strumilin, *Current Digest,* 1960, no. 15, p. 12.

Notes to Table VI.1

Items 1 to 3:

1928–55: Bergson, *Real SNIP,* pp. 128, 134, 165, 225, 252, 255. The per capita figures differ somewhat from Bergson's because of slight differences in the population estimates used for 1950 and 1955. As Bergson does not value communal services in adjusted market prices, item 2 is obtained by increasing the figures underlying item 1 by the ratio of household consumption plus communal services to household consumption alone when both are valued at 1937 factor cost.

1958: Projections based on percentage changes between 1955 and 1958. Household consumption and communal services in current prices are from Olef Hoeffding and Nancy Nimitz, *Soviet National Income, 1949–55,* The RAND Corporation, Research Memorandum RM-2101, April 6, 1959 and Nancy Nimitz, *Soviet National Income and Product, 1956–58.* Household consumption in 1958 is deflated to 1955 prices on the basis of the 1.3 percent rise in the cost of living between 1955 and 1958, indicated by S. P. Figurnov, "K voprosu o metodologii ischisleniia real'nykh dokhodov i real'noi zarabotnoi platy trudiashchikhsia SSSR," *Trud i zarabotnaia plata,* 1959, no. 12, p. 48. Communal services in 1958 are deflated to 1955 prices on the basis of a 14 percent increase in the cost of these services. This is estimated as follows: the official Soviet indexes given in TSU, *Narodnoe khoziaistvo SSSR v 1958 godu* (Moscow, 1959), p. 771 (hereafter cited as *Narodnoe khoziaistvo 1958*); show no change between 1955 and 1958 in retail prices in state and cooperative shops when alcoholic beverages (which are presumably not used in communal services) are excluded. On the basis of Mikoyan's statement (in *Pravda,* November 23, 1959) that average money wages in 1958 were 24 percent higher than in 1950, it is estimated that the increase between 1955 and 1958 in the gross average annual money wage was 10.7 percent. Taking account of the reduction in hours worked (Table VI.1, item 6), this amounts to a 19 percent increase in the cost of labor per hour. Labor accounted for about 72 percent and commodities for about 28 percent of the cost of communal services in 1958, according to computations by Nancy Nimitz based on data in Ministerstvo finansov SSSR, *Raskhody na sotsial'no-kul'turnye meropri- iatiia po gosudarstvennomu biudzhetu* (Moscow, 1958), pp. 46, 71.

Item 4:

Retail sales of goods to households for consumption are deflated by an index of average prices in all Soviet retail markets computed on the basis of given-year weights with 1937 as base year. Retail sales to households for consumption in current prices are from Bergson, *Real SNIP,* p. 46; preliminary 1958 figure is from Nancy Nimitz, *Soviet National Income, 1956–58.* Retail price index is from Chapman, *Real Wages.* For 1944, the only price index in that study is based on 1937 weights; the 1944 price index used in Table VI.1 is based on the assumption that the change in retail prices between 1940 and 1944 was the same with given-year as with 1937 weights. The price indexes for 1950, 1955, and 1958 are interpolated from the Chapman figures for 1952 and 1954 and the official Soviet indexes of retail prices in state and coopera- tive shops and on the collective farm market in TSU, *Sovetskaia torgovlia* (Moscow, 1956), pp. 131, 182 and *Narodnoe khoziaistvo 1958,* pp. 771, 789.

P 1965: Pravda, November 14, 1958; K. Skovoroda, "Tasks in Further Improving Trade Services to the Population," *Current Digest of the Soviet Press,* 1960, no. 12, p. 7.

Item 5:

Real wages are net of income and related taxes and purchases of government bonds.

1928–58: Chapman, *Real Wages,* chap. ix. My computations stop at 1954 and do not cover 1950. The 1950, 1955, and 1958 figures are computed from my 1954 figure and data in S. P. Figurnov, *Real'naia zarabotnaia plata i pod'em material'nogo blagosostoianiia trudiashchikhsia v SSSR* (Moscow, 1960), pp. 192–198.

P 1965: Real wages, presumably gross, are to be about 33 percent above the 1958 level according to S. P. Figurnov, "Chto poluchaiut rabochie i sluzhashchie SSSR sverkh zarabotnoi platy," *V pomoshch' politicheskomu samoobrazovaniiu,* 1959, no. 9, p. 77. I assume, allowing for the fact that income taxes are to be abolished by October 1965, that net real wages are to increase about 35 percent over the 1958 level.

Item 6:

1928–55: Bergson, *Real SNIP,* pp. 425–428.

1958: At the beginning of 1959, the average length of the working day of adults in industry, allowing for the reduced hours on Saturdays and holiday eves, was 7.4 hours (*Narodnoe khoziaistvo 1958,* p. 665). The average number of days worked in industry was 272.1 per worker in 1956 (A. Kats, "Comparison of Labor Productivity in the Industry of the USSR and the Chief Capitalist Countries," *Current Digest,* 1959, no. 32, p. 3). If it is assumed that both figures are representative of 1958, this amounts to a total of 2,013 hours a year or 38.7 hours a week.

P 1965: A rough estimate based on plans for reducing the standard work-week from about 46 hours a week in 1958 to 40 hours by the end of 1962 and to 35 hours by 1968 (N. S. Khrushchev, "On Abolishing Taxes on Workers and Employees and Other Measures Aimed at Raising the Soviet People's Living Standard," *Current Digest,* 1960, no. 18, p. 6).

Item 7:

1928–58: Norman M. Kaplan and Richard H. Moorsteen, "An Index of Soviet Industrial Output," *American Economic Review,* June 1960, pp. 312–313; and *Indexes of Soviet Industrial Output,* The RAND Corporation, Research Memorandum RM-2495, May 13, 1960, pp. 260–261. The index shown is their index of output of final products of industry. The per capita figures differ somewhat from those presented by Kaplan and Moorsteen owing to slightly different population estimates. For consumer goods, the price weights are 1950 retail prices.

P 1965: Based on planned goal of a 62 to 65 percent increase in the total output of consumer goods between 1959 and 1965 (*Pravda,* November 14, 1958).

Item 8:

1928–58: Items 8a, 8g, 8h, 8j, and 8k refer to industrial output and item 8f refers to the fish catch and are from *Narodnoe khoziaistvo 1958,* pp. 302–304, 309 and TSU, *Promyshlennost' SSSR* (Moscow, 1957), p. 372. Items 8b, 8c, 8d, 8e, and 8i refer to net physical output, after allowances for output used in the process of production (seed, feed, eggs for hatching, etc.) and losses, as given in D. Gale Johnson and Arcadius Kahan, "Soviet Agriculture: Structure and Growth," in Joint Economic Committee, 86th Congress of the United States, 1st Session, *Comparisons of the United States and Soviet Economies* (Washington, 1959), part I, pp. 234–235.

P 1965: Skovoroda, p. 7; *Pravda,* November 14, 1958; and *Narodnoe khoziaistvo 1958,* pp. 69, 75.

Item 9:

Except for shoes in 1928, all figures are from *Narodnoe khoziaistvo 1958,* pp. 64–65, 273–274, 293, 302–303; and TSU, *Promyshlennost' SSSR,* pp. 343, 372. Total output of shoes in 1928 is 80 million pairs, the 1928/29 figure in Gosplan, *Kontrol'nye tsifry narodnogo khoziaistva SSSR na 1929/30 godu* (Moscow, 1930), p. 564. This figure includes, it is believed, the output of artisans, handicraft cooperatives, etc., as well as the output of state factories. The total given in *Narodnoe khoziaistvo 1958,* p. 272, is 58 million pairs. *Shoes* are the so-called "leather shoes," which include cloth and leather and cloth and rubber shoes, but exclude footwear entirely of rubber or felt. *Soap* is in terms of soap of 40 percent fat content. *Cigarettes* may include cigarette tobacco sold in tobacco form to be rolled by the consumer.

Item 10:

Items 10aii, 10e, and 10f refer to output; the others refer to quantities allocated to the state and cooperative retail trade systems for sale to the population (*Narodnoe khoziaistvo 1958,* pp. 299–301, 720; and TSU, *Sovetskaia torgovlia,* p. 57).

Item 11:

The figures refer to dwelling space.

1928 and 1937–55: Bergson, *Real SNIP,* p. 316.

1932: Timothy Sosnovy, "The Soviet Housing Situation Today," *Soviet Studies,* July 1959, p. 4. Sosnovy's estimates for 1937 and later years are somewhat lower than the figures shown here.

1958: Computed on the assumption that the increase between 1955 and 1958 in dwelling space was proportional to the increase in total floor space shown in *Narodnoe khoziaistvo 1958,* p. 641.

P 1965: S. G. Strumilin, "What Communism Is: Thoughts About the Future," *Current Digest,* 1960, no. 15, p. 12.

Item 12:

Narodnoe khoziaistvo 1958, p. 870; TSU, *Kul'turnoe stroitel'stvo SSSR* (Moscow, 1956), pp. 317, 322; TSU, *Dostizheniia Sovetskoi vlasti za 40 let v tsifrakh* (Moscow, 1957), p. 293.

Item 13:

Narodnoe khoziaistvo 1958, p. 867.

Item 14:

The figures include students in correspondence courses. Enrollment is taken as a percentage of the total population for lack of data on the age distribution. The figures are affected by changes in age distribution.
1928, 1940, 1950–58: Narodnoe khoziaistvo 1958, pp. 806–809.
1932, 1937, 1945: TSU, *Kul'turnoe stroitel'stvo SSSR,* pp. 77, 122, 201–202. For these years, the number in grades 1 to 4 is assumed to be the same percentage of total enrollment in general schools as is shown on p. 122 of this source for a slightly less comprehensive enrollment.

Items 15a and 15b:

1928–58: Narodnoe khoziaistvo 1958, pp. 879, 882–883, 888.
P 1965: Decree of the Central Committee of the Communist Party and the USSR Council of Ministers, "On Measures for Further Improving Medical Care and Public Health Services for the USSR Population," *Current Digest,* 1960, no. 3, p. 10.

Item 15c:

1928 and 1938: Frank Lorimer, *The Population of the Soviet Union* (Geneva, 1946), p. 134.
1940–58: Narodnoe khoziaistvo 1958, p. 31.

Item 15d:

1926/27: Lorimer, p. 116.
1940–58: Narodnoe khoziaistvo 1958, p. 31.

Notes to Table VI.2

Per capita consumer income:

1869–1955: Simon Kuznets' "flow of goods to consumers," component series, Variant I. In concept, final government services to consumers are included; these are assumed to be equivalent to direct taxes paid by individuals through 1940 and for the war and postwar years are assumed to remain at the prewar fraction of consumer income. The figures are unpublished estimates, provided by Simon Kuznets, underlying those given in *Capital in the American Economy: Its Formation and Financing* (Princeton, 1961),

Table R-40, pp. 633ff. The original figures expressed in 1929 dollars have been converted to 1954 dollars on the basis of the BLS consumer price index.

1956–58: Extrapolations based on the change since 1955 in the Department of Commerce series "personal consumption expenditures," given in U.S. Department of Commerce, *Statistical Abstract of the U.S., 1959* (Washington, 1959), p. 304.

Wages, nonfarm employees:

1890–1928: Money wage figures — average annual earnings per full-time equivalent nonfarm employee — from Stanley Lebergott, "Earnings of Non-farm Employees in the U.S., 1890–1946," *Journal of the American Statistical Association,* March 1948, pp. 76–77. Real wages computed from money wages and Albert Rees' cost of living index for 1890 to 1914, given in *Real Wages in Manufacturing, 1890–1914* (Princeton, 1961), p. 74, linked to the BLS consumer price index for 1914–54.

1929–58: Money wages — average annual earnings per full-time equivalent nonfarm employee — computed from Department of Commerce series on total wages and salaries and on number of full-time equivalent employees in all industries, excluding payrolls and employees in agriculture, forestry, and fisheries. U.S. Department of Commerce, *National Income* (1954 *ed.*, Washington), pp. 180–181, 196–197; *U.S. Income and Output* (Washington, 1958), pp. 201, 211; *Survey of Current Business,* July 1959, pp. 32, 36. Real wages obtained by deflating money earnings by the BLS consumer price index.

Wages, production workers in manufacturing, annual:

1860–80: Clarence D. Long, *Wages and Earnings in the United States, 1860–1890* (Princeton, 1960), p. 155.

1889–1914: Rees, *Real Wages,* p. 33. The Long and Rees figures are shifted to a 1954 dollar basis by means of the BLS consumer price index.

1915–58: Money wages computed from BLS average weekly earnings of production workers in manufacturing, multiplied by 52 weeks, given in U.S. Department of Labor, *Handbook of Labor Statistics* (Washington, 1950), pp. 58–59; *Statistical Abstract, 1959,* p. 227. Rees's series is comparable to this BLS series through 1932 as both are closely related to the Census of Manufactures, but after 1932 the BLS series tends to run somewhat higher than the census series. Real wages are obtained by deflating by the BLS consumer price index, shifted to a 1954 base.

Wages, production workers in manufacturing, hourly:

The series refers to total compensation per hour actually at work; i.e., time on holidays, vacation, and sick leave paid for but not worked is not counted.

1860–89: Long, p. 153. Original data given in 1890 prices were converted to 1954 prices by reference to Rees's cost of living index and BLS consumer price index.

1889–1957: Albert Rees, "Patterns of Wages, Prices and Productivity," in American Assembly, *Wages, Prices, Profits and Productivity* (New York, 1959), pp. 15–16. Original data given in 1957 prices were shifted to 1954 prices on the basis of the BLS consumer price index.

Notes to Table VI.3

Item 1:

USSR: At current prices, per capita household consumption plus communal services was 4,810 rubles per year, according to Nimitz, *Soviet National Income, 1956–58*. At 1954 ruble prices, this is about 4,750 rubles, allowing for the 1.3 percent rise in the cost of living indicated by Figurnov, "K voprosu o metodologii," p. 48. (This is the change for 1955–58 but the official Soviet index numbers show no change in prices either in state and cooperative shops or on the collective farm market between 1954 and 1955.) The figure in 1954 ruble prices is converted to 1954 dollars at the rate of 10 rubles per dollar, the ratio obtained for 1954 with Soviet consumption weights by Norman M. Kaplan and Eleanor Wainstein, *An Addendum to Previous USSR-US Retail Price Comparison*, The RAND Corporation, Research Memorandum RM-1906, May 13, 1957.

USA: From Table VI.2.

Item 2a:

USSR: Gross average annual real wage of all nonagricultural wage earners and salaried employees in 1958 estimated at 9,430 1954 rubles or 943 1954 dollars from 1954 gross average money wage of 8,650 rubles (Chapman, *Real Wages,* chap. vii) and the 9 percent increase in gross wages between 1954 and 1958 indicated in Figurnov, *Real'naia zarabotnaia plata,* pp. 192–198. The Kaplan-Wainstein 1954 ruble-dollar ratio of 10 rubles per dollar is used.

USA: From Table VI.2.

Item 2b:

The net wage in each case is computed on the basis of the tax rates applicable to a person earning the average wage who has three dependents.

USSR: Computed from the income tax schedule in D. V. Burmistov, ed., *Spravochnik nalogovogo rabotnika* (Moscow, 1951), p. 97. The schedule has since been modified by raising the exemption level and reducing tax rates in the lower income brackets but in other respects, it is believed, remained in effect through 1959. Some evidence of this is to be found in examples of current income tax rates given by A. P. Volkov in an interview in *Izvestiia,* July 24, 1960 (*Current Digest,* 1960, no. 30, p. 33).

USA:

1890: No income taxes were levied at that time.

1958: Computed from 1958 federal income tax forms and instructions and 1958 social security employee contribution rates. No account is taken of state or local income taxes.

Item 2c:

Computed by dividing gross annual wages (item 2a) by 52 times the number of hours actually worked per week. The Soviet work week in industry was 39 hours (Table VI.1). The American work week in manufacturing was 54 hours in 1890 and 38 hours in 1957, according to Rees, "Patterns of Wages," p. 20.

Item 3:

The measures refer to the pension that would be received by a worker (and his dependents) who had been earning the average wage during the year and retired at the end of the year. For the United States, only social security pensions are considered.

USSR: The standard individual old-age pension at the average 1958 wage is 65 percent of earnings and for those in dangerous, underground, and hot jobs it is 70 percent of earnings. For two or more dependents, the pension is raised 15 percent; and for continuous length of service the pension may be raised another 10 percent, according to USSR Council of Ministers, "Draft of Law on State Pensions," *Current Digest,* 1956, no. 19, pp. 3–6. The length of service increment is included under item 3b.

USA:

1958: Computed according to the 1958 PIA method, effective January 1, 1959, as outlined in U.S. Department of Health, Education and Welfare, *Social Security Handbook* (Washington, 1960), pp. 66–75. It is assumed the worker earned the average wage each year 1951 through 1958 and the five years of lowest earnings are dropped out, as provided by law. This computation is made in terms of current dollars; the pension as a percentage of the gross average wage in current dollars is applied to the gross average wage in 1954 dollars.

Item 4:

The U.S. figures for all foods but fish refer to civilian consumption. The Soviet figures for flour and sugar refer to output and for all other products but fish to net agricultural output. The fish figures for both countries refer to the catch. The Soviet figure for flour presumably includes all types while the U.S. 1890 figure is for wheat flour only and the U.S. 1958 figure is for wheat flour and corn flour and meal. The meat figures for both countries are in carcass weight but the U.S. 1958 figure includes poultry at dressed rather than carcass weight and the 1890 figure excludes poultry. Also, the Soviet figure includes edible offals but the U.S. figures exclude them.

USSR: from Table VI.1.

USA: The 1890 figures for flour and meat are 1890–99 averages from R. O. Cummings, *The American and His Food* (Chicago, 1940), pp. 236–237. The 1958 fish figure is from *Statistical Abstract, 1959,* p. 705. All other U.S.

figures are from U.S. Department of Commerce, *Historical Statistics of the U.S., Colonial Times to 1957* (Washington, 1960), pp. 186–187, 324.

Item 5:

USSR: from Table VI.1.

USA:

1890 and 1900: Joint Economic Committee, 85th Congress of the United States, 1st Session, *Soviet Economic Growth: A Comparison with the United States* (Washington, 1957), p. 33.

1958: Statistical Abstract, 1959, pp. 806–807, 811–812.

Item 6:

USSR: Item 6a includes sales to the public of radio receiving sets plus output of room loudspeakers. Item 6h refers to sales to the public and collective farms and item 6f refers to output. All other items refer to sales to the public. Data are from *Narodnoe khoziaistvo 1958,* pp. 299–300, 719–720.

USA: Items 6a and 6b refer to output and are from *Historical Statistics,* 1960 ed., p. 491, and *Statistical Abstract, 1959,* p. 825. Items 6c, 6d, 6e, and 6h refer to sales (including exports) and are from *Statistical Abstract 1959,* pp. 558, 852. Items 6g, 6i, and 6j refer to output adjusted for foreign trade as given in Joint Economic Committee, *Soviet Economic Growth,* p. 112.

Item 7:

USSR: Items 7a and 7b are from *Narodnoe khoziaistvo 1958,* pp. 602–603. Item 7c refers to the urban population of the RSFSR only, where ownership is undoubtedly higher than the average for the entire population. Number of washing machines owned by urban RSFSR population from V. Kriazhov and M. Markovich, "The Time Budget and Measures to Improve the Living Conditions of the Working People," *Problems of Economics,* December 1959, pp. 52–53. Urban RSFSR population figure from *Narodnoe khoziaistvo 1958,* p. 10.

USA: Item 7a refers to the number of sets in working order in homes and automobiles in July 1957, given in *Historical Statistics,* 1960 ed., p. 488. Items 7b, 7c, and 7d refer to the number of homes owning one or more of the appliances and item 7e refers to the number of spending units owning one or more, all given in *Statistical Abstract, 1959,* pp. 561, 825.

Item 8a:

USSR: from Table VI.1.

USA:

1958: Estimates of American housing space vary widely. The lower figure is from Louis Winnick, *American Housing and Its Use* (New York, 1957), p. 1, for 1950, which assumes the average room is 12 square meters and excludes kitchens. Timothy Sosnovy, *The Housing Problem in the Soviet*

Union (New York, 1954), p. 179, implies a 1950 figure of 21 square meters per capita, assuming the average room is 16 square meters and counting kitchens. The higher figure, for 1955, is from Joint Economic Committee, *Soviet Economic Growth,* p. 112.

Item 8b:

The number of rooms per person is the reciprocal of the number of persons per room.

USSR: The average number of persons per room is estimated at 3.2 by Sosnovy, "The Soviet Housing Situation Today," p. 5. The figure excludes kitchens.

USA:

1890: A rough guess based on the 1950 figure and Winnick's statement (p. 8) that it seems unlikely that the number of persons per room declined more than 15 or 20 percent between 1900 and 1950.

1950: The average number of persons per room is estimated at 0.8 by Sosnovy, *The Housing Problem in the Soviet Union,* p. 108. The figure excludes kitchens. Including kitchens, Sosnovy's figure is 0.65 and Winnick's is 0.69.

Item 9:

USSR: In item 9a, the urban figure is a guess, but probably the average for all Soviet urban housing falls within the range shown. Of the government-owned housing, which amounts to 67 percent of the total floor space (*Narodnoe khoziaistvo 1958,* p. 641), probably almost all is now equipped with electricity. According to V. Kucherenko, "The Future of Our Cities," *Current Digest,* 1959, no. 43, p. 24, 99 percent of urban houses now being built have electricity. This probably refers only to housing built by the government, although it may well be true of the entire postwar construction program. As early as 1939, 93.8 percent of urban housing belonging to the local soviets of the RSFSR had electricity, but the percentage was apparently lower in government-owned housing built and maintained by industrial enterprises and perhaps also in other areas of the USSR (see Sosnovy, *The Housing Problem in the Soviet Union,* pp. 138–144). Private housing, 33 percent of the total floor space, is, however, less well equipped with electricity; unfortunately no figures are available. The *farm* figure refers to collective farms; probably not all, and perhaps very few, farm dwellings in the electrified collective farms have electricity. It is derived from Artemy Shlikhter, "Certain Questions of Agricultural Competition between the USSR and the USA," *Current Digest,* 1959, no. 36, pp. 7–8. Item 9b is from Sosnovy, "The Soviet Housing Situation Today," pp. 8–9. Item 9c is from *Narodnoe khoziaistvo 1958,* pp. 602–603.

USA: *Historical Statistics,* 1960 ed., pp. 480–481, 510; and *Statistical Abstract, 1959,* pp. 512, 768.

Item 10:

USSR: from Table VI.1.

USA: Item 10a is from *Historical Statistics,* 1960 ed., p. 500. The 1890 figure covers daily newspapers and the 1954 figure covers Sunday and weekly newspapers as well. Total annual circulation is computed by multiplying daily circulation by 312 and Sunday and weekly circulation by 52. Item 10b: Computed from circulation data in *Statistical Abstract, 1959,* p. 521. Item 10c: Sales of books and pamphlets from *Statistical Abstract, 1959,* p. 523.

Item 11:

USSR: from Table VI.1.

USA: from *Statistical Abstract, 1959,* p. 197.

Item 12a:

USSR and USA, 1958: U.S. Department of Health, Education and Welfare, *Education in the USSR,* Bulletin 1957, no. 14 (Washington, 1957), p. 173. The figures include full-time and part-time students. *Historical Statistics,* 1960 ed., p. 210, indicates that U.S. enrollment in college was 29.9 percent of the population 18 to 21 years in 1956. The U.S. figure in the table may be more comparable with the estimate for the USSR.

USA 1890: *Historical Statistics,* pp. 210–211.

Item 12b:

USSR: Graduates of higher educational institutions, including those in evening and correspondence courses, in 1958, are given in *Narodnoe khoziaistvo 1958,* p. 837. Population figures by age group used in computing items 12b and 12c are from USSR Council of Ministers, "On the Level of Education," p. 7.

USA: Number of bachelor's and first professional degrees conferred, given in *Historical Statistics,* 1960 ed., pp. 211–212; *Statistical Abstract, 1959,* p. 24. Population figures by age group for items 12b and 12c are from *Historical Statistics,* p. 10; and *Statistical Abstract, 1959,* p. 24.

Item 12c:

USSR: Number of persons with a complete higher education, given in "On the Level of Education," pp. 3, 7.

USA: Persons 25 years and older with 4 or more years of college education, estimated for 1960, from *Statistical Abstract, 1959,* p. 112.

Items 13a, 13b, and 13c:

The Soviet figures exclude and the American figures apparently include doctors and dentists in military service and beds in military hospitals.

USSR: from Table VI.1 and *Narodnoe khoziaistvo 1958*, p. 881.

USA: from *Historical Statistics*, pp. 34–35.

Items 13d and 13e:

USSR: from Table VI.1.

USA:

  1890: The rates refer to Massachusetts and are from *Historical Statistics*, pp. 26, 30.

  1958: from *Statistical Abstract, 1959*, pp. 62–63.

VII

FOREIGN TRADE

FRANKLYN D. HOLZMAN *

1. INTRODUCTION

The two main purposes of this chapter are to present and explain the major trends in Soviet international trade, and to assess the importance of international commodity and capital flows for Soviet industrial growth.

The concern here is primarily with the period of the five-year plans, but a brief reference should be made to earlier experience. Before World War I, the Russian economy was still basically agricultural although significant industrialization had taken place over the previous 30 years. In 1913, 82 percent of the population still lived in rural areas and only 18 percent in cities.[1] According to estimates of the period, at least 48 percent of the national income of 1913 originated in agriculture, compared with 35

* I am indebted to Abram Bergson, Oleg Hoeffding, J. R. Huber, G. A. Karlsson, Charles Kindleberger, and Simon Kuznets for helpful criticisms; to Catherine Peot for aid in collecting data; to the Social Science Research Council, the Russian Research Center of Harvard University, and the Tufts University Research Fund for financial aid. I was associated with the Far Eastern and Slavic Institute of the University of Washington when this paper was written.
[1] TSU, *Narodnoe khoziaistvo SSSR v 1958 godu* (Moscow, 1959), p. 9.

percent in industry (including lumbering and fishing).[2] The mix of Russian exports in 1913 was what one would have expected from such a nation: 60 percent agricultural (foodstuffs and animals), 34.4 percent raw materials and semimanufactures (largely lumber and petroleum), and only 5.6 percent manufactured goods (primarily cotton textiles). Thus, exports derived almost exclusively from the land: from agriculture and the extractive industries. Roughly half of the agricultural exports were grains, another large part meat and dairy products.

The significance of exports for national income in the pre-Soviet period is reflected in ratios for individual commodities. Exports of wheat, for example, amounted to 46 percent of output in 1886–90 and 38 percent in 1891–95, but fell to only 15 percent in 1913. Exports of barley amounted to roughly one-third of output in pre-World War I years. Exports of cereal grains as a whole comprised 17 percent of output in 1891–95, and still amounted to 12 percent in 1913. Lumber exports, also quite important, constituted, in the decade before World War I, about 25 percent of output. Before the turn of the century, Russia was second largest producer and largest exporter of petroleum in the world. At their peak, exports amounted to 30 percent of output, but by 1913 they amounted to only 12 percent. The pre-1913 markets for Russian gasoline, manganese, and platinum were almost exclusively foreign and for Russian flax were roughly half foreign. None of these commodities loomed large among total exports, however.[3]

The structure of imports in 1913 was also as expected for a nation using its foreign trade to develop new industries and to obtain essential raw materials. It has been estimated that 27 percent of total imports in 1913 could be classified as consumers' goods, a large part luxury items, the remainder comprising producers' goods and raw materials. The two major classes of imports were: machinery and equipment and cotton and other textile raw materials, which amounted to one-sixth, and almost one-fifth of the total, respectively. Coal, ferrous and nonferrous metals, and rubber were also important imports. Tea and coffee, the major consumers' goods imports, amounted to some 6 percent of the total. Manufactured goods (consumers' and producers') were less important than raw and semimanufactured materials in 1913 imports: 32.8 percent as against 48.6 percent.

The heavy Russian import requirements of raw and semimanufactured

---

[2] Paul Studenski, *The Income of Nations* (New York, 1958), p. 369. Alexander Gerschenkron, in *Economic Relations with the USSR* (New York, 1945), p. 50, claims that agriculture comprised 58 percent of total gross output in 1913. He does not explain how this figure is derived.

[3] P. I. Lyashchenko, *History of the National Economy of Russia to the 1917 Revolution* (New York, 1949), p. 519; L. Pasvolsky and H. G. Moulton, *Russian Debts and Russian Reconstruction* (New York and London, 1924), pp. 92ff.

materials reflected not a failure of these industries to grow, for they grew rapidly after 1890, but rather the more rapid growth of industries utilizing these products. Russian industrial development was impressive from 1885 to 1913: the annual rate of growth of total industrial production was 5.7 percent in this period.[4] Russian output of cotton increased fourfold from 1895 to 1912, but the textile industry developed so rapidly that domestic cotton supplied no more than 45 percent of requirements. Rapidly increasing outputs of rolled ferrous metals and copper also failed to keep pace with domestic requirements, and in 1913 imports amounted to about 3 percent and 29 percent, respectively, of consumption. Consumption of lead rapidly outstripped output and in 1913 imports amounted to 97 percent of domestic needs. Russian coal output quadrupled from 1894 to 1913, but consumption more than kept pace and Russia regularly imported about one-sixth of her coal requirements. Russian imports of machinery and equipment increased almost fivefold over the 20-year period before the war. The importance of these imports for the growth of the nation is revealed by the fact that in 1913, imports of machinery and equipment amounted to about 150 to 160 million rubles compared with a domestic output of some 200 to 210 million rubles.[5]

The Russians generally had a favorable balance of trade in the years immediately before World War I. Typically, commodity exports exceeded commodity imports by large amounts — the balance of trade surplus averaged around 25 to 30 percent of exports. At first glance, it might seem that the Russians were exporting capital. In fact, the reverse was true: the Russians borrowed throughout this period. This apparent paradox is explained by the fact that the deficit on invisible account typically exceeded the balance of trade surplus. Most of the invisible account expenditures were in the form of interest and dividends on previously incurred debt. Foreign nationals subscribed heavily to Russian imperial and municipal bonds and invested heavily in Russian railroads and other industries. Just before World War I, annual interest on government debt totaled about 240 million rubles and interest and dividends on industrial investment, 105 million.[6] In addition, tourist and official expenditures abroad typically amounted to 70 million rubles annually. It would seem that prewar Russia was a developing nation, investing too much in residentiary manufacturing industries and not enough in import-competing raw material industries and in potential exportables. The balance-of-payments problem was aggravated by the difficult situation in grain, especially wheat, the

---

[4] Alexander Gerschenkron, "The Rate of Industrial Growth in Russia since 1885," *Journal of Economic History,* Supplement no. 7, 1947, p. 156.

[5] Some of the figures in the preceding two paragraphs are from Pasvolsky and Moulton, *Russian Debts,* chap. 7; others are from Table VII.12 on page 299.

[6] Pasvolsky and Moulton, *Russian Debts,* pp. 27–32. Total debt held by foreigners in 1913 amounted to about 5 billion rubles (p. 40).

major export commodity. Increasing competition on world markets, increasing peasant resistance, and declining prices combined to reduce both the percentage of grain output exported (from 37.8 percent in 1891–95 to 15 percent in 1913) and the foreign exchange earnings on that grain.

Russian exports declined sharply in 1914 after the outbreak of war; imports also declined but then rose sharply in 1916 and 1917. The result was a serious and rising trade deficit which sharply increased Russia's indebtedness and reduced her gold reserves.

The Revolution of November 1917 disrupted Russian society and economy and soon thereafter, foreign trade. Trade almost ceased in 1918 and 1919 because of the foreign blockade, and was still minute in 1920 and 1921. Throughout this period, imports were much larger than exports. The trade deficit was no longer compounded, however, by large interest and dividend payments to foreigners; one of the first steps taken by the revolutionaries was repudiation of all bonds and expropriation of all properties of foreign nationals.

Economic recovery commenced in 1921, at the beginning of the New Economic Policy (NEP) period. Trade also began to rise in 1921 from the 1919–20 nadir, but while the rise was rapid, trade during the NEP never approached the 1913 level. By 1927, exports (in 1913 prices) had risen to only 34.7 percent and imports to 38.9 percent of the 1913 volume. The volume of grain and other food products exported declined particularly sharply relative to 1913. This drop was largely due, of course, to the change in the land-holding pattern with many small peasant farms replacing the large state, nobility, and church estates. Before the war, these estates had produced large surpluses for export.[7] The volume of lumber and lumber products exported recovered more successfully but failed to reach 50 percent of the prewar level. To some extent, the drop in food and lumber exports was offset by increases relative to prewar in exports of furs, coal, petroleum and products, and some other less important commodities.[8] Grain remained the number one export but petroleum dislodged lumber from the number two position.

Imports increased more rapidly than exports and, with the exception of 1923, 1924, and 1926, when small surpluses were experienced, the period before the First Five-Year Plan was one of large deficits. The Russians would have imported even more — to speed reconstruction — but were limited by their inability to increase exports more rapidly or to obtain long-term credits. Their deficits were financed by exports of gold and

[7] Maurice Dobb, *Soviet Economic Development Since 1917* (London, 1948), chap. 9.
[8] The territory of Russia was substantially reduced after World War I, by the loss of Poland, the Baltic States, and other territories, and perhaps a 20 percent downward adjustment in trade figures might have been expected for this reason alone. Cf. D. D. Mishustin, *Vneshniaia torgovlia i industrializatsiia SSSR* (Moscow, 1938), p. 88.

other precious metals and by short-term credits obtained apparently on onerous terms. The short-fall in foreign exchange forced the Russians to cut back imports generally. The biggest cutbacks occurred in consumers' goods, of course. Imports of many industrial items also failed to reach the 1913 level. However, imports of industrial items crucial to reconstruction and development (such as electrical equipment and rubber) by 1927–28 were much higher than in 1913. By the mid-twenties, the planners were in the saddle and the economy was already being oriented sharply toward rapid industrialization.

In section 2 the main trends in the volume and structure of Soviet foreign trade under the five-year plans are described; the conditioning factors, particularly the underlying policies, are considered in section 3; and section 4 examines implications regarding trade and industrial growth.

2. Volume and Structure of Foreign Trade Under the Five-Year Plans

A. *Volume*

Under the five-year plans the volume of Soviet trade has fluctuated widely, and in relation to domestic output it has never regained its pre-revolutionary status (Tables VII.1 to VII.3). Thus, it took a tremendous upward spurt over the First Five-Year Plan period, especially from 1929 to 1931. The increase in volume was substantially greater than that indicated by the trade value figures because of the decline in prices with the onset of the Great Depression. By one index, the volume of exports increased 46 percent, and the volume of imports 61.5 percent, from 1929 to 1931. Interestingly, however, in relation to domestic output exports rose to only a limited extent.

The rapid increase in volume of Soviet exports, large as it was, did not match the decline in export prices and as a result the value of exports declined about 20 percent from 1929 to 1931. Unfortunately for the USSR, the prices of their imports did not fall commensurately with export prices. Thus, while the latter fell from 100 in 1929 to 60.1 and 48.7 in 1931 and 1932, respectively, import prices declined from 100 to 77.1 and 68.0. Therefore, the Soviet commodity terms of trade dropped from 100 to 77.3 and then to 71.6[9] This decline in commodity terms of trade was not counterbalanced by increasing productivity in either agriculture or industry in this period. This implies that the single factoral terms of trade turned just as sharply against the USSR as the commodity terms of trade, which further implies a sharp reduction over these years in the imports the

[9] The USSR exported a large percentage of food and raw materials the prices of which more than halved from 1929 to 1931, and imported primarily machinery and equipment the prices of which declined less than 10 percent.

Table VII.1
USSR: Foreign Trade, 1913–59
(in millions of rubles)

Year	Exports	Imports	Balance of trade	Exports	Imports	Balance of trade
	(at 1950 exchange rate)			(at current exchange rate)		
	(1)	(2)	(3)	(4)	(5)	(6)
1913	5,298	4,792	506	1,520	1,375	145
1918	28	367	−339	8	105	−97
1919	0.3	11	−11	0	3	−3
1920	5	100	−95	1	29	−27
1921	70	734	−664	20	211	−191
1922	286	941	−655	82	270	−188
1923	760	498	262	218	143	75
1924	1,174	906	268	337	260	77
1925	2,119	2,882	−763	608	827	−219
1926	2,527	2,401	126	725	689	36
1927	2,600	2,642	−42	746	758	−12
1928	2,799	3,321	−522	803	953	−150
1929	3,219	3,069	150	924	881	43
1930	3,612	3,690	−78	1,036	1,059	−23
1931	2,827	3,851	−1,024	811	1,105	−294
1932	2,004	2,454	−450	575	704	−129
1933	1,727	1,214	513	496	348	148
1934	1,458	810	648	418	232	186
1935	1,281	841	440	367	241	126
1936	1,082	1,077	5	1,359	1,353	6
1937	1,312	1,016	296	1,738	1,346	392
1938	1,021	1,090	−69	1,353	1,444	−91
1939	462	745	−283	612	986	−374
1940	1,066	1,091	−25	1,412	1,446	−34
1942	301	2,080	−1,779	399	2,756	−2,357
1943	282	6,385	−6,103	373	8,460	−8,087
1945	2,600	3,100	−500	3,444	3,650	−206
1946	2,567	3,039	−472	3,405	4,031	−626
1950	7,200	5,800	1,400			
1951	Exports ⎫	18,000				
1952	plus ⎬	20,900				
1953	imports ⎭	22,000				
1955	13,874	12,242	1,632			
1956	14,446	14,452	−6			
1957	17,526	15,571	1,775			
1958	17,190	17,399	−209			
1959	21,763	20,293	1,470			

Note: Here and for later tables, where sources and methods are not given, see appendix.

Table VII.2
USSR: Exports and Imports, Volume Indexes, 1913–59

	Exports			Imports		
Year	1913 price weights	1929 price weights	Price weights unknown	1913 price weights	1929 price weights	Price weights unknown
1913	100.0			100.0		
1918	0.5			7.7		
1919	0			0.2		
1920	0.1			2.1		
1921	1.3			15.3		
1922	5.4			19.6		
1923	14.3			10.4		
1924	22.2			18.9		
1926	25.1			37.8		
1926	32.2			33.8		
1927	34.7			38.9		
1928	37.7			49.4		
1929	44.4	100.0		48.3	100.0	
1930	56.6	135.7		65.7	141.3	
1931	54.3	146.1		85.3	161.5	
1932	52.2	127.8		71.2	115.8	
1933	48.8	118.5		37.9	62.5	
1934	42.9	102.9		26.3	47.1	
1935		90.5			51.5	
1936		68.2			59.4	
1937		71.5			54.5	
1938 (9 months)		62.4			63.4	
1938			100			100
1946		(64.9)	104		(95.7)	151
1950		(189.1)	303		(160.4)	253
1955		(333.8)	535		(293.5)	463
1956		(353.2)	566		(340.5)	537
1957		(422.4)	677		(364.6)	575
1958		(433.7)	695		(435.6)	687
1959		(571.2)	916		(525.8)	829

Note: Figures in parentheses are obtained simply by linking the index based on 1929 price weights with the more recent index.

Soviet Union could purchase per unit of domestic resources committed to exports.

As a result, trade deficits were incurred in every year from 1928 through 1932, except 1929 which saw a small surplus. The deficits in 1928, 1931, and 1932 were quite large, amounting to 18.6, 36.2, and 22.4 percent, respectively, of exports. Deficits on invisible account added to the balance of

Table VII.3
USSR: Share of Exports in National Income, 1913–59

Year	Percent	Year	Percent
1913	10.4	1934	1.8
1929	3.1	1935	1.3
1930	3.5	1936	0.8
1931	3.0	1937	0.5
1932	2.6	1955	1.7 to 2.0
1933	2.3	1959	2.3 to 2.6

payments problem.[10] These deficits were financed in part by shipments of gold and other precious metals but primarily by high-cost short- and some long-term credits extended by foreign suppliers.[11]

The expansion in trade initiated under the First Five-Year Plan did not long continue. In fact, the upward trend was already reversed toward the end of the Plan, and in the following years the volume of trade tended to decline not only in relation to domestic output but absolutely. Thus, the volume of exports falls to about the 1929 level by 1934 and to 62 percent of the 1929 level by 1938. In the latter years, the Russians exported about 0.5 percent of their domestic output. Here again exports lagged behind imports but the result was a favorable balance of trade, which together with precious metal exports enabled the Russians virtually to extinguish by 1936 the 1,400 million rubles of foreign debt they had accumulated under the First Five-Year Plan.[12]

Absence of Soviet foreign trade statistics for 1939–54 prevents any detailed analysis of foreign trade patterns in this period.[13] Since 1955, foreign trade returns comparable to those of the thirties have been published annually.

Briefly, the trends in volume of commodity trade since 1938 have been

[10] Alexander Baykov, *Soviet Foreign Trade* (Princeton, 1946), pp. 48–49. S. N. Prokopovich, ed., *Quarterly Bulletin of Soviet-Russian Economics* (Prague, May 1941), p. 142, provides some estimates of net invisible expenditures for 1930/31 (in millions of current rubles): contraband, −26; expenditures on trade services abroad and on commissions, −66; interest and dividends, −25; tourism, −5. He estimates the net import of capital as 430 million and export of gold as 110 million rubles. Prokopovich's figures are in either 1936 or 1937–49 ruble exchange rate terms and are therefore not comparable with other data presented for 1930/31. For discussion and appropriate conversion rates see the notes to Table VII.1 in the appendix.

[11] Soviet foreign indebtedness increased from 485 million gold rubles in 1928 to 1,400 million in December 30, 1931, according to Baykov, *Soviet Foreign Trade*, p. 50. See fn. 10 on valuation problems.

[12] Baykov, *Soviet Foreign Trade*, p. 57; Mishustin, *Vneshniaia torgovlia i industrializatsiia SSSR*, pp. 77–78.

[13] Soviet accounts have been built up by some writers from the accounts of Soviet trading partners.

as follows.[14] During the war, as might be expected, exports declined drastically, possibly to less than one-quarter of the 1938 level.[15] Imports, on the other hand, rose sharply as the Soviet Union's Western allies came to her aid.[16] Imports in 1943 were six times the 1937 level by value and possibly four times greater in volume terms. By 1945–46, exports had risen and imports declined to more normal levels so that an import surplus of only about 20 percent was sustained. By volume, exports were up to the 1938 level, and imports exceeded it around 50 percent. Thereafter, the volume of trade increased steadily, exports increasing fivefold between 1946 and 1955, and imports tripling. Between 1955 and 1959, exports and imports both increased about 75 percent with roughly half of these increases occurring in 1959. Since 1955, exports generally have tended to exceed imports. The favorable balance no doubt was used in part to finance Russian foreign credits, although possibly it was also an offset to an invisible deficit.

B. *Structure*

Regarding the structure of exports, the period of the five-year plans is characterized by both continuity and change (Tables VII.4 to VII.6). During the entire period, the Russians continued to rely for a significant part of their foreign exchange on the export of wood products, petroleum, and grain. Nevertheless the shares of these products in exports, especially that of grain, tended to fluctuate, and to a significant extent to give way to other products which had not been exported on any sizeable scale under czarism. Among the latter, the most important are iron and steel products and machinery and equipment. As has often been noted, there are significant trends even within commodity categories, particularly toward a higher degree of fabrication (Table VII.7).

Interestingly, in the first instance the plans actually brought an increase in the role of the czarist staples. In effect, in obtaining foreign exchange under the First Five-Year Plan, the government relied especially heavily on these products. However, they did not maintain their increased impor-

[14] Since this paper was drafted, the new compilation of Soviet trade statistics for the prewar period has appeared; see MVT, *Vneshniaia torgovlia SSSR za 1918–1940 gg.* (Moscow, 1960). As indicated in Table VII.1, Soviet trade roughly halved in 1939 due, probably, to the Nazi-Soviet pact of August 1939, and the outbreak of war afterward. Trade regained its former value in 1940 as a result of a tremendous increase in trade with Germany. From 1939 to 1940 exports to Germany increased from 47 to 556 million rubles and imports from 42 to 316 million rubles (*ibid.*, pp. 533, 558). Trade with Germany amounted to more than half of the Soviet Union's exports and almost one-third of her imports in 1940.

[15] In value terms, exports in 1942 and 1943 declined one-third; since prices had been rising, the decline in quantity terms is still greater (see Table VII.1).

[16] Lend-Lease from the United States cumulated to $9.5 billion as of October 1, 1945, almost $5 billion of which consisted of nonmilitary items.

Table VII.4

USSR: Commodity Structure of Exports (Including Re-exports)

(percent of total)

Commodity	1913	1928	1929	1930	1931	1932	1933	1934	1935	1936	1937	1938	1950	1955	1956	1957	1958
Exports	100	100	100	100	100	100	100	100	100	100	100	100	100	100	100	100	100
Machinery and equipment	0.3	0.1	0.3	0.2	0.6	0.8	0.9	1.3	1.9	1.9	2.8	2.5	11.8	17.5	17.3	14.9	18.5
Fuels and raw materials	42.8	63.1	—	—	—	—	—	—	—	—	—	57.7	64.4	67.9	69.5	64.1	65.9
Coal	0.1	0.6	1.4	1.7	1.8	2.3	2.3	2.6	2.8	3.2	1.9	1.4	0.6	1.9	2.8	4.3	3.7
Oil and oil products	3.3	13.5	14.9	15.1	14.2	18.6	15.3	14.2	12.0	11.8	8.7	7.9	2.4	6.7	7.9	9.1	10.0
Ferrous and nonferrous metals and products	0.6	0.8	0.7[a]	0.7	0.7	1.0	1.2	1.6	2.0	3.2	2.8	1.6	8.5	12.6	15.0	14.7	16.1
Lumber, sawn	6.3	6.8	16.5	16.4	14.0	14.0	15.5	21.4	22.8	26.4	25.3	14.1	1.6	2.8	2.4	3.1	3.2
Other wood products	4.5	5.1										6.0	0.8	1.2	0.9	1.2	1.4
Cotton	—	—	0.3	0.7	2.2	1.0	0	0.6	0.3	0.2	3.2	1.9	9.7	8.7	7.6	5.9	5.6
Flax thread	6.2	3.1	5.3[b]	3.0	2.2	3.7	4.1	5.0	5.5	5.7	2.8	1.7	0.2	0.1	0.3	0.3	0.2
Pelts and raw fur	0.4	15.1	11.5	7.4	6.9	7.3	7.8	7.7	8.2	11.4	8.9	9.4	2.3	1.1	1.1	0.9	0.8
Grain	33.3	33.3	1.1	19.4	18.5	9.6	8.2	4.5	10.1	2.6	14.9	21.3	12.1	8.3	6.3	12.9	8.3
Consumers' goods	23.6	33.5	30.0	23.0	27.0	29.0	26.0	27.0	21.0	23.0	18.0	16.0	11.7	6.3	6.9	8.1	7.3
Meat and milk products	12.0	13.1	6.9[c]	1.5	1.1	3.2	2.5	2.6	2.9	3.4	2.0	0.3	3.5	0.4	1.3	2.4	1.0
Sugar	1.8	4.3	3.8	2.6	4.2	2.2	1.1	1.1	1.5	2.4	2.3	2.5	0.9	0.7	0.6	0.7	0.6
Cloth	3.0	6.5	4.7[d]	4.5	7.5	8.7	6.0	5.5	4.4	4.5	4.1	4.8	2.0	1.2	0.9	1.3	1.3

[a] For 1929–37, only ferrous metals.

[b] For 1929–37, category is "flax, tow, and swing tow."

[c] For 1929–37, category includes butter, bacon, and eggs.

[d] For 1929–37, category includes only cotton cloth.

Note: The dash (—) indicates that data are not available; may be negligible.

Table VII.5
USSR: Structure of Exports by Economic Branch and Use
(percent of total)

	Agricultural			Industrial			
Year	Including manufactured foodstuffs (1)	Not including manufactured foodstuffs (2)	Manu-factured foodstuffs (3)	Not including manufactured foodstuffs (4)	Including manufactured foodstuffs (5)	Consump-tion goods (6)	Produc-tion goods (7)
1913	68	55	13	32	45	24	76
1918	60	32	28	40	68	22	78
1920	56	40	16	44	60	8	92
1921–22	50	33	27	50	77	5	95
1922–23	62	53	9	38	47	5	95
1923–24	63	49	14	37	51	13	87
1924–25	56	34	22	44	66	20	80
1925–26	60	39	21	40	61	21	79
1926–27	57	36	21	43	65	22	78
1927–28	46	19	27	54	81	35	65
1929	39	18	21	61	82	30	70
1930	42	29	13	58	71	23	77
1931	42	28	14	58	72	27	73
1932	32	19	13	68	81	29	71
1933	29	17	12	71	83	26	74
1934	28	15	13	72	85	27	73
1935	27	21	6	73	79	21	79
1936	20	12	8	80	88	23	77
1937	32	24	8	68	76	18	82
1938	36	26	10	64	74	19	81
1939	—	19	—	—	81	23	77
1940	—	45	—	—	55	23	77
1955	23	10	13	77	90	14	86
1956	21	8	13	79	92	14	86
1957	26	14	12	74	86	21	79
1958	20	10	10	80	90	16	84
1959	22	11	11	78	89	18	82

Note: The dash (—) indicates that data are not available.

tance, although the decline in timber products did not come until the Third Five-Year Plan while the downward trend in oil has recently been reversed. For grain, the share in exports has continued to fluctuate with (among other things) the harvests.

Reference was made above to the trends in the relation of exports as a whole to domestic output. For individual products, almost inevitably there are generally parallel trends (Table VII.8). However, different products show rather diverse developments. For agricultural products, particularly grain, the share of domestic output exported rose sharply under the First Five-Year Plan and then declined, although it has continued to fluctuate. For oil products, the share of domestic output exported, which was initially extremely high, tended to decline almost from the beginning, although very recently there may again have been an increase. In the case of lumber products, a sizeable share of output was exported during most of the first two five-year plans, but more recently this share has been reduced. For metal and machinery products, the share of exports

Table VII.6
USSR: Exports, Brussels Classification, 1894–1938
(percent of total)

Year	Animals	Foodstuffs	Raw materials and semi-manufactures	Manufactured goods
1894–98	2.1	59.5	34.9	3.5
1899–1903	2.2	58.7	34.4	4.7
1904–08	1.7	59.9	33.0	5.3
1909–13	1.8	60.5	33.2	4.5
1913	2.3	57.7	34.4	5.6
1929	0.3	21.2	62.7	15.8
1930	...	31.6	53.2	15.2
1931	...	35.2	47.7	17.2
1932	...	22.5	53.5	24.0
1933	...	19.0	58.1	22.9
1934	...	16.1	60.3	23.6
1935	...	19.0	62.0	19.0
1936	...	13.4	66.8	19.8
1937	...	22.9	58.6	18.5
1938	...	30.5	50.4	19.1

Note: The symbol ... indicates that the quantities are negligible.

in domestic output has been limited throughout, but for selected products has been larger recently than it was in the thirties.

Among imports, the outstanding structural feature was the sharp increase under the First Five-Year Plan in the share of ferrous metals and machinery products (Tables VII.9 to VII.11). These products already accounted for nearly a third of total imports in 1928 but toward the end

Table VII.7
USSR: Share of Fabricated (Processed) Commodities
in Exports of Different Goods
(percent of total)

Commodity	1913	1929	1932
Agricultural products	8.0	19.1	20.0
Furs	0.0	17.2	42.6
Flax	1.5	27.1	40.7
Leather	5.0	6.8	51.7
Oil products (percent of gasoline to total)	10.6	26.5	31.8
Lumber	—	67.1	71.9

Note: The dash (—) indicates that data are not available.

Table VII.8

USSR: Exports as Percent of Output, 1913–58

Commodity	1913	1928	1929	1930	1931	1932	1933	1934	1935	1936	1937	1938	1950	1955	1956	1957	1958
Pig iron	0	0.1	—	—	—	—	—	—	—	—	—	0.1	2.1	3.4	3.8	3.5	2.6
Rolled ferrous metals	0.8	0.2	—	—	—	—	—	—	2.6	4.9	—	0.4	2.8	4.3	5.6	4.8	5.0
Autos and trucks	—	—	—	—	—	—	—	—	—	—	—	3.4	4.9	9.9	7.0	7.1	10.2
Tractors	—	—	2.1	1.6	1.7	2.5	2.4	1.7	0.8	0.6	0.2	0.4	1.9	5.0	2.9	3.3	3.9
Crude oil	0	2.1	20.8	19.3	22.9	21.9	22.9	—	0.8	0.6	—	0.6	0.8	4.1	4.6	6.0	8.0
Fuel oil	—	—	—	—	—	—	—	—	—	—	—	—	—	—	—	—	8.5
Kerosene	28.9	36.1	34.0	24.2	18.1	23.3	14.7	9.6	8.5	7.1	—	—	—	—	—	—	21.8
Gasoline	97.4	86.2	91.5	72.1	60.1	68.4	47.4	40.0	21.4	9.9	—	—	—	—	—	—	8.4
Coal	0.3	1.5	3.3	1.8	2.9	2.7	2.4	2.3	2.0	1.5	1.1	0.3	0.4	1.1	1.3	1.9	2.0
Fertilizers	49.4	9.6	12.0	3.8	7.0	36.6	58.8	39.9	26.1	24.8	24.7	9.2	—	11.6	12.9	14.7	17.4
Lumber, sawn	50.2	19.2	23.1	20.2	14.3	18.3	18.0	14.3	18.2	14.2	12.8	—	2.1	3.1	2.9	4.2	4.2
Plywood	46.2	25.2	33.8	22.6	22.7	34.5	33.7	36.5	33.6	27.7	21.8	18.0	7.3	8.5	4.2	8.7	8.8
Raw timber	18.6	5.9	—	—	—	—	—	—	—	—	—	1.4	0.4	0.8	11.7	12.8	13.4
Iron ore	5.1	7.0	6.8	4.2	10.6	2.8	3.5	1.6	0.6	0.1	1.3	0	8.1	12.3	18.6	15.7	15.5
Manganese ore	96.0	71.0	73.6	55.5	83.9	50.0	64.2	40.5	27.0	20.2	36.4	19.6	8.2	17.9	4.7	15.4	7.4
Grain	—	0.7	0.5	9.8	13.7	4.9	4.2	2.0	3.9	1.0	2.2	5.5	6.2	6.6	2.1	9.4	5.1
Wheat	13.3	0.5	0	9.4	18.2	2.6	2.7	0.7	2.3	—	2.2	—	—	4.3	—	—	—
Rye	—	—	—	2.7	4.6	2.0	0.7	0.4	—	—	—	—	—	—	—	—	—
Oats	6.7	—	0.04	2.1	3.0	0.01	0.5	0.7	—	—	—	—	—	—	—	—	—
Barley	34.0	—	2.2	17.4	17.6	8.0	0.7	0.2	—	—	—	—	—	—	—	—	—
Corn	52.9	0.7	0.4	2.0	2.1	8.4	2.6	3.2	—	—	—	—	—	2.1	2.4	1.2	1.3
Flax	87.9	14.0	24.9	22.3	18.1	22.1	22.9	25.7	15.6	14.0	8.7	6.0	—	2.8	7.7	10.8	10.2
Sugar	11.1	10.4	15.4	6.6	21.5	9.2	3.9	3.5	3.8	8.0	5.6	4.5	3.3	6.1	—	—	—
Butter	75.0	40.2	32.6	25.6	37.7	47.3	30.0	28.1	19.0	11.8	7.6	—	9.8	1.1	4.7	7.9	3.9
Cotton	—	—	1.1	3.9	11.9	4.5	0.2	2.6	1.5	1.1	6.3	1.2	—	8.2	7.2	7.6	7.1

Notes: The dash (—) indicates that data are not available; may be negligible.

Table VII.9
USSR: Commodity Structure of Imports
(percent of total)

Category	1913	1928	1929	1930	1931	1932	1933	1934	1935	1936	1937	1938	1950	1955	1956	1957	1958
Machinery and equipment	15.9	23.9	29.9	46.4	53.5	55.2	42.4	24.4	22.6	34.0	23.9	34.5	21.5	30.2	24.8	23.9	24.5
Electrical equipment	1.9	5.1	3.9	4.6	4.9	9.3	5.6	3.6	1.8	4.3	3.8	4.2	—	0.7	0.6	0.7	0.7
Transportation equipment	—	—	7.4	11.3	12.9	3.3	3.9	2.4	4.5	—	—	—	—	12.5	11.7	10.3	9.8
Fuels and raw materials	63.4	67.8	...	—	—	...	...	...	...	—	—	60.7	63.3	51.5	55.7	55.5	51.6
Coal	5.5	0.1	...	...	...	...	...	...	...	...	...	...	6.0	3.9	2.9	2.0	1.4
Petroleum and products	0.4	0	...	...	...	...	...	...	...	...	...	1.2	5.2	4.0	3.8	3.0	3.1
Ores and concentrates	0.1	0	.8	1.0	1.5	.9	.7	1.3	1.2	—	—	2.6	5.8	8.2	10.4	11.5	9.3
Ferrous metals and products	4.3	7.8	8.2	13.3	20.6	17.9	22.7	18.6	15.7	9.8	9.0	7.7	7.2	2.3	4.0	4.2	4.2
Nonferrous metals and products	3.9	6.3	6.9	5.2	4.6	4.6	6.8	9.2	11.0	11.5	20.4	18.1		4.3	4.0	3.2	3.1
Natural rubber	2.9	2.5	1.3	1.3	1.2	1.1	1.8	7.1	5.9	4.5	5.8	3.5	3.1	0.9	3.0	2.7	3.5
Raw cotton	8.3	16.3	13.3	5.3	3.7	2.5	2.8	2.8	6.7	1.8	2.5	1.8	2.8	0.7	1.5	3.1	3.1
Other textile raw materials	10.0	10.3	8.1	4.3	3.0	3.6	6.4	5.3	6.1	4.6	6.6	7.9	5.0	4.8	4.5	4.9	4.0
Hides, skins, leather	3.4	5.6	5.3	2.5	2.0	1.5	2.0	3.2	3.3	3.8	2.6	2.4	—	0.9	1.0	1.1	1.1
Peanuts, soybeans, et cetera	0.1	...	...	...	...	...	...	...	...	...	...	0.1	3.7	3.3	2.8	2.0	1.5
Consumers' goods[a]	20.7	8.3	...	...	...	...	...	...	...	...	...	4.8	15.2	18.3	19.5	20.6	23.9
Tea	4.5	3.9	3.3	1.9	1.1	1.1	1.6	2.8	2.8	1.7	2.1	—	—	0.3	0.5	0.7	0.8
Meat and milk	0.7	...	...	...	...	...	...	...	...	...	...	0.3	2.3	4.2	3.2	2.0	2.6
Cloth	2.7	0.1	...	...	...	...	...	...	...	...	...	0.4	3.9	2.9	3.8	3.3	3.0
Sugar	0	0.1	...	...	...	...	...	...	...	...	...	...	3.1	2.8	0.7	2.3	0.8
Fruits and vegetables	2.8	1.8	—	—	—	—	—	—	—	—	—	1.9	0.5	1.4	1.5	1.9	2.4

[a] See Table VII.10 for a more complete series with somewhat different figures.

Notes: The dash (—) indicates that data are not available; they may be negligible.
The symbol ... indicates that quantities are negligible.

Table VII.10
USSR: Structure of Imports by Economic Branch and Use
(percent of total)

Year	Agricultural			Industrial		Consumption goods	Production goods
	Including manufactured foodstuffs (1)	Not including manufactured foodstuffs (2)	Manufactured foodstuffs (3)	Not including manufactured foodstuffs (4)	Including manufactured foodstuffs (5)	(6)	(7)
1913		25			75	27	73
1918		12			88	73	27
1920		2			98	64	36
1921–22		14			86	43	57
1922–23		14			86	28	72
1923–24		14			86	18	82
1924–25		37			63	28	72
1925–26		30			70	18	82
1926–27		16			84	10	90
1927–28		35			65	10	90
1929		29			71	12	88
1930		16			84	11	89
1931		12			88	5	95
1932		13			87	7	93
1933		16			84	6	94
1934		20			80	12	88
1935		26			74	11	89
1936		17			83	9	91
1937		21			79	7	93
1938		17			83	7	93
1939		21			79	5	95
1940		15			85	11	89
1955	28	14	14	72	86	24	76
1956	25	13	12	75	87	26	74
1957	25	13	12	75	87	26	74
1958	23	12	11	77	88	29	71
1959	21	11	10	79	89	30	70

of the Plan, the share rose to nearly three-fourths. Significantly, only about 10 percent of the machinery and equipment imported during the First Five-Year Plan were for the production of consumers' goods, the remainder having been imported to produce other machinery and equipment.[17] More recently, the share of machinery and ferrous metals has fallen, although it still remains sizeable. The expansion in the share of these imports was carried out at the expense chiefly of agricultural raw materials and processed consumers' goods. In more recent years the share of agricultural raw materials has remained low but in the last several years, there has been a sharp increase in the share of processed consumers' goods.

The period of the five-year plans also witnessed notable declines in the relation of imports to domestic consumption (output + imports − exports) (Table VII.12). This decline is quite general but is especially marked for many products which the Russians initially entirely or almost entirely imported, for example, the nonferrous metals and rubber.

Surprisingly, the share of imports in consumption of machinery taken as a whole was relatively limited under the First Five-Year Plan; neverthe-

[17] Mishustin, *Vneshniaia torgovlia i industrializatsiia SSSR*, p. 52.

Table VII.11
USSR: Imports, Brussels Classification, 1894. 1913, 1929–38, 1955–59
(percent of total)

Year	Animals	Foodstuffs	Raw materials and semi-manufactures	Manufactured goods
1894	0.7	18.4	54.4	26.5
1913	1.3	17.3	48.6	32.8
1929	1.4	8.4	43.6	46.6
1930	2.1	8.9	25.3	63.7
1931	2.4	4.2	19.2	74.2
1932	2.6	7.5	16.5	73.4
1933	3.9	4.6	25.5	66.0
1934	4.7	9.4	38.9	47.0
1935	3.9	8.7	43.9	43.5
1936	4.1	6.5	34.9	54.5
1937	3.4	6.4	49.9	40.3
1938	3.8	9.0	39.6	47.6

Year		Raw materials	Prepared products	
1955		35.0	65.0	
1956		39.2	60.8	
1957		40.5	59.5	
1958		36.3	63.7	
1959		31.5	68.5	

less the shares for selected products were quite high. Imports of machine tools, for example, totaled 66 percent of consumption in 1932. Just as high and higher ratios are recorded for metal-cutting machines, turbines, generators, boilers, tractors, and automobiles (presumably not passenger automobiles), buses, trucks. Already towards the end of the First Five-Year Plan, the share of machinery imports in domestic consumption declined sharply and probably it remained at a low level thereafter except during the war, although more recently there might have been a slight increase. The degree of independence achieved by the USSR in the machinery area in general is indicated in a table presented by Mishustin which shows the percentages which have been imported of *new* machines installed in Soviet factories.[18] The percentages are high, on the whole, in 1929–31: for 18 of 39 types of new machines more than 50 percent were imported. By 1934, the number of cases with over 50 percent imports has been reduced to only 2. An unweighted average (for what it is worth) of the percentage of imported machines to total new machines in Soviet factories

[18] *Ibid.*, pp. 204–205.

Table VII.12
USSR: Share of Imports in Total Consumption, 1909–58
(percent)

Commodity	1909 to 1913	1913	1928	1929	1930	1931	1932	1933	1934	1935	1936	1937	1938	1950	1955	1956	1957	1958
Copper	29.1		46.3	50.1	38.1	46.6	29.3	19.9	20.8	33.7	58.3	41.5		10.1	0 or ···			
Lead	98.8		100	89.0	88.4	73.0	64.4	54.4	40.7	46.0	36.9	54.8		10.5	5.6			
Tin	100.0		100	100	100	100	100	100	100	100	100	100	100		0 or ···			
Nickel	100.0		100	100	100	100	100	100	82.7	75.7	78.9	82.0						
Zinc	100.0		100	92.2	90.3	72.5	43.6	25.9	13.7	3.0	0.2	4.0		21.1	18.4			
Aluminum	100.0		100	100	100	93.5	74.1	26.2	2.3	0.3	6.2				0 or ···			
Rubber		100	100	100	100	100	100	91.7	81.3	60.3	44.1							
Cotton	45.2	41.0	30.2	17.8	15.4	6.0	5.5	5.6	9.3	2.8	3.2	1.8			0.5	1.3	2.7	3.4
Wool	26.1	16.8	18.5	20.1	26.4	29.9	34.5	31.7	31.8	22.9	23.5	19.1			16.9	17.1	17.8	15.9
Rolled ferrous metals	2.7	3.0				23.0	17.0	8.1	3.3	2.0					0.3	1.6	1.9	1.9
Pig iron	0.8	0.2													1.8	1.4	0.4	0.4
Iron and steel pipes and tubing			···	0	0	1.5							0.7	0.9				
Turbines, generators, boilers			29.0	13.7	10.7	26.0	11.4	19.5	10.3	5.5	3.3							
Machine tools					89.0	78.0	77.0	19.0		14.0		10.0						
Metal-cutting machines					58.1	58.7	66.0											
Machinery		44.0	66.4	56.7	19.0	13.0	7.3	2.4	1.0	1.0					2.0	2.5	2.6	2.8
Automobiles, buses, trucks					66.4	43.1	3.9	0.8	0.5	0.2	0.1				0.0	0.1	0.3	1.0
Tractors		100	75.4	76.6	81.2	59.3	0	0	0	0	0.1				0	0	0	0

Note: The symbol ··· indicates that quantities are negligible.

is 48.6 percent in 1929–31, declining to 23.9 in 1933, and to 19.1 percent in 1934.

Almost inevitably the period also witnessed in the case of many products a shift in the Russian position from that of a net importer to that of a net exporter (Table VII.13). The figures, however, appear more dramatic

Table VII.13
USSR: Imports Transformed into Exports
(millions of rubles at 1936 exchange rate)

Commodity	Imports				Exports			
	1909–13 annual average	1927/28	1929	1933	1934	1935	1936	1937
Hard coal	190.1	2.6	2.6	0.4	—	43.6	42.8	31.1
Coke and brickets	28.3	—	—	—	0.7	1.6	1.5	0.8
Magnezite	1.0	—	—	—	1.2	1.9	0.3	0.5
Pig iron	3.8	—	0.7	—	5.1	16.0	24.0	16.0
Motor transport and parts	52.3	42.2	54.0	13.3	6.1	10.5	13.6	24.5
Tractors and parts	—	45.8	121.0	10.5	0.1	0.2	0.4	1.1
Agricultural machinery	177.5	62.3	254.0	0.5	1.7	2.1	2.9	3.8
Textile machinery	9.7	—	46.0	—	3.5	8.4	0.9	4.3
Sewing machinery	37.7	13.1	4.0	1.0	1.5	1.3	1.2	1.9
Asbestos	1.2	0.9	1.0	—	14.2	9.7	9.1	9.1
Cement	9.1	—	0.2	—	3.4	6.4	5.8	4.9
Balsam-turpentine	2.1	—	0.1	—	5.6	5.2	4.1	2.4
Tanning extract	29.1	—	0.2	—	0.8	—	.04	0.2
Dressed and dyed pelts (furs)	26.3	—	—	—	—	27.2	22.5	17.1
Paraffin	6.1	—	0.5	—	6.2	6.1	5.3	3.3
Threads-fibers	8.8	—	—	—	—	4.6	2.7	3.0
Fertilizers	31.0	40.6	50.0	—	22.6	19.0	24.0	29.0
Salt	5.5	—	—	—	2.4	2.5	2.6	2.8
Electric light bulbs	13.5	—	0.6	—	0.9	0.8	0.6	0.4

Note: The dash (—) indicates that data are not available.

than they are, for the actual values involved individually and in the aggregate are not large.

3. Conditioning Factors

A. *Underlying Politics*

The course of Soviet foreign trade has been dominated by manipulation by the USSR government to achieve its other objectives. Foreign trade was nationalized shortly after the Revolution and has since served as an "arm of the state." Every aspect of Soviet foreign trade is and has been under direct state control.

Perhaps the single most important objective of the Soviet leadership has been to develop the economic and military power necessary to guarantee continued safety and independence in a world of (what they believe to be) essentially hostile capitalist nations. The adaptation of their foreign trade to this over-all objective has resulted in at least three foreign trade policies which differ in degree, if not in kind, from those of most Western nations. Each of these policies was pursued with greater intensity before, say, 1950 than at present.

First, Soviet trade has been heavily oriented to the needs of the state in its industrialization drive. This was particularly true before World War II, but still seems to be a valid generalization. The shaping of trade to the requirements of rapid industrialization is attested to by: the emphasis in the first few five-year plans on imports of capital goods at the expense of consumers' goods; the emphasis on imports of Type A capital goods which are used to produce means of production rather than on Type B capital goods which are used to produce consumers' goods; and the large-scale export of consumers' goods (especially grain and other food products) in the early thirties when the standard of living was very low and declining. In these respects, Soviet foreign trade and domestic economic policies were in complete harmony.

Second, the USSR has attempted to minimize trade — it has followed a policy of autarky or self-sufficiency. Although this policy has not been pursued to its ultimate limit — the complete closing of the Soviet economy — for reasons to be mentioned below, the direction of Soviet efforts has been unmistakable. Most Western nations, on the other hand, have had as their goal the expansion of trade to its profitable limits. While this policy has not always been pursued faithfully because of balance of payments problems, to protect certain domestic industries in response to pressure groups, or for development considerations, et cetera, there seems little doubt that the latter have typically represented minor deviations from a "maximizing trade" goal.

The policy of autarky would seem to be in apparent contradiction to the policy of utilizing trade to assist the industrialization drive. This contradiction is in part a real one in that the Soviet Union might have been able to industrialize more rapidly had it not been averse to expanding trade. Why autarky when a larger volume of trade could have facilitated industrialization? The policy of autarky stems from the prior objective of securing and maintaining military and economic independence from the capitalist world. For military reasons, the Russians have wanted to be as self-sufficient as possible so that in the event of war they would not be cut off from any essential materials. The economic rationale for autarky relates to the nature of a planned economy. Planning for a whole economy is a complex matter. Planners like to control as many economic variables as possible. Because of the interrelatedness of separate sectors of the economy, an error in any one sector can reverberate through the system to multiply many times the damage of the original error. While there is no reason to believe *ex post* that domestic economic fumbling in the thirties didn't cause as much damage as could have been caused by foreign trade supply difficulties, it was natural for the planners to want to avoid the uncertainties of the (hostile) world market. Finally, it is worth noting that in one important dynamic respect the autarky and "industrialization through trade" policies were not in conflict — industrialization through trade had the effect of freeing the USSR more rapidly from outside dependence for a large variety of crucial commodities. The Russians consciously followed a policy of importing producers' goods which would make them more self-sufficient in the future. That is to say, the bulk of their imports, especially in the thirties, was designed to help them develop import-competing industries. In the words of one Soviet scholar: " . . . Imports into the U.S.S.R. are planned so as to aid in quickly freeing the nation from the need to import . . . " [19]

Third, the Soviet planners are primarily interested in imports rather than exports. Foreign trade is conducted to obtain essential goods which are either temporarily or permanently unavailable. Exports are viewed as a necessary evil—necessary to pay for imports — and are limited to the value required to pay for desired imports.[20] The Russians thus strive for balanced trade.[21]

[19] D. D. Mishustin, ed., *Vneshniaia torgovlia Sovetskogo Soiuza SSR* (Moscow, 1938), p. 9. This same source also states: ". . . In the years of the First Five-Year Plan the task before us was to liquidate in 10 years those 50–100 years in which old Russia lagged behind other countries . . ." (p. 91); ". . . in the execution of the plan for socialist industrialization [it is necessary to] import the most finished equipment and newest machines for the construction of 'giants', for the organization of our own production of these very machines, to secure our technical-economic independence from capitalist nations . . ." (p. 95).

[20] "The basic task of Soviet exports . . . to earn foreign exchange to finance expenditures on imports and to accumulate the foreign exchange reserves of the country . . . The U.S.S.R. exports its goods only in order to pay for a comparatively small quantity of imported goods which are necessary for the speedy execution of the national economic plans. Therefore, the dynamics of the quantity of exports is defined by the plan which is constructed in connection with the planned volume of imports." (Mishustin, ed., *Vneshniaia torgovlia Sovetskogo Soiuza SSR*, p. 10).

[21] Conceptually, it is useful to divide Soviet imports into two classes: goods which are unavailable in required amounts in the USSR, for example, tin (prewar), natural rubber, tropical fruits, and those which could be produced but not as quickly as desired or at low enough cost. Into the latter category fall such imports as recent Soviet purchases abroad of oil pipeline and chemical plants. Similarly, exports can be conceived as falling into two classes: permanent and temporary. The permanent exports include such items as manganese ore, lumber, and furs — commodities easy to produce in surplus for export, for

In capitalist nations, trade is conducted largely by private businessmen and exports and imports assume parallel importance to the individuals concerned. To the extent that there are national points of view regarding exports and imports, exports probably assume greater positive importance than imports. Although some imports are considered important for development or for strategic purposes, most do not fall within the purview of national policy except for the negative purpose of restricting them to achieve a balance in payments. Exports, on the other hand, have been encouraged by many nations for their employment effects and as a matter of general balance of payments policy.

These, then, are three basic ways in which the conduct of Soviet trade differs from that of capitalist nations. These Soviet policies underlie the trends depicted in section 2. The intensity with which any one of the above policies has been pursued has varied over time, however, and the consequences for trade have been mediated by other forces and circumstances. The interplay of policies and circumstances may best be brought out through a brief review of some of the highlights of changes in the volume and structure of Soviet trade.

B. *Before World War II*

The major statistical indicators of the Soviet policy of autarky in the prewar period are the low volumes (below 1913 levels) of exports and imports absolutely and as percentages of national income. Immediately after the 1917 Revolution, of course, trade almost ceased as a result of economic and political chaos. It increased slowly over the succeeding decade as the new regime gradually achieved some stability in both internal and external political and economic affairs. The more than doubling in volume of imports and rapid rise in exports from 1927 to 1931 was clearly due, as we have already indicated, to an invocation by the USSR of a policy of using foreign trade to speed up industrialization. Even at its peak in 1931, however, the ratio of exports to national income was only about one-third of the 1913 ratio (see Table VII.3).[22]

The rapid trade expansion over the years of the First Five-Year Plan was not easy to achieve and was not without its cost. The big problem was: how to pay for the large projected increase in imports? The USSR would probably have been more than willing to have run a large import surplus

---

which there are steady markets. These exports can be viewed as paying for part or all of permanent imports. In addition, the USSR has to export many other commodities to finance the remainder of their imports. This class of exports ranges from commodities in which the Soviet Union has a short-run advantage *vis-à-vis* specific trading partners (say, passenger automobiles) to commodities which are not produced by plan in surplus but which are in temporary surplus or are diverted from internal needs to pay for essential imports (e.g., aluminum and tin in 1958).

[22] The import: consumption percentages were approximately 9 in 1913 and 4.25 in 1931.

on the basis of long-term low-interest-rate loans. But this was impossible because of the political situation. The political situation also made it extremely difficult for them to increase exports commensurately with imports. As one Soviet writer has put it, exports had to be increased in the face of ". . . embargoes, customs and currency restrictions, higher tariffs, and other anti-Soviet measures . . ."[23] This was also a period of rapidly declining world trade — Soviet exports had to be pushed against rapidly shifting (to the left) foreign demand schedules. In 1929–31, the very period when the volume of Soviet exports expanded 46.1 percent, world trade declined 15 percent in volume and 42 percent in value, reflecting the world-wide depression.[24] These facts led to the decline in Soviet commodity terms of trade mentioned earlier.

The volume of trade declined after 1931 even faster than it expanded in the immediately preceding years. What factors were responsible for this sharp change in policy? Professor Gerschenkron feels that Soviet fear of war led them to autarky:

The decline (of exports) which coincided with the initiation of the Second Five Year Plan, sprang from the specific situation in the 'thirties which were pregnant with war. The loosening of their economic ties with the rest of the world did indeed seem to the Russians to be a necessary element in their plan to increase the military power of the country. Therefore foreign trade was consciously and deliberately throttled.[25]

No doubt fear of conflict with the West was a factor in the Soviet decision to strive for autarky. In a sense, however, it was secondary to and dependent on the fact that the huge producers' goods imports plus large domestic investment in basic plant and equipment of the 1928–32 period had made the USSR much more independent of other countries by 1932–33 than it had been a few years earlier. Without question, the Soviet Union could in 1933 come much closer than ever before to satisfying its requirements in areas considered important by the planners.[26] Autarky (given the desired growth rate) had become a more feasible (that is, less costly) policy. Had the USSR been unable to meet so many of its own strategic requirements, imports probably would not have declined so precipitously.

Two other factors argued for a reduction in trade. For one thing, the commodity terms of trade (and, certainly, also the single factoral terms of trade) had fallen from 100 in 1929 to 77 in 1931 and 71.5 in 1932 and 1933, a clear indication that the gains from trade were much smaller than they would have been under other normal circumstances (Table VII.14).

---

[23] Mishustin, ed., *Vneshniaia torgovlia Sovetskogo Soiuza SSR*, p. 10.

[24] *Ibid.*, p. 92. The volume of world trade declined another 12 percent in 1932.

[25] Gerschenkron, *Economic Relations*, p. 140.

[26] Mishustin, *Vneshniaia torgovlia i industrializatsiia SSSR*, pp. 73–74; Mishustin, ed., *Vneshniaia torgovlia Sovetskogo Soiuza SSR*, p. 10.

Table VII.14
USSR: Export Price, Import Price, and Terms of Trade Indexes, 1929–59

Year	Export price index	Import price index	Terms of trade index
1929	100.0	100.0	100.0
1930	82.7	85.1	97.2
1931	60.1	77.1	77.3
1932	48.7	68.0	71.6
1933	45.2	63.2	71.5
1934	44.0	56.0	78.6
1935	44.0	52.8	83.3
1936	49.3	54.1	91.1
1937	60.4	63.9	94.5
1938 (1st 9 months)	51.1	59.2	86.3
1938	100	100	100
1946	245	188	(112.4) 130.3
1950	233	210	(95.8) 111.0
1955	254	243	(90.2) 104.5
1956	250	247	(87.3) 101.2
1957	254	251	(87.3) 101.2
1958	242	232	(90.0) 104.3
1959	233	224	(89.7) 104.0

Having satisfied their most urgent needs for machinery and equipment, it seems most reasonable for the Soviet Union to have decided that the costs, in terms of exports, of many less urgently needed imports had become too high. For another, the Soviet import surplus proved costly to finance. By the end of 1931, foreign indebtedness had become burdensome and it was considered urgent to reduce this debt as rapidly as possible. The decision on this matter explains the much more rapid decline in imports than in exports.[27]

At least two objective economic conditions mentioned earlier help to explain the tapering-off of the downward trend in exports after 1935 and the slight increase in imports after 1934. First, the terms of trade which had declined from 100 in 1929 to 71.5 in 1933 began to rise in 1934 and by 1937 had reached 94.5. This shift was probably due both to the changing composition of Soviet exports and to improving trade conditions as the Western world recovered from the Great Depression. Second, as more

[27] According to Mishustin (pp. 77–78) the indebtedness was to be cut not only by developing an active balance of trade but by mining more gold. He claims that the debt was costly to service and that from now on (during the Second Plan), trade would only be conducted on reasonable terms—that is, the Soviet Union would no longer take low prices for exports and pay high interest rates for credit. Gold production, incidentally, tripled between 1927 and 1933 and doubled from 1933 to 1937 (S. N. Prokopovich, ed., *Quarterly Bulletin of Soviet-Russian Economics,* April 1940, p. 149).

friendly relations developed with some Western nations, the USSR was granted five-year credits in 1935 and 1936 on what it considered reasonable terms by Great Britain, Czechoslovakia, and Germany. It seems significant that obtaining credits should have led to a widening of imports. It suggests that under the existing conditions the Soviet Union was finding it difficult to expand exports at prices which made trade (as it viewed it) profitable.

The rise in Soviet imports as terms of trade and credit relations improved after 1934 suggests the possibility that these factors, rather than a policy of autarky, may have been responsible for the decline from 1931 to 1934, and that under more normal circumstances the volume of trade might have risen uninterruptedly throughout the thirties and have achieved levels which bore a more normal relationship to GNP than recorded. This seems highly unlikely, for although the volume of trade increased slightly after 1934, exports and imports as a percentage of national income continued to decline sharply (see Table VII.3). This steadily declining trend after 1931 is clear evidence of a dominating policy of autarky whereas the small rise after 1934 represents a fluctuation around this trend resulting from a change in the profitability of engaging in trade.

C. *Postwar Period*

The figures in Tables VII.2 and VII.3 for the postwar period bear out the well known fact that the Soviet Union has foregone the extreme autarky of the mid-thirties. The volume of exports and imports has increased many times relative to 1938 levels and their percentages of national income, while still below the early-thirties peak, have been rising steadily. This increase is undoubtedly due to the fact that the Russians are no longer isolated politically but are surrounded by a sizeable group of friendly nations. Within this group of nations, efforts are made to increase trade and effect a division of labor rather than to minimize trade with *all* nations as was true before World War II. Autarky has been redefined in practice to refer to trade policy *vis-à-vis* nonbloc nations.[28]

The data in Table VII.15 show that the USSR now conducts a much greater share of its total trade with other bloc nations than it did before World War II; the same is undoubtedly true for each bloc nation. While "comparative advantage" among the nations now constituting the Soviet bloc has undoubtedly changed over the past 30 years, it is not to this that the great relative increase in intra-bloc trade must be attributed, but rather to the formation of what is, in effect, a sort of customs union. Development of trade within the bloc is a result of diversion from what would otherwise be its most profitable channels.

---

[28] We cannot say, of course, how close trade among bloc nations is to the free trade optimum.

Table VII.15
USSR: Trade (Exports plus Imports) with Bloc Nations, 1930, 1937, 1959
(percent of total)

Country	1930	1937	1959
Hungary	. . .	. . .	4
Germany	22	10	20
German Democratic Republic (GDR)	—	—	18
Federal Republic of Germany (FRG)	—	—	2
Poland	2.5	0.5	7.5
Romania	. . .	. . .	4.5
Czechoslovakia	1.5	1	11
Bulgaria	. . .	. . .	5.5
Albania	0	0	0.5
Mongolia	2	3	1
China	1	0.5	19.5
Totals			
Including Germany	29	15	73.5
Excluding Germany	7	5	53.5
Including GDR, excluding FRG	—	—	71.5

Notes: The dash (—) indicates that data are not available.
The symbol . . . indicates that quantities are negligible.

Trade between the Soviet Union and China is a good case in point. Trade with China has risen from 1 percent to 20 percent of total Soviet trade since 1930; over the same period, trade with the Soviet Union has risen from 1 percent to between 55 and 65 percent of total Chinese trade. From 95 to 98 percent of this trade is conducted by (very expensive) overland railway transport.[29] This fact alone must substantially reduce the profitability of trade between the two nations, granting that some is between Soviet Siberia and China.[30] Furthermore, as a result, both nations had to invest heavily in new railway transport facilities. This runs counter to the traditional Soviet policy of minimizing investment in rail transport and to the policy established in and maintained since the Third Five-Year Plan, of keeping down length of haul. Trade between the two nations might nevertheless be profitable if the commodities traded were costly to produce at home and were unavailable from other sources. This is certainly not the case from the Soviet point of view. Food, agricultural raw

[29] M. I. Sladkovskii, *Ocherki ekonomicheskikh otnoshenii SSSR s Kitaem* (Moscow, 1957), p. 350. Soviet trade with China must be the primary reason why the railroads now carry about 55 percent of Soviet trade whereas in 1938, they were responsible for less than 5 percent (estimated from MVT, *Vneshniaia torgovlia SSSR za 1959 god.* [Moscow, 1960], p. 13).

[30] In fact, Sladkovskii, *Ocherki ekonomicheskikh otoshenii SSSR s Kitaem,* p. 348, suggests that railway freights from Siberia to China are comparable to (would not exceed) ocean freights from England and America to China. This implies a much higher cost of shipping from European Russia to China.

materials, and other consumers' goods have predominated among Soviet imports from China. These commodities are not likely to be high on the Soviet priority list. Machinery and equipment and industrial raw materials have dominated the list of Soviet exports to China. While the Soviet Union undoubtedly has a comparative advantage in the production of these commodities, it has been argued that these exports have been on such a large scale that they have competed seriously with Soviet domestic requirements.[31] From the Chinese side, the trade was undoubtedly more profitable. Certainly, the machinery and equipment they imported from the Soviet Union were essential to the industrialization drive and highly desired by the authorities. On the other hand, it is only fair to ask: Under more normal political circumstances, couldn't much of this machinery and equipment have been obtained on better terms from Japan, Western Europe, and the United States and couldn't China have found more willing markets for her exports? [32]

Under the Council for Mutual Economic Aid (CEMA), established in 1949, the European bloc nations have made some attempts to gear their economies to each other, increase specialization, and thereby expand mutually profitable trade. While these attempts may bear substantial fruit in the future, it is the opinion of most western observers that, as of 1960, very little integration had in fact occurred. Several reasons may be adduced, all of which may be attributed to wholesale adoption of Soviet-type policies by the nations of Eastern Europe. First, each nation has attempted to industrialize as rapidly as possible, and has developed industries of dubious comparative advantage in pursuit of a higher degree of self-sufficiency than appears economically warranted.[33] In other words, mutually profitable trade based on comparative advantage was foregone in the interest of diversified industrialization. Secondly, most of these nations have followed the Soviet policy, even with each other, of concentrating on imports, and viewing exports as a necessary evil. In pursuing this policy each nation pays too little heed to the requirements of its partners for healthy trade relations. One major problem that has arisen in the bloc because of these two policies is that the inordinate stress on industry has developed a greater demand for agricultural and industrial raw materials than can be supplied from within the bloc. This explains, in part, the interest of these nations since 1954 in trading with the underdeveloped

[31] Walter Galenson, "Economic Relations Between the Soviet Union and Communist China," in N. Spulber, ed., *Study of the Soviet Economy* (Bloomington, 1961).

[32] Obviously, Western political restrictions on trade with both the Soviet Union and China have played an important role in China's dependence on the USSR.

[33] This and the other policies to be mentioned below have been documented in United Nations publications. See, for example, the *World Economic Survey, 1958* (New York, 1959), especially pp. 137ff, 161ff. See also A. Zauberman, "Economic Integration: Problems and Prospects," *Problems of Communism,* July–August, 1959, pp. 23–29.

nations. Third, each nation has been concerned to avoid depending too heavily on imports not only from the West but also from fellow bloc nations in order to maintain the integrity of internal planning. The incentive to follow this policy has been reinforced by rather mediocre "delivery" experience within the bloc.[34] Finally, with few exceptions, trade between bloc nations has been conducted on a basis of bilateral balancing. This may be attributed in part to the requirements of central planning. Even if this is *a* cause, it seems clear that bilateral balancing must remain the rule rather than exception so long as the economies of the bloc nations are characterized by chaotic pricing systems and "disequilibrium" exchange rates.[35] In this respect, the Eastern European nations have again followed Soviet practice and policy. All of these factors have contributed to a lower level and less than optimal distribution of trade within the Soviet bloc.

While trade with bloc nations amounts to about 75 percent of the Soviet total at present, trade with nonbloc nations has expanded quite rapidly since 1953 although from very low levels.[36] The big increase in Soviet (and bloc) trade with the underdeveloped nonbloc nations certainly reflects the scarcity within the bloc of raw materials required for its new and expanding industries. Thus we can ascribe economic motivation to the expansion of trade with these nations which is similar to, although somewhat less intense than, the motivation behind Soviet trade of the early thirties designed to speed industrialization. However, while Soviet trade during the First Five-Year Plan obviously was pursued only with industrialization in mind, the expansion of trade with the underdeveloped nations is more complex and has obvious political overtones. The planners are certainly aware that the smaller nations will be susceptible to politico-economic pressures as they become dependent on the USSR for sales of agricultural and raw material surpluses as well as for imports of spare parts and additions to plant, machinery, and equipment. The political nature of Soviet trade with underdeveloped nations has nowhere been so clearly illustrated as where they have acted as "buyers of last resort," purchasing at world prices otherwise unsaleable surpluses of food and raw materials. The classic examples of several years back were Soviet imports of Burmese rice and Egyptian cotton. While these purchases reflect purely

[34] Zauberman, *Problems of Communism,* p. 24.

[35] Disequilibrium exchange rates in the sense that the internal prices of exportables are not equated among nations.

[36] Between 1955 and 1959, for example, the value of total Soviet trade (exports + imports) increased more than 60 percent. Trade turnover with Western Europe, the United States, and Canada increased almost 70 percent, and with the underdeveloped nonbloc nations of Asia, Africa, and South America, roughly 190 percent. Despite its rapid increase, trade with the latter group of nations amounted to only about 8 percent of the total in 1959.

political motivation, the bulk of Soviet trade with underdeveloped nations reflects a fortunate confluence for them of economic and political factors.[37]

Soviet aid to underdeveloped nations, on the other hand, must be considered economically unprofitable and motivated largely by political considerations. This aid which amounted, as of mid-1961, to about $2.75 billion,[38] has been given in the form of medium- and long-term low-interest (2 to 2.5 percent) credits repayable in some instances in kind. Premier Khrushchev recently attacked the State Planning Commission for building large dams, canals, and other projects which tie up huge amounts of capital for long periods of time.[39] Implicit in this attack is the idea that capital is still too scarce, and the real interest rate too high, for such projects to be economically feasible. Medium- and long-term loans to underdeveloped nations at low interest rates are comparable to dams — the payoff is small and far in the future. In fact, the loans may often appear less desirable to the planners since the products of dams and canals are more highly valued than the rice, cotton, and wool in which the loans will eventually be repaid. A loan to India, for example, involves exporting a blast furnace today in exchange for jute, rice, and tea to be delivered ten years hence!

Unlike trade with underdeveloped nations, Soviet trade with Western Europe and the United States seems to be motivated almost exclusively by economic considerations. Within an autarkic framework, the Soviet Union is willing to export 100 rubles worth of goods to the West if it can import much-needed commodities which would cost much more than 100 rubles to produce within the bloc. Trade is expanding now only because in the past it had been held to abnormally low levels by strategic restrictions which are gradually being relaxed. If the autarkic policy which has characterized Soviet trade in the past is maintained, and I believe it will be, then we should witness only a further mild expansion which will stop far short of the optimum volumes of trade with the advanced nations of the West.

The economic motivation implicit in the "industrialization through trade" policy of the thirties and in most Soviet trade at present, can be crudely documented by relating changes in the structure of Soviet trade to changes in the internal price structure. As the USSR has industrialized, prices (since about 1928) of finished industrial products have risen two- to fourfold whereas prices of primary agricultural and mineral products

---

[37] Franklyn D. Holzman, "Moscow's Motives — Profits or Politics: Soviet Trade and Aid," *Challenge*, April 1961, pp. 13–17.

[38] *New York Times*, Oct. 17, 1961, p. 39.

[39] Gregory Grossman, "Communism in a Hurry: The 'Time Factor' in Soviet Economics," *Problems of Communism*, May–June 1959.

have risen six- to ten- to even fifteenfold. These relative price changes suggest that Soviet "comparative advantage" has moved from the latter to the former.[40] If the USSR has been guided by an over-all profitability criterion, this changed comparative advantage should be reflected in an appropriately changed structure of trade; and it is. Agricultural exports were about 60 percent and industrial exports 40 percent of the total in the 1920's; since 1955, the ratios have averaged 22 percent for agricultural and 78 percent for industrial exports (see Table VII.5). In the early thirties, machinery, equipment, and metal products constituted about three-fourth of total imports; at present they constitute less than one-third (see Table VII.9). This evidence, and the argument it supports (first made by Berliner),[41] would require, for complete rigor, an analysis of the meaning of Soviet prices and their role in economic decision-making which cannot be attempted here. Nevertheless, as it stands, the evidence is suggestive.

4. Trade and Industrial Growth

International transactions can affect growth through exports; imports; related to these, the exchange of exports for imports;[42] capital flows; and migration. We consider here the importance of the first, second, and fourth categories.[43] Briefly, exports encourage growth in that they induce investment in productive capacity in either export or export-supplier industries.[44] Commodity imports are important for growth because they permit development of industries for which nations do not have indigenously all the needed capital goods or raw materials or where the costs of import substitutes are relatively high. Imports of producers' goods may also facilitate growth by embodying technological developments beyond those already known in the importing nation. However, there is little necessary correlation between the quantity of imports and the "quantity" of technology imported: a prototype machine, a blueprint, a technical book, or a technician can (but may not) suffice to transfer the "know-how." Long-term capital inflow into a developing nation facilitates growth largely by providing additional savings, thereby enabling the recipient to raise its rate of domestic investment. Where savings are adequate to

[40] Unless world terms of trade between these groups of commodities have moved to offset Soviet price changes, which has not been the case.

[41] Joseph Berliner, *Soviet Economic Aid* (New York, 1958), chap. 7.

[42] That is, the exchange leads to higher income which leads to higher savings which in turn makes possible a higher level of investment.

[43] Migration was inconsequential for the USSR; and my major concern is with growth in productive capacity, particularly industrial capacity.

[44] See Richard Caves and Richard Holton, *The Canadian Economy* (Cambridge, Mass., 1959), pp. 81ff; and Ingvar Svennilson, *Growth and Stagnation in the European Economy* (Geneva, 1954), pp. 223ff.

finance the desired level of investment, a nation still may not be able to generate quickly enough exports which can be used to finance essential capital goods imports. Here, capital inflow facilitates development by easing the balance of payments problem induced by growth.

The significance of exports can be appraised from the data on the relation of exports to output, both in aggregate and by individual commodities. It is also illuminating to consider the data on total imports and imports of individual commodities in relation to consumption.

It should perhaps be stressed that it is necessary to look not only at the aggregate ratios but at the ratios for individual products as well; and that the more skewed the individual ratios, or the more exports and imports are concentrated in a few products, the greater the importance of the trade for the economy. The reasoning behind this argument follows.

The difficulty with using the aggregate export : output and import : consumption ratios as measures of the importance of trade is that each unit, respectively, of exports to GNP and imports to consumption is likely to have a unique importance to the economy. What we really want to measure is the equivalent of "consumer surplus" on the import side — what we might call "importer surplus"; and the equivalent of "producer surplus" on the export side — what might be called "exporter surplus." And since growth in industrial capacity has been such an over-riding objective of the Soviet planners, these "surpluses," especially "importer surplus," have to be valued very much for their contribution to growth.

Obviously, it is impossible to derive accurate measures of these surpluses. A slightly closer approximation is achieved, however, by dividing the two aggregate ratios into as many export : output and import : consumption ratios for commodities and commodity groups as possible. It is then argued that the higher the ratios for individual commodities (that is, the more that exports and imports are each concentrated in a few commodity groups), the greater the impact of trade on the economy and the greater the gains from trade. This is *likely* to be the case for exports because: (i) the higher the ratio, the more likely it is that the existence of trade has called into use an otherwise unusable resource;[45] (ii) the higher the ratio, the more likely it is that any increase in exports will produce pressure on capacity and new investment rather than diversion from domestic use;[46] (iii) the higher the ratio, the more likely it is that exports are responsible for increasing returns to scale. In the case of imports, the implication of

---

[45] A classic example is Kuwait oil.

[46] This is especially true if the ratio of exports to output is rising at the same time that output is rising, that is, there would be a high *incremental* export:output ratio. Incremental ratios would be a better measure of the importance of exports for growth over any specific period of time, but we did not compute them. They are indicated however by trends in average ratios: rising average ratios imply still higher incremental ratios; falling average ratios, still lower incremental ratios.

high import: consumption ratios for a few commodities is that, in the absence of trade, the deficiencies would be more difficult to overcome — the cost per unit of import-substitute would be much higher than in a situation in which low ratios are spread over many commodities.[47]

For both exports and imports, exceptions can undoubtedly be cited — the infant industry case for one — but the approach seems a reasonable enough expedient. While disaggregating provides a little more information than the aggregate ratios, the improvement should not be overstated. Changes in the skewness of the disaggregated ratios undoubtedly are suggestive of the changing importance of trade to a single nation. On the other hand, these measures are less useful as clues to the relative importance of trade to different nations. Our use of these measures is further weakened because output figures, hence ratios, for many individual exports and imports are not available. For this reason, no formal measures of skewness were attempted. Finally, the extent to which trade in commodities carries technology may be of overwhelming importance to an importing nation. The "importer surplus" created thereby, however, is one to which individual import: consumption ratios would be completely insensitive.

In appraising the role of commodity trade in Soviet growth, U.S. experience will be used as a benchmark.[48] Major aggregative indicators suggest that American growth, 1869–1913, owed more to trade than Soviet growth, 1928–59. Thus, American imports and exports each averaged around 6 to 7 percent of GNP [49] over the relevant period, compared with a Soviet average of, say, 1 to 2 percent.

The lower Soviet ratios were a result, of course, of deliberate policy and of political circumstances. The Soviet Union undoubtedly would have been happy to raise its imports through long-term borrowing but was unable to do so. It also pursued a deliberate policy, in what it believed to be a hostile world, of becoming as self-sufficient as possible. American trade, except for a fairly high protective tariff, was relatively free to expand to the optimum. This suggests not only that Soviet growth benefited less from trade than American growth, but also that Soviet growth may have

[47] Assume two situations, one in which a nation consumes only five commodities and imports 20 percent of its requirements of each; another in which the nation consumes five commodities and imports 100 percent of its requirements of one commodity and produces domestically its total requirements of the other four. Unless one specifies abnormal supply conditions, the nation is likely to have a very great "comparative disadvantage" in the production of the one commodity in the latter case, and the costs of overcoming this deficiency without trade would in all probability be higher than in expanding by 25 percent (in the first case) the domestic output of each of the five commodities.

[48] A lengthy analysis of the role of trade in U.S. growth, documenting much of the material presented below, will be published elsewhere.

[49] U.S. Department of Commerce, *Historical Statistics of the United States, Colonial Times to 1957* (Washington, 1960), p. 542.

been retarded by failure to engage more freely in trade on international markets. The relatively high Russian ratio of exports to national income of around 10 percent in 1913 and subsequent sharp decline suggest the extent of these losses in the interwar period.[50]

What about differences between the two nations in composition of trade and in export : output and import : consumption ratios? Like Soviet exports, American exports were concentrated in the raw material and fuel categories. Unlike Soviet exports, this concentration was in agricultural commodities, primarily in cotton and wheat which comprised between 40 and 80 percent of exports over the five decades under consideration. On the average, exports of cotton, the single largest export category, amounted to about one-third of output; a high of 60 percent was registered in 1870 and a low of 20 percent over the years 1896–1900. Exports of wheat averaged 15 percent of output. Not until 1900 does the United States export anything (for which we have data) except cotton and wheat which has an export : output ratio exceeding 10 percent. The United States was, however, very favorably situated for producing and exporting cotton and wheat. Cessation of trade would have involved substantial curtailment of output in both instances since the surpluses which would have resulted could not have been absorbed domestically. In both instances, the United States would have suffered losses in that a valuable natural resource would have gone unused.

The USSR also benefited from its natural endowment. Moderately high export : output ratios were realized in the thirties in petroleum products, lumber products, manganese ore, and flax. With large supplies of underemployed labor available, exports of the first three items would probably have been stepped up were it not for the depressed state of world markets and adverse trend in terms of trade.[51] However, these exportables accounted for a smaller percent of total trade and, *a fortiori,* of output and of national income in the USSR than wheat and cotton exports in the USA before 1900.

Neither country exported a sufficient percentage of the domestic output of manufactured commodities to suggest that exports might have been responsible for substantial economies of scale. A few items might be cited for each nation which would seem to contradict this statement (for example, Soviet fertilizers), but in each instance the percentages of export to total trade and to GNP were small.

---

[50] Since the U.S. is probably better endowed with resources than the Soviet Union, one would expect that unrestricted trade would lead to a lower trade to GNP ratio in the former than in the latter.

[51] In fact, if not for the world depression, Soviet inability to borrow at reasonable rates from other countries would not have hurt since the Russians could easily have expanded output and exports of these products as well as of furs and some others. I am indebted to Raymond Vernon for this observation.

Exports, as a stimulator of investment and growth, are much more important to a free enterprise economy like the United States than to a Soviet-type planned economy. The rate of investment is a major variable in the calculations of the Soviet planners and is probably determined largely autonomously of the investment (lack of investment) required to support an expansion (contraction) in exports. A rise (fall) in investment in export industries would undoubtedly be offset by a fall (rise) in investment elsewhere. On the other hand, in free market economies, induced investment in export industries is probably largely additive to other investment and therefore more important to growth.[52] In addition, the secondary, tertiary, et cetera, spending effects of autonomous increases in exports spiral their way through the economy via the multiplier process, and these additions to demand may have still further accelerator effects.[53] These considerations suggest that heavier weight be placed on American than on Soviet export : output ratios as indicators of the importance of exports to growth.

Three final points regarding Soviet exports. First, during the First Five-Year Plan, when they reached a post-Revolution peak, exports taken by themselves probably seriously inhibited rather than stimulated growth. The increase in exports, it will be recalled, was in the form of unprocessed agricultural commodities. The direct effect of sales of these commodities abroad was to reduce the standard of living. The indirect consequences, which cannot be measured, stem from several facts. Export of agricultural goods at this time was a contributing factor to the repressed inflation, to the need for rationing in the consumers' goods market, and to the blunting of incentives. The decision to increase substantially such exports was a basic factor behind the decision to collectivize agriculture. Aside from the human suffering connected with collectivization, large losses of animal and physical capital were sustained.[54] While much of this loss was borne by the Soviet peasants and consumers, this catastrophe probably had serious negative side effects for Soviet industrialization. Finally, as indicated earlier, the decision to export large quantities of agricultural commodities in a declining world market involved the USSR in deteriorating terms of trade and sharply raised the cost of imports in terms of the exports required to pay for them.

Second, despite an aggregate export : output ratio in 1959 almost as high as during the First Five-Year Plan and much higher than during the Second Five-Year Plan, the gains in "exporter surplus" are undoubtedly

[52] That this is the case is stressed by Caves and Holton, *The Canadian Economy*, pp. 81ff.; and by Svennilson, *Growth and Stagnation in the European Economy*, pp. 223ff.

[53] The repercussion effects of cotton exports in the 1830's and 1840's were, according to Douglass North, *Economic Growth of the United States, 1790–1860* (New York, 1960), largely responsible for the acceleration in U.S. growth in this period.

[54] Naum Jasny, *The Socialized Agriculture of the USSR* (Stanford, 1949), chap. 13.

much less at present. Table VII.8 shows that the distribution of individual ratios is much less skewed than it was in the earlier period: only one commodity has a ratio above 20 percent.[55]

Finally, as might have been expected from our outline of Soviet trade policies above, the skewness of individual import:consumption ratios is considerably greater than that of individual export:output ratios.

Both the USSR and the USA were quite dependent on purchases abroad for particular commodities in the early stages of the periods under consideration.[56] The Soviet Union had high import:consumption ratios in the early thirties in nonferrous metals, rubber, cotton, wools, fibers, trucks, tractors, and various types of machinery and ferrous metal products. These products constituted some half of total imports in this period and, therefore, about 1 percent of GNP. The United States had rather high import:consumption ratios in iron and steel products, industrial machinery and equipment, copper refinery products, manufactured silk, raw wool, coffee, fibers, and raw sugar. These constituted about one-half of U.S. imports in the 20 years after the Civil War and, therefore, about 3 percent of GNP. In later years, the commodities with high ratios were preponderantly in the consumers' goods sphere. While the U.S. percentage of imports to GNP for these products was higher than the corresponding Soviet ratio, it should not be inferred that American growth was enhanced *each year* by these imports to a greater extent than Soviet growth. *The Soviet imports were concentrated to a much greater extent than American imports in growth industries* — cessation of imports would probably have resulted in a greater slowing down of Soviet than of American growth. On the other hand, the Russians had these high import:consumption ratios in most instances for only a few years; the high American ratios persisted for some 20 to 25 years. In fact, between 1928 and 1959, the skewness of both the Soviet export:output and import:consumption ratios is sharply reduced, whereas the skewness of the U.S. ratios changes little.

In view of the high Soviet import:consumption ratios in important growth industries such as nonferrous metals, rolled ferrous metals, ma-

---

[55] While gold is not usually considered a commodity in international trade, here it appears relevant to consider it one, since the Soviet Union, second largest producer in the world, obviously produces gold almost exclusively for export. Actually there are no firm figures on current Soviet gold output. It is known that more than 5 million ounces were produced annually in the late thirties and it is believed that production equals or exceeds that amount at present. Sales of gold since 1953 have been large, amounting to from 2 million ounces in 1955 to a maximum of 7.5 million ounces in 1957. In other words, in some years, the USSR may have exported 100 percent or more of current output. A 100 percent or larger export:output ratio for gold is probably much less significant, however, than for other commodities, because stocks of gold are undoubtedly so much larger relative to current output or to sales than those of other commodities.

[56] Our disregard of Lend-Lease imports here should not be taken to imply that they were not important in Soviet postwar recovery.

chinery and equipment, and rubber during the First Five-Year Plan, we may ask whether industrialization would have been at all possible if the Soviet economy had been closed. These imports were undoubtedly chosen more carefully for their growth effects than has ever been done by any other nation; the "importer surplus" generated must have been very large. Nevertheless, it seems reasonable to argue that while a halt in trade would have seriously slowed growth for many years, growth would still have been possible, since the USSR faced temporary absolute bottlenecks in only two commodities, tin and rubber. Imports of nonferrous metals taken as a group, for example, amounted to 122,000 tons in 1927/28 and 1931; by 1932, however, they had already declined to 78,000 tons. Even more important, by 1937–38, outputs of copper, lead, nickel, zinc, and aluminum were all greater than consumption of these metals had been during the First Five-Year Plan.[57] The same was true of rubber. With the exception of tin, therefore, the lack of imports could probably have been compensated for by increased domestic production, although this would no doubt have been costly and would have diverted resources from other essential tasks. Just how costly it would have been is impossible to say. In this connection, however, it is worth noting that at their peak in 1929, the value of nonferrous metal imports amounted to only 6.9 percent of total imports, declining to 4.6 percent in 1931 and 1932; imports of natural rubber constituted roughly only one percent.

What we have said of nonferrous metals is also true of rolled ferrous metals. Despite substantial dependence on imports during the First Five-Year Plan, by 1933, the USSR was meeting expanded requirements largely out of domestic production. The trend in import:consumption ratios in machinery and equipment parallels those already mentioned: dependence on imports rapidly declines over a 3- or 4-year period. The situation here, however, is complicated by the fact that machinery imports confer a substantial "importer surplus" by virtue of the modern technology and know-how they often carry and must have carried in this period in Soviet development. As already noted, this aspect of "importer surplus" defies measurement. Furthermore, it is difficult to distinguish the importance of the imports from other "carriers" of technology, for example, foreign technicians who were hired during the First Five-Year Plan; and the books, blueprints, et cetera, which were imported and which, it might be argued, were as important as prototype machines. Furthermore, if only prototype machinery and equipment had been imported, the value of imports in this category might have been cut to a fraction of the amount actually imported. In fact, according to Soviet economists, this was a main factor

[57] S. N. Bakulin and D. D. Mishustin, eds., *Vneshniaia torgovlia SSSR za 20 let, 1918–1937 gg* (Moscow, 1939), pp. 36–37.

behind the reduction in machinery imports during the Second Five-Year Plan: to a much greater extent, machinery imports were confined to prototypes since by this time the USSR could meet most of its regular requirements out of domestic production.[58]

To sum up: If the Soviet economy had been closed completely during the First Five-Year Plan, industrialization would have been seriously retarded if not almost completely stopped for a number of years. Soviet efforts to import in this period despite great handicaps attest to the importance they attributed to imports. On the other hand, the really crucial imports, those which conferred the greatest "importer surpluses"—prototype machines, nonferrous and ferrous metals, and rubber — probably amounted to less than one-fifth of total imports. A sharp reduction in trade which left the Russians still importing these categories would have retarded growth, but certainly would not have precluded a fairly creditable pace of industrialization. And the handicap would gradually have been overcome since the Soviet economy was destined eventually, by virtue of natural resources and domestic investment policies, to achieve virtual self-sufficiency.

Imports were, of course, much less important for growth in the Second than in the First Five-Year Plan. The aggregate import: consumption ratio averaged only about one-third of the earlier level because the Soviet economy had become much more self-sufficient. Gross imports of producers' goods declined as a percentage of gross investment from 12 to 14 percent in the First Five-Year Plan to 2 percent in the Second. Individual import: consumption ratios nevertheless remained quite high, suggesting that substantial "importer surplus" was still being earned through trade. In other words, while the Soviet Union was now less dependent on trade in an absolute sense, its imports were more concentrated than before in categories crucial to the economy! As indicated above, machinery imports were now more in the prototype class than during the first plan; and nonferrous metals rose in importance as a percentage of total imports, although the tonnage imported and import: consumption ratios declined. Thus, while the Soviet economy was virtually closed by 1937, and while the USSR undoubtedly could have grown quite rapidly if the economy had been completely closed, the few imports certainly did increase the pace at which it industrialized.

Imports at present (1955–59) are relatively unimportant to the Soviet economy although the aggregate import: consumption ratio is several times the mid-thirties level. Imports now probably contribute much less to growth than they did then. The Soviet Union is presently able to supply virtually every industrial ingredient necessary to growth. The individual import: consumption ratio for no commodity (for which we have data) ex-

[58] Mishustin, *Vneshniaia torgovlia i industrializatsiia SSSR,* pp. 80ff., 85ff.

ceeds 20 percent. Potential losses from absolute cessation of trade are therefore less, per unit of trade, than ever before.

What is the significance, in aggregative terms, of imports for growth in productive capacity? We have estimated the relation of gross and net imports of producers' goods to the value of gross capital investment. Hoeffding estimates gross investment in 1928 in current prices to have been 6.8 billion rubles. Imports of producers' goods in similar prices are estimated to have amounted to 1.09 billion rubles or to *16.0 percent* of total investment.[59] A net figure is calculated by deducting exports from imports of producers' goods and relating the result, after adjustment, to gross investment. Following the procedure and sources used for imports, we estimate producers' (industrial) goods exports at 706 million rubles. Net imports of producers' goods amount then to 384 million rubles or *5.6 percent* of gross investment. Similar calculations were made for 1931, the peak year for trade in the interwar period, but unfortunately, the estimates are even more heroic than those for 1928. The results, rough as they are, are a proportion of gross investment goods imported to gross investment between *12 and 14 percent;* and a proportion for net imports of producers' goods to gross investment of *2.9 to 3.4 percent.* Strangely enough, the aggregative significance of trade as a percentage of investment or of GNP seems to have been somewhat less in 1931 than in 1928. This is the result not of a decline in imports of producers' goods but of the faster growth of investment, GNP, and exports of producers' goods.[60]

The percentages are much smaller during the Second Five-Year Plan and in the postwar period. Gross imports of producers' goods in 1937 amounted to 1,252 million rubles or only *2.2 percent* of Bergson's 56.1 billion ruble figure for gross investment. Since exports of producers' goods totaled 1,425 million rubles in the same year, there was a net *export* (rather than import) of producers' goods in 1937 of *0.3 percent* of gross investment.

Imports of producers' goods were approximately 4.1 billion rubles in 1955. Making the appropriate rough adjustment for undervaluation and comparing the resulting figure with that for gross investment in 1955 [61] yields a ratio of imports to domestic output of investment goods of about *2.5 percent.* This is barely larger than the 2.2 percent of 1937, a year when

---

[59] Total imports for 1928 were 953 million rubles. Imports of producers' goods are given (Baykov, *Soviet Foreign Trade,* Table II) as 86.4 and 88.4 percent of total imports for the years 1927/28 and 1929, respectively. We assume 87 percent for 1928, or 829 million rubles. This figure is adjusted upward for the 32 percent overvaluation of the ruble in 1928 noted above for exports. We assume the same overvaluation for imports. The adjusted figure for imports of producers' goods is 1.09 billion rubles.

[60] Actually, gross imports of producers' goods (adjusted) rose from 1.09 billion rubles in 1928 to 1.81 billion in 1931.

[61] Oleg Hoeffding and Nancy Nimitz, *Soviet National Income and Product, 1949–55,* The RAND Corporation, Research Memorandum RM-2101, April 6, 1959, p. 9.

trade had virtually shriveled up. Furthermore, exports of producers' goods were about as large as imports so that industrialization in the USSR received no aid from this source.

It is generally agreed that the Soviet Union industrialized without much aid from other nations. This view is supported by the data. The usual approach is to treat the current account deficit as the amount of net foreign investment in one's country. Here we are largely confined to working with the trade deficit for lack of firm figures on invisible items. In 1928, the Soviet Union incurred a trade deficit of 150 million rubles. Adjusting this figure for overvaluation of the ruble, we get 198 million rubles, or 2.9 percent of gross investment and 0.6 percent of GNP. Extrapolating to 1931 indicates that the importance of capital inflow was declining. The passive balance of trade in 1931 is estimated to be only 0.5 percent of gross investment and 0.2 percent of GNP.[62] These figures are somewhat less than a Soviet estimate that foreign credits in the First Five-Year Plan period amounted to 2.7 percent of capital investment.[63] The difference is due in part to the deficit on invisible account.[64] It should also be recalled that the deficits in this period proved very expensive for the Russians to finance.

While some aid was received from abroad during the First Five-Year Plan, the Second Five-Year Plan was a period largely of repayment, and large balance of trade surpluses were enjoyed in every year except 1936 when trade was roughly balanced. Even if there was a deficit on invisible account, the Soviet Union probably repaid some foreign debt during 1933–37.

It is impossible to say definitely that the net capital flow since 1955 has been outward, but there is some evidence to that effect: (a) for the five-year period, 1955–59, a favorable trade balance of about 10 percent of ex-

[62] Estimates for 1931 were made as follows: Hoeffding's GNP, of 32.6 billion rubles in 1928, was projected on the basis of an 11 percent increase per year, yielding an estimate of 43.4 billion rubles. Gross investment is assumed to be from 30 to 35 percent of GNP or from 13.0 to 15.2 billion rubles. This is a much higher rate of investment than for any of Bergson's years and is based on the well-known fact that the standard of living declined during the First Five-Year Plan while national income increased. Exports and imports had to be adjusted to the 1928 level of current internal prices (since the investment and GNP projections are in these prices). Both exports and imports are assumed to be valued at 32 percent below their appropriate value in 1928 due to the overvaluation of the ruble in that year. The ruble was further overvalued in the period 1928–31 due to the decline in foreign trade prices (see Table VII.14). The export and import figures and balance of trade in 1931 were then adjusted upward for undervaluation.

[63] *Den'gi i kredit:* 1960, no. 8, p. 86.

[64] Crude figures for invisibles in 1927–28 indicate a net deficit on invisible account of roughly 100 million rubles. Inclusion of invisibles would make the current account deficit about 5.0 percent of gross investment. Gold exports in 1927/28 are estimated to have been 155 million rubles and the above figures can be adjusted or not for these exports depending on the reader's preference. Figures are from S. N. Prokopovich, ed., *Quarterly Bulletin of Soviet-Russian Economics,* May 1941, p. 142.

ports was sustained; (b) the USSR has been exporting substantial amounts of gold since 1953; (c) available information suggests that Soviet credits to members of the bloc and to the underdeveloped nations have exceeded credits extended to the Soviet Union by other nations.

In contrast, foreign nationals helped finance American investment throughout the post-Civil War period. Total foreign holdings in the United States rose from $1.5 billion in 1869 to $7.2 billion in 1914. However, the flow of capital was not in one direction: American holdings abroad rose from $0.1 billion in 1869 to $3.5 billion in 1914. The change in the ratio of *net* foreign indebtedness to gross investment averaged 2.8 percent over the whole period, 1869–1913. The net inflow reached highs of 11.9 and 7.8 percent, over the periods 1869–73 and 1887–91. On the other hand, the net capital flow was out, rather than in, over three quinquennial periods with a peak of −5.5 percent of gross investment in 1897–1901. The net inflow which averaged 5.5 percent for 1870–90 virtually ceased after 1890. In comparison, the smaller Soviet net capital import of the First Five-Year Plan probably ended, as noted above, with the expiration of that Plan in 1932.

We have not mentioned migration in connection with the economic growth of the USSR because the Soviet Union was probably even more of a closed economy in this respect than with respect to commodity trade. Migration was, however, very important to U.S. economic development in the period under consideration — much more important than commodity or capital flows. About one-fifth of our labor force comprised foreign-born workers in the years between the Civil War and World War I. The importance of these workers is even greater than this figure implies. In Simon Kuznets' words:

Since immigration brought in a large labor force the cost of whose rearing and training was borne elsewhere, it clearly represented an enormous capital investment that dwarfed any capital inflows of the more orthodox type — a conclusion that stands with any reasonable estimate we can make of the money value of labor.[65]

Let us now consider, from a larger perspective, the low ratios of trade to GNP of both nations and what this implies about gains from trade and, indirectly, about growth. Basically, trade among nations takes place because of relative differences in the following: factor endowments; tastes; technology; and the relative extent of external and internal economies. The major natural barrier to trade is cost of transport. Both the United States and the Soviet Union are adequately endowed with good quality

---

[65] Simon Kuznets, "Long-Term Changes in the National Income of the United States of America Since 1870," in Simon Kuznets ed., *Income and Wealth of the United States, Trends and Structure* (Cambridge, England, 1952), p. 198.

natural resources and have large climatic ranges; employ relatively advanced technologies;[66] have sufficiently large internal markets to achieve economies of scale for most commodities demanded; and are relatively well-advanced in sectors which give rise to external economies.

These conditions largely explain the low trade:GNP ratios as well as the low individual export:output and import:consumption ratios in the United States (in producers' goods and raw materials) and the Soviet Union. Under such circumstances, a nation can specialize in almost everything and conduct most of its trade internally rather than externally. From another point of view, there are few commodities for which the domestic and world prices[67] will be sufficiently different to make international trade profitable after transport costs have been taken into account. Small ratios spread over many commodities imply smaller comparative advantages and disadvantages. The production-possibilities curves or hyper-surfaces of the United States and the Soviet Union will roughly parallel those of the rest-of-world trading community for most commodities. Consequently, both the relative volume of trade and profits per unit of trade are small.

The above analysis need not be changed, substantially, for differences in tastes. For example, the cost of producing automobiles in the United States would not change much if demand fell off to, say, 2 million a year or rose to, say, 12 million a year. Given time for adjustment, marginal costs are probably relatively constant over a wide range of output — over most of the relevant range. This would be true of most industrial products. Adjustment is not, of course, frictionless, since existing capital stock cannot always be shifted, or at least easily, from one line of production to another. On the other hand, labor inputs tend to be highly substitutable among industries.[68] Thus, differences in tastes, even if substantial, are not likely to alter comparative costs over the preponderant range of commodities of large, industrialized nations.

The preceding analysis elaborates economic causes of the relatively minor importance of foreign trade in the United States and the Soviet Union. However, as we indicated earlier, the lower Soviet trade:GNP ratio, a consequence of the political decision to seek self-sufficiency, implies opportunities for profitable trade which have been deliberately foregone.[69] While from the point of view of static analysis, the Soviet

[66] A major exception is Soviet agriculture.

[67] Assuming hypothetical equilibrium exchange rates.

[68] This tendency is not as marked for land and raw material (extractive) resources. But as nations industrialize, the shares in national income of these sectors decline.

[69] The various ruble-dollar price ratio studies of a wide range of commodities which have been conducted by The RAND Corporation and by government agencies show a wide dispersion of relative prices and thus support the hypothesis that all opportunities for profitable trade have not been exploited by the USSR.

policy of producing domestically commodities which at least in part might be imported more cheaply involves a misallocation of resources and reduced real GNP in any particular year, the question remains whether this is true when viewed dynamically. Dynamic considerations will be more important than static considerations[70] if the Soviet policy of concentrating investment in import-competing industries rather than in industries producing exportables was responsible for enhancing the rate of growth by an amount which more than compensated for static allocation losses. Concentration on import-competing products will, of course, mean a lower level of trade than what it would be (over the "medium-run") if all efforts are concentrated on increasing the output of exportables.

The argument for the Soviet policy, a variant of the infant industry argument, is based on the following considerations: Assume the USSR has a choice between (i) investing in agriculture, exporting agricultural products, and importing final industrial products and (ii) investing in import-competing industrial products, thereby reducing or eliminating trade.[71] Assume also planners' sovereignty. If the USSR followed policy (i), the volume of trade (per unit of GNP) would rise as would gains from trade.[72] Domestic productivity would also rise as a result of investment in agriculture, but relatively slowly because agriculture is an industry with constant or decreasing returns and provides little scope for either internal economies of scale or external economy benefits to the rest of the economy. Policy (ii) on the other hand, would reduce the volume of and gains from trade but would result in larger increases in domestic productivity because of economies of scale and external economies.[73]

This may be illustrated diagramatically (see chart). Let TT be the initial production possibilities curve, T_aT and TT_i those which would result at some future date if the Soviet Union concentrates on expanding agricultural and industrial capacity, respectively. The indifference curves are drawn to show a high income-elasticity of demand by the authorities for industrial goods and low income-elasticity for agricultural goods. The combination of a greater expansion along the horizontal (industrial) than vertical (agricultural) axis both with respect to possible volume of output and desired consumption-mix combine to make expansion of industry lead to a higher planner welfare position (m on I_4) than expansion of agriculture (q on I_2) in the absence of trade. And the planners might be better off

[70] See Gottfried Haberler, *International Trade and Economic Development* (Cairo, 1959), pp. 10–11 for a discussion of dynamic and static benefits from trade.

[71] These are extreme assumptions, of course; and are not in accord with recent U.S. experience of rapidly increasing agricultural productivity.

[72] This assumes that the Soviet Union is a competitive seller in a large world market and its sales cannot affect the terms of trade.

[73] See G. Warren Nutter, "On Measuring Economic Growth," *Journal of Political Economy*, February 1957.

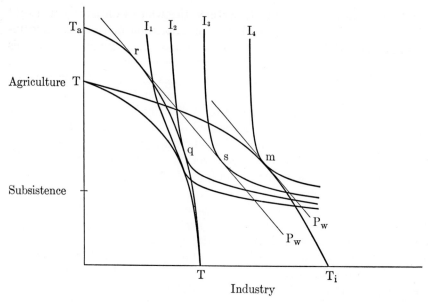

expanding industry and not engaging in trade than expanding agriculture with trade unless the terms of trade, P_w, were very favorable to agriculture. In the chart, given a world price ratio P_w, concentration on expanding agricultural capacity would lead to production at point r and consumption after trade on point s which is on indifference curve I_3. Expansion of industry plus autarky leads to production and consumption at m on the higher indifference curve.[74]

This sort of analysis does suggest a justification, of the infant-industry type, for the extreme Soviet concentration on investment in import-competing industries. It should be pointed out, however, that in the First Five-Year Plan period, the USSR got the best of both worlds by exporting agricultural goods on a *relatively* large scale and importing producers' goods[75] which enabled them to set up import-competing industries. Undoubtedly, the USSR could have benefited from an expansion and continuation of this policy at least through the Second Five-Year Plan. Had it not been for the adverse shift in terms of trade and high cost of borrowing abroad, such a policy might have been adopted more broadly.[76]

[74] We have assumed that the domestic price in TT_i is equal to the world price line P_w. This assumption is not necessary, but does not change the analysis. If the domestic price ratio was not equal to P_w, the nation could rise to a still higher position by engaging in some trade.

[75] The planners' objectives were directed not only at amassing industrial commodities but also at developing *capacity to produce* domestic products.

[76] To some extent this policy is still followed. For example, in 1958 the Soviets announced a Seven-Year Plan to promote the development of bigger chemical and synthetic materials industries. Instead of developing factories through direct domestic investment, they attempted to purchase whole plants from other nations.

The conclusions are: that while the Soviet Union does not fully exploit foreign trade to its profitable limits, the losses are not as large as would appear from the point of view of static comparative advantage; further, that its policy has reduced the profitable limits of trade below what they would otherwise have been had it followed more normal trade and investment policies.

APPENDIX

Notes to Table VII.1

1913–40: Ministerstvo Vneshnei Torgovli SSSR (hereafter MVT) *Vneshniaia torgovlia SSSR za 1918–1940 gg.* (Moscow, 1960), p. 14.

1942–43: N. Voznesensky, *The Economy of the U.S.S.R. During World WAR II* (Washington, D.C., 1948), p. 40.

1945, 1950: Vneshniaia torgovlia, 1958, no. 4, p. 21.

1946: TSU, *Dostizheniia Sovetskoi vlasti za 40 let v tsifrakh* (Moscow, 1957), p. 31.

1951–53: S. D. Sergeev, *Ekonomicheskoe sotrudnichestvo i vzaimopomoshch' stran sotsialisticheskogo lageria* (Moscow, 1959), p. 106.

1955–59: from annual supplements, beginning 1956, to *Vneshniaia torgovlia SSSR.*

The USSR values its goods in foreign trade primarily on a basis of world prices. When the exchange rate changes, the prices at which it buys and sells in world markets remain unchanged; its foreign trade accounts do reflect, however, the change in the international value of the ruble. Currency revaluations therefore cause a sharp discontinuity in Soviet foreign trade return series. For comparability, all previous trade returns are valued at the new exchange rate after a revaluation has occurred. Columns 1 to 3 present Soviet trade returns at the 1950 exchange rate of 4 rubles to $1. Columns 4 to 6 present Soviet trade returns at the actual values at which they were recorded, with the exception of those for 1913–24, which are in constant 1913 prices. Conversion to 1950 rubles was made by multiplying by the following coefficients: 1913–35: 3.4851; 1936: 0.7957; 1937–49: 0.75472 (MVT, *Vneshniaia torgovlia SSSR za 1918–1940 gg.,* p. 9). For discussion of this matter and of the history of Soviet revaluations, see F. D. Holzman, "Some Financial Aspects of Soviet Foreign Trade," in Joint Economic Committee, 86th Congress of the United States, 1st Session, *Comparisons of the United States and Soviet Economies* (Washington, 1959), pp. 427–443. All foreign trade data after 1924 are in current prices.

Notes to Table VII.2

Indexes based on 1913 and 1929 price weights are from S. N. Bakulin and D. D. Mishustin, *Statistika vneshnei torgovli SSSR* (Moscow, 1940), pp. 287 and 290.

Indexes based on 1913 price weights are based on Soviet 1913 prices for 1918–24 and on a British Board of Trade price index (with a 1913 base) for 1924–34.

1938–59 data are from MVT, *Vneshniaia torgovlia SSSR za 1959 god* (Moscow, 1960), p. 11.

Notes to Table VII.3

1913, 1929–37: These figures are taken from Bakulin and Mishustin, *Statistika vneshnei torgovli SSSR*, pp. 293–294. They are based on a revaluation of national income in 1926/27 prices to 1913 prices and revaluation of exports as shown in the trade returns also to 1913 prices. These figures may be too high as a result of the understatement of Soviet national income estimates which are based on the Marxist practice of excluding services. Two estimates of Russian national income for 1913 place it at 13.3 and 16.4 billion rubles, respectively (L. Gatovsky *et al., Sovetskaia sotsialisticheskaia ekonomika, 1917–1957* [Moscow, 1957], p. 168; and M. Kaser, "Estimating Soviet National Income," *Economic Journal*, March 1957, p. 84). We raise these figures 10 to 15 percent to take account of excluded services. Dividing the adjusted figures into Russian exports which amounted to 1.52 billion rubles in 1913 yields ratios of exports to national income within the 8- to 10-percent range.

Rough calculations for 1928 and 1931 corroborate the above Soviet estimates. Soviet national income in 1928 in current prices has been estimated to be 32.6 billion rubles by Oleg Hoeffding, *Soviet National Income and Product in 1928* (New York, 1954), pp. 46–47. The value of exports in 1928 is reported by the USSR as 803.4 million rubles. However, the ruble was overvalued in 1928 and exports were sold 32 percent below domestic prices, according to I. Aizenberg, *Voprosy valiutnogo kursa rublia* (Moscow, 1958), p. 74. Revaluing exports in domestic prices gives a figure of 1,060 million rubles. So valued, exports in 1928 amount to 3.2 percent of GNP. The 1931 ratio can be approximated by extrapolation. If we assume with Bergson that national income increases about 11 percent a year from 1928 to 1931 (in 1928 prices) and the volume of exports 59 percent (Table VII.2) and further assume that the domestic prices of exportables follow the over-all price level, the ratio of exports to GNP in 1931 is 3.9 percent.

The Soviet estimate agrees closely with an independent estimate based on Bergson's Soviet national income figure in current prices and the Soviet 1937 export figure. My own calculations ("Soviet Foreign Trade Pricing Policies," unpublished) indicate that the Soviet ruble exchange rate was neither seriously over- nor undervalued in 1937, the 77-percent devaluation of April 1936 having brought internal and external prices, particularly of producers' goods, more or less into line. Exports in 1937 amounted to 1,729 million rubles which is 0.6 percent of Bergson's 291.8 billion ruble GNP for that year.

1955, 1959: Soviet GNP in current prices has been estimated to be 1,202 billion rubles in 1955 (Oleg Hoeffding and Nancy Nimitz, *Soviet National Income and Product, 1949–55,* The RAND Corporation, Research Memorandum RM-2101, April 6, 1959, p. 9). Exports in 1955 totaled 13.9 billion rubles. As was the case before the 1936 devaluation, the 1955 foreign exchange ruble was overvalued and foreign trade figures must be adjusted upward for comparability with goods valued in domestic prices. I have estimated the overvaluation in 1955 to be between 50 and 75 percent. Appropriately adjusted, exports amount to 20.8 to 24.3 billion rubles or 1.7 to 2.0 percent of GNP. The figure for 1959 can be approximated roughly by extrapolation. We assume that real national income increases 7 percent a year. The volume of exports increased, according to Soviet sources, 71.3 percent from 1955 to 1959. The ratio of exports to national income is then estimated to be between 2.3 and 2.6 percent in 1959. This figure is somewhat below an estimate of 3 percent for 1955 by O. T. Bogomolov, presented without explanation (cf. A. Nove and A. Zauberman, "A Dollar Valuation of Soviet National Income," *Soviet Studies,* October 1958, p. 146). However, Bogomolov undoubtedly used the Soviet definition of GNP which excludes depreciation and services. One can make a good case for increasing Soviet GNP at present about 20 percent to allow for these items, and this would account for at least half of the difference between our ratio and Bogomolov's.

Notes to Table VII.4

1913, 1928, 1950, 1955–58: Taken from TSU, *Narodnoe khoziaistvo SSSR v 1958,* p. 800.

1929–38: Taken from Baykov, Tables IV and V of the appendix.

1929–37: Ferrous metals, computed from S. N. Bakulin and D. D. Mishustin, *Vneshniaia torgovlia SSSR za 20 let, 1918–1937* (Moscow, 1939), p. 56.

1929–37: Consumers' goods, taken from MVT, *Vneshniaia torgovlia SSSR za 1918–1940 gg.,* p. 17. This source gives a figure for 1938 of 19 percent.

Notes to Table VII.5

1955–59: All figures are from *Vneshniaia torgovlia SSSR* (annual issues).

1913–40: Columns 1 and 4 are from Baykov, Table II of the appendix; columns 2, 5, 6, and 7 are from MVT, *Vneshniaia torgovlia SSSR za 1918–1940 gg.,* p. 18; column 3 represents difference between columns 1 and 2 and between columns 3 and 4.

1955–59: Columns 6 and 7 are estimated from detailed trade returns and differ from official estimates in Table VII.4.

Notes to Table VII.6

1894–98 to 1909–13: Taken from S. N. Bakulin and D. D. Mishustin, *Statistika vneshnei torgovli SSSR* (Moscow-Leningrad, 1935), p. 265.

1913–38: Taken from Baykov, Table III of the appendix.

Note to Table VII.7

Taken from Mishustin, p. 105.

Notes to Table VII.8

The major sources and abbreviations used below are:
NK 1958 — Narodnoe khoziaistvo SSSR v 1958
Baykov — A. Baykov, *Soviet Foreign Trade*

VT-20 — S. N. Bakulin and D. D. Mishustin, *Vneshniaia torgovlia SSSR za 20 let, 1918–37 gg.* (Moscow, 1939)

VT Postwar — *Vneshniaia torgovlia SSSR* (statement of foreign trade returns published since 1956), Moscow, annually

B&M — S. N. Bakulin and D. D. Mishustin, *Statistika vneshnei torgovli* (Moscow, 1940)

Mish — D. D. Mishustin, *Vneshniaia torgovlia i industrializatsiia SSSR* (Moscow, 1938)

Ind — *Industry USSR, A Statistical Compilation* (Moscow, 1957)

Johnson — D. Gale Johnson and Arcadius Kahan, "Soviet Agriculture: Joint Economic Committee, 86th Congress of the United States, 1st session *Comparisons of the United States and Soviet Economies* (Washington, 1959)

Commodity	*Output*	*Exports*	*Exports/Output*
pig iron	*NK 1958*, p. 188	*VT-20*, p. 73 *VT Postwar*	
automobiles, trucks, and tractors	*NK 1958*, pp. 242–243	*NK 1958*, p. 802	
crude oil	*B&M*, p. 297 *NK 1958*, p. 208	*VT-20*, p. 48 *NK 1958*, p. 802	
fuel oil, kerosene, gasoline			Prewar: *B&M*, p. 297 1958: unpublished estimates of Richard Judy
coal	*NK 1958*, p. 204	Baykov, Table V *NK 1958*, p. 802	*B&M*, p. 297
fertilizer (including phosphates, potassium, salts, nitrogen fertilizer)	*NK 1958*, p. 204	*VT Postwar* Baykov, Table IV	
sawn lumber and plywood	*Ind*, p. 261 *NK 1958*, pp. 254, 803	*VT-20* *NK 1958*, p. 803	*Mish*, p. 101
raw timber	amount hauled *Ind*, p. 249	*NK 1958*, p. 802	
iron ore and manganese ore	*NK 1958*, p. 193	*NK 1958*, p. 802 Baykov, Table V	
grain	Johnson, p. 234	Baykov, Table V *NK 1958*, p. 803	
wheat and corn	*NK 1958*, pp. 418–419	*VT-20*, pp. 34, 35 *VT Postwar*	*B&M*, p. 297 (Prewar)
rye, oats, barley			*B&M*, p. 297
flax	Johnson, p. 235	Baykov, Table IV *NK 1958*, p. 803	
sugar	*Ind*, p. 373	Baykov, Table IV *NK 1958*, p. 803	

Commodity	Output	Exports	Exports/Output
cotton	Johnson, p. 234	Baykov, Table IV *VT Postwar*	
butter	U.N. *Econ. Bull. for Europe*, vol. 11, no. 1, A-18	Baykov, Table IV *NK 1958*, p. 803	Mish, p. 101
rolled ferrous metals	*NK 1958*, p. 188	*NK 1958*, pp. 802–804	Mish, p. 101 (1935–36)

In some instances, export/output ratios provided by Mish and B&M differed from these computed independently.

Fertilizer exports are expressed as percentage of mineral fertilizer production.

Notes to Table VII.9

1913, 1928, 1938, 1950, 1955–58: From TSU, *Narodnoe khoziaistvo SSSR v 1958*, pp. 800–804.

1929–35: Tsentral'noe Upravlenie Narodno-khoziaistvennogo Ucheta, *Socialist Construction of the USSR* (Moscow, 1936), pp. 426–427.

1929–38: Baykov, Tables I, IV, and VI of the appendix.

1955–58: From *Vneshniaia torgovlia SSSR*, annual issues.

1928–38: Machinery and equipment, from Bakulin and Mishustin, *Vneshniaia torgovlia SSSR za 20 let, 1918–37*, p. 18.

Notes to Table VII.10

1913–40: From MVT, *Vneshniaia torgovlia SSSR za 1918–1940 gg.*, pp. 17–18.

1955–59: From *Vneshniaia torgovlia SSSR*, annual issues.

I assume, according to the reasoning presented in connection with the data in Table VII.5, that manufactured foodstuffs are included in column 5 rather than in column 2. Columns 6 and 7 for 1955–59 were estimated from detailed trade returns. These figures differ from official figures presented in Table VII.9.

Notes to Table VII.11

1894: From Pasvolsky and Moulton, p. 73.

1913–38: From Baykov, Table III of the appendix.

1955–59: From *Vneshniaia torgovlia SSSR*, annual issues.

D. D. Mishustin, *Vneshniaia torgovlia i industrializatsiia SSSR*, p. 82, presents the same figures as Baykov for 1934–37 but differs as to the balance between manufactured goods and raw materials and semimanufactures for 1930–33. His figures for manufactured goods are: 1930, 53.7; 1931, 61.6; 1932, 61.6; and 1933, 52.1. The change in classification has not been ascertained.

We assume that in the 1956–59 handbooks the column marked "raw materials" contains foodstuffs. However, it may exclude semimanufactures, which may be included in prepared products.

Notes to Table VII.12

The major sources and abbreviations used below, in addition to those listed for Table VII.8, are:

Shimkin — D. Shimkin, *Minerals: Key to Soviet Power* (Cambridge, Mass., 1953)

League — League of Nations, *Statistical Yearbooks,* published annually in Geneva

VnT — *Vneshniaia torgovlia,* 1960, 9 (monthly journal)

VT-40 — MVT, *Vneshniaia torgovlia SSSR za 1918–1940 gg.* (Moscow, 1960)

Commodity	Output or consumption	Exports	Imports	Imports/ consumption
nonferrous metals	Shimkin, p. 77	*VT-40, VT-20*	*VT-40, VT-20*	
	League	*VT Postwar*	*VT Postwar*	
rolled ferrous metals, pig iron, machinery, autos and trucks, tractors				*Prewar: VT-20,* p. 19 *Postwar: VnT,* p. 37 tractors 1928–29: Mish, p. 170
machine tools				Mish, p. 151
iron and steel pipes and tubing				Mish, p. 188
turbines, generators, boilers				Mish, pp. 179–181
metal-cutting machines				*VnT,* p. 37: Mish, p. 144
rubber				*VT-20,* p. 19
cotton and wool	Johnson, pp. 231, 235	*VT-40* *VT Postwar*	*VT-40* *VT Postwar*	Mish, p. 202

Consumption is calculated as output — exports + imports.

Prewar tractor figures based on output in power terms. Slightly lower import/consumption ratio where figures are based on output units.

Discrepancies are sometimes encountered between directly estimated figures and the ratios presented in *VT-20* and Mish.

Tin — The figure cited in the 1950 column is actually for 1949; the 1940 figure, not shown in the table, is 70 percent.

Turbines, generators, and boilers are all destined for use in power stations. The figures are unweighted averages of the three.

Notes to Table VII.13

Data taken from D. D. Mishustin, ed., *Vneshniaia torgovlia Sovetskogo Soiuza, SSR* (Moscow, 1938), p. 103; Gerschenkron, *Economic Relations*, p. 52; D. D. Mishustin, *Vneshniaia torgovlia i industrializatsiia SSSR*, p. 120; and the new handbook (MVT, *Vneshniaia torgovlia SSSR za 1918–1940 gg.*), which appeared after this material was written.

Notes to Table VII.14

1929 to first 3 quarters of 1938: From Bakulin and Mishustin, *Statistika vneshnei torgovli*, pp. 284–287. These indexes are based on 1929 weights.

1938–59: Estimates obtained by dividing indexes of value of exports and imports calculated from trade figures by volume indexes in MVT, *Vneshniaia torgovlia SSSR za 1959 god* (Moscow, 1960), p. 11.

The terms-of-trade index is extended from 1929 through 1958 (the figures in parentheses) by a simple link in 1938 between the two sets of price figures.

Note to Table VII.15

Data calculated from the Soviet foreign trade statistical handbooks cited elsewhere in this chapter.

VIII

A COMPARATIVE APPRAISAL

Simon Kuznets

---

1. Introduction

The tables, on which this chapter comments, bring together some measures of the economic growth of the USSR and a number of other countries. Most of the data on the USSR were assembled from the papers in this volume, from the rich store in Professor Bergson's *The Real National Income of Soviet Russia Since 1928* (supplemented by unpublished calculations which he provided), and from the readily available compilations in the successive Joint Economic Committee documents. This is far less than what one could gather with more time, patience, and skill than I could muster. Nor are the tables for the countries other than the USSR as complete as they might be if more time and effort had been spent on them. I had to draw upon what was easily available, utilizing some of my own summary work. But the main findings for these other countries, used here as a background against which to observe some distinctive statistical characteristics of Soviet economic growth, are not likely to be changed much by refinement and up-dating.

These qualifying remarks are offered as a warning that the comparisons presented here are preliminary and tentative. Nevertheless, the attempt seems worthwhile. If there is some value in statistical measures of the economic growth of the USSR, there is surely more justification for comparing them with those for other countries. Some general questions concerning the rationale of such comparisons will be raised below; they would seem more appropriate after the comparisons have been made than before. We proceed now to comment on the findings that the tables suggest.

2. Over-All Rates of Growth (Tables VIII.1 to VIII.4)

The over-all rates of growth for the USSR are much affected by the year of the price base, when the choice is between the preindustrialization price structure of 1928 and the price structures for 1937 and later years; and by the span covered, when the choice is between a period that excludes World War II (and its immediate aftermath) and the early years of struggle for political and economic supremacy within the country, and the longer period that includes them.

I decided not to use the 1928 price estimates, since what is essentially a nonindustrial price structure, while of interest for some special purposes, is hardly relevant to the measurement of the rate of industrialization and economic growth. Moreover, the estimates for other countries, if they are to be used for comparison, would also have to be based on similarly early price structures; and I doubt that they could be found. Besides, the participation of other countries in a network of relatively free foreign trade should have prevented too high a ratio of industrial to nonindustrial prices. Hence I could not use Bergson's composite indexes; and I settled for the estimates in 1937 prices, since all of Bergson's valuable adjustments are available for these.

The choice of the period raises even more vexing problems. Beginning in 1928 would seem appropriate if we were interested in gauging how the Soviet system worked under the five-year plans and all that such plans betokened. But, on the other hand, the period from 1917 to 1928 witnessed a process by which the Communist minority acquired power and experience, and which laid the foundation for what followed. The very decimation of the population, and in the course of it also of latent opposition, may be viewed as an element of strength that made possible the ruthlessness subsequently displayed. Should we not include the pre-1928 decade as part of the period of economic growth under Communist auspices? Does not every case of Communist economic growth begin with a breakdown of libertarian social and economic institutions followed by recovery, in the process of which opposition is reduced and the way cleared for the forced programs that follow? If there are two distinct patterns of growth — one characterized by an initial breakdown and internal struggles as a precondition and the other capable of attaining realization without such turmoil and strife — should we not seek measures that reflect this difference in the character of successive phases and in their impact on over-all rates of growth?

A similar question can be raised with respect to the World War II period. We may or may not assume that the very occurrence of that war should be debited to the foreign policy that the autarkic and dictatorial Soviet system pursued. We may or may not assume that the war ravages in the Soviet Union, following a virtual collapse of its armies in the early part of the war, were a consequence of a policy that disrupted military organization by trumped-up trials and undermined the loyalty of the population by the repressions and violence of the 1930's. We may debit the war fully to Nazi Germany, and neglect not only the early cooperation of the USSR but also the close link between the strains and stresses within the USSR (or any dictatorship of that type) and the international tensions that they generate. Yet we may still argue that for whatever reasons a major war occurs, its widespread damage and attrition facilitate subsequent growth over and beyond the mere restoration of prewar levels — provided the regime does not collapse. Like many a process of destruction, the war may have removed obstacles to rapid growth, permitting replacement of old by new; accelerating such growth-promoting policies as the movement toward the East within the USSR; and creating a solidarity between the people and the government that had not existed in earlier years. Should we then exclude the war period if what happened during the war provided, at least in part, a base for the growth that followed?

The answers to these questions require a knowledge of the causal interrelations of growth in successive periods in the USSR, a firm theory of sequential phases of growth in the USSR and in other countries, that we do not possess.[1] The questions are raised because the answers to them would clearly affect the comparison, not because firm answers can be given. In the discussion that follows, emphasis is placed on the "best" periods, that is, the 12 years from 1928 to 1940 and the 8 years from 1950 to 1958 — in an attempt to compare the level and structure in these periods of most rapid growth with economic growth elsewhere. But some reference is made also to the longer periods, particularly 1928–58.

An over-all rate of growth in net national product of some 5.2 percent per year (for 1928–40 and 1950–58) is high (see Table VIII.1, line 7, column 3). But it is exceeded over long periods in other countries: in the United States in the 1870's and 1880's, and in Australia in the 1860's and 1870's; and is approximated in Japan in the 1920's and 1930's, and in the Union of South Africa during the first half of this century (see Table VIII.3, column 2, lines 31, 35, 39a, and 44). In the United States and Australia the high rates of growth in national product were associated with

---

[1] For an illuminating discussion of questions relating to the distinction of major phases in the economic growth of the USSR and their importance in the analysis of the record see Naum Jasny, *Soviet Industrialization, 1928–1952* (Chicago, 1961), particularly chap. I.

Table VIII.1
USSR: Rates of Growth per Year in Gross and Net National Product,
at Prevailing Constant Prices and at Factor Cost, 1928–58
(percent)

Item	1928–37 or 1928–40 (1)	1950–55 or 1950–58 (2)	Weighted average of columns (1) and (2)[a] (3)
1928 Prices			
1. GNP, at prevailing prices	11.5		
2. GNP, at ruble factor cost	11.9		
3. NNP, at ruble factor cost	9.3		
1937 Prices			
4. GNP, at prevailing prices	4.9	8.2	6.2
5. GNP, at ruble factor cost	5.5	7.6	6.3
6. GNP, at ruble factor cost extended within retail purchases, 1928 only	4.8	7.6	5.9
7. NNP, at ruble factor cost, extended adjustment	4.2	6.8	5.2
1950 Prices			
8. GNP, at prevailing prices	4.9	8.2	6.2
9. GNP, at ruble factor cost	5.4	7.6	6.3
10. NNP, at ruble factor cost		6.8	

[a] The rates of growth of GNP are for the periods 1928–37 and 1950–55, those of NNP are for 1928–40 and 1950–58. The weighting in column 3 is uniformly by duration of the longer periods, that is, 12 and 8 years, respectively.

Note: Here and for later tables, where sources and methods are not given, see appendix.

high rates of growth in population — the latter far higher than that for the USSR; so that on a per capita basis the growth rates would be significantly lower than in the USSR. But in Japan and the Union of South Africa the rates of growth in per capita product would approach those for the USSR.[2] Naturally, if we include the 1940's, and compare the rate of growth in net national product for the full period, 1928–58, 4.1 percent per year, with the rates in other countries, several more show rates of growth that match or exceed the Soviet rates: Sweden, Canada, and even Argentina; and Sweden would show a particularly high rate of

[2] For Japan, the rate of growth in per capita real income averaged 3.2 percent per year for the full span of sixty years from 1878–82 to 1938–42; and it would not be difficult to find a period of twenty years with an appreciably higher rate of growth (see Kazushi Ohkawa *et al., The Growth Rate of the Japanese Economy since 1878* (Tokyo, 1957), Tables 1 and 3, pp. 17 and 19). For the Union of South Africa the rate of growth in per capita income for the averaged 3.0 percent per year.

Table VIII.2
USSR: Rates of Growth per Year in Population, Total Employment, National
Product, and Household Consumption (Including Communal Services), 1928–58
(percent; product based on constant price totals)

Item	1928–40 (1)	1950–58 (2)	(1) + (2) (3)	1940–50 (4)	(3) + (4) (5)	Pre-1928 decade (6)	(5) + (6) (7)
1. Population	1.19	1.74	1.41	−0.80	0.67	0.45	0.61
2. Workers (total employment)	3.7	1.2	2.7	0.7	2.0	—	—
GNP, 1937 factor cost							
3. Total	4.5	7.2	5.6	2.1	4.4	0.45	3.4
4. Per capita	3.2	5.4	4.1	2.9	3.7	0	2.8
5. Per worker	0.7	5.9	2.8	1.4	2.4	—	—
NNP, 1937 factor cost							
6. Total	4.2	6.8	5.2	1.9	4.1	0.45	3.2
7. Per capita	3.0	5.0	3.8	2.7	3.4	0	2.6
8. Per worker	0.5	5.5	2.5	1.2	2.1	—	—
Household consumption and communal services, 1937 adjusted market prices							
9. Total	1.6	7 8	4.0	1.7	3.1	0.45	2.4
10. Per capita	0.45	6.0	2.6	1.9	2.4	0	1.8

Note: The dash (—) indicates that data are not available.

growth in *per capita* product (Table VIII.2, column 5, line 6 and Table VIII.3, column 3, lines 23, 27, and 42).

One difficulty with the comparison just made emerges when we consider the post-World War II years, which make up almost half of the short, 20-year period used for the USSR and which contribute so heavily to the high rates of growth. The rates of growth for the USSR for the post-World War II years were 7.2 for GNP and 6.8 for NNP (Table VIII.2, column 2, lines 3 and 6). Rates of this magnitude, or larger, or not much smaller, are found for West Germany, Japan, Venezuela, Jamaica, Israel, Taiwan, and Rhodesia and Nyasaland; and rates well above 6 percent are found also for Austria, Greece, Turkey, the Dominican Republic, and Burma (Table VIII.4, column 2). In this melange of countries with high rates of growth, two subgroups can be distinguished: one of countries badly damaged by World War II (Japan, West Germany, Austria, Burma); the other of small countries, either with colonial status or independent, that have profited from intensive exploitation of some natural resource (Venezuela, Rhodesia and Nyasaland, Dominican Republic). It is particularly interesting that the larger countries that were badly damaged by World War II, such as West Germany and Japan, show rates of growth in recent years as high or higher than those in the USSR; and even in Italy the rate of growth of national product was 5.6 percent per year. All of these, including the rate for the USSR, are far higher than the long-term rates of growth before World War II in the

Table VIII.3
Selected Countries: Rates of Growth per Year in Product in Constant Prices, Total and per Worker, and in Labor Force, Long Periods
(percent)

| | Duration of period[a] (years) (1) | Rates of growth per year (percent) | | |
| | | Product (2) | Labor force (3) | Product per worker (4) |
Item				
United Kingdom, NNP				
1. A-E, 1851 + 61	53.5; 60	2.2	0.75	1.5
2. A-R, 1890–99; 1891 + 1901	30; 45	1.7	0.8	0.9
3. H-P, 1870–79 to 1890–99	20	3.0		
4. H-P/L, 1871 + 81 to 1891 + 1901	20		0.8	2.2
Germany, NNP				
5. A-E, 1851–55	59; 56	2.7	1.25	1.4
6. A-R, 1886–95	35.5; 38.5	3.3	1.4	1.9
7. H-P				
a. 1886–95 to 1911–13	21.5	2.9		
b. 1952 to 1958	6	7.1		
8. H-P/L				
a. 1851–55 to 1871–75	20		0.7	2.0
b. 1950 to 1958	8		2.1	4.9
Italy, GDP				
9. A-E, 1861	54; 55	1.3	0.2	1.1
10. A-R, 1891–1900; 1891 + 1901	47.5; 48	3.2	0.45	2.7
11. H-P				
a. 1920–22 to 1938–40	18	2.4		
b. 1946 to 1956	10	6.6		
12. H-P/L				
a. 1921 to 1936	15		0.45	2.0
b. 1950 to 1958	8		1.0	5.5
Denmark, GDP				
13. A-E, 1870	44	3.25	0.9	2.3
14. A-R, 1890–99; 1894	43.5; 46	3.4	1.1	2.25
15. H-P, 1890–99 to 1914	19.5	3.7		
16. H-P/L, 1894 to 1914	20		1.2	2.5
Norway, GDP				
17. A-E, 1865	49.5; 50	2.1	0.8	1.25
18. A-R, 1890–99; 1895	51.5; 50	2.9	1.0	1.8
19. H-P				
a. 1915–24 to 1939	19.5	3.2		
b. 1949 to 1956	7	3.5		
20. H-P/L				
a. 1920 to 1940	20		1.1	2.1
b. 1950 to 1955	5		0.5	3.0
Sweden, GDP				
21. A-E, 1861	54.5; 54	2.95	0.8	2.1
22. A-R, 1896–1905; 1900	55.5; 58	3.3	0.9	2.4
23. H-P, 1926–35 to 1948–52	19.5	4.2		
24. H-P/L 1930 to 1950	20		0.6	3.6
Canada, GNP				
25. A-E, 1867 + 70 + 73; 1870	45.5; 45	3.7	2.1	1.5
26. A-R, 1891–1900; 1890 + 1900	49; 47	3.6	2.0	1.6

Table VIII.3 (Contd.)

Item	Duration of period[a] (years) (1)	Rates of growth per year (percent)		
		Product (2)	Labor force (3)	Product per worker (4)
27. H-P, 1891–1900 to 1911–20	20	4.0		
28. H-P/L, 1945 to 1953	8		0.8	3.1
United States, GNP				
29. A-E, 1869–78; 1874	40	4.3	2.55	1.7
30. A-R, 1889–98; 1894	49; 50	3.1	1.7	1.4
31. H-P, 1869–78 to 1884–93	15	5.5		
32. H-P/L				
a. 1874 to 1889	15		2.8	2.7
b. 1946 to 1956	10		1.45	2.8
Australia, GDP				
33. A-E, 1861–65; 1861	52; 53.5	3.6	2.6	1.0
34. A-R, 1891–1900; 1891 + 1901	44; 44.5	2.8	1.8	1.0
35. H-P, 1861–65 to 1876–85	17.5	5.7		
36. H-P/L, 1861 to 1881	20		3.2	2.3
Japan, GNP				
37. A-E, 1885–89; 1883–87	29; 30	3.75	0.7	3.0
38. A-R, 1900–04; 1898–1902	44; 48	4.65	0.95	3.7
39. H-P				
a. 1920–24 to 1938–42	18	5.1		
b. 1952 to 1958	6	6.8		
40. H-P/L				
a. 1918–22 to 1938–42	20		0.9	4.2
b. 1950 to 1958	8		2.4	4.3
Argentina, GDP				
41. A-R, 1900–04; 1895	53; 60	3.6	2.7	0.9
42. H-P, 1900–04 to 1915–24	17.5	4.3		
43. H-P/L, 1935 to 1955	20		1.9	1.15
U. of South Africa, GNP				
44. A-R, 1918–20; 1919/20	34.5; 32	4.7	1.9	2.7
45. H-P, 1944–48 to 1954–58	10	5.0		
46. H-P/L, 1945/46 to 1951/52	6		1.5	3.5

[a] The first entry is for product and the second for labor force.

A-E: Average for the early period. The dates shown are those of the initial segment of the period, either a year or an average for a number of years. Years joined by + indicate that values for the single years shown were averaged; years joined by − indicate that the values for all years from the first through the last shown were averaged. When two sets of dates are given, the first is for product and the second for labor force.

A-R: Average for the recent period. The dates are as described above.

H-P: The one period among several distinguished (usually about 20 years in duration except for the post-World War II span) with the highest rate of growth in total product. Where the post-World War II span also shows a peak, it is marked b. and the earlier period is marked a. The dates are those of the periods covered for total product.

H-P/L: The one period among several distinguished with the highest rate of growth in product per worker. Lines a. and b. are described above. The dates are those of the periods covered for labor force.

Source: The measures are taken from Simon Kuznets, "Quantitative Aspects of the Economic Growth of Nations, VI. Long-Term Trends in Capital Formation Proportions," *Economic Development and Cultural Change*, vol. IX, no. 4, July 1961, Table 5, p. 11; Table 7, p. 22; Table 9, p. 29; and Table 11, p. 34. Hereafter this paper will be cited as Simon Kuznets, Paper VI, *EDCC*, July 1961; and other papers in the series, of which seven have been published, will be similarly cited.

Table VIII.4
Selected Countries: Rates of Growth per Year in Population and Gross National Product and Private Consumption Expenditures, Total and per Capita, Countries Grouped by per Capita Product, 1950–58
(percent; product and expenditure rates based on totals in constant prices)

Country	Population (1)	Gross national product Total (2)	Gross national product Per capita (3)	Private consumption expenditures Total (4)	Private consumption expenditures Per capita (5)
Group I					
1. Belgium	0.59	2.90	2.30	1.72	1.12
2. Canada	2.76	3.78	0.99	3.94	1.15
3. New Zealand	2.26	1.21	−1.03	2.48	0.22
4. Sweden	0.70	3.03	2.31	2.58	1.87
5. United Kingdom (GDP)	0.31	2.24	1.92	2.00	1.68
6. United States	1.74	2.86	1.10	2.87	1.11
Group II					
7. Denmark	0.70	2.31	1.60	1.76	1.05
8. Finland (GDP)	1.10	3.97	2.84	3.43	2.30
9. France	0.83	4.30	3.44	4.25	3.39
10. West Germany	1.08	7.95	6.80	7.68	6.53
11. Netherlands	1.27	4.46	3.15	3.32	2.02
12. Norway	0.97	3.20	2.21	2.57	1.58
13. Venezuela (1949–58)	3.04	8.23	5.04	—	—
Group III					
14. Argentina	2.07	1.77	−0.29	2.17	0.10
15. Austria	0.15	6.25	6.09	4.95	4.79
16. Chile	2.32	3.49	1.14	3.87	1.51
17. Ireland	−0.50	0.83	1.34	0.20	0.70
18. Israel	5.95	12.84	6.50	11.22	4.97
19. Puerto Rico	0.63	3.96	3.31	3.52	2.87
Group IV					
20. Brazil	2.38	4.44	2.01	5.25	2.80
21. Colombia (1950–57)	2.23	3.07	0.82	1.49	−0.72
22. Costa Rica	3.76	5.94	2.10	5.25	1.44
23. Greece	0.97	6.71	5.68	6.33	5.31
24. Italy	0.56	5.58	4.99	4.29	3.71
25. Turkey (GDP)	2.82	6.94	4.01	—	—
26. Union of South Africa (1951–58)	1.82	4.60	2.73	4.46	2.59
Group V					
27. Dominican Rep.	3.46	6.49	2.93	5.84	2.30
28. Jamaica	1.85	10.68	8.67	7.41	5.46
29. Japan	1.28	7.96	6.60	7.83	6.47
30. Guatemala	2.97	4.97	1.94	4.89	1.86
31. Portugal	0.83	3.51	2.66	3.38	2.53
Group VI					
32. Ceylon (1951–58)	2.54	2.54	0	1.82	−0.70
33. Taiwan	3.26	8.79	5.36	—	—
34. Ecuador	2.99	4.70	1.66	5.21	2.16
35. Ghana	1.55	2.51	0.95	2.60	1.03
36. Honduras	2.71	4.81	2.04	4.74	1.98
37. Peru (1950–57)	2.20	3.53	1.30	4.95	2.69
38. Philippines	2.37	5.74	3.29	5.62	3.17
39. Rhodesia and Nyasaland (GDP)	2.65	7.60	4.82	7.79	5.01
Group VII					
40. Belgian Congo (GDP)	2.35	4.41	2.01	6.81	4.36
41. Burma (GDP)	1.15	6.27	5.06	4.85	3.66
42. Korea, South (1949–58)	1.20	2.50	1.28	1.84	0.63
43. Morocco (1951–58)	1.82	2.99	1.15	2.01	0.19
44. Thailand	1.89	0.67	−1.20	—	—

Note: The dash (—) indicates that data are not available.

same countries; and this significantly higher level for post-World War II rates than for prewar long-term rates is typical of many European countries. The high and quickening rate of growth of the USSR in the post-World War II years is thus shared by a number of other countries in which World War II formed, as it were, a watershed.

When we deal with product *per worker,* quite different results emerge. In the USSR the rate of growth in number of workers, essentially the full-time equivalents of the labor force, was far higher than the rate of growth of population (Table VIII.2, lines 1 and 2). In 1928–40 the total number of active workers grew 3.7 percent per year, whereas population grew only 1.2 percent; and in 1940–50 the rate of growth of workers was also higher than that of population. Only during 1950–58 did the growth of workers fall behind that of population. Implicit in this difference was, of course, a rise in the proportion of workers to population — almost a third from 1928 to 1940 and almost a half from 1928 to 1950. Professor Eason's estimates (Chap. II of this volume) indicate that the rise was due largely to the increasing engagement of women (and perhaps also of some men in agriculture) in full-time occupation.

No such accelerated use of labor relative to population appears to have occurred in other countries. Two conclusions follow. First, the rapid rise in the proportion of labor employed to total population provides a partial explanation of the high rate of growth of national product *per capita* in the USSR — with respect to which, for 1928–40 plus 1950–58, it is approximated only by Japan. Second, with respect to rate of growth of product *per worker,* the record of the USSR is far from distinguished: even for 1928–40 plus 1950–58, the average rates of 2.8 percent for gross and 2.5 percent for net (Table VIII.2, column 3, lines 5 and 8) were approximated or exceeded for an equally long or longer period in several countries.

This second finding deserves further examination. The percentage rates of growth in gross product per worker are 2.7 for Italy; 2.5 for Denmark; 3.6 for Sweden; 2.7 for the United States; 2.3 for Australia; 4.2 for Japan; and 2.7 for the Union of South Africa (Table VIII.3, column 4, lines 10, 16, 24, 32a, 36, 40a, and 44). They may be on the high side *if* the growth of full-time equivalent workers was significantly greater than that of the number in the labor force as measured; and this question requires more detailed study than is possible here. But if we accept the figures as they stand, and take into account the high probability that in all these countries and periods the rate of growth of *capital* input was significantly lower than in the USSR during 1928–40 and 1950–58, it follows that for most of the countries in the list the rate of growth in product *per unit of input* was significantly higher than that in the USSR — especially in Sweden and Japan; and probably also in Italy, the United States, and the Union of

South Africa. This relatively modest showing by the USSR is particularly evident in the period 1928–40, when the rate of growth in product per worker was quite low; and it was not much improved by the decade 1940–50.

In sum, judged by its "best" periods, the USSR stands out with a high rate of growth of total and per capita product — being matched with respect to the former by Japan, the United States, Australia, and the Union of South Africa in some periods, and with respect to the latter by Japan. But the high rate of growth in per capita product in the USSR was due in part to a rapid rise in the proportion of population engaged in work, particularly of females; and with respect to product per worker, the rate of growth in the USSR is matched or exceeded in a number of other countries. The discrepancy between the rates of growth of total, per capita, and per worker product is particularly wide for the USSR during 1928–40.[3]

3. Industrial Structure (Tables VIII.5 to VIII.10)

The industrial classification available for the USSR is not quite the same as that for other countries (Table VIII.5). The A sector in the USSR covers agriculture but excludes fishing and forestry, which are included in that sector in other countries. The M sector for the USSR is an extended one, which includes not only mining, manufacturing, and construction (the M sector for other countries) but also fishing and forestry (rather minor additions), transport, and communication (designated M^+). Correspondingly, the scope of the S sector is narrower for the USSR than for other countries; and we designate it S^-, to distinguish it from S with broader coverage. The product distribution is based on totals in constant prices for the USSR and on totals in current prices for other countries; and there may well be differences in the scope of the labor force totals used. Finally, the comparative findings must be qualified by the errors of estimation: the industrial distributions of both product and workers for the USSR are fairly rough approximations, and those in

[3] In a written comment, Rush Greenslade made the interesting suggestion that a comparison of rates of growth in national product, total and per capita, for the period 1937 (1938)–58 would help to take account of what happened during the war interim and minimize the possibly distorting effect of high rates of growth in the years of recovery from the war. Such a comparison indicates that the over-all rate of growth in the net national product of the USSR (in 1937 adjusted prices) of about 4 percent per year is matched by those in the United States and Canada, but West Germany and Japan, with high rates for 1950–58, in Table VIII.4, show annual rates of growth of 3.4 and about 2.5 percent, respectively. The difficulty with this comparison, however, is that the late 1930's were years of booming war production in both Germany and Japan, and do not provide a proper base from which to measure growth. More important, differences in relative devastation during the war would affect the average for the 1937–58 period, and it is not clear that these effects directly reflect differences in growth performance.

Table VIII.5
USSR: Various Estimates of Shares of Major Sectors
in Net National Product, 1928–58
(percent)

Item	1928 (1)	1937 (2)	1940 (3)	1948 (4)	1950 (5)	1953 (6)	1955 (7)	1958 (8)
Share of A sector (percent)								
1. J.C. Print, 1955, 1937 adjusted prices	—	36	—	28	—	23	—	—
2. J.C. Print, 1957, current prices	42	—	—	—	—	—	28	—
3. J.C. Print, 1959, current adjusted prices	—	—	—	—	—	—	27.1	—
4. B-H-H, RM-2544, current adjusted prices	41.0	30.7	—	—	—	—	—	—
5. Bergson approximation, 1937 ruble factor cost	49.2	30.7	28.9	—	24.1	—	21.0	22.1
6. Growth ratio between dates marked *, NNP, 1937 ruble factor cost	*	1.64	*	1.20	*	1.70		*
7. Growth ratio, agricultural output	*	1.05	*	1.07	*	1.45		*
8. Derived share, A sector	45.1		28.9		25.8			22.0
Share of M+ sector (percent)								
9. J.C. Print, 1955	—	41	—	44	—	56	—	—
10. J.C. Print, 1957	35	—	—	—	—	—	49	—
11. J.C. Print, 1959	—	—	—	—	—	—	41.6	—
12. B-H-H, RM-2544	36.5	45.2	—	—	—	—	—	—
13. Bergson approximation	27.9	45.2	44.8	—	49.1	—	55.3	58.0
14. Growth ratio, industrial output	*	2.63	*	1.40	*	2.02		*
15. Derived share, M+ sector	2.79		44.8		52.3			62.1
Share of S− sector (percent)								
16. J.C. Print, 1955	—	22	—	28	—	21	—	—
17. J.C. Print, 1957	23	—	—	—	—	—	23	—
18. J.C. Print, 1959	—	—	—	—	—	—	31.3	—
19. B-H-H, RM-2544	22.5	24.1	—	—	—	—	—	—
20. Bergson approximation	22.9	24.1	26.3	—	26.8	—	23.7	19.9
21. Derived share, S− sector	27.0		26.3		21.9			15.9

Note: The dash (—) indicates that data are not available.

Table VIII.6

USSR: Shares of Major Sectors in Net National Product and Labor Force, Product per Worker by Sectors, and Total Sectoral Inequality in Product per Worker, 1928–58 (product estimates based on totals in constant prices)

Item	1928 (1)	1940 (2)	1950 (3)	1958 or 1959 (4)
Share in NNP, 1937 factor cost (percent)				
1. A sector	49.2	28.9	24.1	22.1
2. M+ sector	27.9	44.8	49.1	58.0
3. S− sector	22.9	26.3	26.8	19.9
Share in labor force (percent)				
4. Agriculture, Eason	82.0	59.5	55.7	48.4
5. Agriculture, Bergson, adjusted	70.9	50.9	45.8	39.8
6. Other (100 − line 5)	29.1	49.1	54.2	60.2
of which:				
7. M+ sector				
Assumption (a)	17.6	29.4	34.5	38.3
Assumption (b)	20.1	32.1	35.2	38.8
8. S− sector				
Assumption (a)	11.5	19.7	19.7	21.9
Assumption (b)	9.0	17.0	19.0	21.4
Relative product per worker				
9. A sector (line 1/line 5)	0.69	0.57	0.53	0.56
10. M+ sector				
a. (line 2/line 7a)	1.59	1.52	1.42	1.51
b. (line 2/line 7b)	1.39	1.40	1.39	1.49
11. S− sector				
a. (line 3/line 8a)	1.99	1.34	1.36	0.91
b. (line 3/line 8b)	2.54	1.55	1.41	0.93
Intersectoral ratios, product per worker				
12. M+/A				
a. M+$_a$/A (line 10a/line 9)	2.30	2.67	2.68	2.70
b. M+$_b$/A (line 10b/line 9)	2.01	2.46	2.62	2.66
13. A/(M+ + S−)				
(line 9/lines 2 + 3 ÷ line 6)	0.39	0.39	0.38	0.43
14. M+/S−				
a. M+$_a$/S−$_a$ (line 10a/line 11a)	0.80	1.13	1.04	1.66
b. M+$_b$/S−$_b$ (line 10b/line 11b)	0.55	0.90	0.99	1.60
15. S−/(A + M+)				
a. S−$_a$/(A + M+$_a$) (line 11a/lines 1 + 2 ÷ lines 5 + 7a)	2.29	1.46	1.49	0.88
b. S−$_b$/(A + M+$_b$) (line 11b/lines 1 + 2 ÷ lines 5 + 7b)	2.99	1.74	1.57	0.91
16. Total inequality among sectors				
a.	43.4	44.0	43.4	39.4
b.	43.4	44.0	43.4	38.4

Table VIII.7
Selected Countries: Rapidity of Movement Away from Agriculture
in the Distribution of National Product and Labor Force

| Country | Initial values | | Duration of period (in years) over which the share declined proportionately as much as in USSR in: | |
	Date (1)	Share of A sector (percent) (2)	1928–40 (3)	1928–58 (4)
	Share in national product			
1. France	1872	43	49	70+
2. Denmark	1870–79	45	35 to 40	45 to 50
3. Sweden	1869–71	43	40	50 to 60
4. Italy	1876–80	56	45 to 50	60
5. Canada	1870	45	40	50 to 60
6. Japan				
a.	1878–82	64	30 to 35	40 to 45
b.	1908–12	42	15 to 20	25 to 30
	Share in labor force			
7. Denmark	1870–79	51	45 to 50	60 to 70
8. Norway	1875	49	35 to 45	65+
9. Sweden	1870	63	40	50
10. Italy	1871	52	65+	not known
11. Canada	1881	52	40	60
12. United States	1840	69	40	60+
13. Japan				
a.	1878–82	82	35	55 to 60
b.	1898–1902	70	30	40+

Note: The share of the A sector in NNP in the USSR was 49 percent in 1928, and dropped 40 percent by 1940 and 55 percent by 1958; its share in labor force was 71 percent in 1928, and dropped about 28 and 44 percent, respectively (see Table VIII.6, lines 1 and 5).

other countries are not free of error. Judgment must, therefore, be exercised in deciding which of our findings are significant and warrant further analysis.

As in all other countries, economic growth in the USSR meant a decline in the shares of national product originating in, and labor force attached to, the A sector. But the rapidity of this shift was far greater in the USSR than in the other developed countries. As Eason points out in Chapter II, the shift of labor force out of agriculture of the magnitude that occurred in the USSR in the twelve years from 1928 to 1940 took from thirty to fifty years in other countries (Tables VIII.6 and VIII.7). And the same was true of the decline in the share of the A sector in

Table VIII.8

Selected Countries: Movements of the Shares of the A, M (or M+),
and S (or S−) Sectors in Product and in Labor Force

Item	A sector (1)	M (or M+) sector (2)	S (or S−) sector (3)
Share in national product (percent)			
USSR, 1928 to 1958			
1. Initial share	49	28 (M+)	23 (S−)
2. Change in share	−27	30	−3
France, 1835 to 1949			
3. Initial share	51	25	25
4. Change in share	−28	21	6
Germany, 1860–69 to 1905–14			
5. Initial share	32	24	44
6. Change in share	−14	15	−1
Norway, 1865 to 1939			
7. Initial share	34	21	45
8. Change in share	−23	13	10
Sweden, 1869–71 to 1949–51			
9. Initial share	43	20 (M+)	37 (S−)
10. Change in share	−30	39	−9
Italy, 1876–80 to 1950–54			
11. Initial share	56	20	25
12. Change in share	−30	19	10
Canada, 1870 to 1950–53			
13. Initial share	45	24	32
14. Change in share	−31	15	15
United States, 1869–79 to 1947–54			
15. Initial share	21	33 (M+)	46 (S−)
16. Change in share	−14	13	1
Japan, 1878–82 to 1938–42			
17. Initial share	64	10	26
18. Change in share	−47	27	20
Share in labor force (percent)			
USSR, 1928 to 1958			
19. Initial share	71	18 (M+)	11 (S−)
20. Change in share	−31	21	10
England and Wales, 1841 to 1921			
21. Initial share	23	48 (M+)	29 (S−)
22. Change in share	−16	10	6
France, 1866 to 1946			
23. Initial share	43	46 (M+)	11 (S−)
24. Change in share	−22	12	11
Germany, 1882 to 1933			
25. Initial share	34	44	22
26. Change in share	−17	3	14

Table VIII.8 (Contd.)

Item	A sector (1)	M (or M+) sector (2)	S (or S−) sector (3)
Netherlands, 1899 to 1938			
27. Initial share	29	36	35
28. Change in share	−11	0	11
Norway, 1865 to 1950			
29. Initial share	60	19 (M+)	21 (S−)
30. Change in share	−34	28	6
Sweden, 1870 to 1940			
31. Initial share	63	10	27
32. Change in share	−36	27	9
Finland, 1880 to 1940			
33. Initial share	79	11 (M+)	10 (S−)
34. Change in share	−32	22	10
Italy, 1871 to 1936			
35. Initial share	52	36	12
36. Change in share	−12	1	11
Canada, 1871 to 1950–53			
37. Initial share	50	13	37
38. Change in share	−29	22	7
United States, 1870 to 1950			
39. Initial share	50	29 (M+)	21 (S−)
40. Change in share	−38	14	24
Puerto Rico, 1920 to 1948			
41. Initial share	60	17	23
42. Change in share	−21	7	14
Japan, 1878–82 to 1938–42			
43. Initial share	82	6	12
44. Change in share	−37	18	19

national product. This movement away from agriculture in the USSR continued but at a much slower rate after 1940; and for the full thirty-year period, 1928–58, the contrast between the USSR and other countries is less marked. But still a comparable shift took from fifty to sixty years in most other countries; and, interestingly enough, only Japan (on the basis of national product) seems to approximate the speed of industrialization of the USSR (see Table VIII.7, column 4).

The decline in the share of the A sector in national product was compensated for largely by the rise in the share of the M+ sector, not only in the USSR but also in Sweden, Germany, and the United States; in other countries, the share of the S sector in national product also gained somewhat (Table VIII.8). By contrast, the decline in the share of the A

Table VIII.9
Groups of and Selected Countries: Shares of Major Sectors in Product and Labor Force, Product per Worker, and Sectoral Inequality in Product per Worker, Post-World War II Years (product estimates based on totals in current prices except for the USSR)

A. Groups of countries classified by per capita product

	A sector (1)	M+ sector (2)	S— sector (3)
Share in product (percent)			
1. Groups I and II (9 to 13)	15.2	49.5	35.3
2. Groups III and IV (13 to 14)	24.6	34.3	41.1
3. Groups V and VI (12 to 19)	39.0	27.4	33.5
4. Groups VI and VII (18 to 24)	48.6	19.6	32.4
Share in labor force (percent)			
5. Groups I and II (13)	18.9	45.7	35.4
6. Groups III and IV (10)	39.5	30.7	29.8
7. Groups V and VI (11)	53.6	23.0	23.4
8. Groups VI and VII (11)	59.3	18.8	21.9
P/L (relative product per worker)			
9. Groups I and II	0.80	1.08	1.00
10. Groups III and IV	0.62	1.12	1.38
11. Groups V and VI	0.73	1.19	1.43
12. Groups VI and VII	0.82	1.04	1.48

B. Ratios of relative product per worker and measure of inequality

	A: (M + S) (1)	(M+): A (2)	(M+): S— (3)	(S—): A + (M+) (4)	Inequality (5)
13. Groups I and II	0.76	1.35	1.08	1.00	7.6
14. Groups III and IV	0.50	1.81	0.81	1.64	29.8
15. Groups V and VI	0.56	1.63	0.83	1.64	29.1
16. Groups VI and VII	0.64	1.27	0.70	1.70	22.0
17. USSR	0.40	2.72	1.30	1.16	39.4

C. Selected countries

	A sector (1)	M+ sector (2)	S— sector (3)	Inequality (4)
USSR, average, 1950 and 1958				
18. Share in product (P)	23.1	53.5	23.4	
19. Share in labor force (L)	42.8	36.4	20.8	
20. P/L	0.54	1.47	1.13	39.4
United States (I)				
21. P	7.2	46.2	46.6	
22. L	10.9	43.8	45.3	
23. P/L	0.66	1.05	1.03	7.4

Table VIII.9 (Contd.)

	A sector (1)	M+ sector (2)	S− sector (3)	Inequality (4)
Sweden (I)				
24. P	12.9	58.7	28.4	
25. L	18.0	50.2	31.8	
26. P/L	0.72	1.17	0.89	17.0
West Germany (II)				
27. P	11.7	61.7	26.6	
28. L	12.6	54.9	32.5	
29. P/L	0.93	1.12	0.82	13.6
Chile (III)				
30. P	16.7	36.8	46.5	
31. L	29.5	34.7	35.8	
32. P/L	0.57	1.06	1.30	25.6
Italy (IV)				
33. P	26.4	48.0	25.6	
34. L	33.9	40.2	25.9	
35. P/L	0.78	1.19	0.99	15.6
Japan (V)				
36. P	24.4	39.2	36.4	
37. L	28.7	37.8	33.5	
38. P/L	0.85	1.04	1.09	8.6
Egypt (VI)				
39. P	34.7	16.9	48.4	
40. L	52.4	16.5	31.1	
41. P/L	0.66	1.02	1.56	35.4
India (VII)				
42. P	49.9	17.0 (M)	33.1 (S)	
43. L	70.6	10.7 (M)	18.7 (S)	
44. P/L	0.71	1.59	1.77	41.4

sector in labor force in all the countries was offset by rises in the shares of both the M (or M^+) and the S (S^-) sectors. Thus, in the USSR, as in many other countries, the share of the S sector in the labor force rose while its share in national product remained constant or declined. With respect to the direction and magnitude, if not the speed, of changes in shares of major sectors in national product and labor force, the movements in the USSR were similar to those in many other developed countries.

Again, as in many other countries, the early years in the USSR were characterized by product per worker in the A sector that was much below the country-wide and by that of the S sector that was much above the country-wide. But the relative product per worker in the M^+ sector in the USSR also was much above the country-wide — between 1.4 and 1.6 — whereas it was fairly close to 1 in most other countries except for

Table VIII.10
USSR: Illustrative Calculation of the Effect of the Allowance for Yield
of Capital Stock on Sectoral Product per Worker, 1958–59

Item	A sector (1)	M+ sector (2)	S− sector (3)
1. Share in net national product, 1937 factor cost, 1958 (percent)	22.1	58.0	19.9
2. Share in labor force, 1959 (percent)	39.8	38.3	21.9
3. Relative product per worker (line 1/line 2)	0.56	1.51	0.91
Share in capital stock, at 1955 replacement values, end of 1959			
4. Total capital (percent)	14.1	43.0	42.9
5. Nonresidential capital (percent)	20.7	63.0	16.3
6. Relative capital-output ratio (line 5/line 1)	0.94	1.09	0.82
7. Absolute capital-output ratio, assuming 1.5 country-wide (line 6 × 1.5)	1.41	1.63	1.23
8. Yield of capital as percent of NNP:			
a. assuming 10 percent yield (line 7 × 0.1 × line 1)	3.1	9.5	2.4
b. assuming 20 percent yield (line 7 × 0.2 × line 1)	6.2	18.9	4.9
9. Share in NNP, *excluding* yield of capital (percent)			
a. assuming 10 percent yield	22.4	57.1	20.6
b. assuming 20 percent yield	22.7	55.9	21.4
10. Relative product per worker, allowing for capital yield			
a. line 9a/line 2	0.56	1.49	0.94
b. line 9b/line 2	0.57	1.46	0.98

some underdeveloped. The movements in relative product per worker in the USSR were similar to those in other countries, but somewhat exaggerated. The relative product per worker in the M+ sector remained high, and in relation to those in other sectors rose substantially. The relative product per worker in the S− sector declined, as it did in other countries; but far more rapidly and abruptly in the USSR. The relative product per worker in the A sector dropped from 1928 to 1950, and rose slightly thereafter (all of the foregoing from Table VIII.6, lines 9–15).[4]

If we compare the industrial structure of product per worker in the USSR in 1950–58 with those for other countries, marked similarities and

[4] The discussion is based on the allocation of net national product given in lines 5, 13, and 20 of Table VIII.5. The alternative, in lines 8, 15, and 21 would have shown similar movements, with an even more pronounced decline in relative product per worker in the S− sector.

significant differences emerge (Table VIII.9). Relative product per worker in the A sector is well below the country-wide in all the countries, but in the USSR it is 0.54, whereas the averages for groups of countries classified by per capita income range from 0.62 to 0.82. The relative product per worker in the M+ sector is generally above 1; but it is as high as 1.5 in the USSR and it is that high only in the underdeveloped countries, for example, India. The relative per worker product in the S− sector, about 1.1 for the USSR, is not too different from that in the developed Western countries. The distinctive features for the USSR are the rather low product per worker in the A sector and rather high product per worker in the M+ sector. Because of this contrast, and the large weights of the A and M+ sectors in the labor force, the measure of total inequality in the sectoral products per worker is unusually high for the USSR — as high as for quite underdeveloped countries.

The distinctive contrast in the USSR between the rather low product per worker in the A sector and the high product per worker in the M+ sector is puzzling, and analysis of the relative levels of reproducible capital per worker does not explain it. Since total product, the numerator of the product per worker ratio, includes profits and other returns on assets, I thought that by eliminating the capital yield the intersectoral differences in product per worker might be reduced (Table VIII.10). But the effect of such an allowance is minor (compare lines 3 and 10). The contrast between per worker product in the A and M+ sectors remains to be explained; as does the rapid decline in product per worker in the S− sector. Of course, if the yield of the natural resources, so abundant in agriculture, were also eliminated, the contrast would be even greater.

One related finding is of interest. According to Table VIII.2, the rate of growth in net national product per worker from 1928 to 1940 was only 0.5 percent per year. Yet this was the period that saw the marked shift of workers from the A sector to the M+ and S− sectors. The intersectoral shifts in the distribution of workers, without any rise in product per worker *within* each sector, should have raised the country-wide product per worker. Indeed, the indicated intersectoral shifts were sufficient to explain an even greater rise than that shown from 1928 to 1940 in country-wide product per worker. The implication is that product per worker within some sectors actually declined over the period; and the approximate estimates available suggest that product per worker in the S− sector declined substantially, product per worker in agriculture declined slightly, and product per worker in the M+ sector rose moderately. While this analysis needs further checking, the conclusion is supported by the evidence examined so far. It also seems clear that the rise in product per worker during the post-World War II years, that is, 1950–58, while bolstered by further shifts of the labor force out of agriculture, was largely due to substantial rises in product per worker within the A and M+ sectors.

4. Capital Formation Proportions (Tables VIII.11 to VIII.15)

Because national product estimates for the USSR are available only for single years, the proportions of capital formation to national product are limited to these years. Nevertheless, the levels and movements of these proportions can be clearly discerned.

The proportion of capital formation to national product rose materially and rapidly from 1928 to 1940; and in the post-World War II years it was significantly higher than in 1928 and 1940 (Table VIII.11, line 8c). It is difficult, therefore, to strike a meaningful average for the period 1928–58. If we assign to the USSR gross capital formation proportion a range from 20 to 28, we can compare it with long-term gross capital formation proportions in other countries. In Germany, Norway, the United States, Canada,

Table VIII.11

USSR: Various Estimates of Capital Formation Proportions, 1928–55
(percent)

Item	1928 (1)	1937 (2)	1940 (3)	1944 (4)	1948 (5)	1950 (6)	1953 (7)	1955 (8)
1. Kaplan, 1953, current prices adjusted								
a. Fixed gross	—	15.9	13.3	9.2	17.2	—	—	—
b. Fixed net	—	12.8	10.1	6.0	14.5 to 14.9	—	—	—
2. J.C. Print, 1955, gross, adjusted 1937 prices	—	21	—	—	23	—	26	—
3. J.C. Print, 1957, gross, current prices adjusted	23.2	22.9	16.6	13.5	25.6	23.3	—	—
4. J.C. Print, 1959, gross, current prices adjusted	—	—	—	—	—	—	—	25.2
5. B-H-H, RM-2544 gross, current prices adjusted	24.6	25.2	19.0	14.1	27.8	—	—	—
6. Bergson, current prices, gross								
a. Fixed	18.6	12.5	12.4	8.7	—	17.2	—	20.2
b. Other	4.1	8.6	3.1	3.3	—	5.6	—	3.8
c. Total	22.7	21.2	15.5	11.9	—	22.8	—	24.0
7. Bergson, 1937 prevailing prices, gross								
a. Fixed	6.0	12.5	11.9	8.0	—	16.2	—	18.4
b. Other	4.3	8.6	3.5	3.8	—	5.9	—	3.9
c. Total	10.3	21.2	15.3	11.8	—	22.1	—	22.3
8. Bergson, 1937 factor cost, gross								
a. Fixed	8.3 (7.8)	16.5	15.2	9.4	—	20.9	—	24.4 (27.4)
b. Other	4.2 (4.0)	9.4	3.9	3.8	—	6.0	—	3.7 (6.9)
c. Total	12.5 (11.8)	25.9	19.1	13.1	—	26.9	—	28.1 (34.3)

Note: The dash (—) indicates that data are not available.

Table VIII.12
USSR: Incremental Domestic Capital-Output Ratios, Two Periods, 1928–58
(based on volumes in 1937 factor cost)

Item	Gross		Net	
	1928–39 or 1928–40 (1)	1950–57 or 1950–58 (2)	1928–39 or 1928–40 (3)	1950–57 or 1950–58 (4)
Share in total capital formation (percent)				
1. Construction (including installations)	59.8	48.1	58.6	46.9
2. Equipment	28.8	39.0	25.4	32.1
3. Total fixed capital (line 1 + line 2)	88.6	87.1	84.0	79.0
4. Inventories	14.6	12.0	20.5	19.6
5. Livestock	−3.2	0.9	−4.5	1.5
Depreciation and other capital consumption as percent of gross domestic capital formation				
6. Construction (including installations)	30	40		
7. Equipment	37	50		
8. Total capital formation	29	39		
Ratio of capital formation to increase in national product				
9. Fixed capital-output ratio	3.13	3.22	2.32	2.05
10. Inventories-output ratio	0.52	0.44	0.57	0.51
11. Total capital-output ratio	3.53	3.69	2.76	2.60

Argentina, and the Union of South Africa for fairly long periods capital formation proportions were 20 percent or more (Table VIII.13, column 2, lines 4, 10, 13, 14, 16, 21, and 22). If we limit comparison to fixed capital formation in post-World War II years, when the capital formation proportions for the USSR were so high, we again find countries with equally high levels. For gross *fixed* capital formation proportions, the level for the USSR of 24 percent is approached by Japan, Germany, the Netherlands, and Canada; and exceeded by Norway (Table VIII.14, column 1).

The distinctive characteristic of the over-all capital formation proportion for the USSR is not its high level, but the rapidity with which this level was attained. With few exceptions (among them the United States), the long-term trends in capital formation proportions in most countries were upward — although this rise may not have begun until several decades after the country had entered the process of industrialization and may have ceased while the growth of the country was still proceeding vigorously. But with the single exception of Canada for 1896–1900 and 1901–10 among the twelve countries for which we have data, in none did

Table VIII.13
Selected Countries: Capital Formation Proportions and Incremental Capital-Output Ratios, Long Periods

Item	Duration of period (years) (1)	Capital formation proportions (percent)		Incremental capital-output ratios (domestic)	
		GDCF/GDP (2)	NDCF/NDP (3)	Gross (4)	Net (5)
United Kingdom					
1. A-E, 1855	60; 53.5	9.0	7.3	4.1	3.3
2. A-R, 1895	45; 30	10.6	6.0	6.3	3.6
Germany					
3. A-E, 1851	63; 59	19.8	12.9	7.4	4.8
4. A-R, 1891	41; 35.5	20.3	12.7	6.1	3.8
Italy					
5. A-E, 1861	55; 54	12.5	6.5	9.6	5.3
6. A-R, 1896	50; 47.5	18.0	10.1	5.7	3.4
Denmark					
7. A-E, 1870	45; 44	12.6	7.7	3.9	2.4
8. A-R, 1895	46; 43.5	14.7	9.4	4.4	2.8
Norway					
9. A-E, 1865	50; 49.5	13.2	8.2	6.3	4.0
10. A-R, 1895	52; 51.5	20.8	14.4	7.3	5.1
Sweden					
11. A-E, 1861	55; 54.5	12.2	7.7	4.1	2.6
12. A-R, 1901	57; 55.5	18.2	11.8	5.5	3.6
United States					
13. A-E, 1869	45; 40	21.9	13.1	5.1	3.1
14. A-R, 1894	50; 49	20.1	8.4	6.5	2.7
Canada					
15. A-E, 1870	45; 45.5	19.7	10.8	5.4	3.0
16. A-R, 1896	50; 49	20.3	10.1	5.6	2.8
Australia					
17. A-E, 1861	54.5; 52	15.2	10.4	4.2	2.9
18. A-R, 1896	45.5; 44	19.4	14.1	6.9	5.0
Japan					
19. A-E, 1887	30; 29	10.9	6.0	2.9	1.6
20. A-R, 1902	46; 44	19.8	14.1	4.3	3.1
Argentina					
21. A-R, 1900	55; 53	26.9	14.0	7.6	4.2
U. of South Africa					
22. A-R, 1919	37; 34.5	22.9	17.8	4.9	3.8

Table VIII.14

Industrial Countries: Incremental Fixed Capital-Output Ratios and Rates of Increase per Year in Productivity, 1950–58

Countries	GFCF as percent of GDP (1)	Rate of growth per year, GDP (percent) (2)	Capital-output ratios Incremental gross capital-output ratio (1 ÷ 2) (3)	Capital consumption as percent of GFCF (4)	NFCF as percent of NDP (5)	Ratio, rate of growth of NDP to rate of growth of GDP (6)	Rate of growth per year, NDP (percent) (7)	Incremental net capital-output ratio (5 ÷ 7) (8)
1. USSR	24	7.6	3.2	45	15	0.92	6.8	2.0
2. Japan	21.8	7.9	2.8	33	15.7	1.01	7.3	2.2
3. West Germany	20.6	7.4	2.8	44	12.7	1.00	7.5	1.7
4. Italy	19.7	5.5	3.6	44	12.0	1.04	5.5	2.2
5. Netherlands	22.1	4.5	4.9	43	13.9	1.07	4.7	3.0
6. France	17.3	4.3	4.0	54	8.8	0.94	4.6	1.9
7. Canada	21.8	4.0	5.45	46	13.1	0.87	3.8	3.4
8. USA (1950–59)	16.5	3.3	5.0	52	8.6	0.93	2.9	3.0
9. Norway	29.4	3.0	9.8	34	21.6	0.91	2.8	7.7
10. Belgium	14.6	2.9	5.0	64	5.8	(1.0)a	2.6	2.2
11. Sweden	19.9	2.9	6.9	(40)a	13.0	0.91	2.9	4.5
12. Denmark	16.8	2.3	7.3	36	11.5	0.91	2.1	5.5
13. United Kingdom	14.4	2.2	6.5	57	6.8	0.98	2.2	3.1

Annual rates of growth in input and in productivity (percent)

Countries	Labor (1)	Net fixed capital (2)	Combined input L at 8 C at 2 (3)	L at 7 C at 3 (4)	NDP (5)	Productivity Using col. 3 (6)	Using col. 4 (7)
14. USSR	1.2	11.2	3.2	4.2	6.8	3.5	2.5
15. Japan	2.4	8	3.5	4.1	7.3	3.7	3.1
16. West Germany	2.1	7	3.1	3.6	7.5	4.3	3.8
17. Netherlands	1.2	4	1.8	2.0	4.7	2.8	2.6
18. France	0.6	3	1.1	1.3	4.6	3.5	3.3
19. Canada	2.2	7	3.2	3.6	3.8	0.6	0.2
20. USA	1.0	4	1.6	1.9	2.9	1.3	1.0
21. Norway	0.4	5	1.3	1.8	2.8	1.5	1.0
22. Belgium	0.3	3	0.8	1.1	2.6	1.8	1.5
23. United Kingdom	0.9	3	1.3	1.5	2.2	0.9	0.7

a Rough approximation.

Table VIII.15
USSR: Incremental Net Fixed Capital-Output Ratios
by Major Sectors, 1928–40 and 1950–58

Item	1928–40 (1)	1950–58 (2)
Share in net fixed capital formation (percent)		
1. A sector	19	16
2. M+ sector	56	51
3. S− sector	26	33
Share in additions to net national product (percent)		
4. A sector	−3 (+4)	19
5. M+ sector	71	71
6. S− sector	31 (25)	10
Relative capital-output ratio		
7. A sector (line 1/line 4)	∞ (4.8)	0.84
8. M+ sector (line 2/line 5)	0.79	0.72
9. S− sector (line 3/line 6)	0.81 (1.00)	3.30
Net fixed capital-output ratio		
10. A sector	∞ (13.2)	2.2
11. M+ sector	2.2	1.9
12. S− sector	2.2 (2.8)	8.6

the proportion double within a short span of a few years (as Table VIII.11, line 8, shows for the USSR proportions in 1928 and 1937).[5]

The shift in the distribution of gross (or net) capital formation between fixed and other capital in the USSR is similar to that in other countries; the proportion of "other" (largely inventories) in the total declines. In view of the weakness of the underlying estimates of changes in inventories in most countries, no firm inferences as to the timing and magnitude of the trend can be made. But it seems likely that the relative share of changes in inventories in total capital formation also declined at a more rapid rate in the USSR than in most other countries.

The incremental capital-output ratios in the USSR are about 3.5 to 3.7 on a gross basis, and about 2.6 to 2.8 on a net basis (Table VIII.12, line 11). While undoubtedly the ratios fluctuated from year to year or over short periods, the change from the first twelve years to the last eight is minor. The gross ratios rise slightly, with the ratio for fixed capital rising more than the ratio for inventories declines. Thus, there is no evidence of a major shift by which higher rates of growth of product were obtained from the same volume of capital or from the same capital formation proportion.

[5] For trends in capital formation proportions in a number of countries see Simon Kuznets, Paper VI, *EDCC*, July 1961, particularly pp. 9–13 and the appendix tables. The data for Canada appear on p. 102.

The net ratios drop slightly from 1928–40 to 1950–58 — not only for total capital but also for fixed capital and inventories. Yet the changes from 1928–40 to 1950–58 are so slight, particularly in the fixed capital-output ratio, that the safest inference is that they remained about the same in the two periods — with the slight decline in the inventory-output ratio more than compensated by the rise in the relative contribution of the other nonfixed capital item — livestock. (The nonfixed capital-output ratio, obtained by subtracting line 9 from line 11 in Table VIII.12, rises from 1928–40 to 1950–58: from 0.40 to 0.47 for gross and from 0.44 to 0.55 for net.)

How do these incremental capital-output ratios in the USSR compare with those in other countries for the post-World War II years? For this purpose, the ratios for fixed capital formation are perhaps most suitable. Of the countries classified by the United Nations as industrial, only Japan and West Germany have gross ratios lower than that for the USSR, but on a net basis the ratios for Italy, France, and Belgium are also lower (Table VIII.14, columns 3 and 8). If we consider the long-term incremental capital-output ratios, which are for total capital and should be compared with those in Table VIII.12, line 11, their magnitude is about the same in Denmark, Sweden, Australia, and Japan (Table VIII.13, lines 7, 11, 17, and 20). In short, the low level of the capital-output ratio in the USSR is not distinctive: it is matched, both in the long run and in the post-World War II years, by several other countries.

What is distinctive about the USSR is the combination of relatively low incremental capital-output ratios with rather high capital formation proportions. Thus, Denmark and Japan, which in the long run had incremental capital-output ratios as moderate as those of the USSR, had long-term capital formation proportions distinctly lower than those for the USSR; and the same was true of Australia and Sweden in the early periods. On the other hand, while the United States and Germany had fairly high capital formation proportions in the long run, their incremental capital-output ratios were significantly higher than those for the USSR. To put it differently, the distinctive feature of the USSR record is that so much capital formation was possible without an increase in the capital-output ratio to uneconomically high levels.

We observed above that the rate of growth in output per unit of resource-input may well have been as high in several long periods in other countries as it was in the USSR. This was also true of the post-World War II years. The estimates are crude, relating current capital formation to total accumulated capital stock; and they are limited to fixed capital, excluding other types of reproducible capital and all natural resources. If, however, we accept these measures and limit input to labor and fixed capital, the rates of growth per unit of input in post-World War II years are as high in Japan, West Germany, and France, as in the USSR (Table VIII.14, columns 6 and 7). And it may well be that if the sample of countries included other European countries and the Union of South Africa, there would be additional cases with equally high rates of growth per unit of input.

Table VIII.15 indicates that the stability in the USSR of the over-all net fixed capital-output ratio (in Table VIII.12, line 9, columns 3 and 4) was due to a combination of a sharp decline in the ratio for the A sector with a marked rise in the ratio for the S sector — that for the M sector showing but a minor change. If we treat the ratios for 1950–58 as more "normal," we can compare them with the sectoral ratios for other countries (given in Simon Kuznets, Paper VI, *EDCC*, July 1961, Table 15, pp. 46–47). Low or lower ratios for the A and M sectors can be found in other countries (for example, in the United States, for agriculture and mining and manufacturing and in the Union of South Africa, for manufacturing); but the capital-output ratios for the S sector in other countries would tend to be higher mainly because of the greater share in capital formation of residential housing.

5. CONSUMPTION EXPENDITURES (TABLES VIII.16 TO VIII.20)

The share of household consumption outlay plus communal services in the gross national product of the USSR declined from well over 80 percent in 1928 to 56 percent in 1950, and rose insignificantly from 1950 to 1955 (Table VIII.16, column 3). At 85 percent, the share was among the highest; at 56 percent it was among the lowest (see Table VIII.17, column 1). The decline in the share of aggregate consumption expenditures (including communal services) was compensated by an enormous rise in the shares of general administration and defense and of gross capital investment.

Long-term records for other countries of the distribution of domestic product among consumer expenditures, government consumption, and domestic capital formation are limited to eleven countries.[6] But from these and from the cross-section comparisons for recent years in Table VIII.17, we may infer that in most countries economic growth was accompanied by a long-term decline in the share of private consumption outlay in domestic product. In most countries, the shares of both gross domestic capital formation and government outlays on commodities and services in gross domestic product rose. But the decline in the share of private consumption expenditures was more moderate in most countries than in the USSR. The gross capital formation proportion rose usually from somewhat over 10 to somewhat over 20 percent; and that of government outlay on

[6] See Simon Kuznets, Paper VII, *EDCC*, January 1962, pp. 20–23 and appendix Table 4, pp. 72–75.

Table VIII.16

USSR: Household Consumption Outlays and Other Components of Gross National Product per Capita:
Shares in the Total, Rates of Growth, and Shares of Additions to Them in Additions to the Total, 1928–55
(based on totals in 1937 factor cost)

Item	Household consumption outlay (1)	Communal services (2)	(1) + (2) (3)	General administration and defense (4)	Gross capital investment (5)	Gross national product (6)
Share in GNP (percent)						
1. 1928	79.5	4.6	84.1	3.4	12.5	100.0
a. Adjustment extended	80.7	4.3	85.0	3.2	11.8	100.0
2. 1937	52.5	10.5	63.0	11.1	25.9	100.0
3. 1940	49.4	10.3	59.7	21.2	19.1	100.0
4. 1950	45.7	10.2	55.9	17.2	26.9	100.0
5. 1955	48.0	8.7	56.7	15.2	28.1	100.0
Rate of growth per year in component and total per capita (percent)						
6. 1928–37	− 0.2	14.7	1.2	19.1	13.3	4.5
a. Adjustment extended	− 1.0	14.7	0.4	19.1	13.3	3.8
7. 1940–50	2.1	2.8	2.2	0.9	6.5	2.9
8. 1950–55	6.8	2.5	6.1	3.2	6.7	5.8
9. Weighted means of above (24 years)	2.2	7.0	2.6	7.9	9.0	4.1
a. Adjustment extended	1.9	7.0	2.3	7.9	9.0	3.8
10. 1928–55 (27 years)	1.8	6.3	2.2	9.6	6.9	3.8
a. Adjustment extended	1.5	6.3	2.0	9.6	6.9	3.5
Share of additions to components per capita in additions to GNP per capita (percent)						
11. 1928–37	− 3.0	22.7	19.7	26.9	53.4	100.0
a. Adjustment extended	− 18.0	26.0	8.0	30.8	61.1	100.0
12. 1940–50	34.4	9.8	44.2	5.6	50.2	100.0
13. 1950–55	55.0	4.1	59.1	9.1	31.7	100.0
14. Apportionmt. of sum of above	31.6	11.3	43.0	13.3	43.8	100.0
a. Adjustment extended	29.0	11.8	40.8	13.8	45.5	100.0
15. Apportionmt. of additions, 1928–55	29.4	11.1	40.5	22.2	37.3	100.0
a. Adjustment extended	26.8	11.5	38.3	23.0	38.7	100.0

Note: All lines designated "a" are based on the estimates for 1928 with the factor cost price adjustment for 1928 extended within retail purchases by households.

Table VIII.17

Groups of and Selected Countries: Shares in Total Domestic Uses of Private Consumption Expenditures, Government Consumption, and Gross Domestic Capital Formation, Post-World War II Years

(percent based on totals in current prices except for the USSR)

Item	Share in total domestic uses (percent)		
	Private consumption expenditures (1)	Government consumption expenditures (2)	Gross domestic capital formation (3)
Groups of countries classified by per capita product			
1. Group I (8)	64.9	13.9	21.2
2. Group II (7)	61.8	13.6	24.5
3. Group III (3)	69.8	12.8	17.4
4. Group IV (4)	72.7	10.7	16.6
5. Group V (6)	69.3	12.2	18.5
6. Group VI (9)	73.0	11.1	15.9
7. Group VII (8)	71.5	11.7	16.8
Selected countries			
8. USSR, average, 1950 and 1955	56.3	16.2	27.5
9. United States (I)	64.0	18.0	17.9
10. Canada (I)	61.9	13.7	24.4
11. United Kingdom (I)	67.2	17.5	15.3
12. France (II)	66.8	14.4	18.8
13. West Germany (II)	60.6	14.9	24.6
14. Netherlands (II)	61.0	14.3	24.7
15. Austria (III)	64.7	13.5	21.8
16. Italy (IV)	67.5	11.8	20.7
17. Union of South Africa (IV)	65.3	11.0	23.7
18. Japan (V)	60.0	10.5	29.5
19. Rhodesia and Nyasaland (VI)	62.3	8.7	29.0
20. Congo (VII)	59.6	13.1	27.3
21. Nigeria (VII)	86.4	4.1	9.5

consumption from somewhat below 10 to somewhat above 15 percent. The total decline in the share of private consumption expenditures was from somewhat below 80 percent of gross domestic product to between 60 and 70 percent, a drop of 10 to 20 points which may have occurred over a period ranging from 3 or 4 to 8 decades — not a decline of some 30 points in a period of barely over two decades.

This drastic reallocation in the USSR of product by type of use can be described somewhat differently. Consumers received a portion of the gain in per capita product far below their average share in the past. As Table VIII.16 indicates, additions to consumer expenditures, inclusive of com-

Table VIII.18
USSR: Consumption per Capita and Structure of Consumption, 1928–55
(based on totals in adjusted 1937 market prices)

Item	1928 (1)	1937 (2)	1950 (3)	1955 (4)
Consumption per capita, in rubles				
1. Personal food consumption of households (including 0.5 of military subsistence)	1,026	912	985	1,330
2. Housing	63	68	87	92
3. Services (including utilities, transportation, repair, trade union dues, et cetera)	105	177	197	282
4. Other nonfoods (including 0.5 of military subsistence)	248	247	355	545
5. Total personal household consumption	1,440	1,404	1,623	2,248
6. Communal services	78	281	362	407
7. Total consumption	1,518	1,685	1,985	2,655
Indexes, 1928 = 100				
8. Personal food consumption of households (including 0.5 of military subsistence)	100	89	96	130
9. Housing	100	108	138	146
10. Services (including utilities, transportation, repair, trade union dues, et cetera)	100	169	188	269
11. Other nonfoods (including 0.5 of military subsistence)	100	100	143	220
12. Total personal household consumption	100	97	113	156
13. Communal services	100	360	464	522
14. Total consumption	100	111	131	175
Share in total consumption (percent)				
15. Personal food consumption of households (including 0.5 of military subsistence)	67.6	54.1	49.6	50.1
16. Housing	4.2	4.0	4.4	3.5
17. Services (including utilities, transportation, repair, trade union dues, et cetera)	6.9	10.5	9.9	10.6
18. Other nonfoods (including 0.5 of military subsistence)	16.3	14.7	17.9	20.5
19. Total personal household consumption	94.9	83.3	81.8	84.7
20. Communal services	5.1	16.7	18.2	15.3
21. Total consumption	100.0	100.0	100.0	100.0

munal services, were only about 40 percent of the total additions to per capita product (lines 14 and 14a), whereas their average share ranged from 56 to 85 percent. And the growth of consumption per capita, until 1950, was at much lower rates than the growth of gross national product per capita.

The contrast in this respect between 1928–50 and 1950–55 is striking. After 1950, the rate of growth of total consumer outlay (including com-

Table VIII.19
USSR: Total Food Consumption and Its Relation
to Agricultural Food Output, 1928–55
(indexes, 1928 = 100)

Item	1928	1937	1950	1955
1. Total personal food consumption of households, 1937 adjusted market prices	100	96	113	165
2. Line 1 plus 0.5 of military subsistence (at wholesale prices)	100	97	114	168
3. Line 2 including transport and distribution markup of consumption of farm income in kind	100	94	109	158
4. Line 3 excluding fabrication charges from state and cooperative retail food sales to households	100	93	107	151
5. Agricultural output for sale or home consumption, 1958 prices	100	113	125	154
6. Line 5 excluding net output of industrial crops	100	106	116	141
7. Ratio of net agricultural output, 1926–27 price weights to 1958 price weights	1.00	1.13	1.08	1.04
8. Ratio of net output of livestock (L) and food crops (F) weighted L = 7 and F = 3, to net output weighted L = 5 and F = 4	1.00	0.88	0.95	0.98
9. Line 6 multiplied by line 7	100	120	125	147
10. Line 6 multiplied by line 8	100	93	110	138

munal services) per capita slightly exceeded that of GNP per capita; and it was particularly high for the per capita volume of household consumption expenditures, excluding communal services (Table VIII.16, line 8). Food consumption per capita, which in 1950 was still slightly below the 1928 level, rose about a third from 1950 to 1955; and the rise in per capita outlay on nonfoods other than housing was even more marked (over 40 percent for services and over 50 percent for other nonfoods; see Table VIII.18, lines 10 and 11). It would be of interest to have a finer breakdown of this impressive rise not only among the categories of goods (for which some detail is given in Chapter VI of this volume) but also among groups in the population.

Large as the rise in per capita consumption was in the USSR since 1950, it was matched in several other countries during 1950–58: West Germany and Japan had rates of growth in private consumer expenditures per capita of 6.5 percent per year; and in several others the rate was 5 percent per year or more: Israel, Greece, Jamaica, and Rhodesia and Nyas-

Table VIII.20
Groups of and Selected Countries: Shares in Private Consumption Expenditures
of Food, Housing, and Other, Post-World War II Years
(percent; based on totals in current prices except for the USSR)

	Share in private consumption expenditures (percent)				
Item	Food (1)	Beverages (2)	(1) + (2) (3)	Housing (rent and water) (4)	Other (5)
Countries grouped by per capita product					
1. Group I (5–6)	27.2	5.7	32.9	10.7	56.4
2. Groups II and III (6–7)	35.6	6.0	41.6	6.4	52.0
3. Groups IV and V (3–5)	40.2	5.9	46.1	8.4	45.5
4. Groups VI and VII (6–8)	48.4	5.0	53.4	8.4	38.2
Selected countries					
5. USSR, average, 1950 and 1955			49.8	3.9	46.3
6. United States (I)	23.7	3.5	27.2	12.2	60.6
7. United Kingdom (I)	31.3	6.9	38.2	8.7	53.1
8. France (II)	34.4	7.0	41.4	4.2	54.4
9. Netherlands (II)	33.0	2.2	35.2	6.9	57.9
10. Austria (III)	36.5	8.4	44.9	4.6	50.5
11. Italy (IV)	46.6	6.3	52.9	2.7	44.4
12. Ceylon (VI)	54.1	2.9	57.0	2.3	40.7
13. Peru (VI)	39.0	5.5	44.5	20.0	35.5
14. South Korea (VII)	52.9	3.0	55.9	6.4	37.7

aland (see Table VIII.4, column 5). Several of these countries, one may note, had, like the USSR, suffered from the devastating damage caused by World War II.

The structure of consumption (including communal services), that is, its distribution among various types of goods, is not well reflected in the available data for the USSR. As far as one can see, the proportion devoted to food declined, from over two-thirds in 1928 to about a half in 1950 — and this decline occurred despite the failure of per capita consumer expenditures to rise significantly to 1950 (Table VIII.18, lines 12 and 15). And from 1950 to 1955, the proportion spent on food remained constant despite the marked rise in total consumer expenditures per capita. Table VIII.19 indicates that the rise in per capita food expenditures, excluding fabrication charges (based on the assumption of a constant ratio applied to the proportion of food subject to fabrication) was by 1955 somewhat greater than the rise in available food per capita as indicated by output data (compare lines 4, 9, and 10). The difference is quite small and perhaps has no significance. On the other hand, it may suggest that the rise in the relative weight of additional fabrication and other services attached to food helped to sustain the proportion of food expenditures in the total for 1955.

Since 1928 there has been a rise in the shares of services, communal and others, and of nonfoods other than housing. The changes in structure, in association with a rise in per capita income, are thus not unlike those that occurred in other countries;[7] but there is a marked dissimilarity with respect to the food and housing proportions within the different periods and the movements of the former.

Comparison of the structure of consumption expenditures in the USSR in 1950–55 and in other countries in post-World War II years suggests that in the USSR the proportion spent on food was higher than in most developed countries (Table VIII.20). The proportion spent on housing was unusually low — partly a matter of pricing, although in other European countries rent regulation produces a similar downward bias. Little can be said about the proportion of "all other" expenditures in the USSR and other countries: the category is far too heterogeneous for the comparison to be meaningful.

6. FOREIGN TRADE PROPORTIONS (TABLES VIII.21 AND VIII.22)

Of the many aspects of foreign trade of the USSR covered by Professor Holzman in Chapter VII of this volume, it is possible to discuss here only its over-all magnitude in relation to some measure of the country's total economic product. And even such a ratio — of foreign trade, if only for commodities, to national income or gross national product — is not easy to derive. The shares calculated in Table VIII.21 are rough approximations which start with fairly plausible levels for 1928, and are extrapolated by the relationship of the movements of the physical volume of imports and exports (in 1929 prices for most of the period) to the movement of gross national product (in 1937 adjusted prices). The alternative possibility of relating imports and exports in current values to gross national product at current prices yields ratios that are clearly unacceptable, because of the use of differing exchange rates for the ruble, with the recent rates reflecting a marked overvaluation of the domestic currency. And yet although the current volumes, at 1950 exchange rates, greatly exaggerate the levels of the import and export ratios to gross national

---

[7] See Simon Kuznets, Paper VII, *EDCC,* January 1962, pp. 32–36 and appendix Table 6, pp. 80–92.

Table VIII.21
USSR: Approximations to Ratios of Imports and Exports
to Gross National Product, Selected Periods, 1928–58
(based on volumes in constant prices)

Item	1928–37 (1)	1937–50 (2)	1950–55 (3)	1955–58 (4)
1. Index, GNP in 1937 factor cost (initial year = 100)	153	136	144	121
2. Index, physical volume of imports, 1929 prices (initial year = 100)	53	270	183	148
3. Estimated imports as percent of GNP, year at end of interval (1928 = 3.0 percent)	1.0	2.0	2.5	3.1
4. Estimated imports as percent of GNP, average for periods indicated	3.3 (1928–32)	1.2 (1933–37)	2.2 (1928–37)	2.8 (1955–58)
5. Index, physical volume of exports, 1929 prices (initial year = 100)	84	242	176	130
6. Estimated exports as percent of GNP, year at end of interval (1928 = 2.5 percent)	1.4	2.5	3.1	3.3
7. Estimated exports as percent of GNP, average for periods indicated	3.2 (1928–32)	1.9 (1933–37)	2.6 (1928–37)	3.2 (1955–58)

product, the relative movements of the ratios from 1928 to 1950 and 1955 are similar to those in Table VIII.21.[8]

The most striking aspect of the foreign trade ratios for the USSR is their low level — even in the late 1920's and early 1930's, when efforts

[8] If we relate the estimates at the current and the 1950 exchange rates, in Table VII.1 of Chapter VII of this volume, to gross national product in current prices as given in Bergson, *Real SNIP,* Table 3, p. 46, we obtain the following ratios in percent of imports and exports to gross national product: At current exchange rates, imports for 1928 were 3.0; for 1937, 0.5; for 1940, 0.3; for 1950 and 1955 data are not available. Exports (also at current exchange rates) for 1928 were 2.5; for 1937, 0.6; for 1940, 0.3; for 1950 and 1955 data are not available. At 1950 exchange rates, imports for 1928 were 10.3; for 1937, 0.4; for 1940, 0.2; for 1950, 6.4; and for 1955, 10.3. Exports (also at 1950 exchange rates) for 1928 were 8.7; for 1937, 0.5; for 1940, 0.2; for 1950, 7.9; and for 1955, 11.7. Obviously, the use of the 1950 exchange rate yields unacceptable *levels* for the ratios, but the *movement* is quite similar to that observed in Table VIII.21, except that the decline in 1937 and 1940 is much exaggerated. On the basis of the current volumes and 1950 exchange rates, the import ratio declines about four-tenths from 1928 to 1950, and

Table VIII.22

Selected Countries: Ratio of Foreign Trade to National Income Plus Imports, or to Gross National Product, Groups of Countries, 1938–39 and Post-World War II Years

| | Foreign commodity trade ratio. Groups of countries by size of population or per capita product | | | | | |
| | 1938–39 | | | 1950–54 | | |
Item	Number of countries (1)	Average population (millions) or average product per capita (US $) (2)	Foreign commodity trade ratio (3)	Number of countries (4)	Average population (millions) or average product per capita (US $) (5)	Foreign commodity trade ratio (6)
Countries grouped by size of population (cols. 2 & 5)						
1. Large	10	135.4	0.17	10	103.9	0.21
2. Small	22	2.5	0.38	17	1.9	0.41
Countries grouped by per capita product (cols. 2 & 5)						
3. High	10	429	0.29	10	1,021	0.35
4. Low	22	52	0.29	17	95	0.33

Shares of imports and exports in GNP (percent)
Selected large countries (with population over 40 million), 1953–59

| | Share of total flows | | Share of commodity flows | | |
	Imports (1)	Exports (2)	Imports (3)	Exports (4)	Commercial trade ratio (5)
Countries in descending order of population size, except for USSR					
5. USSR (1955–58)	—	—	2.8	3.2	0.06
6. India	8.7	6.8	8.0	5.7	0.14
7. United States	4.6	5.0	3.1	3.9	0.07
8. Japan	12.5	13.1	10.0	9.5	0.19
9. Brazil	8.2	7.6	—	—	—
10. United Kingdom	20.3	21.3	16.2	15.7	0.32
11. West Germany	18.8	22.3	—	—	—
12. Italy	14.0	13.2	11.5	9.0	0.20
13. France	13.8	13.6	9.8	10.9	0.21

Note: The dash (—) indicates that data are not available.

were made to maximize imports of industrial equipment and materials, and in the late 1950's, when rapid growth of production, the emergence of satellites, and the policy drive with respect to underdeveloped countries made for increased foreign trade. This, of course, repeats the conclusions stressed by Professor Holzman. In general, the ratio of foreign trade to national product of a country is affected by its size, as Table VIII.22 shows. But while the USSR is a large country, its foreign trade ratio, 0.06, is appreciably lower than those of the large non-Communist countries. The

then in 1955 is back to the level of 1928; the export ratio declines about a tenth from 1928 to 1950, and in 1955 is about a third higher than in 1928. Table VIII.21 (lines 3 and 6) shows a drop from 1928 to 1950 in the import ratio of a third and then a rise to 1955, but the 1955 value is still somewhat lower than that in 1928 (2.5 compared with 3.0); the export ratio is the same in 1950 as in 1928, and then it rises to a level in 1955 more than a fifth higher than that in 1928.

ratios for the United States are only slightly higher than those for the USSR, but clearly the reasons are different. The United States, whose trade with other countries flows in relatively free channels, although hampered by tariffs, has a low foreign trade ratio largely because its size and high level of per capita product (particularly consumption) prevent the absorption of a large proportion in imports. The explanation for the USSR lies largely in the autarkic policy of the state.

Additional analysis of the foreign trade flows presented in Chapter VII demonstrates the heavy concentration of imports on producers' equipment and in general on capital goods, and the restriction of imports of consumer goods. Only two observations are relevant in this connection. First, the policy in regard to foreign trade is part and parcel of the tight control exercised by the USSR government over the country's inhabitants as producers and consumers; for in addition to monopolizing foreign trade, it controls all foreign flows — of commodities, of men, and of ideas. The percentage shares in Table VIII.21 thus reflect a forced isolation of a large population from contact with the rest of the world, not paralleled in any non-Communist country within modern times. Second, this control over all foreign relations was exercised primarily to enforce the restriction of consumption and the concentration of production on capital goods. Without such control, these goals would have been much more difficult to attain because of the "demonstration" effect of products, ideas, and life in societies more directly concerned with the welfare and freedom of their inhabitants. The foreign trade policy was an example, so characteristic of the economic growth of the USSR, of the combination of borrowing production tools and methods from abroad and withholding from the consumer the welfare benefits of those tools and methods.

7. CONCLUDING COMMENTS

The preceding review can be expanded to include other aspects of economic growth both within the broad topics listed above and by adding others. More details on the industrial structure of product, labor force, and capital, and on subgroups within consumer expenditures, government consumption, and capital formation, would certainly help us to study more precisely the interplay between the over-all rate of growth and the changing allocation of resources in income production and use. Nothing was said of the structure of enterprises, of the financial and fiscal system, of regional diversities, of distribution of income by size, and of a host of other important topics.

But even in this sketchy review, the distinctive quantitative, and the implicit institutional and human, characteristics of the economic growth of the USSR stand out clearly. It is a case of high rates of growth, with large inputs of resources and heavy human costs; of rapid shifts in industrial structure, away from agriculture and with emphasis on the industrial sector — both in terms of shares and relative product per worker — that differed in its speed and concentration from other countries; of limiting consumption and maximizing capital investment, achieved in combination with relatively moderate capital-output ratios to permit rapid aggregate growth; and of deliberate isolation from the rest of the world, so that the selective borrowing of production devices and the very limited exposure to the example of high and free consumption levels in other countries could be assured. Finally, the suggested contrast between the 1928–40 period — with its violent internal shifts, tremendous input of resources, low and falling consumption, and low rates of growth per unit of output — and the period after 1950 — with its apparently rapid rise not only in product, but also in efficiency and in consumption — emphasizes the need for more detailed analysis of the post-World War II period, to help us understand this apparently new phase in the economic growth of the USSR and what it portends.

Rather than discuss the statistical comparisons further, I prefer to raise some major questions relating to the very basis of such comparisons. In particular application to a comparison of the economic growth of a country like the USSR with that of others, two broad groups of questions arise. (i) Are our statistical measures, as usually defined and approximated, applicable to the USSR? (ii) Assuming that we can make (or disregard) the necessary adjustment suggested by a positive answer to the first question, which "other" countries should be selected for a meaningful comparison?

(i) In considering the applicability of our statistical measures, particularly the aggregative, to the study of the economic growth of the USSR, I have in mind problems other than those with which the scholars in the field have struggled so hard and with some success: the omission of items that should be included, such as certain types of services; the prices that have to be adjusted to reflect more reasonably the production relations; and the very scarcity, discontinuity, and errors in much of the primary data, resulting partly from internal inefficiency, partly from built-in biases, and partly from official efforts at a statistical blackout. These problems are serious enough, and without the patient and persistent efforts of a group of Western scholars, little in the way of useful measures would have been available. I have assumed here that these problems have been solved with reasonable success; and have accepted the adjusted estimates for the USSR as broadly comparable, in reflecting the underlying concepts, with the measures for other countries.

My concern here is rather with questions relating to the institutional peculiarities of the USSR experience. There were clearly costs and returns in the economic growth that occurred in the USSR to which counterparts are either absent or of much smaller relative magnitude in the experience of other countries. Thus, there was a substantial loss of human life in the 1930's, occasioned by the violence of collectivization and experiences in labor camps that greatly reduced the life expectancy of their inmates — all in order to force the kind of economic growth that occurred. In our accounts the consumption of material capital is included as a cost but the extra consumption of human capital that may be induced by means aimed directly at economic goals is excluded (except in the minor form of accident insurance). This cost, while present in some periods in other countries, was probably much greater relatively in the USSR. Another omission is suggested by the high rate of absorption of females into the labor force of the USSR. What effect did this absorption have on the provision (unpaid) of services within the private household? Did it, combined with the shortage of residential housing, reduce such services materially? We do not include unpaid services of housewives and other family members within the household in national product — for reasons that can easily be defended; and there probably has been a reduction of such services in other countries in the process of economic growth. But it was apparently much greater relatively in the USSR. Finally, what about the cost of repression of freedom, the losses in human creativeness and welfare, that result from the forceful replacement of the judgment of the members of the community by the judgment of the dictatorial "planners"? The losses that resulted from the dead hand of control, from the conversion of literature, theatre, painting, and all the arts into production-propaganda devices, from the ruthless breaking of family and other group loyalties in service to the state, and from persistent isolation of the community from the rest of the world have been far-reaching indeed — as anyone comparing these fields of human life in the USSR and other countries (including pre-Communist Russia) can see.

In addition to these costs omitted from our economic calculation, there are returns that have escaped account; and these were probably enjoyed in the USSR to a far greater degree than in other countries. The removal of inequalities based on inherited wealth and private monopolies, with the distortions in the consumption and the whole pattern of life that such inequalities introduce, must be considered a major positive contribution. The greater possibility of employment in productive work, and of a rise in the economic and social scale commensurate with ability, in the service of what appeared to be a social ideal, was another positive aspect that we do not include directly in our measures. Removal of much *economic,* if not political, uncertainty was another positive element in the economic growth of the USSR not fully matched in other countries.

Some of the costs and returns just noted could be estimated by dint of statistical ingenuity: the reduction in services of housewives and other family members, the economic value of human capital consumed at rates above the minimum feasible, and even the positive returns involved in removal of undesirable income and wealth inequalities and restraints on economic opportunities. But even for some of these the economic price tag may seem rather irrelevant. For some others, such as restraint of freedom, the curbing of creative arts, and the like, no economic calculus is appropriate. And one may ask whether this whole range of questions is relevant to the study of *economic* growth — bearing as they do upon aspects of life that are far beyond and transcend merely economic processes and values.

Of course, one can define economic growth in terms of the measures that we in fact employ; and if this is done, these questions are ruled out of account. But since the study of a defined process pursues some rational goal, one may ask what that goal is, if the study of economic growth, as gauged by standard methods, may be so overshadowed by ignored important costs and returns as to dwindle into insignificance. I assume that the measurement and analysis of economic growth along what might be called traditional lines is justified in the belief that non-economic costs and returns are not so large and different as to spell misery and failure despite relative success with respect to traditionally measured economic growth. Indeed, an implication of such consonance between economic and other values is woven into the very fabric of economic definitions and measurements — geared as they are to the framework of a libertarian, nonslave society. It is therefore better to raise some of these questions relating to noneconomic costs and returns, rather than dismiss them implicitly as noneconomic.

Whether these missing, and economically unmeasurable, aspects of the economic growth of the USSR are really so large as to overshadow the economically measurable results, is a judgment that must be faced. And such a judgment would benefit from a more intensive study of the institutional and organizational arrangements within the USSR and other countries — a subject with which I am not familiar. But I believe that our interest in the measurement of economic growth proper, even with various adjustments to accepted economic concepts, is conditioned by the general premise that the noneconomic costs and returns, in the USSR and in the other countries, are not so dominant over the economic ones as to make the analysis meaningless — either in the sense that these economic measures will provide no explanation of the economic past and no insight into the economic future; or in the sense that economic success, as measured, is irrelevant or makes only an insignificant contribution to the total positive performance in terms of the whole complex of goals of the societies that are being compared.

The preceding paragraphs were written with a national product concept in mind that has marked welfare implications — if only in the sense that consumption outlay is considered a final product (and that sense affects also the production potential, since final product determines what is *net* product). In the case of the USSR, we could perhaps abandon that concept entirely, and shift to the notion of increase in national power as the only substance of final product. The measures would then be radically recast, since only the increase in certain types of material and human capital would be included — and industrial structure, distribution by type of capital and by type of consumption, et cetera, would be quite different from those shown in the present tables. I am not sure that we know enough about national power to classify capital formation, government consumption, and personal consumption by their contribution to it; but I am sure that such an allocation, for both the USSR and other countries, would yield measures that would differ materially from those we now have.

(ii) Even if we assume broad comparability with other countries, we still must choose those countries and periods that delimit segments of growth experience with which the economic growth of the USSR from 1928 to 1958 can be meaningfully compared. The comparison is meaningful if in ordering the data, it answers a question that is of interest to us; and the interest may arise out of a variety of sources. If, for example, the interest stems from an assumption of latent conflict between the USSR and the United States, the economic growth of the two will be compared in terms and criteria, as well as choice of periods, that bear most directly upon that interest (with perhaps a shift toward a concept of national power along the lines suggested above). If we are interested in comparing the economic growth of the United States and the USSR as typical (or most favorable) examples of free and forced growth, respectively, our choice of aspects and periods will be different. Or we may want to compare the economic growth of the USSR and Japan, because they are the two late-comers among the major countries that have entered upon the phase of industrialization and modern economic growth. Finally, we may be quite catholic in our approach, and assume that all countries entering modern economic growth — early or late, large or small, libertarian or authoritarian — display some significant common characteristics of growth; and that deviations from them, within limits, are reflections of the historical and locational peculiarities of individual countries. In this case we would compare the economic growth of the USSR with that of every other country in which modern economic growth has occurred.

Thus, in general, comparisons could be guided by two types of purpose. The first may be defined as political, in that the interest stems from the possible impacts of differences in rate and structure of economic growth on the relations and balances among nations in a changing world setting. The tendency would then be to compare the economic growth of the USSR with that of other *major* countries on the world scene (not with small nations unless these could somehow be envisaged as acting as a unit) ; and to emphasize aspects and periods that bear most directly upon changes in international relations and balance of power. The second may be defined as analytical, in that the interest in the comparison lies in testing some hypotheses concerning common and divergent characteristics of economic growth and of the factors behind them; and the content of these hypotheses would decide the choice of countries, aspects, and periods for comparison.

In practice, general considerations of the kind just suggested may be qualified by difficulties in the supply of data and in understanding — particularly since the guiding concepts of international relations and national power are subject to alternative definitions, and since we do not have many tested hypotheses concerning characteristics of modern economic growth (particularly with respect to the sequence of phases and to the long-term changes in the quantitative coefficients). It may, therefore, be legitimate to prepare multipurpose measures and make comparisons, in full awareness of their limitations but in the justified trust that in the process (even if it is not directed to sharply defined questions) we will add much to our understanding if only because of our relative ignorance. Yet we cannot disregard the distinction between the two bases of comparison suggested above, and perhaps others that could be formulated, for they obviously would give rise to choices and conclusions that, relating as they would to different questions, would be in different realms of discourse.

APPENDIX

Notes to Table VIII.1

All underlying totals are from Abram Bergson, *The Real National Income of Soviet Russia Since 1928* (Cambridge, Mass., 1961), hereafter cited as Bergson, *Real SNIP*, or from Chapter I of this volume.

Line 1: From Bergson, *Real SNIP*, Table 17, p. 88.

Line 2: From Bergson, *Real SNIP*, Table 32, p. 153.

Lines 3, 7, and 10: From Bergson, Chapter I of this volume, Table I.2.

Line 4: From Bergson, *Real SNIP*, Table 4, p. 48.

Line 5: From Bergson, *Real SNIP*, Table 22, p. 128.

Line 6: From Bergson, *Real SNIP*, Table 51, p. 210.

Line 8: From Bergson, *Real SNIP*, Table 16, p. 85.

Line 9: From Bergson, *Real SNIP*, Table 29, p. 149.

Notes to Table VIII.2

The data in Table VIII.2 are obtained as follows:

Line 1: Columns (1) to (5) are calculated from Bergson, *Real SNIP*, Table K-1, p. 442. Population for 1940 given there was reduced 20.5 million for comparison with the 1928 figure (see *ibid.*, p. 10).

Column (6) is calculated from Frank Lorimer, *The Population of the Soviet Union* (Geneva, 1946), Table 12, p. 30 and Table 54, p. 135, population January 1, 1918 and 1928.

Line 2: Bergson, Chapter I of this volume, Table I.2.

Line 3: Columns (1) to (5) are calculated from Bergson, Chapter I of this volume, Table I.1; the index of NNP, adjusted by the relation between GNP and NNP derived from the tabulation on p. 36.

Column (6) is based on the assumption that per capita GNP (line 4) did not change during the 1918–27 decade.

Line 4: Based on lines 1 and 3. The procedure was: Line 4 = [(100 + line 3) ÷ (100 + line 1) − 1] × 100.

Line 5: Based on lines 2 and 3. For procedure see note to line 4.

Line 6: Columns (1) to (5) are calculated from Bergson, Chapter I of this volume, Table I.1.

Column (6) is based on the assumption that per capita NNP (line 7) did not change during the 1918–27 decade.

Lines 7 and 8: Based on lines 1, 2, and 6. For procedure see note to line 4.

Line 9: Based on lines 1 and 10. For procedure see note to line 4.

Line 10: Columns (1) to (5) are calculated from Janet Chapman, Chapter VI of this volume, Table VI.1, line 2.

Column (6) is based on the assumption that per capita consumption including communal services did not change during the 1918–27 decade.

The basis of valuation in lines 9 and 10 is different from that in lines 3 to 8; and the two sets of figures cannot be compared.

Notes to Table VIII.4

The data in Table VIII.4 are obtained as follows:

Column (1) is from United Nations, *Demographic Yearbook, 1959* (New York, 1960).

Columns (2) to (5) are from United Nations, *Statistical Papers*, series H, no. 10 (New York, 1957), and *Yearbook of National Accounts Statistics, 1958* and *1959* (New York, 1959 and 1960). When constant-price figures were not available, current-price estimates were adjusted for price changes by cost of living indexes, given in United Nations, *Statistical Yearbook, 1958* and *1959* (New York, 1959 and 1960).

Notes to Table VIII.5

The data in Table VIII.5 are obtained as follows:

Lines 1, 9, and 16: Joint Economic Committee, 83rd Congress of the United States, 2nd Session, *Trends in Economic Growth, A Comparison of the Western Powers and the Soviet Bloc* (Washington, 1955), Table X-I, p. 284. This table, prepared by Dr. Herbert Block of the State Department, allocates net national product, in 1937 factor costs (Bergson), but adjusted for higher estimates of imputed land rent. Agriculture excludes forestry and fisheries, included in the M+ sector (together with manufacturing, mining, handicrafts, and construction, as well as transportation and communication shown separately).

Lines 2, 10, and 17: Joint Economic Committee, 85th Congress of the United States, 1st Session, *Soviet Economic Growth: A Comparison with the United States* (Washington, 1957), Table 2, p. 133. The estimates refer to national product or income, current ruble prices, adjusted for turnover taxes and for multiple pricing of farm products. The A sector includes forestry and fisheries; the M+ sector, industry, mining, construction, transport, and communication.

Lines 3, 11, and 18: Joint Economic Committee, 86th Congress of the United States, 1st Session, *Comparisons of the United States and Soviet Economies* (Washington, 1959), part II, Table 2, p. 383. The estimates refer to national income. The calculation by sector of origin follows the Bergson approach. The content of agriculture is not given.

Lines 4, 12, and 19: Abram Bergson, Hans Heymann, Jr., and Oleg Hoeffding, *Soviet National Income and Product, 1928–48: Revised Data,* The RAND Corporation, Research Memorandum RM-2544, November 15, 1960, Table 10, p. 35. The estimates are in current, "adjusted" prices. The A sector includes forestry and fisheries in 1928 but in 1937 they are largely in the M+ sector. The M+ sector includes industry, construction, transport, and communication. For 1937, when "other" and statistical discrepancy are given (amounting to 3.2 percent of the over-all total), the shares were taken to the total excluding these two items.

Lines 5, 13, and 20: Unpublished approximations provided by Professor Bergson. They are for net national product by industrial origin in 1937 ruble factor cost, and are extrapolations of the basic figures for 1937 by quantity indexes. The figures are especially crude for 1955–58. Agriculture is defined as for lines 4, 12, and 19; the M+ sector includes civilian industry, munitions industry, construction, transport, and communication. The shares are taken to the total excluding "other" and statistical discrepancy.

Line 6: From Bergson, Chapter I of this volume, Table I.1 — the ratio of the value for one date, marked by an asterisk, to the value for the preceding date marked by an asterisk.

Line 7: From D. Gale Johnson, Chapter V of this volume. The change from 1928 to 1940 was calculated from Table V.3, second column; for the subsequent periods from Table V.5, first column, but as amended in the text (to an increase between 1950 and 1958 of only 45 percent). The gross output index was used for 1928–40 on the assumption that the difference in trend between it and the index of sale or home consumption would be offset by the difference in trend between gross volume of agricultural output and net value added in agriculture.

Line 8: Derived from lines 6 and 7, with the share for 1940 in line 5 as the base.

Line 14: From Norman M. Kaplan and Richard H. Moorsteen, "An Index of Soviet Industrial Output," *American Economic Review,* June 1960, Table 1, p. 296. The index does not cover munitions, and is limited to industrial output (including construction materials but not construction proper). 1927–28 was used for 1928.

Line 15: Derived from lines 6 and 14, with the share in 1940 in line 13 as base.

Line 21: 100 minus lines 8 and 15.

Notes to Table VIII.6

The data in Table VIII.6 are obtained as follows:

Lines 1 to 3: From Table VIII.5, lines 5, 13, and 20.

Line 4: From Warren W. Eason, Chapter II of this volume, Table II.10. The estimates are apparently not adjusted for full-time equivalence. The entry in column (4) is for 1959.

Line 5: Full-time equivalents.

Columns (1) to (3) are from Bergson, *Real SNIP,* Table K-2, p. 443.

Column (4) is based on line 4, column (4) and the ratio of line 5, column (3) to line 4, column (3).

Lines 7 and 8: The entries in line 6 apportioned under assumption (a) on the basis of Chapter II, Table II.13, the distribution of nonagricultural wage and salary workers between the M+ and S— sectors; under assumption (b) on the basis of Professor Eason's distribution of total nonagricultural employment, with the share of civilian nonwage and salary allocated to the M+ sector and commerce.

Line 16: The sum, disregarding signs, of the differences between the share in NNP and the share in labor force.

Notes to Table VIII.7

The entries, except for Japan, are derived from Simon Kuznets, Paper II, *EDCC,* July 1957, appendix Table 2, pp. 68ff; and appendix Table 4, pp. 82ff. (For more detailed reference designations see notes to Table VIII.3 in the text.) For Japan they are derived from Kazushi Ohkawa *et al., The Growth Rate of the Japanese Economy Since 1878* (Tokyo, 1957), Table 9, p. 26; and Table 11, p. 28. Those countries and periods were selected for which the initial shares were fairly close to those in the USSR in 1928.

Notes to Table VIII.8

The entries for the USSR are from Table VIII.6, lines 1 to 3, 5, 7a, and 8a. For all other countries except Norway they are from the sources cited in the notes to Table VIII.7. For Norway they are from Juul Bjerke, "Some Aspects of Long-Term Economic Growth of Norway," a paper presented at the Conference of the International Association for Research in Income and Wealth, held at Portoroz, Yugoslavia, August–September 1959.

Notes to Table VIII.9

The shares in product and labor force for the USSR are derived from Table VIII.6, lines 1 to 3, 5, 7a, and 8a. The shares for the other countries are from Simon Kuznets, Paper II, *EDCC,* July 1957, Table 3, p. 10; Table 6, p. 13; Table 10, p. 23; Table 13, p. 27; appendix Table 1, pp. 62ff; and appendix Table 3, pp. 75ff.

For this table, the shares for the separate Roman numeral groups were averaged, all groups being given equal weight.

The P/L ratios were calculated directly from the entries for P and L in this table.

The Arabic numbers in parentheses in lines 1 to 8 show the number of countries included (which differ for product because of the varying detail in the available industrial classifications).

The Roman numbers in parentheses in part C indicate the per capita product group in which the country is classified.

The measure of inequality (part B, column 5 and part C, column 4) is described in the note to Table VIII.6, line 16.

Notes to Table VIII.10

The data in Table VIII.10 are obtained as follows:

Lines 1 to 3: From Table VIII.6, column (4), lines 1 to 3, 5, 7a, and 8a.

Lines 4 and 5: From Norman M. Kaplan, Chapter III of this volume, Table III.1. The A sector covers item 1c; the M+ sector: industry, construction, transportation, communications, procurement, material-technical supply and sales; and the S— sector, all others.

Line 7: For the aggregate nonresidential capital-output ratio of 1.5, see Chapter III, p. 133.

Line 9a: Calculated by subtracting line 8a from line 1, and dividing by 0.85, the ratio of net national product, excluding yield of capital, to total net national product underlying line 1.

Line 9b: Calculated by subtracting line 8b from line 1, and dividing by 0.70, the ratio of net national product, excluding yield of capital, to total net national product.

Notes to Table VIII.11

The data in Table VIII.11 are obtained as follows:

Line 1: Norman M. Kaplan, "Capital Formation and Allocation," in Abram Bergson, ed., *Soviet Economic Growth, Conditions and Perspectives* (Evanston, 1953), Tables 2.1 and 2.5, pp. 41 and 47.

Line 2: From Table X-3, p. 284 of the source cited in the note to Table VIII.5, line 1.

Line 3: From Table 1, p. 127 of the source cited in the note to Table VIII.5, line 2.

Line 4: From Table 1, p. 380 of the source cited in the note to Table VIII.5, line 3.

Line 5: From Table 7, p. 32 of the source cited in the note to Table VIII.5, line 4.

Lines 6a to 6c: From Bergson, *Real SNIP,* Table 3, p. 46.

Lines 7a to 7c: From Bergson, *Real SNIP,* Table 4, p. 48.

Lines 8a to 8c: From Bergson, *Real SNIP,* Table 22, p. 128 except for the entries in parentheses. The entries in parentheses in column (1) are the shares in gross national product with the factor cost approach extended to household retail purchases, given in Bergson, Chapter I of this volume, p. 36. The entries in parentheses in column (8) are for 1958 and were calculated from gross investment in 1937 factor costs, provided by Professor Raymond P. Powell, and gross national product, given in Bergson, Chapter I of this volume, p. 36.

Notes to Table VIII.12

The data in Table VIII.12 are obtained as follows:

Lines 1 to 8: All underlying capital formation data, gross and net, are from the study of Soviet capital stock now under way by Professors Raymond P. Powell and Richard H. Moorsteen; and cover the periods 1928–39 and 1950–57.

Lines 9 to 11: For the capital formation data, see the note to lines 1 to 8. The increase in national product, for 1928 to 1940 and 1950 to 1958, is from Bergson, Chapter I of this volume, and is adjusted for changes in territory from 1928 to 1940 on the assumption of a 10 percent increase due to them.

Notes to Table VIII.13

See the notes to Table VIII.3 for a detailed description of the entries. The dates indicate the first year for which the capital formation proportions were calculated. The capital formation proportions are based on totals in current prices. The capital-output ratios are derived by dividing the capital formation proportions by the rates of growth in national product in constant prices.

Column (1). The first entry is for the capital formation proportions, the second is for the rates of growth of product.

The measures are from Simon Kuznets, Paper VI, *EDCC*, July 1961, Table 1, p. 15 and Table 5, pp. 17–18.

Notes to Table VIII.14

Capital-Output Ratios — The measures for the USSR are derived as follows:

Column (1) is from Table VIII.11, line 8a.

Column (2) is from Table VIII.1, line 6.

Column (3) is from Table VIII.12, line 9.

Column (4) is from data supplied by Professor Raymond P. Powell.

Column (7) is from Table VIII.1, line 7.

Column (8) is from Table VIII.12, line 9.

The measures for all other countries are derived as follows:

Columns (1) and (2) are from United Nations, *World Economic Survey, 1959* (New York, 1960), Table I-2, p. 23.

Columns (4) and (6) are from Simon Kuznets, Paper V, *EDCC*, July 1960, appendix Table 2, pp. 80ff. and appendix Table 3, pp. 84ff.

Column (5) is from columns (1) and (4) of this table.

Column (7) is from columns (2) and (6) of this table.

Annual Rates of Growth — the measures for the USSR are derived as follows:

Columns (1) and (2) are from Bergson, Chapter I of this volume, Table I.2.

Column (5) is from column (7) of this table (capital-output ratios).

The measures for all other countries are derived as follows:

Column (1) is from *World Economic Survey, 1959,* Table I-4, p. 26.

Column (2) is from *ibid.*, the table on p. 33 (with the rates for gross additions reduced to rates for net additions by the ratios in column (4) of the capital-output ratios.

Column (5) is from column (7) of this table (capital-output ratios).

Notes to Table VIII.15

The data in Table VIII.15 are obtained as follows:

Lines 1 to 3: Column (1) is from Norman M. Kaplan, "Capital Formation and Allocation," (cited in note to line 1, Table VIII.11), Table 27, p. 52.

Column (2) is from Chapter III of this volume, Table III.4, and the distribution for 1952–59 is assumed applicable to 1950–58.

Lines 4 to 6: The entries without parentheses are derived from Table VIII.5, lines 5, 13, and 20 and the movement in net national product given in Bergson, Chapter I of this volume, Table I.1. The entries in parentheses are derived from the alternative distribution in Table VIII.5, lines 8, 15, and 21.

Lines 10 to 12: The product of the relatives in lines 7 to 9 and the capital-output ratio in Table VIII.12, line 11, columns (3) and (4), respectively.

Notes to Table VIII.16

The data in Table VIII.16 are obtained as follows:

Lines 1 to 5: Derived from Bergson, *Real SNIP,* Table 62, p. 237 except for line 1a, which is derived from *ibid.,* Table 51, p. 210.

Lines 6 to 8: Derived from Bergson, *Real SNIP,* Table 22, p. 128; Table 51, p. 210; and Table K-1, p. 443. The per capita estimates are assumed to be comparable throughout.

Line 14: The distribution is for the additions underlying the three periods in lines 11 to 13.

Line 15: The distribution is for the additions from 1928 to 1955, assumed to be comparable.

Notes to Table VIII.17

The measures for the USSR are from Table VIII.16, lines 4 and 5. All others are from Simon Kuznets, Paper VII, *EDCC,* January 1962, Table 1, p. 4, and appendix Table 1, pp. 62–63. Figures in parentheses are described in the notes to Table VIII.9.

Notes to Table VIII.18

The data in Table VIII.18 are obtained as follows:

Lines 1 to 5: Based on totals supplied by Professor Bergson and population, given in Bergson, *Real SNIP,* Table K-1, p. 443.

Line 6: Derived from line 5 of this table and the ratio of communal services to personal household consumption in 1937 factor costs, given in Bergson, *Real SNIP,* Table 22, p. 128. For 1928, household consumption is adjusted for the factor costs of retail purchases.

Notes to Table VIII.19

The data in Table VIII.19 are obtained as follows:

Lines 1 to 3: From data provided by Professor Bergson. Personal food consumption consists of state and cooperative retail food sales to households, collective farm market sales to households, and consumption of farm income in kind. The last item is from Bergson, *Real SNIP,* Table 37, p. 165. The first item was calculated by disaggregating the data on state and cooperative food and nonfood sales in Bergson, *Real SNIP,* Chapter 10. The disaggregation is based primarily on Soviet official and Chapman data on the structure of retail sales in current prices, and Chapman indexes of retail prices of foods and nonfoods, the latter given in Janet Chapman, *Real Wages in Soviet Russia Since 1928* (forthcoming).

Mr. Bergson suggested that half of military subsistence should be assigned to food, and that the transportation and distribution markup for agricultural food products is about 20 percent of final price (that is, 25 percent of cost, a rough approximation).

Line 4: 40 percent is a rough approximation of the ratio of fabrication costs to food output derived as follows. For 1928 we had the shares in net national product of the net output of agriculture and of industry (the latter excluding munitions) in 1937 adjusted prices (see notes to Table VIII.5, line 5). These were converted to shares of gross national product using the data in Bergson, Chapter I of this volume, p. 36; and the output of agriculture was reduced to eliminate nonfood products (see note to line 6 below). We had from Bergson, *Real SNIP*, Table 22, p. 128 consumption of farm income in kind, which was also subtracted and yielded the output possibly subject to fabrication (all in percentages of gross national product, in 1937 factor costs). From Kaplan-Moorsteen (see note to line 14, Table VIII.5), Table 1, p. 296, we derived the ratio of industrial food production to total industrial output in 1928; and applied this to the ratio of total industrial output to GNP in 1928. This gave us a value added in industrial food production comparable to the value of agricultural food output, excluding consumption on farms. The ratio was 0.35+ and we raised it to 0.4, to allow for possible underestimation of fabrication in the Kaplan-Moorsteen indexes. With fabrication costs 40 percent of the agricultural food output (net of that consumed on farms), and the transportation and distribution margin 20 percent of final price, fabrication costs amount to 23 percent of the final price; and the latter ratio was applied to the Bergson estimate of state and cooperative retail food sales to households. Subtraction of the product from the totals underlying line 3 yielded the totals shown as an index in line 4.

Line 5: From Johnson, Chapter V of this volume, Table V.5. No allowance was made for overstatement in 1955.

Line 6: See D. Gale Johnson and Arcadius Kahan, "Soviet Agriculture: Structure and Growth," in Joint Economic Committee, 86th Congress of the United States, 1st Session, *Comparisons of the United States and Soviet Economies*, part I (Washington, 1959). The proportion of industrial crops to total net output was computed from the percentages cited in the footnote on p. 206, and the indexes on pp. 205 and 206.

Line 7: Calculated from Johnson and Kahan, Table 2, p. 205.

Line 8: The implicit weights used in Johnson and Kahan, Tables 2 and 3 for 1928, were about 5 for livestock and about 4 for food crops (leaving 7.7 for industrial crops). From Nancy Nimitz, "Soviet Agricultural Prices and Costs," *ibid.*, pp. 239–284, it is apparent that in 1937 the prices of livestock were substantially higher relative to prices of food crops than in 1926–27 (see in particular Table 6, p. 251). I was curious to see what would happen if livestock were given a heavier weight; and chose 7 to 3, compared with 5 and 4, for that would correspond to a doubling of livestock prices relative to those for food crops — a movement suggested by the table just referred to. The ratio in line 8 was calculated by applying the two sets of weights to the indexes shown in Johnson and Kahan, Table 3, p. 206; and dividing one weighted index by the other.

In addition to the limitations implicit in the approximations, the comparison is defective because no account is taken of: exports and imports; changes in inventories; output of fisheries and other domestic sources of food not covered by agriculture; or consumption of food included under communal service.

Notes to Table VIII.20

The measures for the USSR are from Table VIII.18, columns (3) and (4), lines 15 to 21. All others are from Simon Kuznets, Paper VII, *EDCC*, January 1962, Table 10, p. 24 and appendix Table 5, pp. 76–79. The entries in parentheses in lines 1 to 4 show the number of countries included in each group (the number varies with differences in detail reported). Those in lines 5 to 14 show the per capita product group in which the country is classified.

Notes to Table VIII.21

The data in Table VIII.21 are obtained as follows:
Line 1: From Bergson, Chapter I of this volume, p. 36 with a 10 percent allowance for change in boundaries after 1937. Here, and in lines 2 and 5, the entry is the relative of the estimate in the terminal year of the interval shown in the column heading to the estimate in the initial year.
Lines 2 and 5: From Holzman, Chapter VII of this volume, Table VII.2. The same adjustment for changes in boundaries was made.
Lines 3 and 6: We assume a share of imports in gross national product in 1928 of 3 percent and exports 2.5 percent (approximations based on the discussion and figures in Chapter VII and Tables VII.1 and VII.2). These initial percentages are multiplied by the relatives in lines 2 and 5, respectively, and divided by the relatives in line 1. The results, shown in lines 3 and 6, would yield approximations to the changing shares of imports and exports in GNP, if the indexes in lines 1, 3, and 5, were expressed in the price levels of the same year.
Lines 4 and 7: Annual indexes of the physical volume of imports and exports are given in Chapter VII, Table VII.2 for 1928–37 and for 1955–58. Annual values of the index of GNP were interpolated along a logarithmic straight line. On the basis of these annual indexes and the approximations of the ratios for 1928, annual approximations were calculated. The entries are arithmetic means of these annual shares.

Notes to Table VIII.22

The data in Table VIII.22 are obtained as follows:
Lines 1 to 4: From Simon Kuznets, *Six Lectures on Economic Growth* (Glencoe, Ill., 1959), Table 10, p. 96. The averages are unweighted arithmetic means; the per capita incomes are in United States dollars; and the foreign trade ratios are the ratios of commodity exports and imports to national income plus commodity imports.
Line 5: From Table VIII.21, column (4), lines 4 and 7.
Lines 6 to 13: Calculated from United Nations, *Yearbook of National Accounts Statistics, 1960* (New York, 1961). The total flows are exports and imports of commodities and services, with the *net* balance of factor income

added to exports if positive or to imports if negative. For Japan and Italy, commodity imports and exports exclude freight and insurance, and are therefore understated. Column (5) is the sum of columns (3) and (4) divided by 100 — for comparability with the foreign commodity trade ratios in lines 1 to 4.

ABBREVIATIONS

Baykov — Alexander Baykov, *Soviet Foreign Trade*, Princeton, 1946

Demographic Yearbook — United Nations, *Demographic Yearbook*

Forty Years of Soviet Power — TSU, *Forty Years of Soviet Power, in Facts and Figures*, Moscow, 1958

Historical Statistics — U.S. Department of Commerce, *Historical Statistics of the United States, 1789–1945*, Washington, 1949

Historical Statistics — U.S. Department of Commerce, *Historical Statistics of the U.S., Colonial Times to 1957*, Washington, 1960

Johnson — D. Gale Johnson and Arcadius Kahan "Soviet Agriculture: Structure and Growth" in *Comparisons of the United States and Soviet Economies*, Joint Economic Committee, 86th Congress of the United States, Sess. 1 (Washington, 1959)

Kul'turnoe stroitel'stvo — TSU, *Kul'turnoe stroitel'stvo SSSR: statisticheskii sbornik*, Moscow, 1956

Mish — D.D. Mishustin, *Vneshniaia torgovlia i industrializatsiia SSSR*, Moscow, 1938

MVT — Ministerstvo vneshnei torgovli SSSR (Ministry of Foreign Trade of the USSR)

Narodnoe khoziaistvo SSSR — TSUNKHU, *Narodnoe khoziaistvo SSSR*, Moscow-Leningrad, 1932

Narodnoe khoziaistvo 1956 — TSU, *Narodnoe khoziaistvo SSSR: statisticheskii sbornik*, Moscow, 1956

Narodnoe khoziaistvo 1958 — TSU, *Narodnoe khoziaistvo SSSR v 1958 godu*, Moscow, 1959

Narodnoe khoziaistvo 1959 — TSU, *Narodnoe khoziaistvo SSSR v 1959 godu: statisticheskii ezhegodnik*, Moscow, 1960

NEP — Novaia ekonomicheskaia politika (New Economic Policy)

O raspredelenii naseleniia — TSU, "O raspredelenii naseleniia SSSR po obshchestvennym gruppam, otrasliam narodnogo khoziaistva i zaniaitiiam i ob urovne obrazovaniia rabotnikov fizicheskogo i umstvennogi truda," *Vestnik statistiki*, 1960, no. 12, pp. 3–21

Promyshlennost' SSSR — TSU, *Promyshlennost' SSSR*, Moscow, 1957

Real SNIP — Abram Bergson, *The Real National Income of Soviet Russia Since 1928*, Cambridge, Mass., 1961

Selkhoz SSSR — TSU, *Sel'skoe khoziaistvo SSSR*, Moscow, 1960

Shimkin — D. Shimkin, *Minerals: Key to Soviet Power* (Cambridge, Mass., 1953)

Sovetskaia torgovlia — TSU, *Sovetskaia torgovlia*, Moscow, 1956

Tsifrakh — TSU, *SSSR v tsifrakh v 1959 godu*, Moscow, 1960

TSU — Tsentral'noe Statisticheskoe Upravlenie SSSR (Central Statistical Administration of the USSR)

TSUNKHU — Tsentral'noe Upravlenie Narodno-khoziaistvennogo Ucheta SSSR (Central Administration of National Economic Accounting USSR)

VT-40 — MVT, *Vneshniaia torgovlia SSSR za 1918–1940 gg.* (Moscow, 1960)

VT-Postwar — *Vneshniaia torgovlia SSSR*, Moscow, 1956 and later years

VT-20 — S.N. Bakulin and D. D.Mishustin, *Vneshniaia torgovlia SSSR za 20 let, 1918–37 gg.*, Moscow, 1939

INDEX